# COMPARATIVE POLITICS

## Interests, Identities, and Institutions in a Changing Global Order

Why are the countries of the world governed so differently? How did this diversity of political orders come about? Will liberal capitalism retain its appeal and spread further around the globe in the 21st century, or will new and hostile challengers come on the scene? These are the questions that guide this new introductory text to comparative politics. Cast through the lens of ten theoretically informed and historically grounded country studies, it illustrates and explains how the three major concepts of comparative political analysis – interests, identities, and institutions – shape the polities of nations. A novel feature of this textbook is its explicit discussion of the international challenges to each country's chosen path of development. These challenges frequently alter domestic interests and identities, and force countries to find new institutional solutions to the problems of modern politics. Written in a style free of heavy-handed jargon and organized in a way that speaks to contemporary comparativists' concerns, this textbook provides students with the conceptual tools and historical background they need to understand the politics of today's complex world.

Please visit the Comparative Politics website at www.cup.org/textbooks/Kopstein.html for more information.

Jeffrey Kopstein teaches comparative politics at the University of Colorado at Boulder.

Mark Lichbach teaches comparative politics at the University of California, Riverside.

# COMPARATIVE POLITICS

## Interests, Identities, and Institutions in a Changing Global Order

✎ Edited by

**JEFFREY KOPSTEIN**

University of Colorado at Boulder

**MARK LICHBACH**

University of California, Riverside

CAMBRIDGE
UNIVERSITY PRESS

PUBLISHED BY THE PRESS SYNDICATE OF THE UNIVERSITY OF CAMBRIDGE
The Pitt Building, Trumpington Street, Cambridge, United Kingdom

CAMBRIDGE UNIVERSITY PRESS
The Edinburgh Building, Cambridge, UK                http://www.cup.cam.ac.uk
40 West 20th Street, New York, NY 10011–4211, USA    http://www.cup.org
10 Stamford Road, Oakleigh, Melbourne 3166, Australia
Ruiz de Alarcón 13, 28014 Madrid, Spain

First published 2000

Printed in the United States of America

*Typeface* ITC Cheltenham 9.75/13    *System* QuarkXPress®     [GH]

*A catalog record for this book is available from the British Library.*

*Library of Congress Cataloging-in-Publication Data*
Comparative politics : interests, identities, and institutions in a changing global order /
edited by Jeffrey Kopstein, Mark Lichbach.
     p.  cm.
   ISBN 0 521 63336-2
     1. Comparative government.  I. Kopstein, Jeffrey.  II. Lichbach, Mark Irving, 1951–
JF51.C6235 2000
   320.3 – dc21

                                                     00-020159


ISBN 0 521 63336 2  hardback
ISBN 0 521 633567  paperback

*To Max Kopstein and to Sammi Jo and Yossi Lichbach:*

*May they someday take the time to read this book
and learn about our world.*

# Contents

## PART ONE. EARLY DEVELOPERS
## Cases

### 1  Britain

PETER RUTLAND
*Wesleyan University*

## 6  China      229

YU SHAN WU
*National Taiwan University*

## Stop and Compare

## PART FOUR. EXPERIMENTAL DEVELOPERS
## Cases

## 7  Mexico      271

ANTHONY GILL
*University of Washington, Seattle*

# Maps

# Preface

This book originated in many hours of pleasant conversation about teaching comparative politics. Out of these conversations emerged the idea of an introductory textbook that would convey to students the main currents in contemporary comparative politics. These currents are summed up here under three rubrics: interests, identities, and institutions. We decided to illustrate this framework through a series of country studies cast in world historical perspective. At the same time, we wanted to avoid weighing down the country studies with a heavy-handed or outdated theoretical apparatus that inevitably discourages even the hardiest of students. The result, we hope, has struck an acceptable balance between conceptual rigor and flexibility.

To the extent that we have accomplished this, most of the credit is due to our contributors who have cheerfully taken on our framework without losing what is interesting and distinctive about their country's experience. We are also grateful to the staff of Cambridge University Press and especially to Alex Holzman and Lewis Bateman for their enthusiasm and good judgment.

Editing this book has been a collaborative act. It represents the tangible result of a long friendship. The order of our names reflects only the order of the alphabet. Our efforts have been equal in every way.

# A Changing Global Order

≈ Jeffrey Kopstein and Mark Lichbach

# INTRODUCTION

Imagine that you could design the political order for a country of your choosing. Where would you start? Who would get to rule? What rules for political life would you choose? Could you make rules that would be fair to everyone? If not, whom would these rules favor and whom would they disadvantage? What would be the rules for changing the rules? These are difficult questions because answering them in a meaningful way requires understanding why and how different countries of the world are governed differently. With so many choices to make, it is easy to see why the job of the constitutional designer would be such a difficult one.

It could, however, be made easier. One might start by evaluating the existing possibilities, the states of the world in which we live. The state is an organization that possesses sovereignty over a territory and its people. Yet, within our world of states, no two countries are ruled in exactly the same way. Why should this be the case? Why are societies run and political orders designed in so many different ways? What consequences do these differences hold for people's well-being?

Comparativists believe that it is possible to provide answers to these questions, and in this book students will begin to understand the craft of comparative politics. Even if it is not possible to design a country as one sees fit, it is possible to understand why countries develop the way they do and why they are ruled as they are. By examining the range of possible domestic responses to global opportunities and constraints, we can begin to offer explanations for why countries develop as they do and evaluations about the trade-offs involved in different political orders.

We have chosen a set of countries to study that encompass a wide range of possible paths of development under a diverse set of global contexts. Before turning to these countries, however, it is worth considering the general framework employed here to examine them. Although our discussion is fairly brief, it is crucial reading because it explains the general perspectives and substantive concerns, as well as the historical developmental context, through which the country chapters are filtered.

## OUR FRAMEWORK

The core idea of this book is simple: Three important aspects of domestic politics – interests, identities, and institutions – are explored in a set of country studies cast in world-historical and developmental perspective. We teach, in short, the following framework:

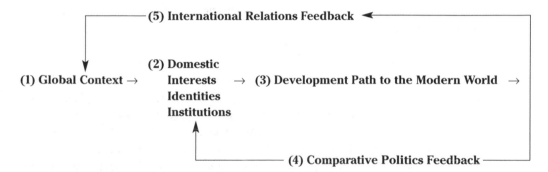

In words: (1) The global context influences (2) domestic interests, identities, and institutions, which produce (3) developmental paths to the modern world, which, in turn, generate (4) comparative-politics feedback effects on domestic interests, identities, and institutions and (5) international-relations feedback effects on the global context. Our approach, which will allow us to raise important empirical questions about comparing governments and significant normative concerns about evaluating good and bad governments, has the following five parts.

### Global Context

Since today's world is small, our book has a "globalist" slant. The global context for comparative politics involves tensions between nations and states, contradictions between global homogenization and local diversity, and conflict among states at particular points in world-historical time.

## NATIONS AND STATES

The first thing to understand about the world is that it is divided into nations and states and that nations and states are often in tension with one another. What are these two sets of things that dominate the globe and why are they in tension?

When we speak of modern sovereign states, we mean first that states have external independence. Governments have armies, navies, and air forces to maintain their external security. They send and receive ambassadors to other states and belong to the global club of states, the United Nations. Sovereignty also has a second dimension, an internal one. The international community of states generally recognizes and accepts the right and power of the government to make laws and monopolize force within its boundaries. This means that states have internal control over their populations. They maintain internal order, collect taxes, regulate economic life, confine people in prisons, and conscript or recruit citizens into the armed forces. However, states vary in how much external independence and internal control they in fact exert. The United States, for example, is a state whose independence is widely accepted in the international arena and one that is able to exercise significant control over its population.

In addition to states, the world is populated by "peoples" who are often called nations. A nation can be defined in a number of ways. Its origins and defining features may be linguistic, religious, racial, or the perception of a common history and shared fate. Nationhood is largely a subjective category; if a people considers itself to be a nation, then we must at least begin to think of it as a nation.

Global society is thus divided into states that are defined organizationally and nations that are defined culturally. Since a state is a set of governing institutions and a nation a community of people, some – the nationalists – argue that the two should coincide in a nation-state. Nationalists maintain that the only proper form of government is one in which the boundaries of the state correspond to the boundaries of the nation. They claim that only in a nation-state, where people identify with the state because the rulers of the state are also members of the nation, will a people accept the government as the legitimate representative of their community, thereby entitled to make laws on their behalf.

While nationalists believe that national identity should coincide with state boundaries, when we look at a map of the world we quickly discover that there is no necessary relationship between state and nation. In fact, they rarely coincide. Very few states are composed of a single national group. Some states are composed of several or even many nations. Some nations are spread out over many states and have never governed themselves. Finally, there are some nations that are spread out over many states and that have one central governing state more or less serving as a focal point for their nationalist aspirations.

State and nation often do not coincide because of history. State building or administrative bureaucratization frequently did not coincide with nation building or national integration. It may surprise you to learn, for example, that late into the nineteenth century, many people in large parts of France did not even speak French as their first language. These people had to be "made" into French citizens. It may also surprise you to learn that two centuries ago, when the United States gained its independence, there were fewer than twenty governments in the world that we would designate today as states. Most entities were principalities, city-states, empires, and tribal areas without fixed territorial boundaries. Today the entire surface of the globe is divided into independent states that make claims to control national territories and their populations. The 19th and 20th centuries have seen the triumph of nationalism and statism, but not necessarily in concert with one another.

## GLOBALIZATIONS AND HETEROGENEITIES

The second thing to understand about the world is that it is a whole with parts and that the whole and the parts are also often in conflict with one another. People think globally but act locally. In other words, there are significant global generalizations and important local heterogeneities.

Consider, first of all, the world as a whole. Regional and global forces respond to and shape a set of common and converging global interests, identities, and institutions. Markets, cultures, and structures operate not only within countries but among them as well.

**THE GLOBALIZATION OF INTERESTS.** The present international political economy consists of a set of interlinked country-level economies that create global markets in land, labor, and capital. Production in multinational corporations is global. Trade, that is, imports and exports, is global. Financial markets are global, too. Immigration and migration, migrant labor and guest workers, war refugees and tourism are global. Communications and transportation, the movement of goods and services, are global. Economic problems are consequently global problems. Growth and prosperity are global problems. Inequality and poverty, the gap between North and South, is a global problem. Diseases and epidemics are global problems – bubonic plague, influenza, and smallpox were problems for humankind and AIDS is now everyone's problem. Environmental problems are also now global. We are part of a single ecosystem, and hence, environmental degradation, global warming, energy conservation, and water pollution are global problems. In sum, it is not possible for a country to isolate itself from global economic trends, cycles, and shocks.

**THE GLOBALIZATION OF IDENTITIES.** Western, and especially American, values are increasingly hegemonic and have come to define social and cultural identities around the entire world. English is the international language used in business and politics, the arts and the sciences. Innumerable technical standards derived from the West define the global business culture. Universal human rights, such as the ideas of crimes against humanity and of war criminals, derived from the Western definition of political culture. At a more mundane level, global pop culture is becoming consumer cosmopolitanism, a common global lifestyle of taste, fashion, and talk in which people define their identity and express themselves symbolically through their material possessions. Many of the global masses, who consume Coca Cola soft drinks, McDonalds hamburgers, Reebok sneakers, Levi blue jeans, Spielberg films, and Gap clothing, attempt to move up the material and status hierarchy and enter the yuppie world of Armani apparel, Chanel perfume, Dom Perignon champagne, and Perrier mineral water. Much of global yuppiedom, in turn, strives to acquire the lifestyles of the rich and famous, the Lear Jets, the Porsche cars, and the transnational managerial classes' Rolex watches.

**THE GLOBALIZATION OF INSTITUTIONS.** Examples of regional or continent-wide Inter Governmental Organizations or IGOs include a European superstate, the European Union (EU) and a North American Free-Trading Zone, NAFTA. Examples of global supranational actors that are part of the global governance network that issues extensive supragovernmental regulations include the United Nations, World Bank, International Monetary Fund, and World Trade Organization. Inter Non-Governmental Organizations or INGOs include the Roman Catholic Church, the International Red Cross, the International Political Science Association, Greenpeace, and Amnesty International. Business Inter Non-Governmental Organizations or BINGOs include transnational organizations and multinational corporations, such as Sony, Exxon, and General Motors, and marketized global governance structures, such as the International Federation of Stock Exchanges and the International Securities Market Association. Non-Governmental, society-to-society, transborder connections are very important. As they become increasingly dense, they create a world civil society: layered sets of networks and connections that are not defined by spatial location and geographic context and that are independent of formal intergovernmental relations.

Global markets, Western values, and international institutions exercise an important common, one might even say homogenizing, influence across borders. Comparativists used to speak of three worlds, a First World of liberal democracy and economic markets, a Second World of communist dictatorships and central plans, and a Third World of poor countries trying to find a third way between the First and Second Worlds. However, the last couple of decades has witnessed a worldwide movement toward the independence of civil society and the corresponding liberalization of political and economic systems. Reform and revolution have moved scores of countries away from dictatorship and central plans and toward democracy and markets. Among the poorest countries of the world, this has meant the decline of authoritarianism and the fall of military regimes. Among the countries of Central and Eastern Europe, it has meant the collapse of communism. And among the countries of the developed West, it has meant renewed confidence in democracy and markets. The world has thus partially converged and the result is diminished diversity of political and economic institutions. The worldwide movement toward variations on a common theme, originally developed in the West, is enforced by the global community of countries. States that are out of tune change to be able to trade their goods and services. Such pressures help explain the end of South Africa's white oligarchy and the demise of the Soviet Union's one-party communist state.

Now that we have examined the world as a whole, consider its parts. In spite of some important global trends, there are equally important heterogeneities at work. States attempt to develop distinctive national economic policies to deal with the global economy and, hence, evolve local institutional variations of democracies and markets. In spite of some global convergence, the idea of different paths to the modern world – for example variations on democracy, authoritarianism, and communism – is still relevant.

It is, of course, paradoxical that so many countries at the same time are responding with similar local variations to global forces. Comparativists often ask whether the principle of sovereignty will remain globally dominant in the twenty-first century. It is too early to answer this question definitively, but there are several challenges to sovereignty from society itself that are turning up in many countries at the same time:

- Various kinds of subnationalisms involving territorial minorities have attempted to separate nations from states. Whether it be Scots in Great Britain, the Baltic peoples in the Soviet Union, or the Sikhs in India, ethnic and cultural groups have sought with varying degrees of success to crown their own sense of separateness with the apparatus of a separate state.
- Religious fundamentalism in Judaism, Christianity, and Islam challenges the individualism, materialism, and secularism of the Western-style state.
- The rise of gender in politics – as shown in the struggles for political representation of women, gays, lesbians, and bisexuals – also challenges the nation-state from below by stressing the politics of diversity and cultural pluralism.
- The authority of the state is challenged from below by libertarians, who want deregulation, privatization, and the control of welfare-state expenditures and public-sector taxes, and by environmentalists who seek to control the effects of economic growth.

Comparativists often study these challenges to the state under the rubric of social movements and revolutions. Student revolts, terrorism, decolonialization, as well as fascist and Marxist revolutions come in waves that affect many countries at the same time. Why? Herein lies another paradox of globalizations and heterogeneities: The source of globalization, the West, is also frequently the source of the challenges to it. Liberalism, democracy, fascism, and socialism, for example, are all Western inventions.

In sum, in your reading you will find contradictory globalist and localist forces that characterize the current world community of nations and states. While the last two centuries have witnessed the consolidation of the world into presumptive nation-states, we have also seen a set of similar challenges to the state from below through the growing independence of civil society, and from above through the growth of regional and supranational forces, that challenge these global trends in global ways.

## WORLD-HISTORICAL TIME AND CONFLICTS AMONG STATES

The global community does not consist of a single sovereign world government or of multiple noninteracting local communities. The world today is divided territorially into nation-states: bounded societies that cooperate and compete, exchange goods and services, and fight militarily for absolute and relative advantage. Trade and imperialism, war and conflict, and violence and instability are thus important aspects of the world. This is global politics, international competition and struggle over plenty, prestige, and power. The world can be a tough neighborhood indeed.

States compete militarily. The search for global and regional hegemony, or mere national survival, leads states to spend a lot of money on armies, navies, and air forces, whereas war and the preparation for war has historically influenced nation building and state building. Modern nuclear weaponry creates the possibility of strategic nuclear competition between the United States and Russia, China and Japan, India and Pakistan, and Israel and Iraq. War is increasingly global. World War II was fought in the Atlantic and in the Pacific, in Europe and Asia, and the geopolitics of the recent Gulf War was equally global.

In addition to competing for military power, states compete for economic plenty. Mercantilism, beggar-thy-neighbor competition to stay on top economically, was more prominent in the interwar period but also occurs today. Many nations decide to close their borders selectively to trade, as in the case of import restrictions. Others restrict the movement of labor across their borders. Some compete with tax breaks, investment subsidies, and export support for companies that invest on their soil. Other states organize regional trade blocks, such as ASEAN and EU, to further their economic ends.

States also compete for cultural hegemony. Travelers to Europe, Latin America, or Asia often notice the huge cultural influence of the United States. Recently some political scientists have maintained that Western, Islamic, and Asian values are destined to clash with one another. Other political scientists, however, point to the high growth rates achieved by Singapore, Taiwan, Malaysia, and Korea during the cold war as evidence that Asian values can work just as well as Western ones in promoting economic development.

Speaking more generally and more historically, *modern sovereign states developed in response to the experiences and challenges of other states.* Our historical point of departure in this book is the profound and irreversible changes that occurred in the northwest part of Europe, and especially Great Britain, approximately 250 years ago. This most important critical juncture in modern history is often subsumed under the rubric of the Industrial Revolution that ran its course roughly from 1780 to 1850. In a very short period, new technologies of mass economic production, the creation of large urban areas containing a growing proportion of the population, the commercialization of agriculture, the increasing ability to manipulate nature due to rapid advances in scientific knowledge, and new methods of organizing people in administrative bureaucracies combined in Great Britain and in a few other countries to generate a new society of unprecedented power that succeeded in the 19th century in conquering much of the rest of the planet.

The rest of the world had to respond to the British challenge, and comparativists have spent much time documenting and explaining these responses. To take just one example, once Great Britain became *the* major power in the world, Germany felt pressure to catch up. In responding, however, Germany could not simply recapitulate the British experience for that would have taken, many Germans believed, far too long. Instead, Germany developed its own set of political and economic institutions that exercised an important impact on its subsequent political and economic history. In fact, as we will see later on, Germany still lives with the institutional legacies of its initial responses to the British "challenge."

Any global order thus involves competition in world-historical space and time that affects the evolution of states. Here are the relevant questions to ask: What was the competitive international situation in which a state found itself when it attempted to modernize and industrialize? Who were its principal rivals and competitors among other sovereign states? In other words, who developed first, had a head start, and could serve as a benchmark? And who developed later, had to play catch-up in order not to be left behind, and hence looked for negative and positive role models?

Different developmental logics of countries thus appear partly because countries begin development in different world-historical eras. Great Britain, for example, developed "first" and thus laid down political, economic, and military challenges to which other states responded. In Europe, France, Germany, and Russia responded to the British challenge out of fear of national backwardness and political humiliation, but did so in their own ways, and hence their developmental histories differ from Britain's and from each other's. Outside of Europe, Japan, China, Mexico, India, Iran, and South Africa, the other countries studied in this book, attempted to find their own ways into the modern world of sovereign states. Each used the resources – human, institutional, and economic – available at the time it responded to the challenges – political, economic, and military – that came from the outside world.

Strategic and defensive modernization to preserve national interests, identities, and institutions is thus crucial. Global political and economic competition affects all countries of the world. Late development brought challenges in the form of malevolent Western colonialism and imperialism. It also brought opportunities in the form of benevolent liberal hegemons and positive and negative models of development that permitted the late developers to learn from the positive experiences and avoid the negative experiences of countries that preceded them historically.

In sum, we stress that domestic politics must be understood in world-historical perspective; that our descriptions and explanations must take into account particular historical situations; and that domestic economies, cultures, and politics are invariably affected by the competitive international environment of states.

## Domestic Interests, Identities, and Institutions

What aspects of domestic politics are affected by the global context of development? We advance three principles that are relatively simple but very powerful. First, people are rational beings who pursue their interests. Second, people are meaning-seeking beings who are defined by their identities. Third, people's interests and identities are shaped by and pursued within institutions. Interests, identities, and institutions are all, in turn, shaped, as shown in our country chapters, by the global context of development. The global context of development, therefore, matters to comparativists because it produces certain constellations of interests, identities, and institutions that persist over time and shape the countries in which we live.

### INTERESTS

Politics is partly about the pursuit of interest. One reason that people get involved in politics is to get the things that they want from government and to ensure that the state enacts laws and policies that advance their interests. Of course, what people want varies greatly. Still, there is no gainsaying that a large part of politics in any society revolves around the question of who gets what. I may want a higher standard of living and you may want a cleaner environment. How these differences in interest are resolved tells us much about a country's politics.

We therefore assume that individuals have preferences, goals, and objectives; that they also face temporally fixed constraints, limitations, and resources; and hence that they make choices among available alternatives in order to reach their goals. Very often it is simply material interests that determine policy preferences. Hence, people react to the incentives in some social context and use some tactic or strategy to pick the alternative that best enables them to satisfy their own material self-interest. In short, people are problem solvers who try to optimize their gains and minimize their losses.

Interest-based analyses therefore focus on material well-being as derived from economic markets. Markets are the dominant mode of resource distribution in modern societies, although societies can organize their markets in a number of ways. Take Japan and Great Britain, for example. Although both have market economies, a close examination of these societies reveals that they are very different kinds of market economies. Contemporary China is a third example: Although it is nominally still communist, it makes wide use of the market in its economic policies; yet, it is very different from a capitalist market economy.

It is particularly important to recognize that global markets often shape economic interests. World markets might make shoemakers in Massachusettes interested in import restrictions and software developers in Silicon Valley interested in free trade.

Such material interests can be pursued collectively. People who share an interest attempt to act as if they were a single individual. This is not easy because of what political scientists call the collective-action problem: People who want to act as a unified group often find that individuals are narrowly focused on their own personal situation and hence do not contribute to collective causes. Yet, people often do band together in pursuit of what they perceive to be their common concerns and join political parties, interest groups, and social movements that become important political actors. For example, professional associations, trade unions, health lobbies, and environmental organizations are but a few of the many kinds of interest groups that people join in order to monitor and pressure the state.

An important category of interest that comparativists believe is often pursued collectively is social class. Class can be a very tricky concept to use because it has so many possible meanings. To Marxists, class means one's place in the production process. Marxists argue that all people with a similar place will think and act similarly. Others adopt a looser definition of class, which means similarity in lifestyles, consumption patterns, and ways of thinking that may or may not coincide with one's position in the economy.

One of the important things that comparativists have noted is the differing degree of strength of interest groups based on class interests or other interests in different countries. More than a century ago, Alexis de Tocqueville observed the propensity among the inhabitants of the United States to participate in associational life. Since then, other comparativists have painted a more complex picture. Some countries, such as Germany and Japan, have relatively high levels of participation in trade unions; others, such as the United States and Canada, have much lower levels. In dictatorial countries, such as Stalin's Russia or Mao's China, it may be very difficult for interest groups to form because the leaders have the power and will to prevent them from coming into existence. One measure of whether a country is becoming more democratic, then, is its people's ability to form interest groups and their capacity to influence political decisions. The kinds of interest groups and their strength determine much about the politics of a country.

*stop*

Of course, it may be the case that there are so many interest groups at work that a country's politics becomes gridlocked. This often seems to be the case in the United States. In countries such as India and South Africa, ethnic interest groups are frequently able to alter the legislative agendas of ruling coalitions and presidents. How conflict and cooperation among interest groups work themselves out in different societies is therefore something in which comparativists are intensely interested. In Great Britain, as in the United States, politics tends to revolve around the competition among interest groups that comparativists call pluralism, which tends toward gridlock. In Japan and Germany, on the other hand, social groups often seek to cooperate and avoid political conflict, even of the peaceful kind, through institutionalized bargaining arrangements called corporatism.

In sum, the pursuit of material interests through interest-group politics is affected by the global context and, in turn, interest groups battle over alternative paths of development. The pursuit of material interests thereby affects the distribution of economic rewards in society and consequently represents one important way of approaching comparative politics.

## IDENTITIES

Politics is also about identity. Although evidence shows that people all over the world often pursue common goals, and thus can be said to share certain interests, people also frequently define what is in their interests differently. Based on particular sets of beliefs and values that we often refer to as culture, they will even define their material interests differently. What people are willing to give their life for, how much hardship they will bear during war, or how many hours on weekends people are willing to work varies across societies. Likewise, the kinds of ideas, political language, and even physical demeanor that people expect from their politicians also varies greatly across nations and states.

Think, for example, about how religion and ethnicity influence politics. If people define their identity primarily in religious terms, if they say to themselves "We are primarily Jewish, Christian, or Muslim, and not German, French or Iranian," they will define their interests differently from people who tend to be anticlerical. In turn, they will support different kinds of governmental policies toward religion, schooling, and popular culture. Ethnicity and national sentiments have a similar kind of influence on how people define themselves. If someone defines herself primarily in ethnic terms, she will tend to care most about how people of her own ethnic group or nation fare in politics. She will tend to define her interests in ethnic terms. It is common, for example, for people of an ethnic group to want a state that will defend its rights to schooling in their language and cultural traditions and to want politics and administration to be controlled by people of their ethnic group.

Just as people with different economic or material interests can clash over their differences, people with different identities also frequently disagree in politics. Although the Soviet Union was a single country, it consisted of many different ethnic groups who never managed to overcome the feeling that their separate national identities were stronger than the Soviet identity that they shared. The result was the largely peaceful breakup of the country in 1991. Often, however, the results of identity politics can be tragic. In the recent Yugoslav civil war, people who speak basically the same language began to define their identities so differently (often in terms of religious and "ethnic" differences) that they were willing to kill one another in order to live in areas that were ethnically "pure."

Of course, people may possess not simply one identity but several competing identities, and it is far from obvious which one will be dominant or how they will ultimately act based on their identities. Someone might be, for example, a Muslim, a woman, and black and feel equally strong about all three of these identities. Leaders often play an important role in mobilizing some identities and neutralizing others. In France, for example, right-wing politicians have tried in recent years to convince the French that their traditional notions of who is French, someone born on French soil, should be changed and that the true French are those who have been born into the French culture. The idea here is to exclude as many immigrants from citizenship and public life as possible. On the other hand, a minority of German politicians have been working in recent years to alter the notion of who is a German, an idea which to this day remains based on blood ties to other Germans, in order to make German identity more inclusive. Similarly, successive Indian governments have worked very hard at catering to the various subnational identities within the country, while simultaneously carving out a distinctive "Indian" national identity that will be more important to people than all their other identities.

Comparativists who study identity are called "culturalists." As the label indicates, culturalists concentrate on the cultural determinants of politics. By culture they mean the dominant belief systems, values, and ideologies in a society. Ethnicity and religion are only two of the more important kinds of cultural identities. One can easily point to a politics of gender, environmental, and regional identities. Each of these identities shapes what people want out of politics, what they are willing to do, and how they define their interests.

The subject can be made even broader, however. Culturalists frequently study attitudes in society toward such issues as the role of government, the kinds of institutions that people want, the degree of commitment to democracy, how much education matters in a society, and the way that people associate with one another. Such studies may be quantitative public-opinion surveys about attitudes and opinions or they may be microlevel ethnographic studies of civic associations, such as Greenpeace, the National Rifle Association, or the Parent Teacher Association.

Sometimes, material interests trump social identities and class politics prevails. In the United States, for example, Clinton won a presidential election with the slogan "it's the economy, stupid." But it is easy to be cynical and to think that people care only about money. In fact, many different types of social identities can trump material interests, allowing identity politics to prevail. For example, in the Iranian Islamic state, Ayatollah Khomeini thought that "economics is for donkeys." The world has seen a revival of traditional communities, religious fundamentalisms, ethnic and racial identities, and gender identifications that have not been washed away by (and arguably have been encouraged by) Western materialism.

On the other hand, social identities can support material interests. Since they can discipline a labor force for development, authoritarian states often try to impose cultures on societies in order to promote economic development. Gorbachev in the Soviet Union and Mao in China were ideological true believers in socialism. They sought an ideological renaissance, a spiritual remobilization, in which the dedication of the masses would be the key to national economic success. It is also possible for liberal and middle-class ideals to rise to the level of a developmental ideology. In the West, the Protestant ethic of hard work being its own reward was probably essential to its economic success: An inner sense of moral duty, rather than an external set of incentives and disincentives, is necessary to maintain a modern work force no less than a modern army. In Iran, secular nationalism replaced Islam in part to encourage economic development; now that secular nationalism is being replaced by Islam, many hope that it, too, will encourage economic development.

## INSTITUTIONS

We now turn from interests and identities to institutions. We first explore how the global context influences domestic institutions and how these institutions, in turn, affect development paths by influencing interests and identities. We then explain why many comparativists consider the study of politics to be synonymous with the study of institutions.

### Institutions as Consequences (of the Global Context) and as Causes (of Interests and Identities)

The state is an organization controlling the people in a territorial jurisdiction. An important factor affecting how societal interests and identities influence development paths is whether a strong or weak state is in control. Moreover, state strength = autonomy + capacity.

Consider autonomy. The state may be autonomous from the interests and identities of civil society. This means that it is not vulnerable to specific groups in society – class interest groups or religious identity groups, for example – that try to penetrate and capture the state and that attempt to use it to pursue their narrow concerns, rather than to pursue the broader concerns of all society. The state's political and administrative leaders could be willing and able to formulate their own preferences and define their own goals with respect to development. Hence, the state could be autonomous in the sense of making its own decisions.

Now consider capacity. The state might also have great power and capacity vis-à-vis the interests and identities in civil society. That is, the state may have the resources and the ability to use those resources effectively, to implement its decisions and strategies so as to address the problems, challenges, and crises of development, in spite of what class interests and religious identities might want.

Many later-developing countries believe that a strong – autonomous and capable – state is good for economic development. A strong state can pursue the general good of all society. It does not have to follow the narrow interests or identities of a single subnational group that has selfish reasons for not contributing to the public welfare. Nor does a strong state have to accept the outcomes of the democratic process – that the public good is the sum of the interests and identities that emerge from voting and lobbying. Rather, a strong state can pursue the true public good of the entire nation. In other words, one needs a strong state to make up for the selfishness found in society: Its diverse interests and identities cannot be counted on to advocate and pursue public goods; the jockeying and give-and-take of group politics does not necessarily yield the optimal policies. The Japanese state, for example, has often operated autonomously of business and labor interests and has had the capacity to implement their choices over their opposition.

Such common democratic institutions as divided government, checks and balances, and federalism were therefore avoided by states that followed the early developers, because they were thought to decrease state power and promote political fragmentation, instability, and gridlock. On the basis of recent experience, however, many later developers have come to believe that a strong state hinders development because it burdens society with high taxes and other policies that are designed to feather the beds of the bureaucrats that constitute the strong state, rather than to foster economic development for everybody else. Ultimately, moreover, former totalitarian states, such as the Soviet Union, proved weaker than the supposedly weak democracies, such as the United States. Democracies, especially those with a powerful president or prime minister, can be strong because they create the state legitimacy that can reinforce national unity and thus resolve political conflicts of interest over interests and identities. Of equal importance is something we will now focus on: how democratic institutions can produce strong states by empowering some interests and identities and disempowering others.

**Democratic State Institutions.** One definition of democracy is simply procedural. In a democracy, political parties compete over who controls government. Democracy thus means that the rulers are chosen in free competitive elections with a wide franchise: All citizens are entitled to vote.

The problem is that under majority rule, such a system could be all-powerful if the majority always has its way. In wartime, for example, democracies can be very strong states. More generally, politicians, who represent citizens, are recruited via well-defined electoral procedures and hence charged by citizens to adopt their policies. The debate and discourse surrounding elections creates popular sovereignty and hence political legitimacy. Government, in turn, can channel popular participation behind government strategies for national development and mobilize its people.

The principle of election, however, means that a different majority can be constructed. Since the "outs" can become the "ins" and the "ins" become the "outs," democracies always have the potential for instability feared by advocates of a strong state.

A more populist approach to democracy allows and even encourages more popular involvement and participation in the public policy-making processes. If people do not get what they want from democratic government, many mechanisms, strategies, and channels of popular involvement may be pursued besides voting, campaigning, and joining a political party: (1) holding town meetings to discuss issues; (2) going to court and filing briefs to support or oppose government policies; (3) drawing upon a set of patron-client ties associated with government officials; (4) formally or informally joining and participating in an interest group; and (5) formally or informally joining and participating in a social movement engaged in peaceful protest activity, such as strikes, demonstrations, or marches, or violent protest activity, such as riots, occupations, and terrorism.

If democracy, whether formal or populist, means government of the people, by the people, and for the people, then how does a democracy choose among the preferences and different visions while producing stable and effective government? How are conflicts of interests and identities resolved and stable policy decisions made?

All democracies influence identities and filter preferences. Several democratic institutions help define and restrict popular preferences so that democratic governments can make choices, avoid endless political instability, and choose a development path.

**Constitutions.** Constitutionalism restrains political authority and limits majoritarian government. It prevents arbitrary and absolute power by setting limits and restrictions on the majority's political power. The U.S. Bill of Rights, for example, secures civil liberties by protecting the individual from arbitrary government action. The rule of law creates separations between the public and the private, the state and civil society, and the government and people. It recognizes that the domain for fulfillment and expression of one's individuality lies not only in government but also in the family, economic organizations, religious institutions, and communal groupings. Constitutions, however, vary. Some constitutions are written, others not. Some are detailed, others sketchy; and some are important, others ineffective. Different types of constitutions empower and disempower different types of interests and identities so that government can get on with the business of governing and make policy choices.

**Separation of Government Powers.** Through a principle known in the United States as checks and balances, government authority can be divided into different branches: executive, legislative, and judicial. But not all governments separate powers. In parliamentary as opposed to presidential systems, the executive is a cabinet that emerges from the majority or plurality party or parties in the legislature, and the head of government is consequently a prime minister and not a popularly elected president. There are also mixed parliamentary/presidential systems as in France. More generally, the forms of executive, legislative, and judicial institutions vary greatly among states. With respect to executives, sometimes the head of state is a ceremonial leader, while the head of government is the effective leader. Sometimes the executive is an individual (a president); sometimes it is a collective. With respect to legislatures, some have a single chamber and others are bicameral, meaning they have two legislative chambers, such as the U.S. Senate and House of Representatives. Some are based on functional representation of interests, and others are based on territorial representations of populations. Some are organized internally by political parties and others by committees. Finally, the independence of courts varies greatly. In the United States, for example, the courts are independent and there is even judicial review of executive and legislative actions. Different types of executive, legislative, and judicial arrangements create winners and losers out of particular interests and identities.

**Participation Restrictions.** Although democracy allows or even encourages participation of different interests and identities, all democracies place limits on the acceptable forms of participation. Voting may be restricted via poll taxes, minimum age restrictions, literacy tests, property requirements, registration procedures, naturalization laws, and race and gender requirements. Democracies also conventionally limit when and where to vote. More populist forms of direct democracy may be limited, too. Initiatives, referendums, and recalls are permitted, if at all, only on certain issues. There are restrictions that bar extremist political parties. Interest-group lobbying is also restricted. For example, there may be limits on campaign contributions. Finally, social movements may be restricted. There may be regulations on such forms of street politics as demonstrations, rallies, picketing, and sit-ins. All forms of violent protest, of course, are illegal. By defining legitimate participation, democracy defines the politically acceptable interests and identities.

**Electoral Rules.** A good example of how institutions screen interests and identities are electoral systems. Voting rules structure vote aggregation. Under single-member district plurality (SMDP) as in the United States, the state is divided into districts and each district has one seat. Candidates run and whoever receives a plurality (the most) votes wins. Under proportional representation (PR) as in contemporary Germany, constituencies are multimember, occasionally consisting of the entire nation. Seats are allocated to parties on the basis of the share of each party's votes in the electorate.

In sum, government of the people, by the people, and for the people is no simple matter. Democracy is complex, and the democratic state is really a set of institutions that activate, restrict, and finally aggregate interests and identities into public policies (e.g., development strategies). To advocates of a strong bureaucratic state, all this democratic complexity is unnerving. It certainly appears simpler to have bureaucrats formulate their government's goals autonomously of its citizens and then to have the capacity to turn the goals into public policy. Our country studies will reveal, however, the great variety of democratic institutions that enable democracies to govern and thereby choose development strategies. Elites in postwar France and Germany, for example, designed institutions to overcome the political fragmentation, instability, and gridlock of prewar experiments in democracy. South Africa and India are examples of multicultural democracies in which democratic institutions are designed to adjudicate fundamental differences in interests and identities.

### Interests and Identities, and the Struggle Over Institutions

We have argued that the competitive geopolitical context generates the demand for economic development that, in turn, generates actors with material interests and social identities. Interest groups and identity groups with different preferences about development then come into conflict with each other.

We have also argued that political institutions empower some groups and constrain others, and thereby transform interests and identities into public policies. Bureaucratic and democratic institutions thus influence the formation of interests and identities, restrict and foster their expression, and finally mold them into policies associated with paths of development.

The various interest groups and identity groups realize that institutions influence the outcome of their policy struggles over a path of development and, therefore, seek to retain or change institutions in order to gain the political power needed to satisfy their own interests and identities. An important part of politics thus involves generally unequal groups fighting over the making and remaking of political institutions. For example, in Britain, middle-class interests fought against monarchs and aristocrats. They sought a parliament to limit the king and preserve their class, status, and power. In Germany, urban industrial elites and rural landowning elites fought against lower-class workers' and peasants' interests. They sought a strong state to preserve their influence. In both cases, democratic and bureaucratic institutions were the outcomes of interest- and identity-driven political struggles. Hard bargains were struck. Whereas some believed that the bargains made everyone in the country better off by permitting development, others believed that the bargains bestowed much greater advantages on some than others.

Since institutions are so central to politics, they stand at a pivotal point in our framework. While the global context influences domestic interests, identities, and institutions, the institutions, which are often contested, shape and filter interests and identities into developmental paths.

## Development Paths to the Modern World

An important manifestation of global competition is a state's selection of a developmental path. States adopt domestic and foreign policies in politics and economics to compete in the global order. What do such policies, paths, and regimes entail?

With respect to domestic policy, states do many things. Governments pursue extractive policies. They take goods and services from their citizens in the form of money (taxes) and time (military service). Governments also pursue distributive policies in which they return goods and services to their citizens, for example, roads and social security payments. Governments pursue regulative policies in which they set the rules for property rights, human rights, and occupational safety. Finally, governments also sometimes attempt to shape equality of opportunity and/or equality of results.

Governments also pursue foreign policies. Some states advance a global revolutionary cause, some pursue global counterrevolution, and others remain relatively peaceful.

These domestic and foreign policy choices often combine into what is called a *development strategy* or *grand strategy* as shown in Table 1. Different world-historical circumstances favor certain grand strategies of development over others. For example, during the cold war, Japan developed its heavy industries and India instituted a green revolution in agriculture. The global trading system may influence whether nations adopt import-substitution industrialization, as in India's attempt to develop its indigenous infant industries, or export-led industrialization, as in Japan's attempt to compete in the world automobile market. World markets might influence whether states are free traders or protectionist, whether they institute a laissez-faire market economy or statist one, and whether they pursue peaceful or aggressive foreign policies.

The third theme of the book is, therefore, democratic capitalism and its alternatives. *There is no single development path to the modern world.* States can and do make their own development choices and often evolve local institutional variations of globally dominant political economies. Theories suggesting that all states moved through common stages and converge in the end, such as modernization theories, are wrong. Looked at historically, there were multiple paths to the modern world; there was no end of history and no inevitable triumph of democracy, markets, openness, and peace. Domestic interests, identities, and institutions combined with the global context to support nondemocratic, socialist, closed, and militaristic paths. And a key source of local variation today is the

**TABLE 1.**

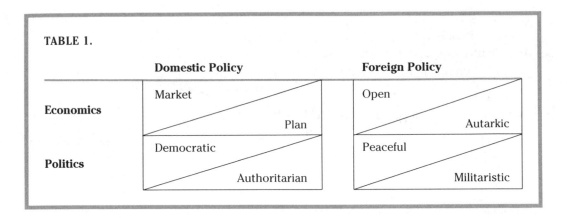

|  | Domestic Policy | Foreign Policy |
|---|---|---|
| **Economics** | Market / Plan | Open / Autarkic |
| **Politics** | Democratic / Authoritarian | Peaceful / Militaristic |

existence of alternatives to and variations on democracy, markets, openness, and peace.

We therefore need to develop a comparative and historical understanding of the alternative paths to the modern world adopted in different international environments. We offer four sets of country studies chosen to exemplify the different developmental logics of countries that began development in different world-historical eras.

**Early Developers: Britain and France.** These countries were among the first to develop domestic and international market economies, individualistic and secular cultures, and the institutions of representative democracy. Both countries set the pattern for liberal democracy in the West and thereby influenced all other countries that developed later. Both were also at the forefront of the colonial empire building of the 19th century that ultimately subordinated most peoples of Africa, Asia, and the Middle East to European domination.

**Middle Developers: Germany and Japan.** Once the "West" developed, all other countries were forced to respond. Germany and Japan were among the first to do so. In general, the later a country began industrial development after Britain, the larger the role of the state in economic development, the weaker developed were the capitalist middle classes, and the more dominant the military component of the developmental strategy. After abortive attempts at representative democracy, both Germany and Japan thus went through a period of fascism, brutal and destructive war, and occupation by outside powers before they were readmited to the world economy under U.S. tutelage. In order to compete in the contemporary period, both fashioned variations on the individualism, markets, and democracy found in the early developers.

**Late Developers: Russia and China.** These countries were late developers that experienced first communist and then (in the case of Russia) anticommunist revolutions aimed at the same purpose: development. Both countries had distinct values and institutions in the communist period, both are currently struggling with the legacy of political authoritarianism and central economic planning, and both are trying to introduce expanded economic markets and to accommodate or contain demands for democracy.

**Experimental Developers: Mexico, India, Iran, and South Africa.** These countries are faced with unique developmental problems characteristic of their respective continents. As part of what once was called the Third World, they sought a middle way between capitalist and communist development, borrowing and innovating in ways they thought fit local circumstances. This third way involved some grand experiments in development that were very different from the early, middle, and late developers. The outcome of these experiments is still uncertain, which reflects the fact that most of Latin America, Africa, and Asia is still coping with the contemporary worldwide trend toward democracy and markets.

Mexico's grand experiment is independence. Is it possible for a country to be autonomous when its northern neighbor happens to be the most powerful nation in the world? Its postrevolutionary development is characterized by a one-party state, which is increasingly challenged by political competitors, and an autarkic economy, which is increasingly threatened by international markets. India's grand experiment is nonrevolutionary democracy. Is it possible for a large postcolonial country to be a democracy when it has had a major independence movement but not a social revolution? It is interesting to note that its one-party dominance and autarkic development have also been influenced by global trends toward democracy and markets. Iran's grand experiment is Islam. Is it possible for a country to be economically and politically powerful when it has had an Islamic revolution that creates an Islamic state? Iran seeks a distinctive path of development that combines democracy and markets in ways that accommodate local religious traditions; one finds here a struggle between pro-Western and anti-Western forces. Finally, South Africa's grand experiment is interracial democracy. Is it possible for ethnoconstitutional democracy and markets to survive in a country that made a relatively peaceful transition from colonialism and apartheid?

These four grand experiments remind us that development is open-ended. Since new challenges to development exist in today's small world, undiscovered paths may still emerge. Yet, the decline of the cold war and the end of the communist alternative has clearly diminished the pride of being part of the Third World and, hence, of seeking a middle way of development. Many former Third World countries are thus redefining their interests, identities, and institutions to compete globally via democracy and markets.

You should note three things about our choice of cases. First, our global and developmental perspective allows us to choose cases on theoretical and substantive grounds and thus to set contemporary issues about policy and performance in a larger setting. Second, we have chosen cases that are today's engines of development for the Western, Middle Eastern, Asian, African, and Latin American regions of the world. Finally, all of our cases have had revolutions of one type or another rooted in world-historical problems of development, which, in turn, influence country-specific patterns of development.

Finally, you should note two aspects of the politics of development paths. First, paths are competing political alternatives. People always debate the choice of a development path, and these debates inevitably involve a power struggle among competing interests and identities. For example, in early-20th-century China, the urban intelligentsia advocated a liberal development path based on urban middle-class interests, Western liberal values, and democratic institutions. The nationalists pushed an authoritarian path rooted in conservative, rural elite interests, a strong nationalist ideology, and statist institutions. The communists advocated a communist path based on peasant interests, Marxist ideology, and totalitarian institutions controlling civil society. Similar debates among liberals, conservatives, and socialists can be located in every Western country during the 1930s. Fascist, communist, and liberal movements that vied for political power also can be found in late-19th-century Russia and late-20th-century Russia. Competing systems of governance captured major states, plunging the global order into World War II.

Second, the debate among proponents of various paths eventually gives way to governing or developmental coalitions, combining state and societal actors, which form behind grand strategies of development and attempt to implement them. Under fascism, rural and urban elites used the state to repress workers and peasants. Under post–World War II "corporatist" systems in Europe, business, labor, and government worked together. Today, neoliberal development coalitions are dominant in many countries. Such policy coalitions, however, face formidable problems. They are vulnerable to shifts in global context and can be quite unstable. Some members leave voluntarily and others are purged. Many have traced the failure of democracy in Weimar Germany to cabinet instability, and others have traced cabinet instability to the failure of the democrats to put together a developmental coalition. Hitler and the Nazi Party then seized power and proposed a new militaristic and genocidal grand strategy for Germany and Europe. This example teaches us that while state-society coalitions are difficult to construct, their success defines development – for better or worse.

In sum, comparativists believe that the world-historical time in which countries modernized or industrialized influences their development strategy. This book, therefore, chooses its cases based on the international situation within which states found themselves when they first attempted to develop.

## Comparative Politics Feedback

A particular developmental policy backed by a specific regime coalition may or may not be successful. Based on the rule of thumb "if it ain't broke, don't fix it," one would expect that when development is working well for everyone in the country, regimes would want to consolidate their development path.

Often a developmental path performs poorly everywhere and for nearly everyone except a very small group of beneficiaries, however. A path, such as the creation of a predatory, nondevelopmental state, could produce little economic growth, wasteful and inefficient allocation of resources, crime and violence, corruption (black markets and bribery), and worker absenteeism, vandalism, and alcoholism. Moreover, developmental strategies can produce misdevelopment, uneven development, or exploitative development. For example, the British approach to colonial development in India involved a divide-and-rule strategy that produced distorted development: Interests, identities, and institutions were constructed so as to favor Britain and not India. And, more generally, development experiments can fail and result in either stagnant or collapsed states. Although some regimes are by definition interim, transitional, and provisional, there are dead-end developmental paths that did not look so dead-end at the time they were adopted. The dustbin of history is littered with colonial administrations, world empires, principalities, city-states, tribal areas without fixed territorial boundaries, bureaucratic authoritarianisms, feudalisms, slave states, apartheid systems, and fascist and communist regimes.

Poor economic performance in failed and misshapen development experiments lead to uncertainty, disruptions, and social tensions: civil disorder and political anarchy, leadership succession crises, illegitimacy and alienation. Developmental models are thus constantly being rethought. For example, until 1990, countries throughout the world sought to emulate Japanese success; now Japan has sunk into a prolonged recession and has been forced to listen to Western advice on how to reform its economy. The result of such new thinking can be evolutionary or revolutionary change of domestic interests, identities, and institutions so as to pursue new developmental paths.

Failed developmental paths can be altered by revolutionary change of interests, identities, and institutions from above. National elites can coalesce into a new regime the purpose of which is to resist the global order. For example, German and Japanese revolutions from above remade social classes, increased national identities, and created militant and strong states so that these middle developers could resist the early developers.

Of at least equal importance, failed development paths are sometimes changed by revolution from below; often after failed attempts at revolution from above. For example, economic and political liberalization under Gorbachev created new interests, identities, and institutions that brought about the collapse of the Soviet Union. It appears that certain development paths and the coalitions behind them run their course wherever and whenever they are tried, and therefore contain the seeds of their own revolutionary demise. Not long ago, for example, many academics and policy makers believed that late-developing countries needed strong states to mobilize resources for industrialization, assure territorial integrity, collect taxes, and staff bureaucracies. As resistance movements began to think otherwise and toppled many such states, global thought shifted. It is now widely argued that strong, populist authoritarian regimes, military and bureaucratic absolutisms, patrimonial states that concentrate power in rulers and their families, and corporatist and state-led industrialization generate problems: bloated public sectors, mismanagement, corruption, waste, and inefficiency that result in such economic imbalances as inflation, currency overevaluation, and balance of payments crises. Neoliberal regimes based on expanded free markets, which have been created in turn, have also generated severe social problems. Some now believe that "shock-therapy" policies of rapid marketization, advocated for many states by the World Bank and the International Monetary Fund, can also produce instability and the possibility of revolution. Different developmental regimes, in short, contain different flaws that eventually lead to the appearance of resistance movements in a set of similarly situated countries.

## International Relations Feedback

There are innumerable ways in which a nation's development influences the global context within which a regime finds itself. Consider some examples. British power helped define the 18th- and 19th-century worlds. In the aftermath of World War II, America imposed its own neoliberal vision on the global economic order. The decision by the U.S. Federal Reserve Bank to raise interest rates from 1979 to 1982 contributed to the world debt crisis. German authoritarianism and fascism plunged the world into global war. Japanese authoritarianism had the same result. The Soviet Union's and China's internal patterns of development led them to try to export communist regimes to the rest of the world. When the cold war was waged, Mexico and India legitimized and encouraged a third way of development for a large number of states. Iran's decision, along with the rest of major oil-producing states, to raise oil prices in the 1970s shook the developed world. Its Islamic revolution shook regimes throughout the Arab and Moslem worlds. And, finally, South Africa's bold experiment in interracial democracy holds worldwide implications.

In sum, developmental paths may contribute to global peace and prosperity. They may also contribute to global war and poverty. A nation's development can thus have an impact far beyond a single nation's borders.

The two feedback loops of our framework – comparative politics feedback and international relations feedback – yield a path-dependent view of development. History, or the legacy of the past, matters. Once a state starts down a development path, where it goes next is affected by where it has been. Choices made at critical junctures in a state's history not only set a state down a certain path but also preclude alternative paths. A state's contemporary problems thus originate in the historical crises and challenges it has faced. The developmental choices a country makes today are partly a result of the choices that were put in place when it began to develop in a particular world-historical context.

For example, interests, identities, and institutions can persist even through revolutions. First, economic markets and the interests they define show continuity. Today's close connection of interest groups and government in Germany, for example, can be traced to the developmental choices of Germany's 19th-century rulers. Second, cultural identities and the values and beliefs people hold dear are resilient. Religion and ethnicity often reemerge after a revolution and affect developmental priorities and choices. Fundamentalist Islam in today's Iran, for example, survived the Shah's regime and was shaped by his industrialization policies. Finally, institutions that define and resolve conflicts among different interests and identities in a country can also survive revolution. Contemporary Russia's interests, identities, and institutions therefore are part of the historical legacy of communism.

The two feedback loops also offer a distinctive view of how the present is shaped by the past. Countries have developmental regimes, supported by developmental coalitions, that are separated by identifiable political crises or critical junctures that produce turning points in a country's history. In other words, a country's global context, its domestic interests, identities, and institutions, and, most significantly, its developmental path to the modern world, can change and lead to a new type of developmental regime. Germany, for example, made the transition from empire, to the democratic Weimar Republic, to Nazism, to a state divided between capitalism and communism, and finally to a new united Germany. Regime changes are often closely identified with leadership changes. Thus, the change from Gorbachev to Yeltsin in Moscow involved a redefinition of Russia's state institutions and national identity. Our country chapters are chronologically organized to take account of the historical changes in regimes associated with changing global contexts, domestic interests, identities, and institutions, and developmental paths.

## WHY STUDY COMPARATIVE POLITICS

Why should we go through all this trouble of studying ten different countries? Why should we bother to compare alternative paths of development? One compares to gain an empirical and a moral perspective on politics.

### An Empirical Perspective: To Explain

All governments grapple with complex global issues: the need to accommodate diverse ethnic and religious identities, the struggle to improve economic security and growth, the quest to provide a strong basis for national citizenship, and the effort to cope with demands for democracy and participation. The world is a laboratory in which countries engage in grand experiments in development. There are a variety of such experiments: many different forms of culture, civil society, economic markets, political democracies, state bureaucracies, public policies, and global systems. The comparativist compares and contrasts how two or more countries conduct these experiments. Much of this book involves describing and explaining similarities and differences among countries.

For example, why are political parties different in Britain and France? Perhaps they are different because of institutions: The British electoral system is a first-past-the-post system that encourages a two-party system, and the French electoral system is a plurality system that encourages the formation of minority parties. On the other hand, perhaps the differences in parties can be attributed to differences in identities: France has a more radical revolutionary tradition than Britain. To take another example, why did Britain and Germany react differently to the oil shocks and budget crises of the 1970s? Perhaps they reacted differently because of the configuration of interests. Interest groups work more closely with government in Germany than in Britain. On the other hand, perhaps the differences can be attributed to identities. German workers value more highly the protections offered by the state against the ups and downs of the market, and were therefore less willing to accept cuts in their benefits than were their British counterparts. We try, in other words, to construct plausible explanations for the variations we observe. Comparison thus allows us to test our ideas about comparative politics. When done well, this sort of comparison provides a good interpretive understanding of the relevant cases.

The purpose of this book is, therefore, not to cram your head with information about politics in faraway places and long-ago times. Comparing cases and explanations helps us do comparative politics because it forces us to *think*. It also forces us to confront in a particularly acute way the problem of applying theories to reality. Ideally, the two types of learning complement one another: To understand cases, you need theory; to understand theory, you need cases.

You are not likely to become a social scientist, however. As policy makers and advisors, or simply as citizens wishing to have input into the policy process, we have two reasons for comparing countries. First, comparison encourages us to broaden our knowledge of political alternatives and possibilities. It allows us to recognize diversity. Such information allows us to offer informed input into the policy-making process. Second, the laboratory of political experiences may be transferable. Nations can learn from one another. They can locate ideas for solving their own problems. They can borrow foreign models or use the information to perfect and adapt their own institutions. In short, comparison allows us to draw positive lessons from successful experiments and negative lessons from failed experiments.

Comparison, in sum, allows social scientists to describe and explain, and policy makers to understand and choose. There are, however, many obstacles to the comparing of countries different in language, size, culture, and organization. The end result of our comparisons might be to recognize the differences rather than the similarities of experiences and experiments. Comparing the ramifications of a central problem of global politics for two or more countries might lead us to conclude that each country is importantly unique. As we probe a case in depth, the highly contextually specific character and direction of politics might be revealed.

For example, Americans might conclude that they are very different than the rest of the world: American exceptionalism is in fact a major theme of comparative politics. However, Americans need to recognize how big, important, rich, and powerful the United States is compared to the rest of the world. And Americans need to move beyond the narrow world of their own familiar assumptions and see the alternatives. In order to understand America itself – to describe, explain, and evaluate American politics – Americans must look beyond themselves. They gain perspective on their own society when they see themselves through the eyes of others. Comparison is therefore the remedy for American ethnocentrism. The features of U.S. government and politics that appear to Americans as constants are, in comparative and historical perspective, variables.

Comparison, therefore, always has been used by both Americans and foreigners to produce a better-informed and more critical understanding of the United States.

## A Moral Perspective: To Evaluate

We also compare to find out what is best. What is the best developmental path? Leaders may want to stay in power, but their citizens ask about the benefits that the leaders have brought. What has the political system achieved? More generally, philosophers ask, What is the good life? What is the best government? Philosophers have offered us many perspectives on the vices and virtues of political orders. Plato valued benevolent rule by a wise elite; Hobbes trusted order and the state; Hegel wanted the nation-state; Rousseau hoped for the natural life in a community; Marx yearned for a classless society; and Jefferson wanted the pursuit of happiness allowed by liberty.

The issue of appraising or critically evaluating the performance of political systems is, therefore, a contentious one. In constructing a checklist for how well a system is doing, two possibilities exist. We could use universal standards of good government set by, say, the United Nations or the World Bank. Or, we could allow every country to define its own standards. The danger of the former approach is that the definition of democracy, for example, might be restricted to Western forms. The danger of the latter approach is that all nations might call themselves democracies: liberal democracies, mass democracies, tutelary democracies, guided democracies, fascist democracies, or communist democracies.

Either type of evaluation is made difficult by two sets of trade-offs. First, there is the potential conflict of the individual and the collectivity. Liberal democracy, for example, values and protects the individual. Respect for the individual human being is an end in itself. He or she has innate qualities and potentials that must be protected, respected, and given freedom to develop. Knowledge and truth are also derived from the judgment of the individual. There is no established truth or transcendental values beyond what individuals want. However, these individual rights and truths often conflict with communal goals and responsibilities. An individual's home might stand in the way of the construction of a highway linking the people on both sides of a town. Moreover, duties to the community seem to be crucial to many of our moral choices. We not only care about ourselves but also want to transcend selfish interests. Identity is wrapped up with concerns for other people, including future generations, the natural environment, and, for religious believers, God.

Evaluations are also problematic because of the contradictions and trade-offs among goals. Consider economics. One goal might be efficiency: the most rational and effective use of human and material resources for given social ends. In a practical sense, people want prosperity and not poverty. They want a political order capable of sustained economic growth and development. Economic well-being allows the opportunity for the advancement and social mobility that are commensurate with one's abilities. A competing economic goal is equity. People also want distributive justice. Those of us who are relatively well-off must not forget that even in the most prosperous of countries, one finds the homeless, the jobless, the helpless, and the hopeless. Hence, a people may want to make certain that all of their fellow citizens receive the benefits of economic growth. Social rights include minimum standards for employment, housing, income levels, welfare, education, and health care. The goal might be, in other words, some equality of result to accompany equality of opportunity. Another competing goal is to ensure a high quality of life. Challenges to economic development brought by science and technology have been mounted by antinuclear activists, environmentalists, and those associated with religious movements.

Competing goals also exist in politics. A country's goal might be to maximize national power, assure domestic tranquility, and keep the international peace. Other goals include having a government that is accountable and respects political equality, the rights of participation, individual freedom, and cultural diversity.

The trade-offs between individuals and collectivities and among different types of goals make it difficult to evaluate alternative paths of development and suggest which is the best. One of the purposes of comparison is to clarify your own value positions on these important questions.

## Our Approach to Comparison

Comparison is essential to comparative politics, and we have made it central to this book. Our approach to comparison involves, first, a common set of tools with which we fashion country studies that reveal distinctive paths of development, and second, explicit comparisons among two or three cases designed to establish the causes and consequences of the significant differences among countries.

First, we have provided a set of tools to study substantive problems, rather than a blueprint to develop a theory of comparative politics. Because politics in Britain is interestingly different than politics in France, which is interestingly different from politics in Germany, we have not forced the chapters into a common, encyclopedia-like framework. That is, for each country we have not devoted three pages to interests, four to identity, and five to institutions. Rather, we have allowed our authors to use our common tools to bring out what is unique and significant about each country. This approach gives students a better sense of British politics, French politics, and South African politics than would be possible if every country's politics were forced through a homogenizing boilerplate framework that drains the countries of their uniqueness. Our framework permits authors to tell the story of their own country in their own way, and hence makes for more interesting reading.

Second, after each part of this book – early developers, middle developers, late developers, and experimental developers – we include a section called "stop and compare." It should really be called "stop and think" because we ask students to use the comparative method to draw empirical and moral lessons from the country studies by establishing the similarities and differences within and among each of our four sets of cases.

Here are the sorts of questions we ask: How are Britain and France variations of early development, and how are they different from the United States? How are Germany and Japan variations of middle development, which are different from the earlier developers? How do our two late developers, Russia and China, differ from one another, and how are they different from the early and middle developers? Finally, what are the similarities and differences among contemporary experimental developers – Mexico, India, Iran, and South Africa – and what sorts of contrasts do they make with the early, middle, and late developers we have studied?

By alternating country studies with explicit sections on comparison, we demonstrate how comparativists think. Comparativists mix the specific and the general. They begin with cases, turn to theory, and then return to the cases in a never-ending sequence of induction and deduction.

## CONCLUSION

This book guides the beginning political science student through the master concepts, dominant theories, and substantive problems of comparative politics. The country chapters you are about to read take you on a journey though space and time. Why would you, a college student, be interested in joining this tour through the countries of today's small world?

Our global framework implies that what happens in other countries is important to you, no matter where you live. Take the United States, for example. Although America is large, important, and rich, and it spans a continent separated by oceans from the rest of the world, we are dependent on the economics and the politics of countries around the world. Our political and economic security, our material welfare, and the well-being of our environment are wrapped up with the rest of the world. The transportation and communication revolutions that have contracted time and space have created global interdependence. The process is accelerating. It is only since the 1960s that we have had pictures of the globe as a "whole" world, and it is only since the 1990s that the Internet has provided instant multimedia communication to people around the world. In short, a state – even a powerful one like the United States – that seeks to be isolated, autonomous, and sheltered from global forces is doomed to fail. A state that accepts that contacts among different societies are inevitable, and hence attempts to integrate itself into today's small and interdependent world, can potentially succeed. Americans thus need to know and understand what is going on elsewhere. Citizens in the United States must be aware of the world in which they live. They need to be cognizant of the potential dangers and challenges, as well as the possible opportunities, that confront them in the decades ahead. This same would apply to any student reading this book in any country of the world.

Our approach exposes you to the theoretically and substantively important currents in contemporary comparative politics. Moreover, we do not expect you to be interested in names and dates for their own sake, but understanding the contemporary world is made easier if you know some of the more important ones.

At critical points along our journey we will stop and compare in order to explain and evaluate what we see. Let's repeat our framework: (1) The global context influences (2) domestic interests, identities, and institutions, which produce (3) development paths to the modern world, which, in turn, generate (4) comparative-politics feedback effects on domestic interests, identities, and institutions and (5) international-relations feedback effects on the global context. And let's begin.

# PART ONE

# Early Developers

## Cases

# 1

# Britain

≫ **Peter Rutland**

# INTRODUCTION

Britain is usually chosen as the starting point for comparative politics textbooks because it has some similarities with the U.S. system, but also some important differences. Also, most people believe that Britain has a successful political system, worthy of study and emulation. Britain is seen as having strong and stable political institutions that have endured for centuries. Britain has a firmly established national identity, and in British society, economic and social interests are clearly defined and vigorously defended.

All of these things are true, but only half true. There are serious contradictions within the British model that undermine the image of stability, and that have provoked a sense of profound political malaise, even crisis. Up until World War II Britain ruled an empire that extended over one-quarter of the globe. This means that for older generations, British national identity is still overshadowed by the legacy of empire. This has made it psychologically difficult for Britain to become an active and committed member of the European Union. The division between Europhiles and Euroskeptics is the most important rift in British politics today. Meanwhile, back at home Britain still faces an unresolved constitutional challenge in dealing with the demands of nationalists in Scotland, Wales, and Northern Ireland for greater autonomy and even independence. Hence, British identity is still very much a work in progress.

Moving from identity to interests, one finds that Britain's entrenched social hierarchy led to a century of class warfare between labor and capital. This struggle polarized the political system, paralyzed public policy making, and hampered

Thanks to Philip G. Cerny and Cecilia Miller for detailed comments on an earlier draft.

Britain's ability to adapt to a changing global economy. Only in the past ten years has the country managed to shake off this legacy of social confrontation, and many fear that it could easily return as prosperity remains elusive for a large and growing underclass.

Britain does indeed enjoy highly stable political institutions, which have been in place for centuries. This much-vaunted stability can be seen as too much of a good thing, however. The system's high level of continuity inhibits much-needed structural reform. Britain's basic political structures have remained largely unchanged since the turn of the twentieth century, while there have been major changes in its economy, global role, and social structure. These changes had only a limited impact on the political system. A reform of Britain's political institutions is long overdue, but over the decades they have grown together in a way that makes it very difficult to alter one without altering all the others.

The past twenty years in Britain have seen a growing chorus of demands to overhaul the political system, in recognition of the fact that the country is heading into the 21st century with 19th-century political institutions. Constitutional reforms currently under debate include the reform or outright abolition of the House of Lords, the upper house of parliament; the introduction of parliaments for Scotland and Wales for the first time in 300 years; and proposals to further integrate British institutions with those of the European Union.

## THE BRITISH MODEL

Over the past century, Britain's prominence as a world power has steadily eroded. Britain's main interest for students of politics is that it pioneered the system of liberal democracy that has now spread to most of the world's countries. However, the way that those democratic institutions work together is unique to Britain. The British political system is less a model and more an exception. Many question whether the British model can survive into the 21st century without serious reform. Since joining the European Union, Britain has come under increasing pressure to adopt the economic and political practices of its neighbors.

The United States sees itself as the most pristine model of democracy, since it introduced the first written constitution in 1787 and has lived under that same constitution for more than 200 years. Britain lacks a formal written constitution, and so it is hard to put a date on the introduction of liberal democracy to that country. Most historians would point to the Glorious Revolution of 1688, when the Protestant William of Orange deposed the Catholic James II in a bloodless revolution and accepted the principle of parliamentary sovereignty. Trying to fix a formal date for the arrival of democracy would go against the main virtue of the British model, which is seen as its capacity to adapt gradually over time. The British model is not based on a set of ideas captured in a single document, but in an evolving set of social conventions. Many of these practices – such as the system of common law, jury trials, freedom of speech, a bill of rights, and the notion of popular sovereignty – were already established by the 17th century and formed the bedrock upon which the U.S. constitution itself was based. But many of the features of the contemporary British model, such as parliamentary sovereignty, constitutional monarchy, and an ideologically polarized party system, stand in contrast to the American model.

The British political system is a product of that country's unique history. There is an old story about the Oxford college gardener who, when asked how he kept the lawn so immaculate, replied: "That's easy, you just roll it every day . . . for 300 years." This continuity argument raises the question of whether Britain's democratic experience can be "exported" elsewhere, or whether other countries are merely supposed to marvel at the unique virtues of the "Westminster model" of parliamentary sovereignty.

The U.S. model of democracy comes more ready for export. Its essence is captured in a short document, based on a fairly simple set of principles: the equality of man, the rule of law, the separation of powers. This has enabled the United States to play the leading role in the spread of democracy around the world over the last half century: It was U.S. advisors who oversaw the writing of new constitutions in postwar Germany and Japan.

The British model is no less important than the American in understanding the global spread of democracy. As the British Empire shrank after 1945, it left a series of democratic political systems modeled along British lines in its wake. The first wave of democratization had come with the independence of the white settler colonies of Australia, New Zealand, and Canada in the 1870s. Then came decolonization in India (1947), Africa (the 1950s), and the Caribbean islands (the 1960s). Cross-national analysis shows that countries that were formerly British colonies are more likely to be stable democracies than are other countries – in part because they are parliamentary democracies (generally more stable than presidential systems). No such correlation can be found for ex-colonies of other European powers. India, the jewel in the imperial crown, has remained a democracy – the world's largest – for half a century despite a very low level of economic development, which elsewhere is inimical to democratization. The British ex-colonies in Africa do not fit this pattern, however. With the exception of Botswana, they have all slipped into periods of military or one-party rule since independence.

## THE LONG ROAD FROM EMPIRE TO EUROPE

### An Island Nation

If you ask someone from England the most important date in their history, they will almost certainly answer 1066. That was when the invading Norman army of

William the Conqueror vanquished the Anglo-Saxon forces of King Harold at the Battle of Hastings. The French-speaking Norman aristocracy took over the country and started the long and bloody process of welding it into a unified state. The date 1066 is symbolically important because it was the last time Britain was invaded. The Spanish Armada was repulsed in 1588, as were Hitler's forces in 1940. The Britons are proud of having preserved their sovereignty against foreign invasion for 900 years, and this feeds a largely unspoken patriotism that has caused many in Britain to regard their country as fundamentally distinct from those elsewhere in Europe.

The fact that Britain is an island meant that it relied on the Royal Navy for its security. Unlike the states of continental Europe, it did not require a large standing army to protect itself from its neighbors. George Orwell once suggested that this reliance on the navy is the reason that Britain became a democracy. In contrast to the absolutist monarchs of Europe, Britain's rulers did not have a permanent standing army at its disposal to put down social unrest. Instead, they had to meet popular discontent with compromise. (The United States, of course, was in the same position as England.) To this day, Britain is the only country in Europe not to require all its young men to perform military service. Although the other European powers introduced compulsory military service in the 19th century, Britain continued to rely on a small, professional, volunteer army (most of which was stationed overseas). Only in the middle of World War I was the military draft introduced – and dropped immediately thereafter. It was reintroduced in 1940, and finally abolished in 1960.

## The End of Empire

By the 19th century, Britain's global naval power and advanced manufacturing industry made it the dominant power of the imperialist world order. Conquest and trade were constitutive of British national identity. Its pantheon of heroes included pirates who robbed Spanish galleons laden with silver (Francis Drake) and the clerk who rose to be the conqueror of India (Robert Clive). British colonies covered one-quarter of the planet, in an empire on which "the sun never set."

After World War I, Britain lost its economic leadership to America and, later, Germany. Britain's economy was simply too weak to sustain the extensive military contingents needed to keep the growing colonial independence movements in check. After World War II, it was forced to grant independence to its colonial possessions – first India and Palestine, then Africa, Malaysia, and the rest. Most former colonies joined the Commonwealth, a loose association of fifty-three countries (founded in 1931), which now has only a ceremonial role, organizing sports competitions and cultural exchanges. Britain clung to a network of smaller possessions around the globe, but these too were slowly jettisoned. In 1968, to save money Britain decided to close all its military bases east of Suez, with the exception of Hong Kong. As Dean Acheson observed in 1963, Britain "had lost an empire but not yet found a role."

Just as memories of empire were fading, the legacy resurfaced in 1982 when Argentina's military rulers decided to seize the Falkland Islands: a worthless, windswept British possession a few hundred miles off the Argentine coast. Prime Minister Margaret Thatcher sent a naval task force to liberate the islands, which was duly accomplished, at the cost of 5,000 Argentine and 125 British lives. The Falklands War was a boost to Thatcher's waning popularity ratings, and helped secure her reelection in 1983. However, Britain had come close to defeat in the war. Victory was only possible thanks to help from the United States (who provided satellite intelligence and the newest air-to-air missiles).

It was not until 1997 that the British Empire finally achieved symbolic closure. In July 1997, the UK returned Hong Kong to the People's Republic of China, its ninety-nine-year lease having expired. China promised to respect the special economic and political rights of Hong Kong for fifty years. These rights did not include democratic government: Only in the last five years of her stewardship had Britain made half-hearted efforts to introduce democratic elections to Hong Kong.

For the most part, Britons look back at the empire with unembarrassed nostalgia, clinging to the myth that British rule brought civilization (from railways to rule of law) to the more primitive corners of the globe. The uglier side of imperial rule was edited out of collective memory. There was no guilt over Britain's role in the transatlantic slave trade, or the 1842 war with China, the purpose of which was to force that country's rulers to allow the import of opium. Visions of empire are sustained in the popular imagination by a steady flow of film and TV dramas.

Although Britain slipped from its previous hegemonic role in the international order, it held onto a place at the table of the leading powers. As one of the "Big Three" powers that won World War II, it was given one of the five permanent seats in the United Nations Security Council in 1945. It developed its own nuclear arsenal in the 1950s, and is one of the world's seven declared nuclear powers. The Labour Party advocated unilateral nuclear disarmament for a few years in the 1980s, a policy that drew little public support.

Britain owes its prominent role in world affairs since 1945 to its "special relationship" with the United States. Britain has dutifully played a role as America's most loyal ally (and "aircraft carrier"). From Korea in 1950 to Kuwait in 1990, Britain has sent troops to support U.S.-led military actions overseas. Britain has been the backbone of the U.S.-led NATO alliance, with 50,000 of its own troops stationed in West Germany until the end of the cold war. There were some rocky periods in the relationship – the United States blocked the Anglo-French seizure of the Suez Canal in 1956, and Britain declined to send troops to support the U.S. effort in Vietnam in 1965. British and American leaders have shown a remarkable ability to find a common language. This began with Roosevelt and Churchill in the 1940s, and continued through Margaret Thatcher and Ronald Reagan in the 1980s (united against the "Evil Empire") to Tony Blair and Bill Clinton in the late 1990s (both seeking an elusive "Third Way").

It is not clear what concrete benefits the UK derived from the U.S. special relationship, apart from assistance in upgrading its nuclear deterrent (and the help during the Falklands War already mentioned). The main benefit was psychological – helping Britain to maintain its self-image as a key player in world affairs. The special relationship also incurred costs. During the cold war, Britain shouldered a defense spending burden greater than what the country could realistically afford. Moreover, the ties across the Atlantic were sustained at the expense of ties across the English Channel. For example, Britain's decision to use U.S. Polaris submarine missiles to provide its nuclear deterrent in 1962 encouraged France to veto the UK's application to join the European Economic Community. (France had been hoping to develop jointly a European submarine missile system). The special relationship with the United States, together with the fading image of empire, were important factors keeping Britain aloof from European integration.

## THE RELUCTANT EUROPEAN

Britain was the dominant European power in 1945, but was a half-hearted partner in the process of building a new political structure in the shattered continent. In 1952 it refused to join the European Coal and Steel Community, fearing that plans for a common industrial policy would infringe upon her national sovereignty. The European Economic Community (launched in 1957) emerged as Britain's major trading partner, and its economic growth outpaced that of Britain. Twice during the 1960s Britain tried to join the EEC but was rejected, mainly because Paris feared that British entry would weaken France's influence.

It was not until 1973 that Britain was granted entry to the renamed European Community. Much of the next decade was spent haggling over the terms of entry. In 1984, the Euroskeptic Thatcher won a reduction in Britain's high contribution to the common budget, half of which went to support inefficient European farmers through the Common Agricultural Policy. Thatcher warily signed the Single European Act (1986), which promoted the free flow of goods, labor, and capital, but also introduced qualified majority voting in place of the veto that the larger countries formerly enjoyed. Thatcher favored free trade but opposed EU-mandated labor and welfare programs. She wanted a Europe of nation-states, rather than one ruled by supranational institutions – bodies that Eurocritics believed lacked democratic accountability. Many conservatives object to the fact that the European Court of Justice has the power to invalidate British laws that contradict EU law. It was splits within the Conservative Party over Thatcher's resistance to European integration that led to her downfall in 1990.

Britain, together with the Scandinavian EU member countries, declined to enter the economic and monetary union that was agreed to at Maastricht in 1991, when the EC renamed itself the European Union. Britain will not join the single European currency (the Euro), which is being introduced in stages that began in 1999. Even so, the gravitational pull of Europe over Britain is ineluctable – symbolized by the opening of the Eurotunnel under the English Channel in 1995. Economic ties between Britain and the Continent continue to multiply, while hundreds of thousands of Britons buy holiday homes in France and Spain, and seek work in Germany. Nevertheless, as the Continent enters the 21st century, Britain's political commitment to the idea of European unity remains uncertain. Ideas of empire and global power status are no longer a significant factor. The main stumbling bloc is the challenge posed by a federal Europe to the principle of parliamentary sovereignty, which lies at the very heart of the British political tradition.

## WHO ARE THE BRITISH? CONTESTED IDENTITIES

We all have an image of who are the British: Lady Diana, the Beatles, Austin Powers. The British, at least in their mass media representations, come across as confident and self-assured, if not complacent. This image of comfortable homogeneity, alas, is an illusion. Britain was always riven by deep social class divisions at home and doubts over the viability (and morality) of its vast empire abroad. These deep divisions have surfaced in political life in recent decades and raise major challenges for the question of British identity.

For the older generation of Britons, their political identity is tied to the old empire, a political institution that disappeared from the world atlas half a century ago. Britain's reluctance to join its neighbors in European integration stems primarily from the worry that such a step could undermine Britain's political identity – which indicates that the latter is more fragile than is commonly supposed. The Scots, Irish, and Welsh are still there to remind us that the "British" should not be conflated with "English." The Celtic periphery makes up 10 million of Britain's 56 million population, and have won increased political autonomy in recent years. Despite 900 years of continuous self-rule, Britain's ethnic identity remains curiously ill defined.

### Forging a British Nation

The inhabitants of the United Kingdom have a complex and shifting hierarchy of identities. At one level they identify themselves as English, Scots, Welsh, or Irish, and at the same time they are aware of themselves as British subjects. Regional identities are quite strong, with many counties and cities having distinct dialects and proud traditions. Contemporary Britain is an ethnically diverse society with strong national communities in Wales, Scotland, and Northern Ireland, which have won increased political autonomy over the past decade. While the empire existed, the four peoples of the British Isles were united in a common endeavor of mutual enrichment through global conquest. With the end of empire, that powerful practical and ideological cohesive force is lacking. Over the past decade an emergent "European" identity has been added to the mix.

The south of England was occupied by Angles and Saxons who crossed from the continent in the 6th to 9th centuries, while Vikings conquered the North. The French-speaking Normans displaced the Anglo-Saxon rulers in 1066 and set about creating a unified kingdom. Already by the 16th century a notion of the English people was quite firmly established – as reflected in the patriotic plays of William Shakespeare. Through the stick of conquest and the carrot of commerce, the English absorbed the Celtic peoples of Wales (1535), Ireland (1649), and Scotland (1707). Local parliaments were dissolved, and a unitary state was created and run out of London.

The process of absorption took place in a different way in each of the three Celtic regions. In Wales, English lords moved in and took over the land, but the peasantry maintained their distinct Welsh identity and even their Welsh language. To this day about one-fifth of the 3 million residents of Wales speak Welsh at home. In Scotland, the indigenous feudal elite was divided over the question of union with England. A majority of the lowland lords sided with London and cooperated in the subjugation of the recalcitrant Highlanders, culminating in the defeat of the Jacobite rebels at Culloden (1745), the last battle fought on British soil. Most of the rebellious clans were deported to America. The Scottish elite played a leading role in the forging of the British nation and the expansion of empire. In the 18th century Edinburgh, home of Adam Smith, rivaled London as an intellectual center and generated the conceptual framework of liberal capitalism.

The 5 million Scots still maintain a strong sense of national identity, although the Gaelic language has almost disappeared. Scotland preserved its own legal and educational systems, independent from the English model. Some Scots believe that the devil's bargain with London has worked to the detriment of their country, not least because its economy lagged behind that of England. These feelings led to the rise of the Scottish National Party (SNP), and were boosted in the 1960s by the discovery of oil and gas in the North Sea off eastern Scotland. Even so, Scotland remained a net recipient of transfers from the national budget, although nationalists complained that this was because little of the oil wealth was staying north of the border.

Also in the 1960s a nationalist movement, Plaid Cymru, arose in Wales. Its main goal was the preservation of Welsh language and culture. The nationalists won concessions from London in language policy – Welsh road signs, a Welsh TV station, and the teaching of Welsh language in schools and universities. Plaid Cymru wins a steady 8 to 10 percent of the vote in Wales in elections, mainly from the Welsh speakers who make up about one-quarter of the population.

Whereas the focus of Welsh nationalism is culture, the Scottish movement is broader, with economic and political goals. As a result, its support fluctuates, depending on the level of voter disaffection with the mainstream parties. The SNP usually wins between 12 and 20 percent of the vote in Scotland, but managed to garner 30 percent in 1974. This led the Labour government to steer more public spending into the Celtic regions. Under the 1974 Barrett formula, Scotland, Wales, and Northern Ireland get 15, 10, and 5 percent of the spending in England – more than their share in the total UK population. Labour also promised to create regional assemblies in each country with the power to pass laws and raise taxes. Scots were split on the idea because the SNP still wanted outright independence. A referendum was held in 1979. Only 12 percent of Welsh and 33 percent of Scots voted in favor of a regional assembly.

The idea of devolution was dropped, but it was revived in the 1990s by the Labour Party under their new leader, Tony Blair. Devolution is primarily an argument between Labour and the SNP, since Conservatives have few supporters in Wales and Scotland, and won not a single seat in Scotland in the May 1997 election. The new Labour government moved quickly to hold referenda on devolution in September 1997. Seventy-four percent of Scots voted in favor of a new Scottish parliament, to be elected in May 1999, and 64 percent approved of granting the body tax-raising powers in the form of an extra 3 percent income tax (the "tartan tax"). The Welsh were more lukewarm about self-government. Their referendum backed a parliament by the slimmest of margins (50.3 percent to 49.7 percent), on a turnout of only 50 percent. Many Britons hope (or fear) that the creation of the Scottish parliament will ineluctably lead to full independence for Scotland.

## The Irish Question

Catholic Ireland was brought under British control only after brutal military campaigns by Oliver Cromwell (1649) and William of Orange (1689). English lords moved in to take over the land, while Scottish Protestants established a colony in Ulster (present-day Northern Ireland). The English banned the Irish language, which survived only in the more remote regions. Unscrupulous landlords, cheap food imports from America, and the failure of the potato crop resulted in famine in the 1840s and a mass exodus from the Irish countryside. A growing movement for Irish independence was met with proposals for autonomy ("Home Rule") from London. These plans foundered – initially over land reform, and later because of opposition from the Ulster Protestants.

The year 1916 saw an abortive nationalist uprising in Dublin. In the wake of World War I, as Ireland sank into civil war the British decided to cut their losses. In 1921 London granted independence to the southern Republic of Ireland, while maintaining Northern Ireland as part of the United Kingdom. Northern Ireland was

granted its own parliament (Stormont), which was controlled by the 1.6 million–
strong Protestant majority. The 800,000 Catholics of the province lived in segregated housing estates and went to separate (denominational) schools. The Protestants controlled the police force and steered jobs and public spending to their
own community.

In 1968 a civil rights movement sprang up, demanding equal treatment for the
Catholics. Its peaceful protests were brutally dispersed by the Protestant police. The
Irish Republican Army (IRA), a long-dormant terrorist group, mobilized to defend the
Catholics, but their goal was a united Ireland. In 1969, 16,000 British troops were sent
to take over the job of policing the province from the discredited Ulster constabu-
lary. Over the next three decades, Northern Ireland was racked by a three-way "low-
intensity" conflict among the British army, the IRA, and sundry Protestant paramilitaries. Riots, bombings, and assassinations became part of everyday life. The British
government fought back with special courts and internment without trial. From time
to time the IRA planted bombs on the British mainland, and managed to kill several
top British officials. All told, the conflict claimed about 3,200 lives. At least the
British army managed to prevent the conflict from escalating into open civil war or
Bosnian-style ethnic cleansing. On occasion human rights went by the board. Six
Irishmen accused of planting a bomb in Birmingham in 1975 were imprisoned for sixteen years before they were declared innocent and released.

The British abolished the Stormont parliament in 1972, but efforts to introduce
power sharing between Catholics and Protestants foundered on opposition from
hard-line Protestant Unionists. The Protestants were living in a 17th-century time
warp, adhering to values of God, Queen, and Country that had long been forgotten
in mainland Britain. The Protestants feared the exchange of their majority status
in Ulster for minority status in a united Ireland – particularly as the Irish Republic's laws were still based on canons of the Catholic faith (banning divorce and
abortion, for example). Britain and Ireland drew more closely together through
integration in the European Union, and in 1985, London agreed to grant Dublin a
direct role in any future peace settlement for the North. To reassure the Unionists,
London insisted that Ulster should join a united Ireland only if a majority in the
North voted in favor. Peace talks resumed in 1993, and on Good Friday in April
1998, a complex peace deal was agreed upon, under the chairmanship of former
U.S. senator George Mitchell. The hope was that IRA and Protestant paramilitaries
would disarm if their convicted comrades were released from prison, and Protestant and Catholic politicians in the North agreed to share power in an assembly
elected by proportional representation. The deal was approved in a referendum,
winning 71 percent support in the North. Despite some continuing violence from
renegade extremists, hopes for peace were high. The leaders of the main Protestant and Catholic parties, David Trimble and John Hume, were awarded the Nobel
Peace Prize. Prisoner releases began, but the IRA refused to disarm and Protestant

leaders balked at sharing power with their Catholic counterparts. The situation remains fluid.

Ireland was the first – and last – British colony. The Northern Ireland "Troubles" are a blot on British democracy and the most painful reminder of the legacy of empire.

## British – and Black

Another important echo of empire was the appearance in the 1960s of a community of immigrants from Asia and the West Indies. The immigrants broke the image of social homogeneity that had prevailed in Britain for decades past (and which had, anyway, disguised the multinational community of Scots, Irish, Welsh, and English).

Facing a labor squeeze, Britain started to recruit workers from Jamaica and Trinidad, former colonies in the West Indies. These black workers were joined by a flow of migrants from India and Pakistan, a process accelerated by the expulsion of Asians from Kenya and Uganda in 1965. More restrictive immigration laws were introduced, which slowed but did not stanch the flow. By 1998 there were 1.6 million Asians and 900,000 blacks in Britain, about 4 percent of the population. Race was not the only issue. The Asian migrants were Hindus and Muslims, posing a challenge to Britain's avowed status as a Christian nation.

Few Americans realize that the Church of England is the established state religion, with the Queen as its official head. Anglican religious education used to be legally compulsory for all pupils in state schools; there are separate (state-subsidized) schools for Roman Catholics and Jews. With the appearance of large numbers of Muslim and Hindu pupils in the 1970s, the practice of religion in state schools was progressively abandoned. In reality, less than 10 percent of the British population are regular churchgoers. The new immigrants forced Britain to acknowledge the fact that it was in reality a secular, urban, individualist culture, and that its old self-images of Queen, church, and empire were sorely outdated.

Immigration was also a political challenge. Many older Britons harbored racist attitudes from the days of empire, while some young workers saw the immigrants as a threat to their jobs and state housing. The racist National Front Party arose in the late 1960s, and there were occasional street battles between racist skinheads and immigrant youth throughout the 1970s and 1980s. The situation began to change as the first cohort of British-born blacks and Asians passed through the educational system and entered the professions. Whereas their parents had kept a low social and political profile, the second generation was more assertive in demanding a full and equal place in British society.

Although some racist attitudes persist (in parts of the police force, for example), general race relations have considerably improved in the space of a single generation. London is a relaxed, multicultural city. Intermarriage rates across racial lines are high (in comparison with the United States) – around 50 percent for both blacks and Asians. The media deserve much of the credit for helping to redefine Britain as a multiracial community. Immigration is no longer a contentious issue for the main political parties. In 1987 four minority candidates won seats in parliament, rising to 10 in 1997 (all but one for Labour). However, accusations of racism in the police force were highlighted by the failure to prosecute the skinheads who killed a black youth, Stephen Lawrence, in London in 1997.

## THE CHARACTER OF BRITISH DEMOCRACY

The British system is characterized by the emergence over time of cohesive, well-defined social groups, each with its own strongly defined economic, social, and political interests. Its legendary landed aristocracy was later joined by a resilient and rapacious commercial bourgeoisie, and these two groups went to war in the middle of the 17th century to decide which institution would rule – the monarch or the elected parliament. The institutions that emerged as a compromise in the wake of the civil war – parliamentary sovereignty and constitutional monarchy – have persisted to the present day.

While the lowly peasantry were shut out from the political system and never emerged as a politically significant force, in the 19th century the industrial proletariat forged a powerful trade union movement and later a parliamentary political party to defend its interests. Each of these social classes – lords, peasants, capitalists, and workers – lived a different life, went to different schools, and even spoke different dialects.

Despite this highly stratified social system, Britain emerged as a peaceful, stable democracy. Strong political institutions emerged that were able to express and absorb these competing class interests. The British example suggests that strongly defined and well-organized social interests beget strong political institutions.

The most widely praised attribute of the British political system is its stability. Britain has functioned with the same set of political institutions, without coups or revolutions, since 1689. There are few nations in continental Europe that can make such a claim. Germany has gone through four regimes since its formation in 1871; France is on its fifth republic since 1815. The last battle fought in mainland Britain was at Culloden in 1745, when a Scottish rebel army was quashed. The general level of social unrest and political violence (Northern Ireland excepted) has been quite low.

Britain's stability stems from the fact that the key political institutions – parliamentary sovereignty, constitutional monarchy, and gradually expanding democracy – were flexible and able to adapt to the changing social environment. They emerged gradually over time and were the product of experience rather than design. The operating principle was Anglo-Saxon pragmatism (what works) as opposed to French rationalism (what is best).

In addition, these institutions were embedded in a broad consensus of political values. This consensus was particularly strong among the tightly knit ruling elite, who have shown a high degree of cohesiveness over the years. Prominent among these consensus values was the notion of loyalty to the monarch, church and empire. The very strength of the divisive social class system was also, ironically, a source of stability. Everyone was fully aware of the existence of the class system and their family's location within it. They all "knew their place."

An important part of these consensus values was the recognition of individual rights and the notion of limited government. Over the centuries, medieval England built up a body of common law: the accumulated decisions of court cases that defined and protected individual rights. Such rights included the right to trial by jury and habeas corpus, meaning protection against arrest without a court hearing (literally, the right to one's own body). Such rights to personal liberty and private property were spelled out in the Magna Carta, a contract that was presented to King John in 1215 by a few dozen leading nobles. That document was designed to protect the privileges of a narrow and oppressive aristocracy, but it set the precedent for the sovereigns wielding of a negotiated and conditional power. Over ensuing centuries, the same rights were slowly – very slowly – extended to broader sections of the population. The rights to personal liberty and property did not initially extend to religion. Although the 1689 Act of Toleration granted freedom of worship to those outside the Church of England, it was not until the 1820s that bans on Catholics and Jews serving in the military or in public office were lifted. At the time of writing, Britain still lacks a formal bill of rights guaranteeing individual rights. In 1950 Britain did sign the European Convention on Human Rights, which created a supranational European Court of Human Rights in Strasbourg. Since 1966, British citizens have been able to appeal to that court (and the court has reversed British legal decisions in some fifty cases). The Blair government has pledged to incorporate the European Convention on Human Rights into domestic law by the end of the year 2000.

Despite the absence of a bill of rights, the individualist, rights-oriented tradition still runs deep in British political life. Europeans are bemused by the fact that there is still no national identity card system in Britain (or the United States). An important difference from the United States is that the right to bear arms was not part of the British tradition. On the contrary, British monarchs were keen to keep a monopoly of force in their own hands – systematically tearing down nearly all the castles of the aristocracy in the 16th century, for example. Restrictions on personal gun ownership are very tight. As a result, British police usually patrol unarmed, and handguns cause fewer than 10 deaths per year in Britain (compared to some 20,000 in the United States). After the massacre of sixteen children by a deranged gunman in Dunblane, Scotland, in 1996, private possession of handguns was completely banned.

## THE PATH TO PARLIAMENTARY DEMOCRACY

The U.S. political system is based on the idea of a written constitution, a contract among the founders to form a new state based on certain principles. In contrast, the lynchpin of the British system is the notion of parliamentary sovereignty. The parliament, representing the people, has the power to enact any law it chooses, unrestrained by a written constitution or the separation of powers.

This notion of popular sovereignty, where voters get to choose their leaders through frequent direct elections, is the essence of British democracy. At first, in the 18th century, the number of voters who got to participate was very small – less than 5 percent of the population. It took 200 years of social conflict before the franchise spread to the majority of citizens. It is remarkable that an institution designed to protect the interests of medieval nobles – the parliament – also came to be accepted by industrial workers in the 20th century as a vital instrument for the protection of their interests.

Regional *parlements* emerged in France as a forum for nobles to discuss their mutual interests and resolve disputes. (The word *parlement* means "talking place" in French, the native language of the British nobility at the time.) The institution spread to England in the late 13th century, providing a forum for the monarch to try to persuade the nobles to pay taxes. Over time, the monarch grew more powerful and was seen as the divinely chosen ruler of the kingdom (whose right to rule was subject to approval by the pope). In 1534, Henry VIII broke with the Church of Rome and established a separate Church of England, with himself as head. This removed an important external prop to the legitimacy claims of the British monarch. The rhetoric of king and parliament gradually shifted from divine right to that of serving the interests of the people and nation. However, there remained many fierce disputes over economic interests, political power, and religious identity.

The upper chamber of parliament – the House of Lords – consisted of hereditary peers, lords appointed by the monarch whose title automatically passes down to their eldest sons. The lower chamber – the House of Commons – consisted of representatives elected by property owners in the public at large. The parliament is known as "Westminster" because it is located in Westminster Palace on the bank of the Thames.

Conflict between king and parliament over the right to raise taxes erupted into civil war (1642–8). The parliamentary forces defeated the royalists and executed Charles I in 1649. After thirty years of military-theocratic rule by Oliver Cromwell, in the Glorious Revolution of 1688 the parliament welcomed back William of

Orange as a constitutional monarch with limited powers. In the 18th century, the parliament's role developed into what has come to be known as the Westminster Model. One of its most important features was its division into two parties – those in power (Her Majesty's Government), and those not in power (Her Majesty's Opposition). The idea that one can disagree with the government without being considered a traitor was novel. The notion of a "loyal opposition" is one of the most important contributions of the Westminster Model. It is also the source of the two-party system that became a structural feature of British democracy.

In his classic 1971 book *Polyarchy,* Robert Dahl argued that liberal democracy develops along two dimensions: contestation and participation. "Contestation" means that rival groups of leaders compete for the top state positions; "participation" refers to the proportion of the adult population who play an active role in this process through elections. In this century, many countries have made an abrupt transition from closed authoritarian regimes to competitive, democratic regimes. In these cases, contestation and participation develop in parallel. In the British case, however, the politics of contestation were firmly established long before mass participation appeared on the scene. Prior to the 19th century, property requirements meant that only 2 percent of the adult population had the right to vote. Parliamentarism, initially reflecting the interests of landed elites, preceded popular democracy by several centuries.

## The Impact of Industrialization

From the 17th century on, Britain emerged as the preeminent maritime power, pulling ahead of Holland, Spain, and finally France. This was due to the skill, enterprise, and ruthlessness of its sailors in trade and in war. Napoleon described England as a "nation of merchants" (often mistranslated as "a nation of shopkeepers"). Trade was the main source of England's wealth, and it generated a new capitalist class that gradually merged with the old landed aristocracy.

Britain was the first country to experience the agricultural revolution. Peasants were driven from their subsistence plots to make way for extensive farming methods. These peasants had a very limited range of political opportunities. Many opted for emigration. About one-quarter of the population left the British Isles (some unwillingly, as convicts) for America, Canada, Australia, and other outposts of empire. This provided an important safety valve, reducing the surplus population and easing social discontent. In a TV interview, Mick Jagger was asked why there had never been a revolution in England. He replied that it was because all the people who did not like the place had left. Whereas America was formed as a nation of immigrants, Britain was a nation of emigrants.

Britain was also the first country to experience the Industrial Revolution, in the first decades of the 19th century. Industry and empire grew together. Britain became "the workshop of the world," selling its manufactured goods throughout its global trading network. However, the ruling elite were terrified that the example of the 1789 French Revolution could be replicated in Britain. A growing protest movement within the expanding industrial working class was initially met by a mixture of repression and reform. The 1832 Reform Act loosened the property requirements for voting, but even then only 5 percent of the adult population were enfranchised. A two-party system emerged in the House of Commons, with reformist and reactionary elements grouping themselves into the parties of Liberals and Conservatives (also known as Tories). Further Reform Acts in 1867 and 1884 gave the vote to 20 percent and then 40 percent of the population.

It was the arrival of organized labor that forced open the doors of parliament to the mass electorate. Faced with mounting labor unrest, Britain's ruling class opted for compromise rather than confrontation. By giving workers the right to vote, they provided an outlet for their political frustrations and turned them away from industrial violence. Trade unions had started to form on a craft basis in the 1840s, and by the 1880s they were expanding to the masses of unskilled workers in the docks and construction trades. Heavily influenced by the Methodist revival, British workers were generally deferential to their masters and accepting of the status quo. Their initial focus was on improving wages and conditions, rather than political rights. For decades they had precious little to show for their loyalty, as they were crowded into Dickensian slums and labored long hours in the "dark satanic mills" of the Industrial Revolution.

Union organization and strike activity did slowly improve the workers' lot. In 1900 the unions formed the Labour Representation Committee to advance their interests in parliament. The unions realized that they urgently needed legislative protection after a court case had threatened severe civil penalties for strike action. The LRC renamed itself the Labour Party and won fifty seats in the 1906 parliamentary election in alliance with the Liberal Party.

The Liberal government that ruled from 1906 to 1914 introduced some of the basic elements of a welfare state in Britain – rudimentary public health care, school meals, and the like. These measures were not merely a response to the rise of labor. They were also prompted by the shocking discovery that one-third of the recruits for the British army in the Boer War (1899–1902) were medically unfit to serve. In order to match the mass armies of Germany and Russia, the British state would have to start looking after its workers a little better. This realization was articulated by Joseph Chamberlain as the philosophy of "social imperialism" – welfare spending for the working classes in return for political loyalty in imperial ventures. This program was clearly an echo of Bismarck's model of welfare capitalism in Germany. The Industrial Revolution had transformed Britain forever – bringing new social classes into existence, and forcing the ruling class to compete with (and borrow from) other nations.

While the workers were organizing, the ruling class was also developing new institutions to streamline its role. The 19th century saw the spread of the public schools, designed to forge a new elite of like-minded young men by means of a rigid regime of sport and Latin. (The schools were called "public" because they were open to anyone who could pay the stiff fees, irrespective of social origin.) In 1854, public officials were organized into an independent, structured civil service, in which recruitment and promotion were to be based on merit, rather than political connections. Overall, however, the British elite came through the Industrial Revolution with its medieval institutions remarkably intact. The aristocracy plied their way from country house to royal court to London club, educating their sons at Oxford and Cambridge and sending them off to fight in the colonies in the family regiment.

## Labour's Rise to Power

The first major challenge to the integrity of the British state was the bloodbath of World War I, which Britain would have lost had the United States not intervened. That conflict killed about 10 percent of the adult male population, drained the economy, and sapped the enthusiasm of the British state for foreign ventures. Still, Britain got off lightly – the war caused the complete collapse of the political systems of Germany, Russia, and Turkey. In recognition of the people's sacrifices for the war effort, in 1918 all adult males were given the vote, irrespective of their property holdings, as were women over the age of 28. (The 18- to 28-year-old "flappers" were enfranchised ten years later.) Thus it was not until 1929 that one person, one vote became the law in Britain, showing that democracy is a quite recent historical development.

The Labour Party fought the 1918 election as coequal of the Conservatives and Liberals, and in the 1924 election emerged as the largest single party. Although they did not control a majority of seats in the Commons, their leader Ramsey Macdonald was invited to form a minority government. This was a remarkable achievement. It had taken only two decades for the trade unions to emerge from the political wilderness to the very pinnacle of power. The euphoria was not to last, however. The 1924 government fell within a year, and economic recession triggered a decade of poverty and industrial conflict.

It was not until World War II that one saw a major shift in the distribution of power in the British political system. British patriotism blossomed in 1939–41, when the nation fought alone against Nazi-occupied Europe under a coalition government headed by Conservative Winston Churchill. In return, the people demanded a brighter future once the war was won. In 1942 the government released the Beveridge Report, promising full employment and state-provided health care, insurance, and pensions. This was not enough to satisfy the voters. In 1945 they turned out Churchill and for the first time in history elected a majority Labour government.

The Labour government moved quickly to implement a radical socialist program, including the nationalization (taking into state ownership) of large sections of private industry. They introduced the basic institutions of the "welfare state" – a National Health Service, state pensions, and state-funded higher education. They expanded state-subsidized housing (called council housing, because it was provided by local councils). Health care, jobs, and housing were seen as social rights to which everyone was entitled. (Bear in mind that in 1945, one-third of Britons were still living in houses without bathrooms.) Laws were passed taking about one-quarter of private industry into public ownership, including coal mines, electric and gas utilities, steel mills, docks, railways, and long-distance trucking. The expropriated private owners, who were paid compensation, opposed the nationalization of their firms but were powerless in the face of Labour's parliamentary majority. The postwar government also oversaw the speedy granting of independence to such colonies as India and Palestine. The Labour government did, however, support the United States in forming NATO to oppose Soviet expansionism, and reintroduced the draft to help fight the cold war. The new commitment to socialism at home and cold war abroad provided a double anesthetic to dull the pain caused by the loss of empire.

## The Postwar Consensus

In the 1950s, British politics slipped into a familiar pattern that was to last until 1979. The Labour and Conservative parties alternated in power, and they both agreed on the basic institutions of postwar Britain. The Tories realized that it would be political suicide to try to dismantle the welfare state. They also acquiesced in the retreat from empire. Labour, in turn, acknowledged that the postwar nationalization program had gone just about as far as the British public wanted, not least because problems soon emerged in the management of state-owned industry. Postwar governments from both parties accepted the economic analysis of John Maynard Keynes, who had argued in the 1930s that state intervention with public spending could have avoided the horrors of the Great Depression.

This high level of consensus left little for the two parties to argue over. It is ironic that a political system built around two-party adversarial politics should have produced such a consensus. Anthony Downs offered one explanation for this in his 1957 book *An Economic Theory of Democracy*. In a two-party system, Downs reasoned, leaders will compete for the "median voter" in the middle of the policy spectrum. Hence, both party programs will tend to converge.

In the 1950s and 1960s, successive governments managed to avoid another depression. However, they were too ambitious in trying to "fine-tune" the economy by adjusting interest rates and money supply to ensure simultaneous economic growth, low inflation, and full employment. The country fell into a debilitating "political business cycle." Attempts by Conservative governments to lower inflation typically led to a recession and a rise in unemployment, causing a surge of support for Labour. In turn, efforts by Labour to boost economic growth and cut unemployment would cause inflation, and on occasion caused embarrassing financial crises when international investors deserted the pound sterling (in 1967 and 1976).

Despite the introduction of the welfare state, the institutional structure of private industry remained largely unchanged. Workers still remembered the desperate struggles of the Great Depression, and relations between labor and management were tense and confrontational. Unlike in Germany or Scandinavia, after the war there was no attempt to introduce corporatist institutions, such as works councils, to give labor a say in the management of private industry. With unemployment held at 3 to 4 percent, workers were able to threaten strike action to push for better wages and conditions. The economy was plagued by successive waves of strikes, which came to be known as the "British disease."

At the same time, managers were slow to reequip British industry with the latest technology. Britain was overtaken in industrial output by Germany, France, Japan, and even Italy. London was still a major center of international finance, however. The easy profits from banking, or the prestige of a career in the civil service, tended to draw the "brightest and best" away from careers in industry.

The 1960s were not all gloom and doom. While industry was rusting, London was "swinging." A whole new youth subculture was invented in Britain and exported to the rest of the world. Music and the arts flourished, putting Britain back on the world map as a cultural superpower. By the end of the 1970s, Britain was earning more from exports of rock music than it was from steel.

The 1964–70 Labour government tried to address the problem of industrial stagnation by promoting tripartite negotiations among the state, employers, and unions to set prices and incomes. Labour's main liability was that it was too closely tied to the trade unions. The unions were the main source of finance for the Labour Party, and in selecting parliamentary candidates and the ruling National Executive Committee, the 10–12 million union members outvoted the 250,000 or so individual members of the Labour Party.

Industrial unrest led to the Labour Party's defeat in 1970, and a prolonged strike by coal miners brought down the Tory government in 1974. The 1974–79 Labour government tried unsuccessfully to negotiate a "social contract" with the unions. Strikes by garbage collectors, railway workers, and nurses culminated in the 1978 "winter of discontent." Adding to the confusion was the fact that Labour failed to win a clear majority over the Tories in the February 1974 election, and only formed a government thanks to support from the Scottish and Welsh nationalists. They failed to improve their position in the second election that they called in October 1974, and defections and deaths eroded the Labour majority.

Exasperated by the dominant role of unionists and left-wing radicals in their party, a group of centrist Labour leaders broke away to form a new Social Democratic Party (SDP). Their centrist program appeared to reflect the views of the majority

**TABLE 1. PRIME MINISTERS SINCE 1945**

| Election Date | Year of Appointment* | Prime Minister | Party |
|---|---|---|---|
| 1945 | | Clement Attlee | Labour |
| 1950 | | | |
| 1951 | | Winston Churchill | Conservative |
| 1955 | | Anthony Eden | Conservative |
| | 1957 | Harold Macmillan | |
| 1959 | | | |
| | 1963 | Alec Douglas-Home | Conservative |
| 1964 | | Harold Wilson | Labour |
| 1966 | | | |
| 1970 | | Edward Heath | Conservative |
| 1974† | | Harold Wilson | Labour |
| | 1976 | James Callaghan | Labour |
| 1979 | | Margaret Thatcher | Conservative |
| 1983 | | | |
| 1987 | | | |
| | 1990 | John Major | Conservative |
| 1992 | | | |
| 1997 | | Tony Blair | Labour |

* In these years the prime minister was changed, even though no election took place.

† There were two general elections in 1974, in February and October.

of voters. However, the winner-take-all party system (see Table 1) makes it very difficult for third parties to gain a foothold in the parliament. In the 1983 election, the SDP-Liberal alliance won 26 percent of the votes – only 2 percent less than Labour – but they won only 23 out of the 635 seats in the Commons at that time. The SDP eventually merged with the Liberal Party to form the Liberal Democrats.

By the end of the 1970s, the "British model" seemed to be in irreversible decline. The economy stagnated while inflation hit double figures. Journalists began to write about the "ungovernability" of Britain and a system "overloaded" with the demands of competing interest groups.

## Thatcher to the Rescue?

At this point, change came from an unexpected source – the Tory party. At the urging of regional party leaders, in 1975 the Conservatives selected a woman – Margaret Thatcher – as their new leader. Thatcher was a low-ranking party leader, having served as education minister in the 1970–4 government. Thatcher was an aggressive intellectual with an iron will and razor-sharp debating skills. Unusual for a Tory leader, she came from humble social origins – her father had been a grocer. She had earned a Ph.D. in organic chemistry at Oxford before switching to a career in law in order to have more time to raise her children. She then embarked on a political career.

Thatcher was influenced by the writings of the libertarian Friedrich Hayek and the monetarist economist Milton Friedman. Her philosophy of popular capitalism drew heavily upon American ideas of rugged individualism and free-market economics. Thatcher concluded that the British model was not working, and her solution was to try to minimize state interference in the economy and society. Thatcherism was to have a profound impact on the British political system, shattering the postwar consensus on the welfare state and locking Labour out of power for eighteen years.

Thatcher's bracing New Right rhetoric caught the attention of the British public and gave the Conservatives a clear victory in the 1979 election. She had ambitious plans to deregulate the economy and to privatize large chunks of state-owned industry, and pledged to follow a tight monetary policy in order to control inflation, whatever the effect on unemployment. Unlike in the United States, the New Right in Britain did not have a social agenda (abortion had been legal since 1967), although they promised to be tough on crime.

Thatcher's first task was to break the power of the trade unions. She introduced new legislation to make it more difficult to call strikes (requiring prestrike ballots and cooling-off periods). She doubled spending on police, and equipped them with shields and other riot gear so that they could go up against rock-throwing strikers. The coal miners had been the main source of labor unrest over the previous decade, and they led the battle against Thatcher's government. Thatcher used the courts to seize the assets of the miners' union when they mounted an illegal strike in 1984, and went on systematically shutting down most of the state-owned mining industry. There had been 300,000 coal miners in Britain in the 1960s; by 1990 their number had shrunk to 50,000. These measures succeeded in breaking the back of organized labor. By the end of the 1980s, labor unrest had shrunk to historically unprecedented levels and was lower than in almost any other country in Europe.

Economic growth was sluggish during Thatcher's first term, and it was probably only her victory in the 1981 Falklands War that won her reelection in 1984. One of the most successful elements of her "popular capitalism" was allowing tenants to buy public housing with low-cost mortgages. From 1979 to 1989, home ownership leapt from 52 to 66 percent of all households, including a majority of manual workers. One after another, major nationalized enterprises were sold off – British Telecom, British Gas, and the electric and water utilities. Privatization generated cash for the budget, and profits for financial brokers and for the millions of citizens who applied for shares in the new companies. Tax rates were cut: The top personal income tax rate fell from 90 to 40 percent. Workers were encouraged to opt out of the state pension system and invest some of their payroll taxes in a private retirement account. This investment should cut state pension spending to a projected 6 percent of Gross Domestic Product (GDP) by 2030, compared to 14–17 percent in continental Europe.

Thatcher was less successful in tackling some of the other sacred cows of British industry. She was not able to introduce more competition into professions, such as law and realty. The City of London was rocked by several major financial scandals, showing the limits of the self-regulation regime that prevailed in the stock market and insurance industry. Nevertheless, a deregulatory program for the financial markets in 1983–6, called the "Big Bang," enabled London to reinforce its position as the world's leading international financial center.

By the late 1980s the economy was growing, living standards were rising, and there was a boom in productivity and corporate profits. The fruits of progress were unevenly distributed, however. Although average incomes rose 37 percent in real terms in 1979–93, the earnings of the top 10 percent of the population leaped by 61 percent, while those of the bottom decile fell 18 percent. Unemployment climbed to 10 percent, from a level of 5 percent in the 1970s, but fell again to 5 percent by 1989. Still, one-third of the population lived in poverty, and there arose a large underclass of jobless youth that led to a surge in drug use and crime. It is ironical that demographic changes and the rise in unemployment caused state welfare spending to rise despite the Thatcher revolution.

In 1988 Thatcher introduced an ambitious "New Steps" program to change the way state services were delivered – reforms that provided much of the intellectual inspiration for the "reinventing government" movement in the United States. State agencies were obliged to introduce independent cost accounting for each stage of their operations. State services were contracted out to private companies or voluntary agencies through competitive tendering. Many state offices were turned into independent agencies, which then bid to provide government services, from sewage to prisons. Local governments, the National Health Service, and the education system were forced to adopt these reforms. Individual schools were encouraged to opt out of local-authority financing and receive direct grant funding. From 1979 to 1993, the number of civil servants was slashed by 30 percent, while about 150 new semi-independent government agencies were created. This reform created more than 40,000 new patronage positions for central ministers. The reforms increased efficiency and cut costs, but led to increased corruption. They triggered widespread protests, especially over the local "poll" tax, introduced in 1988, that replaced the former local property tax with a flat per-capita tax.

## The Fall of Thatcher

Thatcher secured reelection to an unprecedented third successive term in 1989. However, after ten years under the "Leaderene," strains were beginning to show in the upper ranks of the Tory party. Many traditional conservatives disliked Thatcher's radical reforms, while her authoritarian style alienated many colleagues. Her vocal opposition to further European integration, such as the introduction of a single currency, lost her the support of the internationalist wing of the party. Between 1979 and 1992, membership in the Tory party slumped from 1.5 million to 500,000.

Thatcher's departure came not with a bang but with an uncharacteristic whimper. Her popularity steadily eroded throughout the 1980s, dipping to 29 percent in 1990, and she came to be seen as an electoral liability. The Conservative leader is selected by an annual ballot of members of parliament (MPs). Usually, no candidates run against the incumbent, but in 1989 an obscure MP came forward to challenge Thatcher, winning 33 votes. The next year she faced a serious opponent in the form of ex-Defense Minister Michael Heseltine. Thatcher beat Heseltine in the first round by 204 votes to 152 (with 16 abstentions). Under party rules, a candidate winning less than two-thirds of the vote has to face a second round. Even though she would almost certainly have won, Thatcher chose to resign, partly in order to clear the way for her chosen successor – John Major.

Major, like Thatcher, came from humble origins. His father was a circus trapeze artist turned garden-gnome manufacturer. Major left school at sixteen to be a bus-ticket collector, and later worked his way up from bank teller to bank director before entering politics. Major was reasonably popular, but he lacked Thatcher's charisma. Despite a deep recession that began in 1990 and saw the GDP fall by 3.6 percent, Major was able to win the election in 1992, thanks mainly to the inept Labour campaign.

Major pressed ahead with privatization of British Rail and the nuclear power and coal industries. But his administration was dogged by a series of crises. The Tory party was badly split over Europe, with a hard-core right wing opposing further integration. The British public was skeptical about the Brussels bureaucracy but generally favored EU membership. (In a 1996 poll, 42 percent approved and 24 percent disapproved.) In 1990 Britain joined the Exchange Rate Mechanism (ERM), the precursor to the single European currency. But in 1991 Britain opted out of the "social chapter" of the Maastricht treaty on European integration. This would have introduced the EU's generous labor legislation to Britain (longer vacations, shorter working hours), and was opposed by employers.

The key turning point in the Major administration was September 1992, when the pound came under speculative attack. Despite desperate government efforts, including spending $5 billion (U.S.) to defend the exchange rate, the British pound was forced to leave the ERM. This was a major humiliation and left the government's financial strategy in ruins. Major's approval rating plummeted from 49 to 25 percent after the devaluation crisis, and it never recovered.

The Tory party's credibility was further battered by a series of sex and corruption scandals. Tory MPs were caught taking cash to ask questions in the Commons, and government officials were implicated in illegal arms sales to Iraq and Malaysia. The biggest policy disaster came with the 1996 discovery that "mad cow" disease (BSE), an incurable virus that attacks the brain stem, had spread from cattle to humans, killing 14 people. The government initially downplayed the problem and delayed ordering the mass slaughter of cattle. (A minister even appeared on TV feeding hamburgers to his daughter.) Major protested a subsequent EU ban on British beef by blocking all EU business for several weeks, bringing UK-EU relations to an all-time low. Eventually all of Britain's cattle had to be killed and burned.

Dissent over relations with the EU was ravaging the Tory party, and John Major found it increasingly difficult to control his MPs. In 1995, Tory rebels defeated a government proposal to introduce extra tax on heating fuel, a measure that would have hurt the poor. The same year, eighty-nine Tory MPs voted against Major's reappointment as their leader. Clearly, the Tories had been in power for too long. But was Labour in a fit state to replace them?

## The Rise of New Labour

After the 1992 election, the Labour Party was alarmed that it might never be able to defeat the Tories – and might even be replaced by the Liberal Democrats as the main opposition party. In 1994 the party selected the young, charismatic Tony Blair as its new leader. Blair set about fashioning a new Labour Party that would be able to recapture the middle-class and working-class voters who had defected to the Tories.

Following their defeat in 1979, the Labour Party had been split between parliamentary leaders anxious to improve the party's electoral chances and trade-union bosses keen to retain their control. The party's 1918 constitution had given Labour MPs the right to choose the party leader, but in 1981 an electoral college was introduced, with 40 percent of the votes in the hands of the trade unions. In 1983 Neil Kinnock took over as Labour leader, and he waged a vigorous campaign to diminish union power and expunge left-wing militants from the party. He closed down some local Labour Party branches that had been taken over by a secretive Trotskyist group called Militant.

After their defeat in 1987, the leadership started to expunge leftist policies from the party program, dropping their commitment to reverse Thatcher's privatizations, strengthen union power, and give up Britain's nuclear weapons. Intraparty reforms shifted the balance of power away from union bosses toward the parliamentary leadership. The union vote at the annual party conference was cut from 90 to 50 percent, while the share of union contributions in the party budget fell from 80 to 40 percent, thanks in part to an influx of cash from sympathetic business interests. Union influence had been weakened by Thatcher's defeat of the miners' strikes, and by changes in the economy. Manufacturing industry saw its share of total employment fall from 38 percent in 1956 to 19 percent in 1990; and the proportion of the workforce in unions fell from a peak of 53 percent in 1978 to 30 percent in 1995.

Kinnock stepped down following the humiliating 1992 electoral defeat. After the untimely death of his successor, John Smith, in 1994 Tony Blair took over the leadership. Blair sought to turn Labour into a modern, European, social-demo-cratic party of the center. He wanted to redefine Labour's identity in order to convince the middle-class voter that Labour no longer favored the redistributive, "tax and spend" policies of the past. Britain had become a society of "two-thirds haves and one-third have-nots," and Labour would never get back into power by appealing to the latter group alone.

But what would "New Labour" stand for? Blair used focus groups to try out ideas, such as communitarianism and the "stakeholder society," before hitting on the formula of the "Third Way." As Andrew Marr explained (*The Observer,* 9 August 1998): "The Third Way can be described, so far, by what it is not. It isn't messianic, high spending old socialism and it isn't ideologically driven, individualist conservatism. What is it? It's mostly an isn't." Many of the planks of Blair's new program were pulled straight from 19th-century liberalism. The state should stay out of economic management while providing moral leadership, investing in education and welfare, and devolving power to the regions. The centrist Third Way was encapsulated in the Labour slogan "Tough on crime, tough on the causes of crime." New Labour agreed with Thatcher that free markets are the best way to create prosperity, and did not seek to reverse her reforms of public-sector management. In 1995 the Labour Party finally removed from its constitution Clause IV (put there in 1918), which called for state ownership of industry. All this change was anathema to old-style socialists in the party.

Blair described New Labour as a "pro-business, pro-enterprise" party, albeit one with a compassionate face. He even said in May 1998: "I know it is not very PC [politically correct] to say this, but I am really proud of the British Empire." As recently as 1983, the Labour Party had called for Britain's withdrawal from the EU, which it saw as a capitalist plot. Blair, in contrast, was committed to EU membership, while echoing some Tory concerns over a "federal Europe."

New Labour was also more open to women. In 1993 the party decided that half of the new candidates being selected by local parties for the next parliamentary election must be chosen from women-only shortlists. (In 1996, a court struck down this rule as discriminatory.) As a result of these efforts, in the 1997 election 102 women were elected as Labour MPs, alongside 13 Conservatives. The total number of women MPs rose from 60 in 1992 to 120 in 1997 (18 percent of the total).

Blair turned to an expensive and sophisticated American-style media campaign to sell the New Labour image to the public. Along with a new Labour, there was to be a new Britain – sophisticated, multicultural, and hip (from "Rule Britannia" to "Cool Britannia"). Labour's main slogan was the patriotic "Britain Deserves Better." Campaign innovations included posters above urinals in pubs, saying "Now wash your hands of the Tories." In a bid to reassure the voters that their tax-and-spend policies were behind them, Labour pledged to maintain the Conservative government's planned spending limits for at least two years after the election. No new welfare initiatives were planned, beyond a new workfare program for 250,000 unemployed youths, paid for by a tax on the windfall profits of the recently privatized utility companies.

Labour won a landslide victory in the May 1997 election. The Conservatives lost half their seats, and 10 percent of voters switched from Tory to Labour – the largest swing this century. Major went down to defeat despite a strong economic recovery, scotching the widely held notion that British election results are driven by economic performance. In June 1997 he was replaced as party leader by the 36-year-old William Hague.

Voters did not choose Labour because they preferred their program to that of the Tories, since their policies were nearly identical. Rather, the Tories were seen as divided, corrupt, and inept, while New Labour was trusted to do a more competent job of governing the country. The only significant policy difference between the two parties was over Europe. Most Tories were skeptical about European integration. Whereas Major pursued a vague "wait and see" line, two-thirds of Tory candidates spoke out against the EU. Blair was adamantly pro-Europe, although he promised to hold a referendum before taking Britain into the single European currency. One of the first acts of the New Labour government was the granting of independence to the Bank of England: a striking example of their rejection of the old policies of Keynesian demand management.

## BRITISH POLITICAL INSTITUTIONS

The British political system is characterized by a high level of stability in its institutional structures. The main strength of the British system is its capacity to develop institutions able to defuse the deep conflicts in British society before they turn violent. The core features of the Westminster Model – parliamentary sovereignty, prime ministerial government, and two parties alternating in power – have remained basically unchanged for more than a hundred years. There have been no significant changes in these institutions since 1945, except a slight rise in the importance of minor parties. The most important structural reform of the postwar era was the Thatcher government's campaign to decentralize and marketize the provision of state services.

The centerpiece of the British political system is the House of Commons, and the essence of British democracy is Prime Minister's Question Time. For thirty minutes once a week, the prime minister stands before the Commons and answers questions, largely unscripted, from MPs of both parties. The ritual often strikes foreign observers as rather silly. The questions are not really intended to solicit information, but to score political points and make the other side look foolish. MPs from both parties shout, whistle, laugh, and jeer to express their encouragement or displeasure. The drama is enhanced by the fact that the two main parties sit on ranked benches facing each other, just yards apart.

The spectacle seems juvenile, more akin to a college debating competition than a legislative assembly. However, the game has a serious purpose: public accountability. Week after week, the members of the government have to take the stand and defend their policies. It is a kind of collective lie-detector test, in which the failings of government policy are ruthlessly exposed to ridicule by the opposition. Problems or scandals are speedily brought to light: A controversial newspaper article will stimulate questions in parliament within days. (And a minister who is caught lying to the Commons must immediately resign.)

Question Time illustrates the radical difference between the American and British legislatures. The American president never has to confront his political adversaries face to face. His communications with the public are carefully managed through public statements, photo-ops and the occasional press conference. Since 1989, Question Time has been televised. MPs were wary of exposing their at-times childish behavior to the cameras, but the broadcasts seem to have boosted public respect for the Commons.

## Prime Ministerial Government

The House of Commons consists of 659 members of parliament (MPs), elected from single-member constituencies. Although a handful of members sit as Independents, the vast majority of MPs run for election as members of a political party. The Commons must submit itself for election at least once every five years, in what is called a General Election. (If an MP dies or resigns between elections, an individual by-election is held for that seat.) The leader of the party with a majority of MPs is invited by the queen to form a government. If no single party has an absolute majority, party leaders negotiate and the monarch appoints a coalition government. That has not happened since 1935, because the winner-take-all electoral system typically throws up two strong parties.

The head of the government is known as the prime minister (PM). The PM nominates a cabinet of about twenty ministers, who are appointed by the queen to form Her Majesty's Government. There are another 70 to 90 ministers and deputy ministers without cabinet rank. Individual ministers are not confirmed by the legislature, as in the United States. By convention, all ministers must be sitting members of parliament and must account for their actions, individual and collective, to that body. (At least two cabinet ministers must be from the Lords.) A Tory

PM can pick whom he or she wants to be a minister; a Labour PM is constrained by the fact that the parliamentary party elects a shadow cabinet when they are in opposition.

The cabinet meets weekly in the PM's residence, No. 10 Downing Street. The PM chairs and directs cabinet meetings, and votes are usually not taken. The most senior ministers are those heading the Foreign Office, the Treasury and the Home Office (dealing with police, prisons, etc). The ministers rely on the permanent civil service to run their departments, with only one or two personal advisers brought in from outside. The total number of outside appointees when a new government takes power is fewer than thirty, compared to more than 2,000 political appointees in the United States.

There is no separation of powers between the executive and legislative branches. On the contrary, the two are fused together. The public elects the House of Commons, knowing that the majority party will form the executive. The PM comes from the party with a majority in the Commons, and this majority always votes according to party instructions. This means that the legislative program of the ruling party is almost always implemented. The government rules as long as it can sustain its majority in the Commons. A government will resign after defeat in the Commons of what it deems to be a vote of confidence.

This system gives the prime minister tremendous power, in what Tory Lord Hailsham called "an elective dictatorship." The power of the prime minister is augmented by the fact that he chooses when to call an election. The Commons can vote to dissolve itself at any time, leading to a general election just six weeks later. Thanks to his control over the majority party in the Commons, the prime minister can choose when he has to face the electorate. This gives a tremendous political advantage to the incumbent government. PMs carefully monitor opinion polls and economic data, and choose to call an election when their support is at a peak (although an election must be called no later than five years after the previous election).

If the U.S. Congress is a policy-*making* legislature, Westminster is at best a policy-*influencing* legislature. In Britain, the government is responsible for introducing virtually all legislation: It is extremely rare for a bill proposed by an individual MP to make it into law. MPs are expected to vote in accordance with party instructions (the party "whip"), except when a vote is declared a matter of conscience. An MP who defies the whip may be expelled from the party and denied its endorsement at the next election, which will usually prevent her reelection. Even so, in about 10 to 20 percent of votes in the Commons, a small number of rebels defy the party Whip. The parliaments of 1974–9 and 1992–7 saw frequent revolts by dissident MPs from the ruling party, but they had only a marginal effect on the government's capacity to enact its program. In an attempt to bolster the parliament's powers, in 1979 fourteen new committees giving MPs oversight over ministry activities were introduced.

Still, some commentators suggest that the power of prime ministerial government should not be overrated. Globalization of the economy means that the British state, like all states, has become "hollowed out," and now has much less discretion in national economic policy than it did in the 1950s and 1960s. Increasingly, policy is driven by informal networks of transnational corporate elites, not represented in the institutional structures of the Westminster Model.

The upper chamber of parliament, the House of Lords, has a limited capacity to block or delay government legislation. The judicial branch has only a limited ability to interfere with the government's actions, since there is no written constitution to which they can appeal to declare a law invalid. Any act that is passed in three readings by the Commons and Lords and signed into law by the queen supersedes all preceding laws and precedents and must be implemented by the judiciary. The lack of a bill of rights has troubled many liberal observers.

Britain has a unitary system of government. There is no federal system that can block the powers of the Westminster parliament. There are separate ministries for Scotland, Wales, and Northern Ireland, the main tasks of which is spending regional development funds. Local governments have very limited powers, and the national government sets the rules by which they raise and spend money. Eighty percent of the funding for local councils comes from the national government, and there are strict rules over how it can be spent. Thatcher was so annoyed by the policies of the Labour-controlled Greater London Council that she had parliament abolish the council (which had been created only in 1964). Unique among the world's capitals, London has no city council and no mayor. The New Labour government of Tony Blair set about reversing the centralization of the Thatcher years, moving ahead with plans for the introduction of new parliaments in Wales and Scotland.

## The Electoral System

Britain operates a first-past-the-post or winner-take-all electoral system, similar to that in the United States. This produces clear winners and strong alternating majority parties in the House of Commons. However, it is criticized for offering voters an exceptionally narrow range of alternatives (two) and denying third parties adequate representation.

Each of the 659 members of parliament is elected from a single-member constituency in which the candidate with the highest number of votes wins. This first-past-the-post electoral system works to the advantage of the two leading parties, which tend to finish first and second in every race. Britain's third-largest party, the Liberal Democrats, has 15 to 25 percent support in nearly every constituency in the country, but this is not enough to displace a Labour or Tory incumbent with 40 to 60 percent support. Hence, the Liberal Democrats win very few parliamentary seats.

Also, as several candidates compete for each seat, the winner may not have an absolute majority of the votes cast. Similarly, at the national level there is no guarantee that the party that wins the most seats will have won a majority of the votes. In fact, no governing party since 1945 has won more than 50 percent of the votes cast in a British election – yet this did not prevent those governments from having absolute control of the Commons and pursuing an aggressive legislative program.

The first-past-the-post system is unpredictable in the degree to which voter preferences are translated into parliamentary seats. Table 2 shows the results of the 1992 and 1997 elections (excluding Northern Ireland). The third column illustrates the hypothetical case of how many seats each party would have won if they had been allocated in strict proportion to the share of total votes cast – a system of proportional representation, or PR. In 1992 both Labour and Tories won more seats than they would have had under a PR system, while the Liberal Democrats got only one-fifth of the seats they would have had under PR. In 1997 the Liberal Democrats won twice as many seats as they did in 1992 – although they garnered fewer votes than in the previous election. The Conservatives did worse in 1997 than they would have under PR, while Labour scooped up two-thirds of the seats with only 44 percent of the national vote.

The unequal relationship between votes and seats is exacerbated by the unequal geographical concentration of voters, and the economic divide between the prosperous Southeast and the depressed North and West. Labour does well in London and in northern cities, but usually wins few seats in the southern suburbs and rural seats. (An exception was in 1997, in that Labour did well even in the South.) The gap in regional voting patterns actually increased during the 1970s and

**TABLE 2. 1992 AND 1997 GENERAL ELECTIONS** (excluding Northern Ireland)

| | 1992 Election | | | 1997 Election | | |
|---|---|---|---|---|---|---|
| | Share of Vote (%) | No. of MPs | No. of MPs under PR* | Share of Vote (%) | No. of MPs | No. of MPs under PR* |
| Conservatives | 42.8 | 336 | 273 | 31.4 | 165 | 199 |
| Labour | 35.2 | 271 | 222 | 44.4 | 419 | 286 |
| Liberal Democrats | 18.3 | 20 | 114 | 17.2 | 46 | 109 |
| Scots/Welsh nationalists | 2.4 | 7 | 16 | 2.5 | 10 | 16 |
| Referendum Party† | – | – | – | 2.7 | 0 | 17 |
| Others | 1.3 | 0 | 0 | 1.7 | 0 | 0 |

* This is a purely hypothetical case of proportional representation, based on dividing total votes by total seats.

† The Referendum Party was formed by billionaire industrialist James Goldsmith to push for Britain's exit from the EU.

1980s. As a result of this pattern, four out of five constituencies are "safe seats" that rarely change hands between parties in an election. Despite this, voter turnout is relatively high, usually around 80 percent, slipping to 72 percent in 1997.

Under the first-past-the-post system, minor parties with a regional concentration, such as the Scottish and Welsh nationalists, can win seats on their home turf. The third-largest party in Britain, formerly the Liberals and now called the Liberal Democrats, mainly win seats in the alienated periphery where their supporters are concentrated – Scotland, Wales, and the Southwest. Elsewhere, they win few seats.

There are growing calls for a reform of the British electoral system, in order to make the results more representative of voter opinion. The Liberal Democrats have the most to gain from the introduction of European-style proportional representation. Most advocates of PR suggest a compromise system, such as that operating in Germany, where half the seats are reserved for single-member races (to ensure that there is an MP responsible for each district) and half for party lists (to ensure proportional representation).

Proponents of the existing British system argue that it produces strong governments with the power to implement their legislative program. PR would spread power among three or more parties, requiring coalition governments of more than one party. This may be undemocratic, since in most countries, coalition governments are usually formed in backroom deals that take place after the election. Neither Labour nor Tories are likely to introduce PR, since this would undermine their capacity to form single-party governments. The Liberal Democrats hope that if a future parliament is equally split between Labour and Conservatives, the Labour Party might introduce PR in return for Liberal Democratic support. Some Labour politicians suggest merging with the Liberal Democrats and then introducing PR, a strategy that could permanently exclude the Tories from power. In 1993 Labour promised to hold a referendum on electoral reform if they were elected to office.

## Political Behavior

Voters' loyalty to political parties is quite high in Britain, although it has fallen since the war. In 1950, 40 percent of those polled "strongly identified" with a single party, but this figure had halved by 1992. In the 1950s, social class and income level were a good predictor of voting behavior – although even then a quarter of industrial workers voted Conservative and not Labour (which was attributed to deferential or patriotic values). The protracted economic crisis of the 1960s and 1970s eroded party loyalties as voters started to shop around for new ideas. Social-class origin could explain 70 percent of voting behavior in the 1950s, falling to 50 percent by the 1970s. Voting became less a matter of habit, and more a matter of choice. Voter behavior became more volatile, harder to predict, and more likely to be swayed by party campaigns.

Given the large number of "safe" seats, the parties pour their efforts into winning the "marginal" seats, those that may change hands at every election. In marginal seats, the parties canvass every household and record the voting intentions of each family member. On election day, party volunteers stand outside polling stations to record voters' registration numbers. The data are collated at party headquarters, and supporters who have not voted are reminded to go to the polls.

Tight limits on campaign spending have mostly prevented the spread of American-style money politics in Britain. There are no limits on donations to national parties, however, fueling repeated scandals. It is the role of the media, rather than money, which is a source of controversy in British politics. The British are avid newspaper readers (average daily circulation is 14 million). In contrast to those in the United States, most British papers are not politically neutral, but actively campaign for one of the parties. The papers are not controlled by political parties, as in much of Europe, but are owned by quixotic business magnates who enjoy playing politics. In 1997 the *Observer* newspaper concluded that the second most influential man after Prime Minister Tony Blair was Rupert Murdoch, the Australian who owns one-third of Britain's newspapers. Two-thirds of the newspapers usually back the Tories, but in 1997 most papers switched to Labour, which helps to explain Labour's dramatic victory that year. Most newspapers are hostile to Europe, causing a problem for Europhile Tony Blair. Unlike the press, the television stations are required to be politically neutral, and are highly valued for their objectivity. The BBC is state financed, while three other stations are commercially owned and depend on advertising.

Civil society is deeply rooted in Britain, with a broad range of interest groups. Such groups expanded in the 1970s as voters became disillusioned with the mainstream political parties and turned toward "postmaterialist" values. The environmentalist group Greenpeace saw their membership swell tenfold to more than 400,000, in part thanks to media coverage of their spectacular protests. Groups protesting new road construction and defending animal rights continued to be active throughout the 1990s. However, environmental issues did not enter the agenda of the mainstream political parties.

## THE DIGNIFIED CONSTITUTION

Elizabeth II ascended to the throne in 1953. She is the head of state but has only limited influence over the affairs of government. The queen meets the prime minister each week for a private chat, over tea. The most important function of the monarch is to invite a prime minister to form a government, usually after a general election. If that government wins majority support in the Commons, the monarch's effective role is at an end.

The last time the monarch played a significant role in British politics was in 1910. The House of Lords blocked a high-spending welfare budget passed by the

Commons. Liberal Prime Minister Lloyd George called an election, which he won, and he asked the king to create enough new peers to tip the voting in the upper chamber. The Lords gave in and accepted a new law abolishing its right to delay bills involving public spending. They retained the right to return nonspending bills to the Commons, although if passed a second time by the Commons, such bills become law after a two-year delay (reduced to one year in 1949).

The House of Lords is a bizarre anachronism. In a democracy, it does not make sense to give a legislative role to the descendants of medieval knights. The Lords consists of 750 hereditary peers and 600 life peers. Hereditary peers are exclusively male, and they pass their title to their first sons. The system of life peers was introduced in 1958. They are mostly retired politicians, men and women, who are nominated by the PM and appointed by the queen. Their seat in the Lords does not pass to their heirs.

The ultraconservative hereditary peers give the Tories a guaranteed majority in the upper chamber, so Labour has a strong interest in reforming the upper chamber. However, reform of the Lords has proved difficult, since the House of Commons does not want to create a new elected second chamber that could rival its power. In 1998 the Blair government announced plans to phase out hereditary peers over several years.

The monarchy, like the Lords, is not likely to be abolished anytime soon. The idea of replacing the monarch with a president has never attracted much sympathy in Britain, since the existing system has worked pretty well for 300 years. The main argument is over money. Each year the Commons votes a budget for the queen and her extended family in recognition of their public duties. In the 1990s, as the royal family fell prey to divorce and scandal, the public began to wonder whether they were getting value for money. The queen's vast personal wealth is exempt from tax, but in response to public criticism in 1995, she voluntarily started to pay income tax. Defenders of the monarchy often fall back on the argument that royal pageantry is good for the tourism industry.

The life of the royals is a real-time soap opera that provides endless copy for the tabloid press in Britain and throughout the world. Princess Diana was probably the most well-known woman on the planet. Her untimely death in August 1997 produced an extraordinary outpouring of emotion in Britain, equivalent to that following the death of John F. Kennedy in the United States. Diana, whom Blair called the "people's princess," has come to represent the new England, breaking down barriers of class, gender, and race through her charity work.

## CONCLUSION

Britain has a robust and successful political system that seems to have recovered from the economic stagnation and class warfare of the 1970s and 1980s. The Westminster Model is no longer the "envy of the world," as was complacently assumed by many Britons in the 19th century. But the parliamentary system, with strong parties competing for office, has proved its mettle in producing strong governments, capable of exercising leadership to tackle Britain's social and economic problems. The experience of countries in the "third wave" of democratization, in the 1970s and 1980s, seems to confirm that parliamentary systems are more successful than presidential systems in reconciling conflicting interests in society and, hence, promoting less violence and greater stability.

The major challenge facing Britain is the same one that confronts the other European countries – crafting transnational institutions to manage the global economy while maintaining the capacity to tackle social problems that arise at the national and regional levels, and while preserving national and subnational identities. Britain has been a follower rather than a leader in this process of international institution building (such as the European Union), which is a reflection of its diminished role in the international system since the end of empire.

## BIBLIOGRAPHY

Butler, David and Denis Kavanagh. *The British General Election of 1997.* New York: St. Martins Press, 1998.

Dunleavy, Patrick, Andrew Gamble, Ian Holliday, and Gillian Peele, eds. *Developments in British Politics No. 5.* New York: St. Martins, 1997.

Geddes, Andrew, and Jonathan Tonge, eds. *Labour's Landslide.* New York: Manchester University Press, 1997.

Will Hutton. *The State We're In.* London: Jonathan Cape, 1995.

Denis Kavanagh. *Thatcherism and British Politics: The End of Consensus?* New York: Oxford University Press, 1990.

Anthony King et al, eds. *Britain at the Polls 1992.* London: Chatham House, 1993.

David Marquand, and Anthony Seldon. *The Ideas That Shaped Modern Britain.* London: Fontana Press, 1996.

Lynton Robins, and Bill Jones, eds. *Half a Century of British Politics.* (New York: Manchester University Press, 1997.

Anthony Seldon. *Major: A Political Life.* London: Trafalgar Square, 1998.

Margaret Thatcher. *The Downing Street Years.* New York: Harper Collins, 1993.

## IMPORTANT TERMS

**British Commonwealth**   cultural association linking fifty-three former colonies of Britain.

**The "British disease"**   a high level of strike activity, caused by powerful trade unions taking advantage of low unemployment to push for higher wages.

**Devolution**   the creation of regional assemblies in Wales and Scotland, debated since the 1970s and introduced in 1999.

**Exchange Rate Mechanism (ERM)**   the common currency band of European Union currencies, which Britain joined in 1990 and was forced to leave in 1992.

**Falklands War**   the 1982 conflict after Argentina had seized the British-owned Falklands Islands and a naval task force was sent to recapture them.

**Glorious Revolution**   1688 removal of the Catholic king James II by Protestant William of Orange, who accepted the principle of parliamentary sovereignty.

**Greenpeace**   the environmental action group that saw its membership expand in the 1980s.

**Hereditary peers**   members of the House of Lords appointed by the monarch whose title automatically passes down to their sons.

**Her Majesty's Opposition**   the second largest party in the House of Commons, which is critical of the government but loyal to the British state, as symbolized by the monarch.

**John Major**   Conservative Party leader who replaced Thatcher as prime minister in 1990, and resigned after losing the 1997 election.

**Keynesianism**   a philosophy of state intervention in the economy derived from the work of John Maynard Keynes, who argued that state spending could have avoided the Great Depression.

**"Mad-cow" disease scandal**   a political scandal in 1996 that followed the Conservative government's delay in taking urgent measures to stop the spread of the BSE disease, which was infecting humans.

**Magna Carta**   the contract guaranteeing the rights of noble families that King John agreed to sign in 1215.

**"Marginal" seats**   seats in the House of Commons that are closely contested and are likely to change hands between parties in an election (the opposite of "safe" seats).

**1984 miners' strike**   the coal miners' strike that was defeated by Margaret Thatcher, clearing the way for legislation limiting the power of trade unions.

**Neil Kinnock**   Labour Party leader in the 1980s who introduced reforms to decrease the power of trade unions in the party.

**"New Steps" program**   Thatcher's program to cut state bureaucracy and make it more responsive to citizens' interests.

**No. 10 Downing Street**   the prime minister's residence, the place where the cabinet meets.

**Parliamentary sovereignty**   the power of parliament, representing the people, to enact any law it chooses, unrestrained by a written constitution or the separation of powers.

**Plaid Cymru**   the nationalist party in Wales that advocates more rights for the Welsh people, including use of the Welsh language.

**Prime Minister's Question Time**   the thirty-minute period once a week during which the prime minister stands before the House of Commons and answers questions from MPs.

**Referendum Party**   a new party formed by billionaire industrialist James Goldsmith to campaign for a referendum demanding Britain's exit from the European Union.

**Rupert Murdoch**   the Australian-born magnate who owns one-third of Britain's newspapers and has considerable political influence.

**Social Democratic Party**   a group of moderate socialists that broke away from the Labour Party in the early 1980s.

**"Third way"**   the new, moderate philosophy introduced by Tony Blair after he became Labour Party leader in 1994.

**Tory**   colloquial name for a member of the Conservative Party.

**Unionists**   the Protestant majority in Northern Ireland, who want to keep the province in the United Kingdom.

**Welfare State**   the program of state-provided social benefits introduced by the Labour Government of 1945–51, including the National Health Service, state pensions, and state-funded higher education.

**Westminster Model**   the British system of parliamentary sovereignty, prime ministerial government, and two parties alternating in power.

**William Hague**   leader of the Conservative Party who replaced John Major in 1997.


## STUDY QUESTIONS

1.  What were the main features of the bipartisan consensus in British politics that lasted from the 1950s to the late 1970s?

2.  Why did some observers argue that Britain was "ungovernable" in the 1970s?

3.  Which aspects of British society were the targets of Margaret Thatcher's "revolution"?

4.  Why did Margaret Thatcher fall from power in 1990?

5.  What does Tony Blair mean by the "Third Way"?

6.  What factors have been holding back Britain from fuller participation in the European Union?

7.  When did most British citizens get the right to vote, and why?

8.  Why did Labour defeat the Conservatives so soundly in 1997?

9.  How does the power of the prime minister compare with that of the U.S. president?

10. What are the strengths and weaknesses of the first-past-the-post electoral system, compared with proportional representation? Is Britain likely to introduce PR in the near future?

# 2

# France

≋ **Arista Maria Cirtautas**

# INTRODUCTION

Politically, the predominant image of France today is that of a stable democratic government presiding over the second-largest country in Europe after Russia, covering an area of 211,208 square miles with a population of 56.5 million, including 4.4 million immigrants. Economically, France is securely ranked as an intermediate power sustained by an active trade sector that places France in fourth position after Japan, the United States, and Germany in terms of the volume and value of foreign trade. In addition, France produces one-quarter of the European Union's total agricultural production. Every now and then, strikes, popular protests, corruption scandals, and hostility against immigrants generate headlines, yet without seriously disrupting the viability of the existing political system. Although largely taken for granted now, the strength and stability of France's post–World War II governing institutions do represent a remarkable achievement as the country has, beyond a doubt, experienced one of the most turbulent, complex, and contradictory paths of development toward democratic government that history has produced. Since the French Revolution (1789), democracy in France has been challenged and modified, attacked and replaced and, ultimately, fully stabilized only after 1958 in the form of the current Fifth Republic. Whereas the United States has had only one constitution with twenty-six amendments in 200 years, France has endured three monarchies, two empires, and five republics, as well as thirteen written constitutions during the same time period.

During the course of this unique history, the French have made significant contributions both to the evolution of modern democracy and to its principal competitors. Indeed, what makes the French case of development extraordinary from a comparative perspective is the nation's complicated relationship to democracy. As the birthplace of continental European democracy, France is clearly a case of early development that set the terms for later developers throughout Europe. However, France is also the country that first experienced tremendous difficulties in institutionalizing a stable democracy when competing ideologies and interests mobilized to resist this new form of government. The French case consequently manifests characteristics of both early and late development and can, therefore, best be introduced as a country that bridges these two categories of development.

On the one hand, the French Revolution represents one of the earliest and most important articulations of liberalism – in circumstances that were arguably more difficult than the English and American cases. Whereas England gradually and largely peacefully evolved into a modern democracy, ultimately granting full political, civil, and social rights to all of its citizens, and whereas the United States was, according to some observers, born a modern rights-oriented society that simply had to rid itself of the traditional monarchy in order to flourish as a democracy, French democrats had to struggle simultaneously against active supporters of the monarchy, against foreign invaders coming to the aid of the French king, and against their own destructive schisms and factions. In spite of these difficulties, French democrats promulgated and defended the Declaration of the Rights of Man and Citizen (1789), a powerful and eloquent statement proclaiming the natural rights of the individual citizen against the tyranny of monarchical government, second only to the American Declaration of Independence in terms of its impact.

On the other hand, because of its excesses, the revolution soon gave rise to a reactionary form of conservatism as supporters of monarchical authority recovered throughout the 1800s and attempted to restore some type of monarchy, which, in their opinion, remained the only appropriate and legitimate government for France. Although conservative traditions are not unknown in the United States and Britain, there is a fundamental difference between the French and Anglo-American manifestations of conservatism. Whereas conservatism in the latter countries has tended to support reform efforts within the existing framework of liberal democratic government, in France and in later developers around the world, the drive to defend and conserve a nation's traditional way of life against the modern socioeconomic and cultural attributes associated with liberalism has produced profound ideological and institutional challenges to liberal government on the part of conservative political forces.

In France itself, the conflict between traditional and republican values proved to be of long duration, doing much to prevent the smooth institutionalization of a democratic form of government until the late 1800s. To this day, the gap between what has often been called the "two faces of France" – one conservative, Catholic, and rooted in rural peasant life, the other progressive, secular, and anchored in urban life – remains a central feature of French political culture.

In addition, the revolution also gave birth to nationalism, an ideology that subordinates all rights and interests to those of the nation and its designated leaders. In the course of defending the new republic from foreign intervention, the French revolutionaries began to equate the natural rights of individuals to exist on free and equal terms with the equally natural right of the nation to exist on the terms determined by its own population and not by outside forces. The nation, as a collective entity comprising all French citizens, was thereby elevated to a transcendent status. This new ideological legitimation, when combined with the inherited bureaucratic and administrative structures of the centralized monarchical regime, provided a firm basis upon which to ground the enhanced authority of the postrevolutionary state. As noted in Chapter 1, the expansion of state authority is a basic institutional characteristic of later developers. Interesting to note, it is in France, an early developer, that a compelling new foundation for state-building efforts was created, as it was here that the justification for this expansion was first expressed in terms of a rational need for the state to play a greater role in promoting and preserving the nation's rights and interests. This tendency culminated in post–World War II programs for national economic development and planning initiated and extensively coordinated by the French state. Like the Japanese, the French have not hesitated to use the state in order to protect and promote domestic industries.

Finally, socialist principles as well were first expressed during the French Revolution when revolutionaries from the lower social orders, the "sans-culottes," (literally: without short pants – meaning those without proper attire) and their more privileged supporters began to question the value of citizenship rights that proclaimed political equality in the context of substantial social and economic inequalities. How could all French citizens exercise their rights equally, not to mention their duties, if a majority remained disadvantaged in terms of wealth and education? Unlike the American case, where substantial income disparities did not divide the colonists and render their civic equality meaningless, or the English Glorious Revolution of 1688 where the right of representation for the upper social orders took precedence over the rights of liberty and equality for all, the French Revolution attempted to reconcile not just individual and collective rights but also political and socioeconomic rights.

In the process, the traditions of democratic socialism and, ultimately, even Marxism were born. Marx, for example, used what he perceived to be the failure of the French Revolution to provide for the full emancipation of man from all scarcity and want as one of the crucial points of departure for his philosophical rejection of liberalism. This radicalization of opposition to democratic government on the part of the Left is another characteristic of later-developing countries. Faced with unfavorable social and economic conditions, which democracy itself can do little to ameliorate in the short run, groups hoping for more immediate reforms have tended to turn away from liberalism and toward ideologies such as Marxism, which hold up the promise of more complete forms of social justice.

In short, the French experience of attempting to build democratic institutions while coping with ideological challenges from both the conservative Right and the radical Left, as well as finding ways to control the power of state institutions that have been given enhanced authority, represents the earliest manifestation of a pattern of political development that later-developing nations would find themselves replicating in part, if not in whole. Given France's unique position as a bridge between early- and later-development paths, the question arises as to how and why France came to occupy such intermediate ground. To begin, we will examine the historical factors that led to, and account for, the problematic French experience with democracy. Three major periods of French history will be surveyed briefly: From Absolutism to Revolution, 1760–1789; From Postrevolutionary Restoration to Republic, 1789–1870; and, finally, The Third Republic, 1870–1940. In each period, one can determine how the interplay between conflicting identities and interests led to specific institutional outcomes that subsequently generated the conditions for new conflicts to emerge, which, in turn, culminated in new institutional arrangements.

## HISTORICAL DEVELOPMENT

### From Absolutism to Revolution, 1760–1789

Over the centuries much has been written about the French Revolution. Indeed, it is one of the most studied of historical phenomena, a remarkable example of the collapse of a regime considered to be among the most powerful of European monarchies. From the reign of Louis XIV (1643–1715) on, the French monarchy had undertaken a highly successful program of consolidating the king's rule. Over time, the powers of the nobility to rule their lands as miniature kings had been broken, providing for the greater stability of the monarchy's borders and ensuring that the king's decrees would be followed from one end of the land to the other. Monarchical authority was thus increasingly centralized and rendered more absolute. Although the autonomy of the nobility undoubtedly suffered in this process, ordinary French subjects benefited, as the monarchs were able to provide higher levels of law and order, freeing the countryside from bandits and improving the transportation infrastructure. As a result, the country as a whole grew more prosperous. Between 1713 and 1789, for example, French foreign trade increased fivefold. According to some accounts, half of the gold coins circulating in Europe on the eve of the revolution were French. Moreover, France was the center of the intellectual movement of the Enlightenment. Throughout Europe, French was considered the principal language of the educated and aristocratic circles, allowing French literature, science, and philosophy to be read and followed far beyond French borders. In light of these successes, how could the monarchy fail? How could the French Revolution, unlike the Russian or Chinese revolutions of the 20th century, take place in what was perhaps the most admired and most advanced country of the day?

While many explanations have been put forward there is, for the most part, a general consensus that the revolution was the by-product, if not the direct product, of an emerging middle class of professionals and entrepreneurs who felt disadvantaged by existing feudal institutions that privileged the monarchy and the aristocracy at their expense. Of special concern was the extent to which their non-noble blood denied them access to the higher appointments in the bureaucracy and in the military. Had they never had access to such appointments, perhaps the concern would not have been as great. But the French monarchy had, for a brief period of time, opened the doors of advancement to men of talent, not simply men of the right blood, only to close those doors in the wake of aristocratic protest. Frustrated interests and ambitions on the part of an increasingly educated and wealthy social group was the inevitable result.

By the mid–18th century, ordinary farmers and peasants, small craftsmen, and shopkeepers also became frustrated with their constrained living conditions and limited opportunities for advancement. For example, Alexis de Tocqueville, one of the first great historians to study the revolution and the collapse of the "ancien régime" (the old regime), has emphasized the extent to which French peasants, especially, felt their interests and their dignity violated by old feudal obligations owed to the nobility and to the Catholic clergy. Again, had the French peasants never experienced the freedom of owning their own lands, if they had remained fully dependent on the nobility, they might not have so greatly resented the restrictions they lived under. However, as de Tocqueville points out, the destruction of some medieval institutions over the course of centuries made those that survived all the more intolerable. The erosion of these institutions, encouraged in part by monarchs interested in limiting the feudal powers of the nobility, had enabled the peasants to acquire some land of their own, which, in turn, made them eager to acquire more land and greater freedom to define and pursue their interests.

Even the aristocracy became increasingly aware of the need for change as the French monarchy grew ever more incapacitated and unable to manage the growing complexities of the bureaucratic machinery of the state – including the raising of sufficient tax revenues to offset costs, such as the financial assistance given to the American revolutionaries. Successive efforts of the monarchy throughout the 18th century to rationalize the operations of the state, to enhance efficiency and productivity, had fallen short of the desired effects. Instead, these reform efforts served mainly to antagonize the nobility as their outdated privileges, including exemption from taxation, had come under attack from reform-minded ministers appointed by the king. An "aristocratic resurgence" was the result as members of the nobility, in their turn, began to contemplate reforms that would curtail the powers of the monarchy by giving the aristocracy and the clergy greater authority to rule the nation alongside the king.

One might note here the irony of unintended consequences. As the French monarchs developed an absolutist regime to strengthen their rule, they also set in motion the very social, political, and economic forces that would undermine that rule. Economic prosperity and the decline of feudal institutions, both encouraged by the monarchy, created the conditions for the development of new propertied interests, both small and large, that by the late 1770s stood on the threshold of mobilizing to defend themselves against a system of privilege increasingly seen as corrupt and illegitimate. This distaste for the existing system was shared by members of the nobility for whom the corruption and venality of the ancien régime was also becoming offensive, thereby providing further motivation for their efforts to reclaim ruling powers from the monarchy.

According to the historian R. R. Palmer, this widespread social discontent with the existing state of affairs had, by the 1760s, developed into a "revolutionary situation" characterized by the existing regime's loss of legitimacy and credibility, as previously accepted social, political, and economic circumstances were no longer considered valid, just, or reasonable. Although actual revolution need not follow, such a precarious setting provides the context in which groups begin to contemplate a fundamental change of the established system, as well as envisioning a new, more just and legitimate, political community. It was in the effort to determine the exact nature of such a new community that opposing ideas and interests began to struggle against one another in France. These struggles would culminate in the revolution, which can be understood at its most basic level as series of conflicts between incompatible conceptions of the kind of polity that should replace the discredited monarchy.

Ultimately, the French king himself, Louis XVI (1774–92), provided the mechanism that would transform the revolutionary situation into an actual revolution. In 1788, hoping to obtain popular approval for new taxation measures, the king called for a meeting of the Estates-General to be held the following year. Comprised of the three main groups in French society – the nobles, the clergy, and the middle orders – the Estates-General has been called a "proto-parliamentary" body; it originated in the Middle Ages before the era of monarchical absolutism. Earlier French kings, lacking the ability to impose their will unilaterally on society, had used this rudimentary representative institution to gain acceptance for their policies.

In the context of 1788–9, however, calling out the Estates-General created the opportunity for people to reinterpret their frustrated interests as unendurable grievances that validated their calls for an entirely new system of government. From the very beginning of this process, however, the various groups involved were divided over what kind of government and community should replace the old regime. The nobility, for example, envisioned something like a constitutional monarchy that would guarantee certain crucial rights, such as "personal liberty for all, freedom of speech and press, freedom from arbitrary arrest and confinement." The king would henceforth have to share authority with the Estates-General, which would become a permanent parliamentary body with the aristocracy as its most powerful component. In order to achieve this vision of a new community, numerous members of the aristocracy were even willing to give up their privileges and become more equal members of society. By and large, a constitutional monarchy along these lines would have been quite similar to the English model of government, and French nobles were no doubt influenced by what the English had achieved.

Unfortunately for the aristocracy in France, the world had changed since 1688 when the English nobility had successfully limited monarchical powers in favor of parliamentary authority. Most importantly, the Enlightenment had transformed the world of ideas. French philosophers, such as Voltaire, Diderot, Rousseau, and Montesquieu, provided the philosophical and moral basis upon which the French middle orders, and quite a few nobles as well, began to contemplate an entirely new community – one that would be founded on the fundamental equality of all men; that could do without the monarchy entirely; that would reanimate the ancient republican traditions of self-government and civic virtue; and that would preserve and protect the inalienable rights of all citizens. The American Revolution that had just taken place across the Atlantic proved to many Frenchmen that these ideals of the Enlightenment could be given concrete form and substance in the creation of an entirely new form of government. Accordingly, the middle orders called for a parliament that would represent all the people of France equally without giving undo weight and power to the nobility. Such a parliament would serve to protect the fundamental equalities demanded by those of non-noble birth: equality in the state, equality in taxation, and equal access to public office and to the civil service. No longer would men of talent and merit be held back by hereditary privileges that denied them the right to pursue their interests and objectives.

The type of community they envisioned, rooted in individual rights and liberties, is not too far distant from what was achieved in the United States. Why, then, did this program for revolutionary change fail to replicate the success of the American case? Here the answer lies less in the realm of changed global circumstances and more in the particular nature of French society. In this context, Palmer reminds us of the "deep native roots" of the French Revolution. Although the French might have been exposed to outside influences, their revolution was rooted in the specific nature of earlier French history. France was not, at the time, challenged to maintain a competitive international position. Consequently, feelings of backwardness did not animate or promote institutional changes in order to facilitate development and progress. Indeed, according to de Tocqueville, it is precisely the "progressive" nature of French feudalism in particular that created the conditions for an active land-owning peasantry to emerge in France. Although feudalism, as a system of privileges granted to the aristocracy and the clergy at the expense of the peasants who actually worked on the land, existed throughout Western Europe, it was in France that the system had actually decayed the furthest by the mid–18th century. As more and more French peasants had become landowners in their own right, they did not hesitate to demand the complete destruction of the old feudal order during the years of the revolution. Often these demands took the form of armed rebellion in the countryside, rebellions that swept over into the cities as poor harvests and high food prices inflamed the urban laboring classes.

With much passion, and often quite violently, urban groups demanded both basic economic necessities, such as lower bread prices, and political representation on their own terms. They too wished to have an active voice in governing the new political community – one that they envisioned in terms of universal economic and social rights, not just in terms of civil and political rights. In other words, their ideal community would provide for both equality of outcome and equality of opportunity. Centuries of economic oppression and deeply ingrained social, cultural, and institutional patterns had relegated peasants and wage laborers permanently to the lowest positions in the social hierarchy. It is not surprising, therefore, that their vision of the new republic provided for the most complete levels of equality. In this vision they were supported by radical members of the more privileged classes, who interpreted Rousseau's writings, in particular, as a call to arms, not just for a political revolution but also for a profound social revolution.

The widespread political mobilization of these groups was, ironically, facilitated by the degree to which France had been unified into one state under the monarchy. Events in one region were relatively rapidly transmitted throughout the country by publications and by word of mouth. Violent uprisings, whether in Paris or in the provinces, were therefore difficult to contain and to localize. Ultimately, this level of mobilization, while perhaps empowering for those who participated in it, went a long way toward preventing the successful implementation of any coherent program for change – be it one put forward by the aristocracy, the middle class, or the laboring classes. Stable institutional and constitutional outcomes along American lines could not be achieved in revolutionary France as there were too many competing interests and ideas, not just articulated but also most actively pursued during the revolution. In this highly charged environment, achieving viable compromises among competing groups became impossible. Since all groups believed that they had not only the best and most just vision for the future government of France, but also a reasonable chance of implementing that vision, their incentive to cooperate with one another was decidedly diminished. Unfortunately, the single-minded and often extremely violent pursuit of these competing identities and interests, both on the part of democratic revolutionaries and their counterrevolutionary opponents, would lead to the loss of republican liberty within ten years as Napoleon finally stepped in to restore order in 1799. The spirit of the republic was, however, to live on and animate future democrats to resume their pursuit of a democratic political community.

## From Postrevolutionary Restoration to Republic, 1789–1870

Although unsuccessful in their efforts to institutionalize and consolidate a democratic form of government, the first generation of revolutionaries did implement policies that went a long way toward constituting a new order, albeit in a piecemeal and haphazard fashion, and always against a turbulent background of social unrest, political and military conflicts, and economic hardships. Unfortunately, resistance to these policies grew over time, thereby creating the conditions for a successful restoration of nondemocratic regimes.

In the two-year period from October 1789 to September 1791, the National Assembly in Paris undertook the enormous task of doing away with the entire feudal system of special privileges and unequal rights. For the most part, the edicts and laws passed during this period, as well as the constitution-writing process (the Assembly disbanded in 1791 with the promulgation of the first French constitution) reflected the transformations desired by members of the Third Estate, the middle class. Since their agenda for change was heavily based on individual rights, including property rights, and a subordination of church authority to the authority of the state, it had a profound effect on political, economic, and social life.

Politically, the constitution of 1791 replaced monarchical absolutism with a parliamentary system of government in which the king and his ministers, the executive branch, had very little power. Almost all of the powers of government resided in a unicameral elected assembly (elected by limited male suffrage because a direct tax was required to exercise voting rights and stand for election). In subsequent years, the absence of any checks on the legislative branch would leave the country to be ruled by a "debating society," which was often unable to reach the compromises necessary for effective government. The tendency of French democrats to associate proper democratic governance with a preponderance of powers given to the legislature – a tendency overcome only after World War II – originated in the early days of the revolution when the highly uncooperative behavior of Louis XVI prevented a compromise. From that time on, executive powers came to be associated with antirevolutionary, antiliberal forces. However, governing without a strong executive branch led to problems that pushed French moderates, conservatives, and reactionaries alike to support the reintroduction of "strong man" rule. Consequently, for almost the next one hundred years, French governments oscillated between the soft authoritarianism of the restorationist regimes and the efforts to return to republican, that is, legislative rule (see Table 1 at the end of the chapter).

Economically, the National Assembly enacted numerous laws that promoted "free economic individualism." The passing of laws, such as the confiscation and sale of all church properties on terms that benefited existing property owners, as well as the Le Chapelier law, which effectively prohibited collective bargaining and labor organizations of any kind, have led many historians to conclude that the revolution promoted middle-class interests almost exclusively. Undoubtedly, the middle class benefited from the revolution, but these benefits did not lead to long-term political support for republican government. As the laboring classes mobilized to demand more rights and greater equality than the revolutionary leadership was willing to provide, the larger property owners began increasingly to favor more conservative, even authoritarian, forms of government that would safeguard the gains they had already acquired. In this turn away from democratic government, such groups were joined by substantial numbers of the peasantry. Having achieved the destruction of the feudal system of rents and obligations, the better-off peasants were also satisfied with what had been accomplished. Moreover, they were becoming increasingly dissatisfied with the social and cultural policies of the revolutionary leadership.

In particular, the Assembly's efforts to subordinate the church to the authority of the state alarmed the more traditionally minded groups in French society. Having divested the church of its property, the Assembly made financial provisions for the church out of the state budget and mandated a full administrative reform of the church hierarchy. Parish priests and bishops were no longer to be appointed by Rome, but were to be elected by the citizens, including Protestant, Jewish, and agnostic citizens. This new dependency of the church on the state was largely intended to facilitate state control over the crucial realm of education, which was at that time largely in the hands of the clergy. Not surprisingly, the pope reacted negatively to this effort to transform the formerly independent Catholic Church into a national church, and in 1790 he condemned the entire revolution and all that it had accomplished. In response, a year later, the Assembly demanded that the clergy swear an oath of loyalty to the new constitution. Although half of the clergy did take the oath, half did not, including most of the bishops. French society was immediately polarized between those who supported the pope and the church, believing that the revolution had now gone too far, and those who supported the Assembly and its continuing efforts to pursue a new political, economic, and social order. Overall, the Assembly's effort to subordinate the church became "the greatest tactical blunder of the revolution," a blunder that had long-reaching consequences, as throughout the 19th century the church was to be officially antidemocratic and antiliberal, while democrats and liberals in most cases became committedly anticlerical. Not until World War II did the hostility of the church and its followers toward republicanism fade away, leaving behind only residual conflicts over the role of the church in education.

In short, the earliest phase of the revolution created both winners and losers that were unwilling to support a fully democratic, representative form of government. Instead, clear losers, such as the royal family (although Louis XVI was beheaded in 1792 for treason against the revolutionary authorities, he left behind a brother who would continue struggling from abroad to restore the throne), the nobility, and the clergy, wished to overturn the revolution and return to the past. Moreover, the newly enriched property owners and the wealthier peasants, while they would not endorse a full restoration of monarchical powers, did ultimately come to support any form of government that could restore order and guarantee the rights and properties they had already obtained. Given this constellation of interests, and the violent excesses and weaknesses of the First Republic (proclaimed in 1792, this Republic was immediately embattled, facing civil war and foreign invasions), it is not surprising that considerable social support existed for Napoleon's seizure of power and for all of the subsequent restorationist regimes. This support only intensified as the Terror, in particular, frightened propertied France with nightmare images of lower-class rebellion and radicalism.

Indeed, the First Republic is mainly associated with the years of the Terror, 1793–5, when the unrest and violence of the laboring classes, along with armed conflict against the enemies of the revolution, created a momentum that influenced the new legislature, the National Convention, to undertake extreme measures. These measures were designed to attack both the internal and the external enemies of the revolution. Under the leadership of Robespierre, head of the radical Jacobin group that held a dominant position in the Convention, about 40,000 people from all social backgrounds were killed as enemies of the republic. At the height of the Terror, even members of the Convention were put to death, including, ultimately, Robespierre himself. Yet, in spite of the political violence at home, the French republican armies were sweeping across Europe, chasing foreign invaders back into their own lands. These successes on the battlefields abroad ultimately gave Napoleon, as a rising general, the prestige and the manpower he needed to take over the government in 1799.

Napoleon's rule itself did much to convince the French that one-man rule was preferable to the republican forms of government to which they had been introduced during the revolution. Almost immediately, Napoleon restored internal order by using both the stick of an enhanced police force and the carrot of a general amnesty that would allow the nobility to return to France, so long as they gave up their efforts to restore the monarchy. In another move to reconcile the conservative Right to his rule, Napoleon made peace with the Catholic Church. These moves were balanced, however, by policies designed to please the middle classes. For example, fiscal and economic order was restored as the tax codes were rationalized, abolishing all tax exemptions based on birth, status, or special arrangement. French legal codes were also rationalized by providing for universal legal equality. Although Napoleon's citizens might not have enjoyed political rights in the sense of choosing their representatives, they all did enjoy the same civil rights. In addition, careers in the judiciary and in the state administration were permanently opened to men of talent, regardless of birth and breeding.

Although Napoleon's regime came to an end in the wake of his military defeats, the subsequent restorationist governments, beginning with Louis XVIII (Louis XVI's brother) who reestablished the Bourbon throne in 1814, successfully continued his policies of reconciliation. Louis XVIII's regime, for example, managed to please most of the French by promising legal equality, including the equal eligibility of all citizens to hold public office, and a parliamentary government in two chambers. Napoleon's policies and reforms were recognized, and the redistribution of property that had taken place during the revolution was allowed to stand. Basically, the restored monarchy continued the process of abolishing the remnants of feudal privilege. Consequently, even though voting rights were confined to a small group of large property holders, the regime did enjoy considerable support among the population as property holders, large and small, were finally able to go about their business in peace.

In effect, during all of the restorationist regimes, a majority of French citizens were willing to sacrifice extensive political rights, such as universal suffrage and truly representative parliaments, for the guaranteed maintenance of their civil rights and their property rights. In the face of this trade-off, even such moderate republicans as de Tocqueville began to express considerable concern. In their view, the dearly won rights of the revolution were no longer seen as important by the majority of the French inasmuch as violations and evasions of these rights did not seem to arouse concern or opposition. Instead, after decades of turmoil during which the conflicting interests and identities or worldviews of the conservatives, on the one hand, and the radical republicans, on the other hand, had often led to armed conflicts, the stability of the French state, even under the leadership of restorationist rulers, came to be valued more – at least in the short run. In the long run, however, de Tocqueville need not have worried, since the transformations wrought during the revolution also created the conditions that eventually led to the establishment of the Third Republic, which, in the French context, lasted a remarkably long time, from 1870 until 1940 and the outbreak of World War II.

## The Third Republic, 1870–1940

Fundamentally, the revolution succeeded in paving the way for the emergence of a more modern France as exemplified in a progressive, rationalized, state administration staffed by men of talent and merit, rather than of birth and breeding, and in a more uniformly prosperous society – a society, moreover, in which crucial social groups and individuals remained committed to republican values. Consequently, the belief that socioeconomic development was, in and of itself, insufficient and incomplete if unaccompanied by political democracy was maintained over time. This belief represents perhaps the most significant positive legacy of the revolution, a legacy that would set France apart from other modernizing European states, like Germany, that were content to pursue development without democracy.

The socioeconomic development of France was, ironically perhaps, pursued most diligently by Louis-Napoleon, the last authoritarian ruler (1848–70), who was greatly interested in the economic development of his country and the general well-being of all of his countrymen – not just the wealthiest. Consequently, his economic and social programs, including giving workers a legal right to strike in 1864, not only modernized France but also helped to bridge the income disparities in French society. These programs eventually provided the lower classes with a stronger resource base that would ultimately help to overcome the long-standing division between moderate, prosperous republicans, on the one hand, and the more radical, less-well-off republicans, on the other hand – a division that had undermined the First Republic and even a Second Republic proclaimed in 1848 after the ouster of King Louis Philippe (who had taken over from Louis XVIII in 1830 after popular protests had forced the Bourbon king to give up his throne).

Unfortunately, the Second Republic immediately faced intense social conflicts between the moderate republican government and a radicalized working class. A class war raged in Paris for three days, during which time 10,000 people were killed or injured and 11,000 insurgents were imprisoned. As a result of these conflicts, the republic fell but new heroes and martyrs of republican belief were created, thus serving to sustain republican sympathies among many French citizens. For, in spite of the benefits of the restoration regimes, significant groups in French society, especially the lower middle classes, the growing working class, and peasant families that had benefited from the land redistributions of the revolutionary era, remained committed to republicanism, by virtue both of their interests and their identities. Based on a combination of socioeconomic interest and heroic republican identity forged originally during the revolution, and subsequently carried forward in new periods of conflict and contestation, an enduring commitment to republicanism was maintained over time among these groups. Taken together, a powerful modernizing state, an increasingly prosperous society, and the commitment of significant social groups to republicanism provided the context in which a third, and successful, republic was finally established.

The Third Republic, which was constituted after Louis-Napoleon's military defeats, especially to Prussia in 1870, initially manifested all of the troubles that had plagued the previous two republics. A civil war raged in and around Paris from March to May 1871 as radical Parisian republicans contested the authority of the newly elected, but largely conservative, National Assembly. In the wake of the defeat of the Paris Commune, as the radicals named their spontaneously formed alternative government, some 330,000 people were denounced, 38,000 arrested, 20,000 put to death, and 7,500 deported. Intense class hatreds and widespread fears that the Terror might revisit French society hardly provided an auspicious beginning for the third incarnation of French republicanism. Additionally, the Third Republic maintained the central institutional weakness of its predecessors. Based on the supremacy of legislative powers and on the weakness of executive powers, the republic was to become known for its revolving cabinets that would come and go with dizzying speed as different parliamentary coalitions formed and reformed. Against considerable odds, however, the republic survived, and was ultimately able to rehabilitate democratic republicanism, in the process rendering it a trusted and respectable form of government for France.

These achievements were largely due to the increasing political maturity and economic well-being of the social groups that had provided French republicanism with most of its support. As we have seen, this support had come mainly from the working classes, the poorer peasants, artisans, mechanics, shopkeepers, and wage workers, and from their more radical middle-class allies. Not surprisingly, the most important political party of the republic, the Radical Party, represented the interests of the small shopkeepers and smaller property owners in general. In turn, the leaders of the Third Republic proved to be remarkably adept at maintaining social support for the republic, even in the context of universal male suffrage. For the first time since the revolution, suffrage was no longer restricted to a narrow circle of property owners. Instead of sinking under the weight of possible populist pressures, as many conservatives had expected, republicans managed to represent these broader social interests without sacrificing the support of the more-well-to-do members of the middle class. The key to this success appears to have been rooted in the decision to seek peasant support for the new government, as opposed to relying extensively on working-class support. In steering clear of radical socialist programs and by dampening working-class expectations, republican leaders were able to present themselves as sensible, center-oriented politicians. Eventually, a functioning democracy was established, based not only on economic interests but also on a growing civic identity that encompassed not just civil rights, but political and, to some extent, social rights as well. This identity was preserved by a willingness on the part of the republican leaders to combat extremism on both ends of the political spectrum. Just as right-wing, conservative conspiracies were overcome, so too was working-class extremism.

By the onset of World War I in 1914, the republic was becoming ever more popular, and its support only increased during the war as many French citizens came to equate patriotism with republicanism. Consequently, France weathered the upheavals of the 1920s and the 1930s as a democracy, even as other European nations fell to fascism, and even as French extremists on the left and the right increasingly advocated nondemocratic solutions to the country's problems. Like the rest of the world, the French experienced the hardships of the Great Depression, having to cope with unemployment and declines in industrial production. Although the republic's protectionist policies managed to prevent the severe economic dislocations that plagued other European countries, considerable social unrest ensued, stoked by both fascists and communists. As a result, the republic was weakened but managed to survive nonetheless, ending only in the wake of Hitler's invasion of France in 1940 and the establishment of the collaborationist Vichy regime in occupied France.

In conclusion, it should be clear that the legacies of the revolution decisively shaped French political development from 1789 on. The central division of the revolution – between those who were for or against the republican form of government – determined the highly conflictual nature of French political life and the resulting oscillations between political regimes, while the secondary division within the republican camp – between moderates and radicals – fundamentally undermined efforts to establish republican governments prior to the end of the century. The intensity of these political cleavages, which tended to be reinforced by socioeconomic cleavages, began to diminish only in the early 1900s as the economic well-being and social security of all levels of French society were enhanced. Over time, this evolution facilitated the reconciliation of both the upper and lower classes to republicanism. However, even such a gradual process of reconciliation would not have been possible without the commitment of individuals and groups who, at critical junctures in French history, struggled to preserve the ideals of the revolution in the face of formidable opposition. The birth of the Third Republic represented one such critical juncture, just as the founding of the Fifth Republic represents another.

## CONTEMPORARY POLITICS

### The Interplay of Interests and Identities in the Fifth Republic

Founded in 1958 by General Charles de Gaulle, leader of the Free French (unoccupied France) during World War II, the Fifth Republic, like the Third, experienced a tumultuous and inauspicious beginning. Many observers at the time believed that this latest republic would be as short-lived as the postwar Fourth Republic, which had survived only thirteen years (1945–58) before succumbing to parliamentary paralysis in the face of numerous postwar crises. Among these crises, the most significant was the inability of the French government to manage a peaceful process of decolonization. Instead, wars raged in Indochina and in Algeria as the

French colonial presence was violently resented and resisted. The war in Algeria proved to be especially costly, as members of the French armed forces, dissatisfied with the conduct of the war, staged a putsch in Algeria that brought down the Fourth Republic, thereby paving the way for de Gaulle's ascent to office. Although this means of coming to power awakened fears of a return to one-man rule in the tradition of the Bonapartes, the political and military impasse was so great that both existing political parties and the general public were willing to entrust de Gaulle with the formation of a new government.

Although de Gaulle himself was apparently not involved in the military rebellion, he took advantage of it to present himself as an alternative to the stalemated rotating cabinets of the existing government – an alternative capable of containing the military, ending the conflict in Algeria, creating an effective form of government, and overcoming the political threat posed by a large and active French Communist Party. Since the ultraconservative traditional groups on the right side of the political spectrum had been discredited by their allegiance to the Vichy regime, the greatest challenge to republicanism now appeared to be on the left, as workers, feeling unrepresented and overlooked, gravitated to the radical agenda of the Communist Party. Finally, in addition to rescuing republicanism, de Gaulle intended to restore France to a leading position in the world, a position that had been eroded before and after the war as first Germany and then the United States and the Soviet Union overshadowed France in international importance. In pursuit of these objectives, de Gaulle and his supporters hoped to create a republic that would be strong enough institutionally to respond to the challenges of the postwar environment. It is remarkable that de Gaulle did preside over the creation of a lasting republic, giving it constitutional and institutional form and substance. In the process, de Gaulle also established the basic parameters of the crucial policy domains – foreign, economic, and social – that remain in effect to this day. Following a brief overview of these policies, the remainder of this chapter will focus on the contemporary institutions and policy-making mechanisms of the Fifth Republic. Like the Third Republic, the Fifth Republic has largely succeeded in muting the historical clash of interests and identities in the French polity by channeling them into more routinized and productive patterns of state-society relations.

Under de Gaulle's leadership, the new republic withdrew from Algeria and provided a new purpose for the military by establishing France as a nuclear power. Although the price of Algerian withdrawal was high – another attempted military putsch in 1961, an attempt on de Gaulle's life in 1962, and, ultimately, a reanimation of ultraconservative right-wing nationalist forces – de Gaulle had the support of the vast majority of the French population, which favored decolonization. While fraught with fewer dangers, the development of an independent nuclear arms capacity also came at a price – conflict with the United States and withdrawal from NATO command structures. In spite of these difficulties, de Gaulle persisted in his policies because he believed they were crucial prerequisites to the attainment of the active international role he envisioned for France. For de Gaulle, even in a bipolar cold-war world, France, as a unique source of universal culture, rights, and freedoms, had to retain its historic position of aloof grandeur, succumbing neither to the patronage of the United States nor to the blandishments of the Soviet Union. Overall, French foreign policy adheres, to this day, to the course set by de Gaulle: alliance with the West, while maintaining independent maneuverability in the pursuit of national objectives.

To restore France's international position further, a state-led program of economic development and recovery was initiated after the war in order to enhance the competitiveness of French industries. Again under de Gaulle's leadership, state control over such crucial sectors as energy, transportation, insurance, and banking was established, while key companies, such as Renault, were nationalized. For the next thirty-odd years, until the mid-1970s, the payoffs of this "directed" economy (l'économie dirigée) were considerable. France had the highest annual growth rate, 5.8 percent on average, of all industrialized nations, including the United States. By the mid-1980s, after a second wave of nationalizations initiated by the socialist government of President François Mitterand (1981–95), state control extended over 24 percent of the French economy. While the process of nationalization has come to an end, and many firms were even reprivatized during the late 1980s, state control over the economy remains considerable. State-controlled financial institutions, for example, still distribute two-thirds of French credit. Even a growing awareness of the extent to which planning might impede competitiveness and growth has, for the time being, failed to produce a sustained rolling back of the state's involvement in the economy. The reason for this failure lies in the political and social benefits that are thought to accrue from the policies of state-regulated capitalism. De Gaulle himself clearly believed that the state provided the best means, as he put it in a 1944 speech, "to direct the economic struggle of the whole nation for the benefit of all, to improve the life of every Frenchman and every Frenchwoman." In France, trust in the state's ability to transcend narrow sectoral and individual interests in pursuit of the greater general interest, a trust that goes back to the days of the French revolution, obviously outweighs any faith in the "invisible hand" of the market.

In addition to state-led economic planning, de Gaulle and other French postwar leaders, such as Robert Schuman and Jean Monnet (principle architects of what was to become the European Union), recognized the value of European economic integration as a means of asserting French influence in a new forum. In its earlier phases, European economic integration also dovetailed quite nicely with French economic policies, providing additional resources with which to target specific sectors for growth and development, while protecting threatened, but politically essential, sectors, such as French agriculture, from unacceptable levels of decline. To assure the success of integration efforts, French postwar leaders were even willing to reconcile with Germany. Indeed, this reconciliation possibly represents de Gaulle's greatest foreign policy accomplishment, as the Franco-German relationship has become the pivotal axis in determining the course of European integration, and has provided a vital guarantee for peace in Western Europe. For the most part, de Gaulle also set the tone for French policy toward the European Union. For de Gaulle and subsequent French leaders, the process of integration should be based on intergovernmental cooperation, leaving national sovereignty as intact as possible, and not on the creation of a supranational authority to which member states would have to cede their sovereignty.

In terms of social policy, de Gaulle's government initiated a state-led program of welfare measures designed to enhance the living conditions of postwar French society. At the time, France was in the midst of a population boom that required specific measures above and beyond the typical characteristics of the European welfare state, such as guaranteed health care and pensions, and greater job security. For example, the government embarked on an extensive construction project of subsidized housing throughout France. To this day, 13 million people in France, almost a quarter of the population, live in such housing projects. In addition, the state developed an extensive network of child-care facilities, French nursery schools are deemed to be among the best in the world, as well as providing direct financial subsidies to families with children. In regard to health-care as well, an extensive state-sponsored system was established that currently takes up 10 percent of the gross domestic product (GDP), the highest level of spending in the European Union. Although these provisions failed to diminish every source of social discontent (de Gaulle himself ultimately resigned the presidency in the wake of student uprisings in 1968), they did ensure that postwar economic recovery was not limited to too narrow a section of French society. Indeed, most observers are struck by the rapid pace of change in French society over the last fifty years. From a tradition-bound, rural, Catholic, peasant-based society, France has been transformed into a postindustrial society where all classes can, in theory at least, share similar lifestyles and consumption patterns.

Against the background of these considerable achievements, even de Gaulle's abrupt departure from political office in 1969 cannot be taken as a weakness or failure for the new republic. Instead, the successful transfer of presidential power and authority to de Gaulle's successor, Georges Pompidou (1969–74), represented a point of consolidation for the new regime, inasmuch as the party and governing institutions de Gaulle had founded were able to continue functioning effectively even in his absence. Fears that the republic was too closely dependent on the leadership of its founder could thereby be laid to rest.

The success of de Gaulle's government in overcoming both its early problems and in laying the policy groundwork for all subsequent governments of the Fifth

Republic, whether under Gaullist or socialist leadership, can be explained with reference to three principle factors: the leadership abilities of de Gaulle himself, the impact of World War II on France, and the novel institutional arrangements of the republic. First and foremost, the Fifth Republic was a product of what one historian has called de Gaulle's "inexhaustible originality." Drawing on considerable resources of intelligence, courage, and a not-insignificant amount of self-confidence, de Gaulle was capable of envisioning a completely new form of government for his beloved France, while his practical skills as a politician ensured that he would have sufficient support to carry out his plans. In forming his own political party/movement in the late 1950s, which still exists in today's political arena, de Gaulle was able to rally to his cause a significant number of center-right political interests, ranging from republicans to nationalists to Christian democrats. Mindful of the limits of sectarian party politics, however, de Gaulle made every effort to appeal to the population at large for his mandate. The birth of the Fifth Republic was, therefore, validated and legitimated by a series of referenda beginning with a vote on the new constitution (approved in September 1958 by 80 percent of the voters in a turnout of 85 percent) and ending with a vote on the direct election of the president (approved in October 1962 by almost 62 percent of the voters). In this context, de Gaulle was one of the first political figures to use the new medium of television with remarkable effectiveness. His physical stature, his voice, his use of language and song to convey his message all resonated quite powerfully with the wide new audience that television could provide. Quite simply, de Gaulle was the right man at the right time.

Even though de Gaulle did not turn out to be a 20th-century Bonaparte, he remains a controversial figure, however. For some critics he was too much the populist demagogue, for others he was too much the high-handed autocrat, but both sides agree he was not a republican in the traditional French understanding of the term. His disdain for conventional party politics and for parliamentary government as practiced by the first four French republics was quite apparent. Yet had de Gaulle been alone in this disdain, he would not have succeeded in his objectives, no matter how much talent and charisma he possessed. The fact that de Gaulle's attitudes were representative of broader social and political opinions and interests in the aftermath of the war represents an additional factor that promoted both his career and the rise of the Fifth Republic.

In many ways, the impact of the war on French political culture had been a positive one, allowing old conflicts to be overcome and paving the way for a new consensus to emerge in its aftermath. In the interests of promoting national survival, long-standing conflicts among classes, among political camps, and between clerical and anticlerical groups were set aside, if not entirely forgotten. A consensus emerged that France, in order to survive after the war, would have to reform both its economy and its polity in order to enhance competitiveness and efficiency. For the first time in the country's postrevolutionary history, the impact of the outside world made itself felt in France in direct and consequential ways. No longer could France afford the luxury of its weak parliamentary-based republics. Nor, having just fought a reactionary fascist regime, did the soft authoritarianism of France's own conservative governments seem attractive any longer. The only solution was a strong liberal government that could ensure national survival. Such a government was not just desired on instrumental grounds, however. A new consensual identity, one based on the commonalities inherent in both Christian and socialist humanism, had also emerged. In the face of the Nazi regime, French Catholics and socialists in particular, old antagonists since the days of the revolution, discovered that the values they held in common far outweighed their differences. Consequently, the political ideals (a fusion of patriotism, liberalism, and humanism) and the interests that underlay the founding of the Fifth Republic, though most clearly articulated by de Gaulle, were widely shared.

The time was, accordingly, right for a new type of republic, one that would be based not on legislative supremacy but on a strong executive branch capable of providing efficient and timely leadership. The institutional innovation of the Fifth Republic was, therefore, to rehabilitate executive leadership (which had, since Napoleon's regime, been associated with undemocratic, conservative forms of government), by embedding it in a constitutional context. The role of the presidency in the new republic thereby took on tremendous significance. Like the American president, the French president is empowered to provide national leadership – initiating legislation, conducting foreign policy, and overseeing military and strategic concerns. Beyond this, however, the French president, like the British monarch, also serves as a national symbol of unity, transcending political interests and conflicts. To facilitate this transcendent role, the constitution of the Fifth Republic provides as well for a prime minister (drawn from the parliamentary majority), whose role it is to conduct the daily affairs of government. In addition to removing the presidency from the wear and tear of mundane politics, this dual executive system, wherein the president is head of the state and the prime minister is head of the government, was designed by de Gaulle to promote two kinds of leadership, innovation and implementation. The president innovates, while the prime minister implements. For all of its complexity, this system has generated able leadership since the republic's founding, and has survived even "cohabitation" periods when presidents and prime ministers from different parties are forced to cooperate. To a great extent, the establishment of a strong presidency, a "republican monarchy" that fuses traditional and democratic bases of authority, was the vital institutional ingredient needed to stabilize the French republic. By the late 1980s, therefore, eminent French historians, such as François Furet, felt safe in reaching the conclusion that the Fifth Republic was finally a "normal" democracy, sharing the essential characteristics and attributes of all other Western democracies. French "exceptionalism," brought on by the haunting legacies of the revolution, had been overcome once and for all. For the most part, this is an accurate assessment, as France has more in common with its European neighbors than ever before. However, in spite of the homogenizing processes of democratic consolidation and economic integration, globalization, and interdependence, France, as we shall see, continues to manifest unique characteristics that are rooted in the country's distinctive past.

## INSTITUTIONS OF THE FIFTH REPUBLIC

All liberal democratic governments are based on an institutional separation of powers, often accompanied by a territorial separation of powers between the federal and state levels of governments. Whereas the United States represents the most extreme case of separating and offsetting the three branches of government (executive, legislative, judiciary) with the checks and balances system, Western European democracies follow suit by distinguishing between the rights and responsibilities of the executive and the legislative branches, even if the judiciary does not always retain an independent role. In France, however, the executive branch has been given such extensive powers that a considerable institutional imbalance exists, leading some observers to claim that the French presidency has resulted in a "quasi-monarchical system." Indeed, given the specific need to stabilize the French republic after the war with strong executive leadership, the constitution does grant the president substantial formal powers, which have been supplemented over time by the authority and prestige that has accrued to the office.

The French president is elected by direct universal suffrage for a seven-year term. The electoral mechanism was designed to confer maximum legitimacy upon the winner, since he must receive an absolute majority of votes cast – either in a first round of ballots (which no one ever has to date), or in a second run-off round of ballots where voters must choose between the top two candidates produced in the first round. Such an electoral mandate tends to invest the presidency with even greater legitimacy than the popularly elected National Assembly (the lower chamber of parliament). Although presidential candidates initially come out of the party system, representing a particular party, the electoral mechanism tends to encourage the notion that the elected candidate represents more than just his party, that he represents the nation at large. Consequently, even such committed party activists as François Mitterrand, a longtime leader of the Socialist Party, acted, once in office, counter to the interests and program of his own party. While presidents obviously have the greatest room to maneuver when their own party controls a majority in the Assembly, consequently determining the prime minister and the cabinet, even periods of cohabitation have strengthened the perception that the presidency stands above party politics.

In terms of his formal powers, the French president appoints the prime minister, presides over the Council of Ministers (the cabinet), often determining the agenda of the council's meetings, signs decrees and ordinances, and appoints three members of the Constitutional Council (including its president), as well as senior-level civil servants. Additionally, the president can call for a referendum, dissolve the National Assembly, and in crisis periods exercise extraordinary powers for as long as he deems necessary. More conventionally, the president is also the commander in chief of the armed forces and head of the diplomatic service. By and large, given these powers, the president has set the agenda for the government as a whole, except in periods of cohabitation. In turn, the government has determined the agenda for the legislature, thereby giving rise to the imbalance in the governing institutions of the Fifth Republic.

If the general functions of a democratic parliament are to play a major role in initiating legislation, to oversee the executive, and to represent its given constituencies, then the French legislative branch tends to fall short on all counts. In terms of initiating legislation, the role of the French parliament is severely restricted, as more than 90 percent of all laws start out as government bills. While this trend is not unknown in other Western European democracies, what is unusual in France is the extent to which the government can manipulate the lawmaking process in its favor. For example, during the period in which the upper chamber (the Senate, elected for nine years by regional electors, usually local elites or other notables) and the lower chamber (the National Assembly, elected for five years by direct popular vote in single-member districts) attempt to reconcile their respective drafts, the government more or less dictates the outcome, either by using the upper house to block the lower house or by ignoring the upper house altogether since, in the case of a failure to agree on a compromise draft, the government can ask the Assembly to vote on whichever draft is favored by the government – the joint committee's or the Assembly's. If all else fails, the government can bypass the lawmaking process altogether and simply promulgate a decree, ordinance, or regulation. Although certain key areas of legislation are constitutionally reserved for the parliament – areas such as budget and tax matters, civil liberties, and penal law – the constitution also gives the government the authority to ask the parliament to delegate its powers in these specific areas to the government, which is then free again to legislate by decree.

In terms of oversight, as well, the parliament is hampered by the constitution, which allows it only six permanent committees. Oversight committees can, therefore, be constituted only on a temporary basis, and since membership is determined by a proportional representation of the parties, they are dominated by the majority party, which determines the cabinet as well. Minority or dissenting reports are not allowed, effectively ruling out an unbiased inquiry or control procedure. High levels of absenteeism also hinder the legislature's ability to monitor and/or question the government's actions and policies, even in the traditional "question-and-answer" setting. Although the French parliament is not quite a rubber-stamping body, since debates and disagreements with the government do arise, its ability to act efficiently and to carry out even the duties and responsibilities allocated to it by the constitution are impeded by further problems in the realm of representation.

First and foremost, the unique French practice of allowing elected officials to hold more than one office at a time (*le cumul des mandats* or accumulation of elected offices) has meant that members of both the upper and lower chambers also hold local or regional offices, usually as a mayor or member of a municipal council, which, while not making them less representative of their communities, does tend to diminish their ability effectively to represent their constituency at the national level, since their time and attention is divided between two offices. In addition, problems of actual representativeness do plague the Senate which, in the eyes of its critics, is not directly elected, serves for too long, and gives too much weight to rural interests.

Evidently, to see how executive powers might be balanced in the absence of a strong legislature, we must look elsewhere. Although the judiciary in France does not constitute a fully independent branch of government, much like in England, a 1974 constitutional reform has given expanded powers to the Constitutional Council, a body roughly analogous to the American Supreme Court, that has the authority to review proposed legislation for its constitutionality. However, the right to review is restricted to the period before a law is actually enacted, rendering the council much weaker than its American or German counterparts. Since the republican tradition in France was hostility to the judiciary as agents first of the monarchy and then of counterrevolutionary regimes, the judicial branch has on the whole been subordinated to the executive branch, as exemplified by the fact that the courts are placed under the Ministry of Justice, which has the authority to determine the career advancement of judges and prosecutors, as well as the extent to which cases will be prosecuted. If it were not for the existence of the Council of State, a court with jurisdiction over matters concerning the state administration, and the Constitutional Council, the executive branch in particular and the state administration in general would be completely free from judicial oversight.

An additional, and not insignificant, check on executive powers does, however, exist in the form of popular opinion and the willingness of disgruntled groups to contest the government's policies through strikes and protests. In this context, the revolution has provided both a legacy of and a model for popular protest that continues to animate contemporary French citizens, be they workers, students, civil servants, or farmers, all of whom have vehemently protested government policies at one time or another. Even before protests reach the streets, popular opinion can constitute a barrier to executive intentions. De Gaulle, for example, resigned the presidency in 1969 when a referendum he initiated failed to pass. In the absence of a strong legislature and an independent judiciary, the final check on the government, that of popular pressure, remains true to a pattern established in the past when powerful executives ruling in the name of the people were ultimately forced to bow to the will of the people, most notably in 1830 and 1848.

## POLICY MAKING IN THE FIFTH REPUBLIC

In view of the preponderance of powers given to the executive branch in the interest of efficient leadership, it is not surprising that the state administration, as embodied by both appointed civil servants and career bureaucrats, plays the predominant role in policy making as well as in policy implementation. The scope and reach of the French bureaucracy is, of course, also consistent with the historic pattern of a strong, centralized, unitary (as opposed to federal) state administration dating back to the days of the monarchy. In crucial ways, the administration of today is quite like past administrations of notables. French civil servants, especially at the highest levels, represent a closed and elite group of specially educated and usually well-born or well-connected men and, to a far lesser extent, women, who move easily from one management position to the next, regardless of whether it is in the public domain or in the private domain. The resulting interpenetration of elites (administrative, political, and economic) is the most extensive in Western Europe, which is perhaps, in turn, the result of the *grandes écoles* system, wherein future civil servants and managers are trained at very prestigious and highly competitive national schools – again a system without counterpart in Western Europe.

Although this background has certainly produced a state administration characterized by efficiency, stability, and expertise, it is not a system designed to promote equal opportunity, transparency, or democratic accountability. For example, a recent survey determined that two-thirds of the chairmen of the top-forty-listed French companies are graduates of this system, while two of the past three presidents, six of the past eight prime ministers, and more than half of the current cabinet are all graduates of just one of the top schools – the prestigious École Nationale d'Administration. Nor is the state bureaucracy an impartial one, designed to stand aside from politics like the British civil service. Instead, the level of interpenetration has produced a bureaucracy that fully serves the government, even to the extent of failing to implement and enforce laws enacted by the legislature. It has also produced an increasingly corrupt interplay among business interests, elected officials, and state administrators.

In spite of these drawbacks, the centrality of the state administration is unlikely to be contested, given the weak position of the political parties and interest groups in the French political system. Whereas political parties in a democracy are generally responsible for producing coherent policy initiatives, agendas, and objectives, even when in opposition, as well as for mobilizing popular opinion in support of their initiatives, French political parties tend to be too fragmented and too personalistic in their orientation to fulfill these functions fully. Certainly, French parties are spread across a conventional left-center-right spectrum, with the Communists (the PCF) and Socialists (the PS) located on the left, along with a number of other smaller parties; the Christian Democrats and old-style Republicans (the UDF) in the center; and the Gaullists (the RPR) on the right, with Le Pen's Front National (an ultraconservative, anti-immigration party) located on the far right. However, party leaders, rather than party platforms, tend to stand out in the mobilization process, as well as in the party-formation process. This personality-oriented political arena is perhaps a logical outcome of the example set by de Gaulle himself when he created a party/movement in his own image. Most recently, the Front National has split into two groups, a division that is driven by leadership disagreements, not by any programmatic concerns. Multiple changes in the electoral system, shifting from a two-ballot majority system to a proportional representation system and back again to the majority system, have doubtlessly contributed as well to the fragmentation of the parties. More generally, the weakness of French parties is also a reflection of a political tradition dating back to Rousseau that views parties with deep suspicion as divisive and particularistic bodies incapable of transcending their narrow interests.

For this reason, France was also very late in developing a pluralist system in which interest groups have a legitimate role to play as well in the process of mobilizing interests and articulating policy preferences. While in theory French interest groups operate in much the same way as do American groups, in practice their impact and influence tend to be much lower because of their fragmented nature and the relatively institutionalized relationship the principal interest groups have with the state administration. At first glance, this latter feature would seem to guarantee French interest groups, such as employers' associations and trade unions, a considerable voice in the policy-making process. However, since this relationship is at the discretion of the state, the role of interest groups tends to be reduced to a consultative one. Fragmentation, as well, especially among the trade unions, which are the weakest in Europe with a combined membership of only 2.5 million, has taken its toll on the ability of interest groups to participate effectively in the policy-making arena.

In short, the state administration has been able to acquire considerable power and prestige as the sole player in the policy process that represents and indeed is held to embody the public's general interest, as opposed to all other players that represent only narrow sectoral or ideological interests. Although this perception clearly obscures the extent to which special interests are actually involved, even at the state level, and the extent to which civil servants might pursue their own specific interests, it is consistent with French political traditions that allow the state administration to appropriate, as it were, the definition of the public good, without allowing for that good to emerge from an interplay of interests and public debates. While a preference for state-based leadership and a correspondingly weak concept of pluralism is not novel in the context of continental European traditions, what renders France unique is the extent to which this constellation is validated by democratic ideals (the state as reflection of the general will), as opposed to simply conservative traditions or an instrumental need to overcome economic backwardness by using the agency of the state. As a result of this particular path of development, the sheer size and influence of the French state remains remarkable – even as the United States and Great Britain attempt to minimize the impact of their state bureaucracies. For example, the French state today employs one in four workers, endowing them with very substantial benefits, and, partly as a consequence, spends 54 percent of the GDP, one of the highest rates of public spending in the European Union. As one observer has noted, the state in France is "regulator, educator, protector, and planner," a multiplicity of roles that the French have come to expect from their state. Consequently, although the powers of the state and the executive branch represent a considerable deviation from the liberal democratic norm, they are consistent with French democratic traditions and are unlikely, therefore, to be fundamentally contested or altered in the future.

## CONCLUSION: IDENTITIES, INTERESTS, AND INSTITUTIONS IN FLUX?

While the powers of the state per se are not a cause for concern in France, the scope and nature of state policies are. In particular, there are growing concerns regarding the state's inability to find solutions to the problems generated by newly emerging inequalities in French society. As we have seen, French republics are strongest when socioeconomic inequalities are kept to a minimum, thereby limiting social support for alternative forms of government, either of the conservative right or the radical left. Currently, however, there are three divisions in French society that together constitute a formidable challenge to the future stability of the Fifth Republic. First and foremost, there is an ever-expanding divide between "the haves," those who are a part of the working population, well paid and well endowed with state-mandated benefits, and "the have-nots," those who are jobless and dependent on government handouts. Unemployment levels in the late 1990s have remained stubbornly high at about 11.5 percent, with structural unemployment estimated at between 9 and 10 percent. Moreover, 12 percent of the population is estimated to be living in poverty. As a consequence, social problems are growing, especially in the housing projects where young people without work and without prospects are becoming increasingly restive. Basically, the French *économie dirigée* has failed to create a flexible job market that would allow younger, unskilled or part-time workers to find a place in the economy. As a result, the level of jobs created in the private-sector services in France falls far below that of the United States and Britain. Logically, employers overburdened by the benefits they must provide to their existing employees are extremely reluctant to hire new workers. As a survey of France in *The Economist* recently concluded (5 June 1999), "because the government taxes employment so heavily, joblessness remains high, which in turn means the government has to keep on taxing heavily to pay for it."

In a related context, a second divide has emerged between the French and the immigrant population of North African Muslims who wish to retain their culture and traditions. In the past, France readily granted equal citizenship rights as long as immigrants became French and accepted a French identity based in large part on the republican myth, born during the revolutionary era, of a single, united, and unifiedly French nation. The question now arises as to how such a different population can be treated equally, both legally and socially. When combined with the fears and frustrations caused by high levels of unemployment, problems of assimilation have all too easily turned into problems of blatant hatred and racist exclusion. For example, in a 1999 poll, two-fifths of the respondents openly declared that they were racist, while 51 percent were of the opinion that there were "too many Arabs" in France. Such sentiments are, unfortunately, nothing unusual in Europe today, as these traditionally homogenous countries are struggling to come to terms with multiculturalism. France, however, is unique in fielding the most significant right-wing extremist party in Europe, the Front National, which can draw on a long tradition of reactionary conservatism that has never been discredited to the same extent as have similar traditions in Germany and Italy. Not surprisingly, the Front managed to achieve 15 percent of the vote in national elections during the mid-1990s.

Finally, recent corruption scandals involving high-ranking civil servants and elected officials have resulted in considerable levels of public dissatisfaction with, and alienation from, the privileged elites of their society. The exclusive *grandes écoles* system has been called into question, as has the educational system in general with its blatant advantages for the better-off members of society. Additionally, the taxation system, which contains parallel privileges, has come under increasingly critical scrutiny. For many ordinary French citizens, these privileges no longer seem just or warranted. Consequently, a gap is emerging between those who govern and the people in whose name they exercise their authority. This gap has manifested itself most directly in the growing propensity of the French electorate to create cohabitation situations. Three times in recent years, in 1986, 1993, and in 1997, when the current government was voted in, a different political party from that of the president's received the popular mandate to constitute the government. While splitting the vote between Congress and president is nothing new for American voters, this tendency does represent a considerable departure for the French electorate.

It would appear obvious, at least to English and American observers, that the French state must fundamentally alter its relationship to the economy and to the society by reducing its public spending, freeing the labor market from current burdens and restrictions, and transferring responsibility for many social programs, such as pension funds, to the private sector. Unreformed, for example, state pensions could comprise up to 20 percent of the GDP by 2040, up from 12 percent today. While the situation is clearly urgent, progress to date in reforming the scope and nature of state policies has been slow, hindered in large part by public resistance, political stalemate, and ideological reluctance to change. President Jacques Chirac, upon assuming office in 1995 as a representative of the Gaullist center-right, did immediately attempt to reform public-sector spending. His efforts were substantially undermined, however, in 1996 when a massive strike of public-sector employees brought the entire country to a standstill. The understandable reluctance of these employees to give up substantial benefits, including secure lifelong employment and earlier retirement, longer holidays, and higher pensions than private-sector workers, is further compounded by the extent to which these benefits are seen, not as privileges but as accustomed rights. Not surprisingly, when Chirac called for a parliamentary election in 1997, which he hoped would strengthen his hand for reform, the electorate responded by returning a socialist majority and, correspondingly, a socialist prime minister. Although this cohabitation situation represents less of a stalemate than one might assume, given the French Socialist Party's pragmatic tendencies, it still represents an institutional barrier to innovative policy making and sustained reform. A further barrier is represented by ideological reluctance on all sides of the political spectrum to exchange France's unique republican model of development, which is based as much on social development as on economic development, for the Anglo-American liberal model. As Prime Minister Lionel Jospin has declared, "Yes to the market economy, no to the market society." From this perspective, creating a quantity of low-quality, low-paid jobs is just as disruptive to social solidarity as are persistently high levels of unemployment. French policy makers are thus caught in a bind between accepting the necessity of responding to a changed global context in which the Anglo-American model dominates, and a desire to maintain the distinct quality of social life in their country – even as that social life is increasingly threatened by internal divisions.

Clearly, this is an unenviable position to find oneself in, especially in France with its history of evolution through dramatic revolution, as opposed to piecemeal reform. While it would be an overstatement to say that revolution is likely in the near future, it is evident that France has reached a watershed. The accommodation of historically hostile interests and identities that postrevolutionary socioeconomic development fostered, and that the institutions of the Fifth Republic finally consolidated, is now increasingly open to renegotiation if these institutions and the elites that inhabit them fail to generate and implement sustainable policies of continued socioeconomic development. Accordingly, based on historical precedent, there is a possibility that a long period of open contestation among a moderate republican center, a conservative right and a radical left might ensue as these interests and identities clash again over the appropriate institutional and policy remedies. Just as likely, however, is the possibility that the changed global context will force even contentious French interests and identities to seek solutions within a constructive framework. As President Mitterand learned early during his tenure in office when his plans to implement an extensive program of socialist transformation ran aground on the basic constraints posed by an increasingly globalized economy, French elites no longer have the luxury to engage in extreme forms of political experimentation, ideological contestation, and institutional instability.

It is probable, therefore, that the European Union will provide that constructive framework within which France, in conjunction with Germany, will seek to make the necessary changes to their respective economic models, while attempting to preserve the levels of social solidarity that both countries value over the Anglo-American model of liberal capitalism. If this latter scenario unfolds, it will provide powerful evidence of the positive impact that global conditions, in conjunction with committed domestic actors, can have on the promotion of solutions to substantial socioeconomic problems, while remaining within a democratic context – an overall outcome that is not limited, it is hoped, to the postwar democracies of the Fifth Republic and the Federal Republic, but that can be reproduced as well in the postcommunist democracies of Eastern Europe.

## BIBLIOGRAPHY

Agulhon, Maurice. *The French Republic, 1879–1992.* Oxford, Eng.: Blackwell, 1990.

Corbett, James. *Through French Windows: An Introduction to France in the Nineties.* Ann Arbor, Mich.: University of Michigan Press, 1994.

"Country Survey, France." *The Economist,* 5 June 1999.

Denomme, Robert T., and Roland H. Simon. *Unfinished Revolutions: Legacies of Upheaval in Modern French Culture.* University Park, Penn.: Pennsylvania State University Press, 1998.

Furet, François. *Revolutionary France 1770–1880.* Oxford, Eng.: Blackwell, 1988.

Goux, Jean-Joseph, and Philip R. Wood, eds. *Terror and Consensus: Vicissitudes of French Thought.* Stanford, Calif.: Stanford University Press, 1998.

Hoffmann, Stanley, et al. *In Search of France: The Economy, Society and Political System in the 20th Century.* New York: Harper Torchbooks, 1963.

Lefebvre, Georges. *The Coming of the French Revolution.* Princeton, N.J.: Princeton University Press, 1989.

Meny, Yves, and Andrew Knapp. *Government and Politics in Western Europe.* London: Oxford University Press, 1998.

Soboul, Albert. *The Sans-Culottes.* Princeton, N.J.: Princeton University Press, 1980.

Tocqueville, Alexis de. *The Old Regime and the French Revolution.* Translated by Stuart Gilbert. New York: Anchor Books, 1983.

Tombs, Robert. *France 1814–1914.* London and New York: Longman, 1996.

Willis, F. Roy. *France, Germany and the New Europe 1945–1967.* London: Oxford University Press, 1968.

Wright, Gordon. *France in Modern Times.* 4th ed. New York: W. W. Norton & Co, 1987.

## TABLE 1.  KEY PHASES IN FRENCH DEVELOPMENT

| Dates | Regime | Global context |
|---|---|---|
| I. Upheaval | | Monarchical absolutism/ |
| 1789–1792 | Revolution | Enlightenment |
| 1792–1799 | First Republic (Terror) | |
| 1799–1804 | Napoleon's takeover | |
| II. Reaction and counterreaction | | Industrial Revolution/ |
| 1804–1814 | First Empire (Napoleon) | 1848 Revolutions |
| 1814–1830 | Bourbon restoration | |
| 1830–1848 | Constitutional monarchy | |
| 1848–1852 | Second Republic | |
| 1852–1870 | Second Empire | |
| III. Republic restored | | Franco-Prussian War (1870–1) |
| 1870–1940 | Third Republic | Imperialism/World War I |
| 1940–1944 | Vichy (Occupied France) | Great Depression/World War II |
| 1945–1958 | Fourth Republic | |
| IV. Republic consolidated | | Decolonization/Cold War |
| 1958–present | Fifth Republic | European integration/growth of global free market |

### Interests/Identities/Institutions

I.  Interests: Rising middle class and rioting lower classes
    Identities: *Liberté, Egalité, Fraternité*
    Institutions: Parliamentary sovereignty v. one-man rule

II. Interests: Propertied classes (upper/middle/peasant)
    Identities: Conservative/clerical/economic liberalism
    Institutions: One-man rule/executive supremacy

III. Interests: Small and medium producers/property owners and peasant farmers
     Identities: Political liberalism/economic protectionism
     Institutions: Parliamentary sovereignty

IV. Interests: Middle class; business and financial elites
    Identities: Patriotism/humanism/liberalism
    Institutions: Presidential democracy

### Developmental path

I.   Reconstituting the state: From feudalism to liberalism
II.  State-sponsored economic development
III. State-protected economic stability
IV.  State-led development plus social welfare

## IMPORTANT TERMS

**Accumulation of elected offices**   the practice whereby elected officials are allowed to hold more than one office at a time, which tends to diminish further the role of the National Assembly.

**Algeria**   France's most significant colony. The number of French living in Algeria and considering it their home made the process of decolonization a long and conflict-ridden one. Currently, Algerians living in France are the focus of considerable anti-immigration sentiment.

**Charles de Gaulle**   military leader of the Free French during World War II and subsequently the first president of the Fifth Republic. De Gaulle had immense influence in shaping the institutions and policies of the contemporary French government.

**Cohabitation**   the term used to describe the situation when the president and the prime minister represent different political parties. At first it was feared that this situation would lead to political deadlock, but it has proven to be much more manageable than originally thought. During these periods, the prime minister logically has a greater range of maneuverability vis-à-vis the president.

**Conservatism**   in the French case, an ideology that emerged in the wake of the French Revolution, rooted in the conviction that traditional customs and institutions should be protected at all costs against the onslaught of modern republican thought.

**Constitutional Council**   a judicial body, roughly analogous to the American Supreme Court. However, the Council can only review laws before they are enacted, which considerably weakens the powers of judicial oversight.

**Declaration of the Rights of Man and Citizen, 1789**   one of the founding documents of liberal democracy, along with the American Declaration of Independence, anchoring the universal rights of equality and liberty.

**Democratic socialism**   yet another modern ideology that was first articulated during the French Revolution on behalf of and by lower social orders demanding more extensive rights, not just civil and political rights but also social rights that would promote greater equalities of condition in a deeply divided society.

**Directed economy (L'économie dirigée)**   the high degree of state involvement in economic planning and the direct state ownership and control of critical sectors of the economy since World War II. The French economy thus represents a different path of development from the Anglo-American "free"-market economy.

**Dual-executive system**   as established by de Gaulle, the executive branch of the French government, which is divided between a directly elected president and a prime minister selected from the winning majority in parliament. Within this division, the president has more authority and influence than the prime minister, especially in regard to foreign policy.

**Estates-General**   a protoparliament originally divided into the three basic orders of society – the aristocracy, the clergy, and the middle orders – that was convened by Louis XVI in a last effort to save his throne on the eve of the revolution.

**Feudalism**   a social and political order that developed during the Middle Ages, based on hierarchies of power and authority that linked peasant to lord and lord to king in a network of duties and obligations.

**Fifth Republic**   the current government of France, characterized by a dual-executive system in which the president traditionally wields considerable authority, and the state administration in general holds the preponderance of power.

**François Mitterand**   the first socialist president of the Fifth Republic. Mitterand's regal manner of leadership further solidified the authority of the office of the president.

**French Revolution**   next to the American Revolution, the most consequential democratic revolution, paving the way for the expansion of democracy throughout continental Europe.

**Front National**   the most significant radical right-wing party in Europe, representing an anti-immigration nativist platform.

**Grandes écoles**   the elite universities of the French educational system that train professionals for careers in the state administration, business management, and politics. It is virtually impossible for someone without a degree from one of these universities to reach the top ranks of his or her chosen profession.

**Jacques Chirac**   the current president of the Fifth Republic. He is faced with the challenge of fundamentally restructuring the French welfare state, and furthering the process of market liberalization.

**Monarchical absolutism**   a form of government, best exemplified in the reign of Louis XIV, in which the monarch's powers are supreme, in contrast to constitutional monarchy in which royal powers are limited and shared by a representative body.

**Napoleon Bonaparte**   emperor from 1804 to 1814. While exercising dictatorial powers as the first of a series of postrevolutionary one-man-rule regimes, Napoleon also acted constructively to stabilize France after the turmoil of the revolutionary era, and even consolidated a significant number of the republican gains made during the revolution.

**National Assembly**   the lower chamber of the French parliament elected for five years by direct popular vote in single-member districts. Constitutionally not as powerful as the executive branch, its powers are further diminished by high levels of absenteeism and, in general, unassertive leadership.

**Nationalism**   another ideology that emerged in the context of the French Revolution, designed to promote patriotism and loyalty to the nation and the state that protects it.

**Radical Party**   the most important party of the Third Republic, representing the interests of small- and medium-size producers and property owners and deriving its identity from the positive legacies of the revolution, mainly promoting the equality of rights for all French citizens.

**Republicanism**   what might be called the French form of liberalism as an ideology committed to representative government, broad-based suffrage, and equal protection under the state. But unlike liberalism, French republicanism is more oriented toward the attainment of political, civil, and social rights than the preservation of economic rights as enshrined in the Anglo-American liberal tradition.

**Restoration regimes**   beginning with Napoleon's takeover of power in the wake of the Terror and ending with the rule of Louis Bonaparte, a series of postrevolutionary governments based on executive powers, supported by social groups hostile to republicanism.

**Sans-culottes**   the lower urban classes that played an active and radicalizing role during the French Revolution by demanding rights for themselves.

**The Terror**   the phase of the revolution under the leadership of extremists, such as Robespierre, that has come to be equated with revolutionary excess since both innocent members of the aristocracy and moderate revolutionaries were put to death as enemies of the newly proclaimed republic.

**Third Republic**   in spite of its scandals and rotating parliamentary coalitions, the regime that was finally able to overcome the negative legacies of the revolution and firmly consolidate republican government.

**Two-ballot majority system**   the electoral system that has prevailed for much of the Fifth Republic's history. Although based on a majority, in contrast to proportional, representation system, it differs from the Anglo-American, first-past-the-post tradition in that a second, run-off election between the two front runners must be held, if the first election fails to generate a clear majority winner.

**Vichy regime**   the government of Nazi-occupied France. The extent to which Vichy leaders and the French in general collaborated with the occupying forces is currently a contested subject in France.

## STUDY QUESTIONS

1.   Compare the French and American Revolutions in terms of their causes and consequences. What are the principle similarities and differences?

2.   Identify the most significant legacies of the French Revolution. What, in your opinion, rendered these legacies so long-lasting?

3.   Compare and contrast the constellation of interests and identities that supported restoration, as opposed to the interests and identities that supported republicanism. Why did the latter ultimately win out?

4.   While other democracies in Europe fell during the interwar period under the combined pressures of fascism and the Great Depression, what enabled the Third Republic to survive?

5.   What are the costs and benefits associated with the strong state as it has evolved in France?

6.   Discuss the role of de Gaulle in the founding of the Fifth Republic. Does any other

modern democracy owe its existence to such a personalized form of institutional crafting and design?

7. What are the costs and benefits associated with the dual-executive system? Is the French presidency too powerful in your opinion?

8. How can the imbalance between the extensive powers of the state administration and the very limited powers of political parties and interest groups best be explained?

9. What are the costs and benefits associated with the Fifth Republic's model of directed economic growth and development?

10. In your opinion, is France today a "normal" European democracy, or does it remain more of an exception – an enduringly unique case of democratic development?

# ✍ Stop and Compare

## EARLY DEVELOPERS: BRITAIN AND FRANCE

An important part of democracy is the role of parliaments. Much of Great Britain's history has been a constant refinement of the principle of representative parliamentary government. Through a long series of struggles and reforms, British parliamentary government emerged triumphant over the rule of kings and queens. In the course of these changes, the monarchy remained a symbol of national integration and historical continuity, but the real political power came to reside in the prime minister and his or her cabinet of ministers. Of course, even in Britain, parliamentary and cabinet government did not necessarily mean the same thing as democracy: The right to vote – the franchise – was only gradually extended to the lower classes and women, and the final reforms came about in the 20th century.

Despite the important upheavals in British history, political scientists continue to view the British experience as one of successful gradualism, of a gradual extension of the freedoms of liberal democracy to ever-larger groups of people. In the creation of liberalism, the British were undoubtedly aided by the simultaneous and successful rise of a commercial and capitalist economy in the 18th and 19th centuries. This was the age of the Industrial Revolution. Although the transition to a new kind of economy was not easy, for the first time in history an economy generated large amounts of goods that could be consumed by a large number of people. To be sure, at first these goods were enjoyed only by the new "middle" classes, but over time the new lifestyles spread to the working class as well. Accompanying these changes in material living standards came changes in the way people thought about their place in the world. One's position and life chances were no longer set in stone from the time of birth. Upward mobility was now a possibility for people who never would have thought such a world possible a mere century earlier. It was in this context that common people could begin to demand a political voice commensurate with their contribution to the public good. The argument was a powerful one, and gradually the old feudal/aristocratic oligarchy gave way to wider sections of society in search of political representation.

Of course, a further important feature of the British experience was the creation of a global empire between the 17th and 19th centuries. Industrialization both contributed to and was assisted by the military, economic, and political conquest of large parts of Africa and Asia. Empire provided raw materials for manufacture, markets for export, a "playground" for military elites, and a source of national pride that made it easier for the British to try to universalize their particular experience. As other countries in Europe began to compete economically and militarily, however, and as locally subjugated peoples from Ghana to India recognized the incongruity of British ideals of parliamentary democracy and law with continued imperial domination, the costs of empire began to rise. By the beginning of the 20th century, Britain had clearly fallen from the imperial heights it had once occupied, and domestic discussion began to focus on issues of economic decline and how to extricate the country from costly imperial commitments. With Britain divested of its empire, its economy continued to decline throughout the 20th century relative to the other European countries, and much of contemporary British politics has concerned ways to reverse this decline. In Britain's (mostly) two-party system, both parties have proposed cures for what ails the economy, but neither has been able to offer recipes for regaining the national confidence (indeed, some say arrogance) that was once taken for granted.

Notwithstanding its recent troubles, the British experience continues to be the benchmark against which comparativists think about the developmental experience of other countries. The British (or what is sometimes called the Westminster) model of government is the standard against which other countries measure their own progress.

Britain's experience could not be duplicated, however. Even France, the country whose experience we pair with Britain, initially developed in Britain's shadow and bridges early and late development paths. The logic of pairing France and Britain is, nevertheless, compelling. Like Britain's, France's history is largely one of the people emerging victorious over kings. The difference is that in France, the monarchy and the old feudal oligarchy were displaced not through a long series of conflicts and compromises but largely through a major revolution in 1789 in which the monarch was executed and the aristocracy hounded out of political life. Over the course of the next century, French political history was tumultuous, the political pendulum swinging back and forth between democratic development and periods of authoritarian or populist closure. Despite these changes, what remained a constant in French political life was the notion that power ultimately resides with the people. Even such populist demagogues as Napoleon and, later, his nephew Louis Bonaparte never managed to depart fully from the notion of popular sovereignty. Indeed, they could not, if only because postrevolutionary France depended on its people to serve in its armies and mobilize for war.

If the British political experience is one of subjecting monarchical power to representative institutions, the French democratic experience is one of regulating a strong centralized state through plebiscitary mandate. War was a staple of political life on the European continent, and preparing for it an important part of what states did. The French state was no exception; in fact, it became a model for others to emulate (and eventually surpass). Even before the French Revolution, French monarchs and their states played an important part in encouraging economic development and collecting taxes for the purposes of military preparation. The revolution did little to change this and in many ways intensified the power of the French state. In fact, one way of thinking about the revolution is in terms of a rebellion against the taxing power of the French monarchy and its resurrection in the form of more or less democratically elected heads of state who, because of their popular mandate, had more power to draw on private resources for public goals than ever before. Given its pattern of development, it is perhaps not surprising for us to learn that after much experimentation with various forms of representative government in the later part of the 19th and first part of the 20th century, France has settled on a strong, popularly elected presidency with a seven-year term of office.

This contrast between parliamentary rule in Britain and presidential rule in France has become a model one for political scientists. Such differences in democratic institutions have important long-term effects on politics and policies. Given the importance and centralized nature of the French state, it is natural that the state has become highly involved in economic development in the 20th century. French economic planning, a subtle and highly developed system of state guidelines and state-induced market incentives, has often been contrasted with the heavy-handed Soviet communist model, not merely in the differences in style but also because for a very long time, the French model seemed to work so well. Recently, however, the impact of European integration and increased global trade have brought the feasibility of the model under question and led to a debate in France on the future of French-style economic planning and whether it will have to adapt to the competing model of Anglo-American capitalism. Britain has also experienced a debate between Euroskeptics and Europhiles.

Finally, globalization has also meant that both nations are now experiencing immigration problems. Right-wing sentiment against the "foreigners" has emerged, and politicians have raised questions about national identity. Questions of identity are nothing new to Britain and France. British identity has always been contested – the Celtic periphery of Scots, Irish, and Welsh have frequently challenged the hegemony of the English. French identity has long been split between a Catholic and conservative France rooted in the rural peasantry and a secular and progressive France rooted in the urban classes.

# PART TWO

# Middle Developers

## Cases

# 3

# Germany

≋ **Andrew C. Gould**

# INTRODUCTION

In October 1990 the East German state collapsed, losing control of its territory and people to the West German state, even though just over a year before almost no one had expected this to happen. Yet the collapse of East Germany makes sense as part of a path through the modern world where German interests, identities, and institutions have been strongly influenced by the surrounding political and economic conditions. Germany's precarious military-strategic position in Europe traditionally made it difficult for one German polity to rule over everyone who is one way or another conceivably German. As a result, German political organizations frequently competed with one another for people and territory. Only rarely has one king, emperor, or chancellor succeeded in dominating all other German rulers. Even today, millions of German speakers and considerable territories that were formerly ruled by various German polities remain outside of a unified Germany.

The challenges and opportunities that Germans faced were characteristic of their "middle path" through political and economic development. Falling behind the early developers put Germany at a disadvantage. In politics, German rulers could not match French rulers in establishing strong central authority over their vast territory. In economics, German industrial development lagged behind Britain's. Apart from these strategic and economic disadvantages, however, the rapid diffusion of new ideas into Germany offered certain opportunities. Germany's newer bureaucracies skipped over traditional practices and, instead, adopted only the latest organizational techniques. German industries, unimpeded by false starts, implemented advanced technology on a massive scale. The German experience demonstrates that backwardness can have its advantages.

Contemporary interests, identities, and institutions in Germany stem from Germany's path through the modern world. As for interests, the reliance of major German industrialists on the state and big banks for funding, and the struggles of many small- and medium-size firms to stay afloat, were responses to Germany's economic position. The almost bewildering variety of contemporary German identities – from right-wing nationalism, to ecological activism, to recent immigrants seeking a new status – also flows from previous episodes of identity formation and reformulation. On the one hand, some of the key institutional features of the contemporary German state, including the relocation of the capital from Bonn back to Berlin, show the pull of past practice. On the other hand, many German political institutions are explicitly designed to prevent any reemergence of the authoritarian elements of its past. As we explore German interests, identities, and institutions, we will examine how Germany's particular sequence of development created legacies that strongly influence Germany today.

## ORIGINS OF A MIDDLE DEVELOPER, 100 B.C.E.–1800 C.E.

The origins of modern Germany did not lie uniquely in German lands but, instead, in the contact between two societies. Early German and Roman cultures blended and grew together during the expansions and contractions of the Roman Empire across Europe. Roman influence, starting in the first century before the current era, brought a common culture of Christianity, a common elite language of Latin, and a common experience of the Roman legal code. As the Roman Empire declined in the 5th century, Germanic warriors reinvigorated their practice of honor-based pacts of loyalty to provide a political foundation for new feudal kingdoms.

In many ways, Germany at this time resembled the rest of Europe. As in the rest of Europe from the 8th through the 12th centuries, aspiring German kings were usually at war with one another. As in other parts of Europe, strong cities emerged during the 13th through 16th centuries, especially along the Rhine river and the Baltic Sea. In contrast to the traditional style of rule in feudal kingdoms, cities governed themselves through written laws and representative institutions for various social groups.

Germany's divergent path from the early developers, however, began as early as the 17th and 18th centuries when German rulers fell behind the more successful monarchs in France and England. Whereas each of the early developers became unified under absolutist rulers or would-be absolutist rulers, Germany remained politically divided. The persistence of political divisions accentuated other differences, such as the cleavage between Protestants and Catholics and the divide between more economically advanced regions in western and southern Germany and more backward agricultural economies and social structures east of the Elbe River.

## COMPETING MODERN STATES, 1800–1871

German polities were middle developers in building a modern state, that is, in the task of building a political organization that could successfully claim to be the only organization with the right to use violence over the German territory and its people. The two most powerful political units were Austria-Hungary in the south and Prussia in the east, but they competed with each other and with dozens of other would-be states in what is now modern Germany. The winnowing down of German states was accelerated by the military conquests of an early developer. In 1806 the French Emperor Napoleon invaded Germany, consolidated many German states, and imposed a common legal code. German leaders sought both to imitate and resist the French by rationalizing their own bureaucracies and building stronger armies. When the allies finally defeated Napoleon in 1815, Prussia and Austria emerged even stronger than before. As an eastern power, Prussian military might was centered on its capital in Berlin, but the Congress of Vienna awarded Prussia control over many economically advanced territories in the west, along the Rhine River.

Two main social and political groups contended for influence in Germany in the 19th century. The first group included many people energized by the broader European liberal movements for nationalism and constitutionalism. They were liberals in the 19th-century meaning of the term: They favored large and free markets, the separation of church and state, and constitutional-representative government. German liberals sought to build a German nation that encompassed all of the people then divided into various polities; they wanted a national market unhindered by internal boundaries; and they wanted to limit monarchical power by building new political institutions, such as a national electoral system, a parliament, and a written constitution. Leading intellectuals, professors, government officials, industrialists, professionals, and various members of the middle classes played key roles in the liberal movement.

The second group contending for influence were the landed elite of eastern Prussia (Junkers). These owners of large tracts of land employed agricultural labor in conditions of near servitude to produce grain. They were very conservative politically and sought to forestall any political change that threatened their control over land and people. In general, they sought to prevent any change in either the system of German states or in the ways the various states were governed internally. This group produced grain for the world market at very competitive prices, but their approval of market economics did not extend to the conditions of production for their workers. In fact, their economic success rested on political power and exploitation.

German monarchs successfully resisted most of the political demands of the liberal group and allied themselves with the landed elite. For example, in 1830, liberal revolutions took place in France, Belgium, and Switzerland. Liberalism was strong as well in the Rhineland, but the Prussian king in Berlin avoided changes by taking advantage of his government's physical separation from most of the revolutionary action and his additional military resources based in the east. Even less change occurred in Austria-Hungary than in Prussia. During 1848, important political reforms again engulfed many countries of Europe. Widespread revolutionary activity in the Rhineland, Berlin, and Vienna led to a call for the election of a national assembly of delegates. Elections were held in all of the German states, from Prussia to Austria-Hungary and the many other states. The delegates met in Frankfurt to draw up a new constitution for a unified German state, but the Prussian and Austrian monarchs used force to preserve their rule, and the Frankfurt parliament, unable to reform, overthrow, or unify the conservative states, disbanded without achieving any of its intended aims.

The rejection of liberalism had the unintended consequence of setting in motion future revolutionary movements. In the spring of 1841, Karl Marx was a twenty-three-year-old student whose dissertation was accepted by the University of Jena. He had planned for a career as an academic philosopher, but the Prussian government's imposition of strict controls on university appointments meant that Marx had to write for a different audience. His new job as the editor of a newspaper financed by liberals and run by radicals, the *Rheinische Zeitung,* ended abruptly when the Prussian censor closed the paper down for being too critical. Unable to find work in Germany, Marx left for France in 1843, where he met his life-long collaborator, Friedrich Engels. In 1848 he and Engels wrote the *Communist Manifesto,* closing with the statement: "The proletarians have nothing to lose but their chains. They have a world to win. Working men of all countries, unite!" He returned to Germany during the revolutionary movements of 1848 and advocated an alliance with liberal reformers, but the failure of this revolution finally convinced him and many other activists and supporters that real reform was impossible without more fundamental changes in the economy and society.

In the battle for supremacy among the German powers, the Prussian monarchy adopted the economic dimension of the liberal program but used its military strength, both to dominate the smaller German states and reject the political dimensions of liberalism. Prussia sponsored a growing free-trade zone among the German states, and the size of its own market made it costly for other states to avoid joining. Prussia defeated Austria-Hungary in war in 1866, paving the way for the formation of the North German Confederation under Prussian leadership in 1867. The final steps in Germany's first modern unification required that France be forced to accept the change in the German situation. The Franco-Prussian War of 1870 matched two nondemocratic rulers, France's emperor Louis-Napoleon (Napoleon's nephew) against the king of Prussia. The war had widely divergent consequences. Louis-Napoleon lost the war and was replaced by a democratic regime, the Third Republic (1870–1940). Prussia won the war and used its victory to consolidate a larger German state under authoritarian rule.

The Prussian king – advised by his chancellor, Otto von Bismarck – had himself crowned the emperor of Germany while at the French palace of Versailles in 1871. The military victory established the new German borders. Unified Germany encompassed Prussia (including its eastern territories along the Baltic in what is now Poland and Russia) and virtually all of the non-Austrian German states. It also included territory taken from France, the economically advanced provinces of Alsace and Lorraine. Austria and Switzerland remained outside of the new German empire as independent countries.

## UNIFICATION UNDER AUTHORITARIAN LEADERSHIP, 1871–1919

Germany's late unification gave its newly constructed state institutions a great deal of influence over society. The state's initiative played a crucial role in changing Germany, even if the state was not always successful in its efforts. In other words, the development path of late state building gave the state an opportunity to attempt to reshape many other institutions, including those in society, the economy, and in politics.

The leaders of the German state reshaped society in unintended ways when they set about recasting institutions and reformulating identities. First, the mainly-Protestant leaders attacked Catholicism. In the early 1870s, the state leaders pursued a cultural struggle ("Kulturkampf") with laws and regulations to make it difficult for Catholic priests to carry out their work. Political activists responded by founding a political party, the Center Party (Zentrum). The party's top decision makers were Catholic lay leaders, and Center Party candidates received the implicit and explicit aid of the church. The long-term effects of the Kulturkampf, however, were neither what the German political elite wanted, nor what the Catholic Church expected. Instead of a retreat from politics, the struggle against Catholicism induced Catholics to mobilize in their own political party. Instead of increasing the power of the Catholic Church in politics and society, as the Catholic hierarchy would have preferred the Kulturkampf brought about the emergence of professional party leaders who were not priests, even though they were Catholic. The state reconciled with the church in the 1870s, but the Center Party remained to represent German Catholics, and it went on to become one of Germany's largest political parties.

As the regime made its peace with a recast Catholic community, the leaders next turned their attention to the emerging political movements among the working classes. The Socialist Worker's Party was formed in 1875 from various radical groups, and it won only 9 percent of the vote in 1877. Bismarck, however, blamed the party for Germany's economic situation: "As long as we fail to stamp on this communist ant-hill with domestic legislation," he said, "we shall not see any revival in the economy." In 1878 Bismarck won majority support in the Reichstag for severe antisocialist legislation. The government closed Socialist Party offices and publications, prohibited its meetings, and generally harassed its organizers. Many left-wing activists fled from Germany, especially to Switzerland, and sought to keep their efforts alive in exile.

Despite the repression, many workers and other supporters continued to identify themselves as working class and to support the Socialist Party. Most of the antisocialist laws lapsed in 1890, and the party reemerged under a new name as the Social Democratic Party. The Socialists climbed at the polls in 1898 with 27 percent of the vote. In the final elections under the empire in 1912, the Social Democratic Party won even more, 35 percent of the vote. The typical Socialist voter was a young, urban worker who was Protestant but did not go to church, and who was German rather than a member of the Polish or other minority groups. The party attracted little support from Catholics or people living in rural areas. Still, the party had almost a million members in 1912, a substantial accomplishment, as its members were expected to pay regular dues as in many other European parties. Like other mass parties in Europe, the party reached beyond the purely political realm to organize funeral societies, buying cooperatives, book-lending libraries, gymnastic societies, choral clubs, bicycling clubs, soccer teams, Sunday schools, and dancing courses.

The new German state had to foster economic development in difficult circumstances. Most importantly, from 1873 to 1896 there was a European-wide depression. Agricultural prices fell with the introduction of inexpensive Russian and midwestern American grain on world markets; industrial prices also fell, employment figures were unstable, production rose, profits decreased. One response to these difficult conditions lay beyond state control: Many Germans emigrated from Europe to North and South America.

German firms enjoyed some "advantages of backwardness." They could adopt advanced machinery and industrial organization from British examples without having to devise these things themselves. But there were also disadvantages of backwardness. In order to acquire expensive technology and survive early competition with established businesses, many German firms relied on large banks and the state for the necessary capital funds. From 1875 to 1890, both the eastern German grain growers (the Junkers) and the big industrialists sought and won state protection from imports in the form of high tariffs; Germany's relatively large working class would have preferred free trade and cheaper food.

One can argue that the German empire's institutions were on their way to becoming more democratic in the early 20th century. The Social Democratic Party and the Center Party were gaining in strength, and liberal industrialists were gaining in influence over the old Junker elite. As the success of industrialization began to materialize in the 1890s, for example, many leading industrialists saw that they could compete on the world market and broke with the Junkers to seek lower tariff barriers. Industrialists now, like workers, favored low tariffs and the resulting lower prices on food. Several shifts in cabinet formation resulted, followed by a victory for low-tariff delegates in the Reichstag election of 1912.

For all of the democratic gains at the ballot box under the empire, however, Germany's position within the global context made a transition to democracy problematic. German leaders ruled over a middle developer and felt threatened by the early developers. Frustrated in their ambitions to challenge Britain and France as leading imperial powers, the German elite responded to a crisis in southeastern Europe and opted for war in 1914. Their basic hope was for a quick victory to expand Germany's base from which to challenge the established powers. But the quick German victory did not materialize. Instead, the forces of Germany and its ally in this war, Austria-Hungary, bogged down in trench warfare against those of the Triple Entente (Britain, France, and Russia). The German high command's next gamble to win the war quickly – by introducing submarine warfare in the Atlantic – did not weaken Britain and France sufficiently before the feared and ultimately decisive intervention of American troops and resources.

As in other countries affected by the Great War, as World War I was called, massive mobilization had political consequences for Germany. Eleven million men, amounting to 18 percent of the population, were in uniform. Workers and families scrambled to support the war effort. Massive propaganda campaigns encouraged a strong national feeling and the sense that every German person was a valuable member of the nation. Similar campaigns in the other great powers boosted the feelings of national belonging in every state and increased the pressure for political reform to give every member of the nation an equal set of citizenship rights.

Although there was a gradual democratization of political life under the empire, the transition to a full democracy came abruptly. As it became clear that Germany was losing the war, several navy and army units mutinied. This was followed by uprisings in Berlin, the abdication of the kaiser, and the end of the authoritarian German empire. As in France at the end of Emperor Louis-Napoleon's rule, loss in war combined with military defections and domestic uprising sparked the transition from authoritarianism to democracy.

## DEMOCRACY AND COMPETITIVE CAPITALISM, 1919–1933

With the fall of the Second Empire, a democratic, constitutional regime took command of the German state. Under the Weimar Republic, all adult men and women had the right to vote in elections to parliament (Reichstag). Elections were also held to select a president. In turn, the president usually requested the leader of the strongest parliamentary party to serve as the chancellor, form a cabinet, and lead the government. If the chancellor's party could not form a majority on its own, the chancellor had to put together a coalition of parties in parliament in order to govern. Given the absence of a single party that could command a majority, most governments were coalition governments composed of several parties. Not all coalition governments are weak, but in the case of Weimar Germany many were.

The incumbents of the old regime retained considerable influence even under the new regime. The new democratic leaders never purged reactionary officers from the army or police. Instead, the democrats relied on the old authoritarians. For example, the Social Democratic leaders of the new German government called on the army to suppress demonstrations in a bid to restore order to rioting cities, quell the threat of a communist revolution, and prevent a German example of the recently successful 1917 revolution in Russia. In addition, most of the judges had received their legal training under the empire and continued to interpret the law in an antidemocratic fashion. Similarly, many of the highly trained and placed civil servants were holdovers from the previous era. While the first president was a leading Socialist, Friedrich Ebert, the second and only other president, Otto von Hindenburg, was a Junker and former army officer. It was Hindenburg who appointed Hitler as chancellor in 1933.

If the usual distribution of vote shares had been sustained as the country moved into the early 1930s, the Weimar Republic might well have survived. The leading parties in the regime during the 1920s were the Social Democratic Party, which usually received about 25 percent of the vote, and the Center Party, which usually received about 15 percent of the vote. Further to the left, the Communist Party also polled steadily in the 15 percent range. On the center-right, various bourgeois, liberal, and traditional-nationalist parties accounted for most of the remaining 45 percent of the vote. The governments worked reasonably well, so long as parties in the center of the political spectrum remained strong.

Important aspects of the Weimar Republic's demise were the increasing strength of extreme left-wing and right-wing parties committed to the destruction of the republic and the failure of the center-right parties to retain their constituencies. Beginning with the election of 1930, the new National Socialist German Workers' Party (Nazi Party) started to capture a substantial share of the vote, mostly from the old center-right, bourgeois, and liberal parties. In 1933, in the last democratic election, for example, the Socialists received almost their typical amount at 20 percent and the Center Party won its usual 15 percent. The Communists received a somewhat higher than normal 17 percent. It was the collapsing center-right and right-wing parties that provided the Nazis with a plurality of 33 percent of the vote, paving the way for Hitler to be named chancellor.

Our perspective on global contexts and paths to development illuminates important causes of the democratic collapse and fascist takeover that stand up to comparative analysis. First, Germany's size and middle-developer status interacted in ways dangerous for democracy. Germany was a big country, and many of its people had seemingly reasonable expectations that Germany would become the next great power. Yet years of competition with the early developers, especially Britain and its ex-colony, the United States, and now added competition with a late developer, the Soviet Union, seemed to leave Germany lagging behind. For many people in Germany and in other territorially large middle developers (such as Japan, Italy, and Spain), one temptation was to change the nature of the competition and embark on a military strategy to remake the world order with their nation on top. The temptation had already faded in the countries that had suffered permanent defeats in attempts to use force and authoritarianism to improve their global position (Sweden in 1648; France in 1815 and 1870); the temptation was also weak in smaller countries with no realistic hope of a military path to greatness. Thus, one can see World War I, World War II, and the authoritarian regimes that pushed them forward as part of a larger tendency among the large middle developers to improve their global position by military means. It is interesting to note that this remains even today a tendency in several other large countries with frustrated developmental ambitions.

Second, Germany's middle-developer status allowed an antidemocratic class at the top of its social structure to exercise considerable influence. Although Germany's rapid industrial development helped to produce a substantial middle class and working class, both of which are frequently in favor of democratic regimes in other states, there also remained a small but powerful class of landed elites who used labor-repressive modes of agriculture on their estates. These Junkers were also highly positioned in the German state and could use their position to maintain their social and economic position. As we saw above, it was Hindenburg, a Junker president of the Weimar Republic, who appointed Hitler as chancellor. Although most Junkers certainly preferred more traditional conservatives to the Nazis, the Nazis had a better hold on mass support and were seen as useful tools in the larger struggle against communism. Other landed elites using labor-repressive modes of agriculture (such as plantation owners in the southern United States) had fought against full democracy; in these and similar cases, it seemed to require a major military defeat to force these small but powerful groups to relinquish key aspects of their authority.

Third, Germany's path to development set up political institutions that made it more difficult to reach agreements among social and political forces. Other middle-developing democratic regimes (in Sweden, Norway, Denmark, and Czechoslovakia) survived the interwar years without succumbing to domestic fascist movements. These liberal democracies survived at least in part because their democratic regimes were supported by strong coalitions between socialist and agrarian parties. Such a democratic urban-rural coalition did not form in Germany, nor did one form in the two other European countries that succumbed to fascist movements (Italy and Spain). Thus, it may be that the inability of predominantly urban socialists and predominantly rural agrarian parties to reach agreement fatally weakened the German, Italian, and Spanish democracies in the interwar years. Taken together, all three reasons imply that Germany's global position and domestic institutions tended to undermine attempts at democracy and competitive capitalism.

## NAZISM IN POWER, 1933–1945

Germany's Nazi regime was similar to other fascist regimes in several key organizational aspects. Hitler used his legal appointment as Chancellor of the Weimar Republic to consolidate his command of the Nazi Party and put his party in control of the state. Within weeks, Hitler used Communist resistance as a pretext to prohibit and suppress the Communist Party. During the rest of 1933, other parties were strongly encouraged to dissolve and allow their members to join the Nazi Party; for the remainder of the regime's rule the Nazi Party was the only legal party in Germany. In principle, Nazis sought to enroll all Germans from every social class in various party-affiliated organizations. With these steps toward constructing a one-party, mobilizing, authoritarian regime, German Nazism can be seen as similar to the fascism in Italy under Mussolini and, to a lesser degree, Spain under Franco.

What separates Nazi Germany from other cases of fascism, however, is the world war it initiated and the genocide it committed. Widespread support for militarism and expansionism, especially to the east, certainly were part of Hitler's initial program and appeal. Hitler prepared for war from the start and succeeded in annexing Austria in 1938 and the Sudentenland in Czechosovakia in 1939 without provoking a military response; there is evidence that he hoped to avoid having to fight until the middle 1940s, and many Germans undoubtedly believed that a war could be short. Nevertheless, in September of 1939, the German invasion of Poland led the British and French to declare war. When German forces entered Paris in 1940, many Germans hoped for both victory and peace, but as the fighting dragged on, this combined outcome became unlikely. From 1939 until the Nazi regime's fall in 1945, Germany and the rest of the world were at war.

The Nazi regime undertook a brutal and virtually unique policy, the mass murder of civilians based on beliefs about their racial background that both demands and evades explanation. The Holocaust, as the Nazi destruction of European Jewry is called, could not have gone forward without a combination of 1) racist beliefs, 2) the organizational capabilities of a modern state, 3) a fascist political regime, and 4) a leader who favored killing, not just as a means to another end but also as a major policy objective in its own right. Of the three major fascist regimes of the period, only the Nazi regime carried out a campaign to exterminate all European Jews and people belonging to many other groups (Sinti and Roma, homosexuals, psychiatric patients, and the handicapped). In Italy, for example, the early fascist leadership openly included some people of Jewish descent, and Mussolini did not seek a campaign against Jews. Prior to the Holocaust, traditional forms of anti-Semitism were present in Germany (but also throughout much of predominantly Christian Europe), as were modern, scientific forms of racism and population theories (these, too, were present elsewhere in Europe and the United States). Other demagogues sought power in all of the major Western countries, but these potential leaders were less successful than Hitler. Taken alone or in various partial combinations, racist ideas, modern states, nondemocratic regimes, and murderous leaders have contributed to terrible outcomes throughout history and around the world, but the full combination of all four has so far come together only once.

The choices made in the 1930s carried consequences that many Germans would arguably have sought to avoid if the full ramifications had been known. The war eventually brought considerable pain for the society that started it. Even aside from the human suffering, the war weakened all of the European powers, including Germany, and left two other powers at the top of the global military system: the Soviet Union and the United States. This new global context was thus ushered into being by the development path and choices taken by Germany.

## OCCUPATION (1945–1949), DIVISION (1949–1990), AND UNIFICATION (1990– )

The three key periods in post–World War II German politics each helped forge new interests, identities, and institutions. The first period was the Allied occupation from 1945 to 1949 and the temporary administration of Germany in four zones with virtually no central state apparatus. The second period was the division into two German states, the Federal Republic of Germany (FRG), based on the American, British, and French zones in the west, and the German Democratic Republic (GDR), based on the Soviet zone in the east. The third period began with the fall of Soviet communism in Central Europe in 1989 and the unification of the two German states in 1990.

After World War II, Germany's place in the global arena changed decisively. During the occupation, Germany was considerably weakened, compared to the world's two new global powers, the United States and the Soviet Union. Germany was occupied and then divided into two regimes, each closely tied to one of the major powers. In the decades after the war, the FRG moved from being a middle developer in economic terms to becoming one of the leading developers, while the GDR remained tied to the less-successful command economies of the Soviet Bloc. The collapse of the Soviet Union sparked the final decay of the GDR. Reunited Germany now occupies a leading position among the nations of the world and within Europe. As we shall see, these changes influence the makeup of Germany's current interests, identities, and institutions.

The FRG (or as it was often known, West Germany) itself led much of the world's post–World War II economic growth, partly financed internationally by the American Marshall Plan for European Recovery, but also grounded domestically in its close cooperation among top businesses, organized labor unions, and the state. In order to avoid future military conflicts and to guide growing intra-European trade, West German leaders supported the drive for closer economic and political cooperation among European countries. In the 1970s and 1980s, the U.S. and Japanese economies put severe pressures on European industries. In response, West Germany took the lead, along with France, in pushing for a stronger European Union. Unified Germany in the 1990s has continued to support the institutions of the European Union, including monetary union in 1999.

## INTERESTS IN CONTEMPORARY GERMANY

Germany's economic growth puts it in the top rank of industrialized economies. By 1994, the economy yielded a gross domestic product (GDP) per person of $19,097 (in 1990 U.S. dollars). Only four advanced industrialized countries produced more per person (Denmark, Japan, the United States, and Switzerland). This output per person is impressive, especially considering that Germany's population is about 82 million people; if East Germany had not been annexed in 1990, Germany's production would still have been high but with a smaller population of only about 65 million people. Measured by exports, too, Germany is a world leader: German exports in 1992 were valued at $409 billion in 1990 U.S. dollars; only the United States had more, while Japan trailed significantly behind in third place.

Germany benefits greatly from competing economically within the current system, rather than attempting to subvert it through military force as it had attempted to do earlier. Whereas prior to World War II, Germany had achieved impressive economic growth but still lacked the imperial success of Great Britain, now German economic and political ambitions seem well served by the current distribution of power, and it has long since surpassed Britain's standard of living. Germany is a member of the Organization for Economic Cooperation and Development and a leader in the Group of Eight, which is composed of the leaders from the world's eight largest economies. Within Europe, Germany is, along with France, one of the key states pushing for greater economic and political cooperation in the European Union.

Germany is often seen as Europe's preeminent political and economic power. Several constraints on German sovereignty have been lifted with unification since 1990. The German-Polish border was finally settled at the Oder-Neisse line, and the old allies from World War II no longer occupy Berlin. Although Germany is a member of the UN, it still lacks a seat on the powerful Security Council, which includes, by contrast, Great Britain and France.

As a whole, Germany's material interests lie in maintaining and working within the current world economic system. But that does not mean that all Germans have exactly the same interests. What are the various interests in Germany? Which interests emerged as dominant, and how do they seek to position Germany in the world economy? How do they add up to produce a national political outcome?

One way to divide up the economy is to look at the major factors of production: land, labor, and capital. As you might expect, these factors generate different interests. Owners of land favor low costs for the inputs – labor and industrial products – that they use in agricultural production and high prices for their agricultural products. Owners of labor – that is, workers – favor low food prices and high wages. Owners of capital – such as factory owners – favor low food prices, low wages, and high prices for their own products.

Since the end of World War II, the impact of the generally expanding world trade on these different interests has helped to sustain democratic and capitalist institutions in Germany. Productive labor and capital are both relatively abundant in Germany. The German workforce is highly skilled and productive. Germany imported more workers as immigrants, especially in the 1960s, and the German workforce remains one of the world's strongest, even though unemployment in the 1990s rose above 10 percent. As for capital, Germany possesses a massive industrial base, some of which survived from before World War II, but much of which was built after the war along highly efficient lines. To take one measure of Germany's capital abundance, in 1953 West Germany was the seventh most-industrialized country in the world, measured by industrialization per capita, and by 1980 it was the third most-industrialized country (behind only the United States and Sweden). German industry, along with its workers, substantially rely on foreign markets for their goods and do quite well in global competition.

In agriculturally productive land, however, Germany has a relatively scarce supply. In West Germany there are 414 persons per square kilometer of arable land. By contrast, for example, in the land-abundant United States there are only about 41 persons per square kilometer of arable land. Thus, unlike industry and labor, German agriculture was not in a position to produce on a global scale at competitive prices. Owners of agricultural land in Germany would have benefited from a system in which Germans were forced to buy food not from producers around the world but from German agriculture only.

One can see the practical political effects of these economic interests in at least two ways. First, the major political parties agree on the basic outlines of economic policy. Industry and labor have won the fight with agriculture to put Germany in the free-trade camp. German industry and labor now have strong interests in an open international trading system in which they use their strength to compete on a world market and avoid flooding their own market with too many goods. Given the size of these two sectors in Germany, their joint interests overrode those of the opposing agriculturalists. The Social Democratic Party, with a stronghold in the working class, favors free-trade industrialization. The Christian Democratic Party, with strong support from industrialists, also favors free-trade industrialization. Both have pushed for the reduction of trade barriers on a world scale and within the European Union.

The second political impact of interests is that the main parties advocate even greater economic free trade and are willing to compensate the losers in this policy. Even in the late 1990s, when world financial crises unsettled global markets, both major parties remained strongly in favor of the continued economic integration of Europe, including monetary union with ten other European countries. A major concession that the government regularly has to make in order to deepen European integration is to its farmers. As compensation to landowners and farmers for the losses due to economic integration and free trade, to this day the European Union spends the bulk of its budget on support for farmers. Both the Social Democratic Party (SPD) and the Christian Democratic Party (CDU/CSU) have supported the relatively generous welfare provisions of the German state, all of which help cushion the blows of economic competition and allow the employed workforce to maintain its high level of technical skills.

The social classes that make up German society come out of a tradition of stark class distinctions. However, the experiences of fascism, the postwar economic success, and now the transition to a service-oriented economy have dulled long-standing divisions. A key result of the war was the loss of the eastern territories and the final destruction of the last remnants of the political power of the landed elite. Whereas many Junkers welcomed Hitler, at arm's length, in a bid to bring order to a rapidly changing society, the result of Nazism and its failure was their elimination from a role in German politics.

One can take the occupational composition of the workforce as another measure of changes in Germany's class structure. In 1950, 28 percent of workers were in agriculture or self-employment, 51 percent were manual workers (mostly in industry), and 21 percent were salaried, nonmanual workers (so-called white-collar and service workers). By 1994, only 10 percent were in agriculture or self-employment and only 38 percent were manual workers, whereas fully 52 percent were salaried, nonmanual workers. Thus, as in the rest of the industrialized world, Germany has developed a combined industrial and postindustrial social structure.

## IDENTITIES IN CONTEMPORARY GERMANY

Gradually after World War II antidemocratic values weakened. The failure to win world domination shook many people's faith in the fascist alternative to democracy. After the war, many Germans avoided overt politics and turned inward – toward family, work, and the pursuit of personal well-being – and abandoned a belief in grander political ends. The relative economic success of the West German economy in the 1950s and 1960s reinforced the value placed on the pursuit of prosperity.

Support for democracy has grown. In a 1950 survey, German respondents were asked about political competition. Fully 25 percent said that it is better for a country to have only one political party, and another 22 percent were undecided about this question or gave no response. A bare majority, just 53 percent, said it is better for a country to have several parties. It would be hard to say that a political culture is democratic if such a slight majority of people believe that political competition among parties is a good idea. Things have changed, however. In a 1990 survey, just 3 percent of respondents said that it is better to have only one party, and only 8 percent were undecided or gave no response. Now, the overwhelming preponderance of respondents, 89 percent, state that it is better for a country to have several political parties.

Today a strong faith in democracy can be seen at the elite and mass levels. The German political philosopher Jürgen Habermas has described "constitutional patriotism" as the ultimate political value. Support for democracy is also reflected in public opinion polls. According to a recent survey, 50 percent of respondents in Germany state that they are "very satisfied" or "fairly satisfied" with the way democracy is working in Germany; 37 percent say they are "not very satisfied," while only 11 percent are "not at all satisfied." While not as high as in the United Kingdom – where 61 percent report that they are "very" or "fairly satisfied" – the distribution of responses to this question in Germany is about average among EU countries. Still, there are important differences between former East Germany and the West: only 30 percent of East German respondents state that they are "very" or "fairly satisfied," compared to 55 percent in the West. The indicators of public opinion suggest that there is widespread support for human rights as a basic value and broad support for the current version of democratic institutions in Germany.

Still, the more than 82 million people living in Germany do not share a single identity. One dimension on which Germans differ is how they situate themselves with respect to the rest of Europe and the possibility of a European identification that transcends national identifications. In a recent survey, 49 percent of respondents said that they consider themselves to be "German only." Another 35 percent of respondents said that they considered themselves to be "German and European." Seven percent said they considered themselves, "European and German" and 5 percent chose "European only." The distribution of national versus European identity in Germany is about average for the 15 European Union countries. Among the bigger countries, German national identity is located halfway between the weak national identity in France (where just 31 percent chose "French only") and the strong national identity in the United Kingdom (where 60 percent chose "British only").

Many Germans are relatively new residents in the German state. In the post–World War II period of division, from 1949 to 1989, approximately 13 million refugees whom the state identified as German migrated to the FRG from Poland, the Soviet Union, and the GDR. The territory of the GDR in 1948 was home to about 19 million people. The GDR's population shrank during the decades of division, mostly because of legal and illegal migration to the FRG. In 1989 alone, some 344,000 people left the GDR for the FRG, along with 376,000 "ethnic" Germans from the Soviet Union and elsewhere in Eastern Europe. As we have seen, what was left of the GDR's population, 16 million people, came under FRG control in 1990.

Many people live in Germany whom the German state considers to be foreigners. People from Turkey and southern Europe (the former Yugoslavia, Greece, and Italy) arrived in large numbers during the 1960s under the government's policy of encouraging the temporary migration of foreigners to work in German industries that needed more labor. Almost a million people from these groups left Germany during the 1970s, when the government provided incentives for foreign workers and their families to leave Germany. Yet most of the immigrants did not leave; today they number about 7.5 million people, the largest group of foreigners in any European country. In 1997, there were about 2.1 million people the state identified as from Turkey, 1.3 million from the former Yugoslavia, 0.6 million from Italy, 0.4 million from Greece, 0.3 million from Poland, 0.2 million from Austria, and 0.1 million from the United States.

While there are signs of change, the conventional term for foreign workers, "guest workers" (Gastarbeiter), underscores the state's attempt to emphasize the temporary nature of their stay in Germany, despite their deep involvement in the German economy and society. Many of the hardships faced by these immigrant groups are common to the experience of immigrant laborers in other industrialized countries: low wages, dangerous employment, few opportunities for advancement, racism, thuggery, discrimination in housing and employment, and the near-constant threat of legal deportation. The difficult situation of many immigrants defined as nonethnic Germans is exacerbated by their exclusion from the political process. It was virtually impossible for foreign workers, or even their children, to earn the right to vote, become a citizen, or run for public office. The still-strong German legal tradition of defining citizenship by descent, rather than by place of birth, lies at the core of the problem. After assuming power in 1998, Chancellor Gerhard Schröder's government introduced legislation to ease citizenship requirements but was forced to postpone and moderate its plan in the face of widespread opposition.

With the absorption of the East, the long-standing predominance of Protestantism in the population has been renewed, along with a new injection of people not affiliated with any religion. Protestants comprise 45 percent of the population, Roman Catholics 37 percent, Muslims 3 percent, and unaffiliated or other faiths a total of 15 percent. In the West just before the transition, in 1987, Roman Catholics comprised 43 percent of the population, while Protestants (Lutheran-Reformed and Lutheran) comprised an almost identical 42 percent. In addition to these two main groups, there were Muslims (2.7 percent), Reformed tradition (0.6 percent), Jews (0.1 percent), and others, including those officially without religion (12 percent). Meanwhile, in the former East Germany (in 1990), Protestants comprised fully 47 percent of the population and Roman Catholics just 7 percent. Most of the rest were officially unaffiliated, about 46 percent (this figure also includes a very small proportion of "other"). Just several thousand German Jews survived the Holocaust, and only about 30,000 Jewish people live in Germany today, predominantly in Berlin.

The identities of men and women are changing, too. Germany emerged from World War II with gender identities rooted in the past. In the FRG, the law still reflected greater rights for men against those for women, especially in marriage and property. In the GDR, strict legal equality was undermined by pervasive informal occupational segregation by gender. A movement for women's rights developed during the 1970s in the FRG, as in virtually all Western democracies. By force of example, this movement has changed how men and women think of themselves. Institutional changes have reinforced these new conditions, though not as dramatically as in some other countries. Abortion laws were almost liberalized in the 1970s but were turned back by a conservative majority on the Constitutional Court. After unification, the differences in abortion laws between West and East proved to be a difficult political issue: The liberal abortion law for the East expired in 1992, and a moderately pro-choice, all-German law was declared unconstitutional in 1993. Nearly 90 percent of women in the communist East had worked outside of the home, whereas not even half of women did in the West. Pay and working conditions were better in the West, but the advancement of women into the higher ranks of important professions remained slow.

# INSTITUTIONS IN CONTEMPORARY GERMANY

The founding document of the Federal Republic of Germany is the Basic Law *(Grundgesetz)* of 1949. Although political actors use it much like a constitution, it is often not called a constitution, given the prominent role that the occupying Western powers had in its formulation and given the reluctance to recognize as permanent the division of Germany into two parts. Under the Western occupation, political life began to reemerge mainly at the regional rather than the national level. In September 1948, the Allied military governors and provincial leaders convened a constituent assembly of sixty-five delegates to draft a provisional constitution. The aims of the framers were to avoid the perceived weaknesses of the Weimar system, to prevent a renewed fascist movement, and to lock western Germany into the Western alliance. Thus, the Basic Law strengthened the chancellor and the legislature over against the bureaucracy and army, and decentralized power to the various regional governments. The framers placed the rule of law and basic liberal institutions at the very heart of the system. Their proposed Basic Law was ratified by regional parliaments in May 1949.

In part because of the Basic Law's well-crafted institutional design, Germany has sustained its political democracy since 1949. At the most basic level, Germany qualifies as a political democracy because all of the major actors in German society expect that elections for the highest offices in the state will be held on a regular basis into the foreseeable future. This situation contrasts with the Weimar Republic, when many leading political actors either sought to end the practice of elections or at least reasonably expected that elections would be suspended at some point. While not a guarantee, it is certainly important that free and fair national elections in the Federal Republic were held in 1949 and regularly thereafter, including the elections of 1998 that ended seventeen years of Christian Democratic rule and brought the Socialists to power. According to the Basic Law of 1949, elections to the national legislature are held every four years. (The Basic Law's exceptions to this rule occur when the legislature is deadlocked. If this happens, it provides for the federal president to call early elections. So far, this has happened only twice, in 1972 and 1982.) The intervals between German national elections are not quite as regularly spaced as election intervals in presidential systems, such as the United States, but they are more regular than in other parliamentary systems, such as the United Kingdom.

For the most part, the powers of the president are severely restricted, compared to the relatively powerful role for the president under the Weimar system. Although the president is the official head of state, the president's powers are mainly restricted to the calling of elections and ceremonial functions, and one person can serve for no more than two terms. The president can pardon criminals and receives and visits other heads of state. The president promulgates all federal laws with a signature (the authority to refuse to sign is disputed, and presidents have signed all but perhaps five laws). The president is not popularly elected. According to the Basic Law, a federal convention composed of the legislature and an equal number of representatives from the state assemblies meets every five years to select the president. The selection by the federal convention has so far led to presidents who are relatively old politicians, well respected by the political elite, and with moderate views, but who lack a strong basis of prior political support. Still, some presidents have been able to influence national debates by means of skillful speech making, as when Richard von Weizsäcker gave a 1985 speech commemorating the 40th anniversary of the end of World War II that cautioned Germans not to forget the nation's past and to guard against a revival of nationalist sentiment.

The chancellor is the real executive power in the German system. While he or she is responsible to the legislature, as in other parliamentary systems, he or she may appoint and dismiss other cabinet ministers at will, rather like U.S. presidents. The relatively regular interval between elections gives the chancellor a somewhat firm idea about the political struggles that lie ahead and enhances the authority of the legislature and the chancellor over that of the president. Another source of the chancellor's authority is Article 67 of the Basic Law, the so-called constructive vote of no confidence, which states that the legislature may dismiss the chancellor only when a majority of the members simultaneously elects a successor. This brake on the authority of the legislature helps prevent weak chancellors from emerging. For example, the only time that a constructive vote of no confidence succeeded was in 1982, when the Free Democratic Party (FDP) withdrew from the ruling coalition and went along with a vote of no confidence regarding Social Democratic Party (SPD) Chancellor Helmut Schmidt. A new FDP and CDU/CSU coalition in the legislature selected Helmut Kohl as chancellor. With a majority behind him from the beginning and with several election victories thereafter, Kohl served as chancellor from 1982 until 1998. In other parliamentary governments, legislatures can agree to dismiss a sitting government but then may fail agree on a strong successor, agreeing instead only to select weak figures who are not able to take real initiatives on their own.

The legislature is bicameral and, as in other parliamentary orders, produces the executive. The lower house *(Bundestag)* is directly elected, whereas the upper house *(Bundesrat)* is composed of delegates chosen by the sixteen federal states (each state is called a *Land*). The combination of federalism in the state and bicameralism in the leading institutions of the regime gives Germany a substantial amount of institutional overlap that differs both from unitary systems (such as in the UK and France) and from federal systems, which have sharper federal-state distinctions (such as in the United States). The leader of the largest party usually puts together a two- or three-party coalition in the lower house; the coalition in turn supports the party leader as chancellor. The chancellor must maintain a legislative majority in order to stay in power. With majority support, however, the chancellor has a relatively free hand in appointing and dismissing members of the cabinet.

The rules for translating votes into seats constitute another crucial institution. A voter makes two ballot choices in a German election. The first choice is for a candidate to represent the voter's district in the lower house. The second choice is for a national party overall in the lower house. How are these two ballot choices translated into specific seats in the lower house? Germany uses a modified form of proportional representation. In a proportional system, a party usually receives seats in the legislature in proportion to its share of the popular vote. In the German case, half of the seats are awarded according to the first-ballot choices for individual candidates, and the other half are awarded so as to bring each party's representation up to its share of the national vote on the second-ballot choice.

Proportional representation makes it easier for medium-size parties to gain national representation than does the other main type of electoral rule, a plurality system, in which the voter makes only one choice for a given office and the top vote-getter in a district wins the office (as is the case in the United States and United Kingdom). Two German parties have won seats in the legislature by securing a national vote of more than 5 percent on the second-ballot choice, even though their candidates do not win any districts on the first-ballot choice. The FDP has been a crucial player in legislative politics since 1949, while typically wining about 10 percent of the popular vote. Similarly, the Greens have become almost as influential since the 1970s with only around 10 percent to 5 percent of the popular vote.

Germany's proportional system is modified in three crucial ways, two of which aid the largest parties. One important modification is the "5 percent rule": A party must win at least 5 percent of the national vote on the second-ballot choice in order to get its share of seats. Thus, small parties are eliminated from representation, such as the extreme right-wing Republican Party, which won only 3 percent of the vote in 1994. Even the medium-size Free Democrats and the Greens are perennially concerned about falling below the 5 percent threshold; their coalition partners in government have often advocated strategic voting in order to ensure that the medium-size parties do not fall below that mark. The 5 percent threshold thus increases the reliance of the medium-size parties on their larger partners. A second important modification is the "three-district waiver" exception to the 5 percent rule: If a party wins a mandate in at least three districts, then the national 5 percent rule is waived, and the party is awarded seats according to its share of the total vote on the second-ballot choice. This second modification permitted the former East German Communist Party, campaigning as the Party of Democratic Socialism, to win national representation based on its victories in the former East

Berlin, despite its very small national vote share. This second modification is the only one that aids very small parties, and it comes into play only if the small party's supporters are concentrated in a few districts. Finally, the "excess mandate provision" holds that if a party wins more district mandates than the proportion of the popular vote on the second choice would otherwise award the party, then the party gets to retain any extra seats, and the size of the legislature is increased accordingly. While of relatively little consequence for most of the Federal Republic's electoral history, this last rule recently helped the big parties; it gave the CDU 6 extra seats in 1990, and then in 1994 gave the CDU 12 extra seats and the SPD 4.

Germany's federal structure gives the republic's constituent units a great deal of power. Sixteen states *(Länder)* make up the republic. Compared to regional governments in Europe, they possess a good deal of power in relation to the central government. Each state has a premier and a legislature. The state legislatures send delegates to the assembly that elects the president and also send delegates to the national legislature's upper house (the *Bundesrat*). The Basic Law reserves certain powers for the states, including education, police and internal security, administration of justice, and the regulation of mass media. The states are also responsible for administering federal laws and collecting most taxes. Changes since the Basic Law of 1949 have been designed to enhance or at least preserve the states' powers. They now have at least a joint role in higher education, regional economic development, and agricultural reform. Reforms in 1994 were designed to give the various states a voice in policy making at the European level; until then, the federal government had a larger role to play.

The economy itself can be seen as an institution, especially since its key actors are linked in stable relationships that go beyond mere monetary exchange. Many terms have been used to describe the economy of the Federal Republic of Germany: neocorporatism, social democracy, and coordinated market economy, to name three important ones. These terms seek to capture Germany's blend of social and market institutions in a single economy. In fact, a term that Germans commonly use to describe their economic order is a "social market economy." A social market economy rests not only on market principles of supply and demand but also on extensive involvement by the state and societal institutions. Germany has institutions that work hard to ensure the smooth functioning of free economic exchange. Prior to the monetary union, the central bank, for example, was for a long time one of the most independent and powerful central banks in the world. It sought to keep interest rates and inflation low and the currency stable. There is no purer example of a firm commitment to market principles than a central bank free of political influence. On the social side of the equation, the German state guarantees a free university education for all who qualify, and basic health and adequate income for all its citizens. In addition, the state supports organized representation in the workplace and vocational training for workers, rather than letting these matters be handled by firms or unions alone.

At the heart of Germany's social market economy is the "social partnership" of business and labor. According to the political scientist Lowell Turner, social partnership is defined as "the nexus – and central political and economic importance – of bargaining relationships between strongly organized employers (in employer associations) and employees (in unions and works councils) that range from comprehensive collective bargaining and plant-level codetermination to vocational training and federal, state and local economic policy discussions." In addition to labor and business, there are also important "framing and negotiating roles" for two other actors, large banks and the government. In this kind of system, negotiated agreements between the social partners of business and labor shape politics and economics at the national, regional, and local levels. As an example of national, peak agreements, one could point to the Concerted Action of 1967 or the Solidarity Pact in 1993. There are also industry-wide or simply firm-level agreements regarding, for example, vocational training and industrial policy.

The Solidarity Pact of 1993 nicely illustrates a peak bargain under social partnership. The federal government agreed not to let old industries in the former East Germany simply wither away. Instead, it sought an active role for itself in industrial restructuring. Eastern industries benefited from temporary assistance, as did labor, since employment was protected. Western industrialists were also given opportunities for developing infrastructure (such as roads, railroads, and government offices), while they promised to invest in the old eastern industrial core, rather than simply dismantle it and confine their production to the already developed western regions. Unions, in return, promised to hold back wage demands in both East and West and promised to support the program of adjustment in the East, rather than adopt a posture of militant opposition. While this bargain worked to the benefit of all sides, it was the product of institutionalized negotiation, not simple economic logic.

Scholars and policy makers do not agree on the future of German social partnership. In the view of many, the Pact of 1993 was just an isolated episode in a period more noted for conflicting interests. The early 1990s witnessed a new phase of economic globalization: Would the institutions of social partnership survive the neoliberal economic policy atmosphere? Would they hold up against rapid financial movements across international borders? Could they be maintained in the face of widening international economic competition as the costs of communication and transportation continued to fall? In the early 1990s it was plausible that Germany's more moderate social partnership would succumb to the new conditions. Unemployment rose to over 10 percent in late 1995 and grew to over 12 percent in early 1997. Since unions typically find it difficult to maintain their bargaining position in the face of persistent joblessness among workers, German unions will likely find it hard to sustain their influential role. Furthermore, the increasing integration of European economies weakens the position of national-level actors, especially labor unions. Finally, the prospect of extending the European Union to the east introduces the possibility that employers will use low-cost labor in less-developed member countries, rather than continue to invest in the developed core.

Others are more optimistic that German social partnership may be resilient after all. While recognizing the difficulties facing partnership, especially the challenges facing organized labor, one can point to more positive signs. In the first place, the eastern decay has not spread to the West; instead Western institutions have spread to the former East Germany. Employer associations, industrial unions, comprehensive collective bargaining arrangements, elected works councils, and legally mandated codetermination have all taken root in the old East. The economic integration of the East, while not complete, and while not as painless as Chancellor Helmut Kohl argued it would be in 1990, has certainly not led to an economic collapse. According to these optimists, few companies actually relocated to low-wage countries in the 1980s. They further maintain that there will likely be little relocation to the East in the next few decades. Investment in the East, moreover, may serve to stimulate demand for exports from Germany and may also open up even more markets for German goods. In addition to these favorable trends, the international financial crises of the late 1990s – first in Asia, then in Russia, and then in Latin America – have dampened enthusiasm for unregulated free markets, even among global investors. In times of uncertainty, many international financial decision makers seek the greater security provided by more institutionalized forms of industrial organization. European Union institutions also leave a great deal of leeway to national-level institutions, on the principle of subsidiarity, and because each individual government, especially governments of big countries such as Germany, have a major say in what happens at the European level.

The German Federal Bank *(Bundesbank)* is a semipublic institution that has regulated important aspects of the economy with a great deal of freedom from other political institutions. The bank, with a function similar to the United States Federal Reserve Bank and the Bank of England, is the national bank responsible for monetary policy and price stability. Arguably reacting to the broader German experience with ruinous inflation in the 1920s, which destroyed the savings of many Germans and helped set the stage for the Nazi seizure of power, the German Federal Bank has consistently adopted interest-rate policies designed to nip inflation in the bud. The bank's directorate is appointed to fixed eight-year terms by the federal president on the recommendation of the chancellor's government. The membership of the other executive body, the Central Bank Council, is determined mainly by regional banks, the Bundesrat, and state governments. Yet, once appointed, the bank's officials cannot be removed – they answer to no political official – and the bank's day-to-day operations and long-range planning take place with nearly complete autonomy from political leadership. At several key moments in postwar German history, the bank's anti-inflationary bias has clashed with the plans of domestic and international politicians: Chancellor Helmut Schmidt wanted lower interest rates to help the country out of recession in 1981 and 1982, but the bank refused to give in and Schmidt blamed the bank for his fall in 1982. In 1987 the United States pressured the German government to reflate its economy to help pull the United States out of its trade deficit – that is, to encourage Germans to buy U.S. goods – but the bank resisted as long as possible until the stock market crash of the late 1980s made the policy more palatable to the bank. The bank even opposed – albeit largely unsuccessfully – Chancellor Kohl's generous offer during the unification process to exchange East German marks on a 1-to-1 or 2-to-1 basis for FRG marks. Finally, the bank has been the strongest voice for maintaining an anti-inflationary stance in the transition to the new monetary union of the European Union.

The new German judiciary and the legal philosophy of the state is partly the product of a deliberate attempt by post–Nazi era political actors to transform radically an institution that had not protected basic civil and human rights. On the side of institutional redesign, the Basic Law created a Federal Constitutional Court with the power of judicial review. The practice of judges reviewing state actions for conformity with a higher law – in this case, the Basic Law – was completely foreign to the German legal tradition before 1949. The change was strongly championed by the American occupiers, who had at their disposal the model of the U.S. Supreme Court and who were clearly thinking of the old German judiciary that did not strike down any of the Nazi government's decrees.

A distinctive and controversial aspect of German law and legal institutions, however, concerns what Americans would call freedom of speech. Unlike in the United States, "hate speech" is unconstitutional in Germany, and the organizations that promote it are banned after being investigated by the Office of Constitutional Protection (*Verfassungsschutz*). It is illegal, for example, to organize a Nazi party, to deny publicly the historical fact of the Holocaust, or to sell or distribute Nazi propaganda. How does the German state justify actions and policies that Americans would consider unacceptable, and even unconstitutional, departures from liberal democratic practices? Germans view their democracy as a "militant democracy" that is unwilling to permit antidemocratic forces to use the protections of the liberal state to help undermine it. These ideas and the institutions that are in place to back them up are one obvious reaction to Germany's authoritarian past.

The German judiciary nevertheless also shows some continuity in its institutional practices. On the side of persistence, German judges are closely integrated with the state bureaucracy, and their posts are like those of high bureaucrats.

They are rarely former politicians, prosecutors, or other types of attorney, as is often the case in the United States. Instead, aspiring jurists begin their careers as apprentices to sitting judges; they then rise through the hierarchy, and, if they are successful, never leave the judicial branch. The dominant institutional philosophy of judging puts the judge in the role of actively applying the law to individual cases, in a deliberate pursuit of the truth, unlike U.S. judges who more commonly see themselves as impartial arbiters between two conflicting parties. German judges do not set precedents as do their Anglo-American counterparts; the job of German judges is simply to apply the law correctly, not interpret it or adapt it to circumstances unforeseen by the framers of a statute. Despite the otherwise federal structure of the judiciary, the German legal code is uniform across all the various state governments.

## CONCLUSION

The path of German political development was profoundly shaped by its long period as a middle developer (see Table 1 at the end of the chapter). Germany began much like the rest of Europe. Yet compared to England and France, Germany's lateness in developing a single territorial state and a strong industrial base, and then new challenges from even later developers, such as Russia, put Germany in a difficult position. Germany was also a relatively large middle developer, like Japan, and thus it acquired domestic interests, identities, and institutions different from smaller middle developers, such as Sweden and Denmark. The temptation to use a massive state apparatus for military conquest in a bid to improve its global position did not disappear in Germany until after World War II. Germany's persistent reliance on the state to address many important tasks fostered a distinctive set of interests, identities, and institutions that made it hard to develop or sustain democratic political institutions. As a result, for much of its history, Germany's economic development was state led, and its political order was authoritarian.

Germany's global context predisposed it to adopt the state-led path to development. The Second Empire rose by facing challenges from its military rivals. With a heavy reliance on its army and bureaucracy, the state then aided the growth of heavy industry in a bid to catch up with leading industries in Britain. In politics, the state strongly discouraged dissent and refused to permit elections to the highest public offices. The empire never became a democracy. The Weimar Republic departed from this pattern to adopt competitive capitalism and democratic, constitutional government. In stark contrast to the preceding regime, the two political parties at the core of most of its coalition governments were the Socialist Party and the Catholic Center Party. The global context, however, remained unfavorable for capitalist democracy in Germany. In addition to the burden of reparations payments to France and Britain after World War I, Germany still faced stiff industrial competition from its Western rivals. After the establishment of communist rule in Russia in the 1920s, Germany felt threatened and discriminated against, both from the West and the East. The economic crisis brought on by the Great Depression was the final blow to the Weimar Republic. In the end, the Nazi Party offered Germans a chance to take a new version of antiliberal state-led development. Thus, the durability of the Second Empire, the experiment with democracy under Weimar, and the reversion to state-led development under Nazi rule all point to the importance of the state for much of Germany's existence.

The path of state-led development was difficult to change because of the feedback effect through domestic institutions. The legacies of the Second Empire, including strong authoritarian enclaves in the army, bureaucracy, and presidency, made the survival of the Weimar Republic precarious. The Second Empire's support for Protestant nationalism against Catholicism and class-based sentiments left contradictory legacies. On the one hand, Catholic and working-class identities and institutions developed in opposition to the regime and then went on to be bulwarks of the Weimar Republic. On the other hand, the legacy of strong nationalism and the experience of stigmatizing various groups as unpatriotic and non-German fed into support for the Nazi Party and the overthrow of the democratic system.

Germany's state-led development also fed back into the international system itself. German militarism provoked Soviet defensive action and the fortress mentality of communist regimes, and it also provoked the established Western powers to use force in defense of the liberal international order. The defeat of Nazi Germany in World War II laid the groundwork for a new global rivalry between the United States and the Soviet Union. These two main powers occupied and divided Germany. U.S. and international support for West Germany's reindustrialization and reintegration into the world economic and political systems helped to set Germany down a new path.

Germany's new global position as one of the world's leading economic powers supports a revised set of interests, identities, and institutions and a kind of democratic capitalism that can be described as embedded liberalism. Germany stands for strongly liberal economic policies, and its industries are fiercely competitive in the international marketplace. Its institutions are a firmly democratic regime with a constitutional framework. The market is combined with the social partnership of strong labor unions, business leaders, and key administrative agencies. Germany's political parties, labor unions, and federal institutions all consistently support the basic practices of constitutional, parliamentary democracy. As for identities, most political scientists agree that Germany is as solidly democratic today as any country in Europe.

The continuing globalization of the economy presents a new set of challenges and opportunities for Germany. With the collapse of the Soviet Union, a unified

Germany is exercising even greater influence in European and world politics, especially through its leading role in the strengthened European Union. The German social welfare system so far remains relatively intact, despite some cuts in recent years. Germany also maintains a high level of wage equality and keeps government budgets largely in balance, but the price has been a relatively high level of unemployment. The question of how Germany's distinctive set of interests, identities, and institutions will respond to the new challenges remains an exciting issue to follow in the coming years.

## BIBLIOGRAPHY

Bairoch, Paul. "International Industrialization Levels From 1750 to 1980." *Journal of Economic History* 11, no. 2 (fall 1982): 269–333.

Conradt, David P. *The German Polity.* 6th ed. White Plains, N.Y.: Longman, 1996.

Dahrendorf, Ralf. *Society and Democracy in Germany.* New York: Norton, 1967.

Ertman, Thomas. *Birth of the Leviathan: Building States and Regimes in Medieval and Early Modern Europe.* Cambridge: Cambridge University Press, 1997.

Eurobarometer Surveys of public opinion. Recent Eurobarometer Surveys can be accessed at http://europa.eu.int.

Gerschenkron, Alexander. *Economic Backwardness in Historical Perspective: A Book of Essays.* Cambridge, Mass.: Harvard University Press, 1962.

Gould, Andrew C. *Origins of Liberal Dominance: State, Church, and Party in Nineteenth Century Europe.* Ann Arbor: University of Michigan Press, 1999.

Iversen, Torben, and Anne Wren. "Equality, Employment, and Budgetary Restraint: The Trilemma of the Service Economy," *World Politics* 50, no. 4 (1998): 507–46.

Janos, Andrew C. "The Politics of Backwardness in Continental Europe, 1780–1945." *World Politics* 41, no. 3 (April 1989): 325–58.

Luebbert, Gregory M. *Liberalism, Fascism, or Social Democracy: Social Classes and the Political Origins of Regimes in Interwar Europe.* New York: Oxford University Press, 1991.

Maddison, Angus. *Monitoring the World Economy, 1820–1992.* Paris: Development Centre of the OECD, 1995.

Moore, Barrington. *The Social Origins of Dictatorship and Democracy: Lord and Peasant in the Making of the Modern World.* Boston: Beacon, 1966.

Rogowski, Ronald. *Commerce and Coalitions: How Trade Affects Domestic Political Alignments.* Princeton, N.J.: Princeton University Press, 1989.

Streeck, Wolfgang. "German Capitalism: Does It Exist? Can It Survive?" *New Political Economy* (forthcoming).

Suval, Stanley. *Electoral Politics in Wilhelmine Germany.* Chapel Hill, N.C.: University of North Carolina Press, 1985.

Turner, Lowell. "Introduction. Up Against the Fallen Wall: The Crisis of Social Partnership in Unified Germany." In Lowell Turner, ed. *Negotiating the New Germany: Can Social Partnership Survive?* Ithaca, N.Y.: Cornell University Press, 1997.

Wehler, Hans-Ulrich. *The German Empire, 1871–1918.* Leamington Spa: Berg Publishers, 1985.

**TABLE 1. KEY PHASES IN GERMAN DEVELOPMENT**

| Time Period | Regime | Global Context | Interests/ Identities/Institutions | Development Path |
|---|---|---|---|---|
| 1800–1870 | Competing monarchies (authoritarian) | Industrial and political revolutions | Strong landed elite | State building |
| | | | Protestant nationalism and Catholic resistance | |
| | | | Authoritarian institutions evade reform | |
| 1871–1918 | Second Empire (authoritarian) | European imperialism | Industry and landed elite | State important |
| | | | Strong nationalism and working-class and Catholic subcultures | |
| | | | Authoritarian with elections | |
| 1919–1933 | Weimar Republic (democratic) | Rise of U.S. economic power; communist revolution in Russia | Strong industry | Competitive capitalism |
| | | | Socialism, Catholicism, nationalism, weak democratic values, and fear of communism | |
| | | | Democracy with powerful reserved domains for authoritarian office holders in army and bureaucracy | |
| 1933–1945 | Third Empire (authoritarian) | Global depression | Strong industry | State important |
| | | | Fascism and anti-Semitism | |
| | | | Authoritarian | |
| 1945–1949 | Foreign occupation (military) | U.S. and Soviet dominance | Reindustrialization | International aid |
| | | | Fascism discredited | |
| | | | Parties, unions, and local governments rebuild | |
| 1949–1990 | Federal Republic of Germany (democratic) | Cold war and economic growth | Automobiles and high-technology industry | Embedded liberalism |
| | | | Democratic values grow, new immigrants, feminism, and environmentalism | |
| | | | Parties, unions, federal state | |
| | German Democratic Republic (authoritarian) | Cold war | Heavy industry | Leninism |
| | | | Communist indoctrination but strong disaffection | |
| | | | One-party state | |
| 1990– | Federal Republic of Germany (democratic) | Globalization | Advanced industry and services | Embedded liberalism |
| | | | Strong democratic values, feminism, environmentalism | |
| | | | Parties, unions, federal state | |

## IMPORTANT TERMS

**Basic Law** *(Grundgesetz)*  Founding 1949 document of the Federal Republic of Germany that serves as its constitution. Originally designed to be replaced by "a constitution adopted by a free decision of the German people," it was amended to incorporate the new states from the East in 1990.

**Berlin**  city in northeastern Germany, capital of reunified Germany as from 1990. It was earlier the capital of the kingdom of Prussia, the Second Empire, the Weimar Republic, and the Third Reich. It was occupied and divided after World War II. American support in the Berlin airlift (1948–9) kept Soviet forces from taking the western sector. The Berlin wall (1961–89) kept easterners from leaving for the West. Berlin's eastern half was capital of the German Democratic Republic.

**Bonn**  city on the Rhine River in western Germany, from 1949 to 1990 the provisional capital of West Germany. After 1990 it continued to house many federal offices during the move back to Berlin. It was occupied by French revolutionary forces in 1794 and was awarded to Prussia in 1815.

**Bundesrat**  second, or lower, house of the parliament. It represents the sixteen federal states and is composed of 69 delegates chosen by state governments, usually ministers in state governments. Delegates vote in blocs according to state government instructions. The Bundesrat's approval is required in about two-thirds of legislation, when the states' powers are involved. Secondary in importance to the Bundestag, but important when different parties control the two houses.

**Bundestag**  primary, or upper, house of the parliament. It is composed of 656 delegates elected by popular vote, normally every four years. Its approval is required for all legislation, as in most parliamentary systems, and it exercises more oversight of government than do most parliaments. Its majority party or coalition selects the chancellor.

**Center Party** *(Zentrumspartei)*  the political party that emerged in defense of Catholic interests in the 1870s in the Second Empire. It was the second-largest party for much of the Weimar Republic (with 15 percent to 20 percent of the vote), and it frequently was in the governing coalition. Its predominantly Catholic supporters for the most part did not defect to the Nazi Party in the early 1930s, but its deputies voted for the Enabling Act that gave Hitler dictatorial powers in 1933.

**Christian Democrats**  the Christian Democratic Union (CDU) and the Christian Social Union (CSU), allied parties that campaign together and form one parliamentary grouping (CDU/CSU). The CDU operates in all states except Bavaria, where it is allied with the more conservative CSU. The CDU's founding in the post–World War II era broke from tradition by including Protestants as well as Catholics. The two parties usually win 40 percent to 50 percent of the second-vote choices.

**Congress of Vienna, 1815**  great-powers conference after the defeat of French Emperor Napoleon. The powers agreed to give Prussia control over most of the Rhine territories in order to keep France in check, greatly expanding Prussia's role in Germany overall.

**Constructive vote of no-confidence** requirement in the Basic Law that the Bundesrat, in order to dismiss the chancellor, must simultaneously agree on a new chancellor. It was designed to limit the power of the parliament and strengthen the chancellor. Attempted twice but successful only once, it has generally had the intended effect.

**Friedrich Ebert** leader of the moderate wing of the Social Democratic Party and first president of the Weimar Republic.

**Euro** currency unit introduced in January 1999 for Germany and the ten other members of the European Monetary Union. The German mark is now officially just a denomination of the euro, which is scheduled fully to replace all national member currencies in July 2002.

**European Union (EU)** now an organization of fifteen European countries, in which West Germany or Germany has always played a key role. It originated as the six-member European Coal and Steel Community in 1951 and the European Economic Community in 1958, gradually enlarging its membership and becoming known as the European Community (EC) until the Maastricht Treaty of 1991 came into effect in 1993 and enlarged its authority and changed its name for most purposes to the EU.

**Federal Chancellor** *(Bundeskanzler)* head of the government, usually the head of the leading political party. Once the chancellor is selected by the Bundesrat, the chancellor can count on majority support most of the time. He has more authority than prime ministers in most parliamentary systems.

**Federal President** *(Bundespräsident)* head of state with largely ceremonial authority. The president is selected by a federal convention of all Bundestag deputies and an equal number of delegates selected by the state legislatures. The position is usually filled by senior politicians; activist presidents can use the office to influence public opinion.

**Federal Republic of Germany (FRG);** *Bundesrepublikdeutschland (BRD)* the current German state. Founded in 1949 and based on the American, British, and French zones of occupation, it was often known as West Germany until 1990. It acquired the states of the German Democratic Republic (GDR) in the unification of 1990.

**Frankfurt Parliament, 1848–9** the all-German parliament elected in 1848 that met in the city of Frankfurt and attempted to unify and reform the many German states along more liberal or democratic principles. Its inability to do so began a long period of authoritarian predominance in German states.

**German Democratic Republic (GDR);** *Deutschedemokratischerepublik (DDR)* German state based on the Soviet zone of occupation from 1949 until 1990, often known as East Germany.

**Guest worker** *(Gastarbeiter)* frequently used term for immigrant workers that underscores their temporary status in Germany.

**Oder-Neisse line** the contemporary eastern border of Germany with Poland along these two rivers.

**Otto von Hindenburg**   the junker former army officer who became the second president of the Weimar Republic and appointed Hitler as chancellor in 1933.

**Holocaust**   the Nazi attempt to kill all European Jews during World War II. An estimated 5.7 million Jewish people were killed, and other so-called undesirable people – including Roma, homosexuals, psychiatric patients, and the handicapped – were also targeted for destruction. A total of between 6 and 7 million people lost their lives. Auschwitz and Treblinka were two major death camps.

**Junkers**   the landed nobility of eastern Prussia. Their vast estates east of the Elbe River produced grain for Germany and the world market, but only by keeping agricultural laborers in near slavery. They formed the core of the Prussian state administration and of the Second Empire's administration and never fully accepted the legitimacy of the Weimar Republic.

**Kulturkampf (cultural struggle)**   the attempt by the Second Empire to break the authority of the Catholic Church in unified Germany by means of legislation, regulation, and the harassment of priests, mainly between 1871 and 1878. It reduced the church's authority in some areas, but generally sparked revival of political Catholicism and popular religiosity.

**Karl Marx**   founding thinker of modern socialism and communism. Born in 1818 in Trier, in the Rhine province of Prussia, he became involved in various German and French radical movements in the 1830s and 1840s. He wrote *The Communist Manifesto* (1848, with Friedrich Engels) and many other polemical and analytical works. The guiding personality in the Socialist International movement in the 1860s, he died in London in 1883.

**National Socialist German Workers' Party (Nazi Party)**   the fascist party taken over by Adolph Hitler in 1920–1. It became the largest political party in the Weimar Republic in the early 1930s, winning 38 percent of the vote in July 1932 and 33 percent in November. Hitler's appointment as chancellor in 1933 was followed by the end of the republic and the beginning of one-party Nazi rule until 1945.

**Prussia**   the North German state governed from Berlin by the Hohenzollern dynasty from 1701 that grew in military strength and gained control of most of what is now Germany and western Poland in the 18th and 19th centuries. It formed the core of the Second Empire in 1871. Subsequently a state within Germany, it was disbanded during the Allied occupation in 1947.

**Social Democratic Party**   Germany's oldest political party, generally on the left but recently similar in its political program to the Democratic Party in the United States. It emerged in the 1870s as a working-class protest party, and its main wing helped to found and frequently govern the Weimar Republic. It governed in West Germany alone or in coalition from 1966 to 1982 and returned to power in a reunified Germany in 1998.

**Social market economy**   the term for a tempering of the free market with concern for social consequences. It is based on a "social partnership" of business and labor, along with the state and banks, to shape politics and economics at the national, regional, and local levels in order to cushion and guide economic change.

**Two-vote ballot procedure**   the voting procedure to select delegates in the Bundesrat. The first vote is for a candidate to represent the voter's district. Half of the seats are awarded as a result. The second vote is for a party overall. The other half of the seats are distributed so that the overall seat shares for each party match the second-vote choices.

**Weimar Republic**   the German state and democratic regime that was formed after the fall of the Second Empire in 1919 and lasted until 1933. It was named for the city where its constitution was written. Bitter and polarized partisan competition from the communist left to the extreme nationalist right wing made it difficult for the moderate and mostly Social Democratic and Center Party governments to operate.

## STUDY QUESTIONS

1. Consider Germany in 1815. In what ways was it like the rest of Europe? How was it different?
2. Why were Germany's political institutions under the Second Empire authoritarian rather than democratic?
3. Why did the Weimar Republic fail to survive as a democracy?
4. What were the main features and policies of the Nazi regime?
5. How did the Allies reshape interests, identities, and institutions in occupied Germany from 1945 through 1949?
6. What were the major differences between the FRG and the GDR between 1949 and 1989?
7. How did Germany's interests, identities, and institutions change as a result of reunification in 1990?
8. What are the major political parties in the FRG?
9. What impact has the FRG had on Europe and the world since World War II?
10. How is the global context after 1990 affecting Germany?

# 4

# Japan

## ❧ Robert W. Bullock

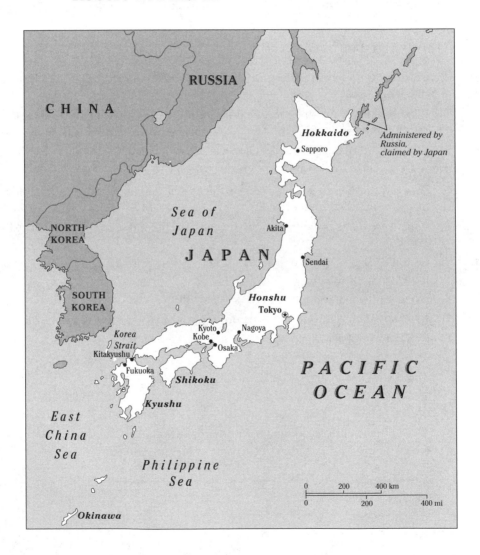

# INTRODUCTION

Japan has attracted considerable attention as the most successful of the formerly "backward" nations in becoming an industrial power. From 1955 to 1973, Japan's real (inflation-adjusted) growth rate averaged 9.8 percent. Even in the decade following the 1973 oil shock, growth remained 3.7 percent, the highest in the industrialized world. A great many studies have been devoted to discovering the "secrets" of Japanese success and have stressed, above all, industrial policy and the role of the powerful state bureaucracy in creating it.

In the 1990s, however, political instability and economic crisis – with growth averaging just 1.5 percent annually – have forced a rethinking of the "Japanese miracle." Analyses have swung from one extreme to the other as the image of yesterday's economic superstate has given way to stories of bureaucratic bungling and political corruption. Today, analysts risk underestimating the country's strengths in the present, just as we have overestimated them in the past.

In this chapter, we step back from the headlines to take a long, historical look at modern Japan. Specifically, the chapter stresses three themes that run through its history: bureaucratic dominance of policy-making even in a context of increasing democracy, pervasive state intervention in the economy and society, and the political foundations of Japan's catch-up development.

The third theme is perhaps the least obvious and most fundamental. In brief, my sense is that Japan's economic performance has attracted so much attention that it has crowded out the study of politics and obscured the political bases of late development. This narrow, economics-first bias in the literature remains pronounced even in the late 1990s. This chapter attempts to help correct this bias by re-situating the focus on Japan's economic performance in a truly *political* economy. Indeed, the very idea of modern Japan was formed in the crucible of international politics – to confront the threat of Western imperialism in the mid–19th century and to retain national independence. Today, when Japan is an advanced, powerful nation, it is easy to forget that catch-up development was never simply about getting rich.

A second, perhaps less heroic, sort of politics has also shaped modern Japan – the politics of contesting competitive, democratic elections. Following its defeat in the Pacific War (1941–5), Japan became a parliamentary democracy with universal suffrage and powerful socialist and communist parties. Rule by the conservatives – they became the Liberal Democratic Party (LDP) in 1955 – could no longer be taken for granted. First, if the Left were to win power, pro-business economic policy and the bureaucrats behind it would be among its first targets. Second, even as conservative hegemony began to assert itself, whether the LDP would *remain* the hegemon was always in doubt. For even as the Left threat receded, the conservatives' worst enemies became themselves – most conspicuously, in the fractious, intra-LDP battles for seats in Japan's multimember election districts. Long-term LDP dominance thus represents a contingent outcome, not an environmental constant, of postwar Japan. And while conservative dominance has provided the political stability necessary for long-term economic planning and industrial policy, it has depended on distributional policies – payoffs to political supporters – that threaten to undercut the economic miracle. The emphasis on distributional policy, most notably in rewarding Japan's politically powerful farmers, has only increased in the current context of poor economic performance and political flux.

The organization of this chapter is chronological: first, we briefly survey Tokugawa-era Japan (1603–1868) and explore in more detail the Meiji Restoration (1868), treated by most historians as the beginnings of "modern Japan." Then we trace Japan's political and economic developments to the turn toward militarism in the 1930s and the Pacific War. Following this, we turn our attentions to the postwar: the American occupation of Japan (1945–52), the importance of industrial policy and the bureaucracy, and the political foundations of rapid growth. Last, we survey the dramatic changes of the 1990s and attempt to put them into their historical context.

## THE BIRTH OF MODERN JAPAN

It may be hard to imagine today, but little more than a century ago, Japan was an isolated, feudal, predominantly agricultural society. The country was sealed off from contact with the outside world by government decree (only the Dutch, Koreans, and Chinese held limited trading privileges), frozen into rigid social strata, and governed, as in European feudalism, by local clans (han) that were self-governing, even as they paid tribute and owed allegiance to a central government known as the *bakufu*. The bakufu was originally a military government, one ruled by a shogun. Below the shogun were some 280 *daimyo,* or feudal lords, who ruled their own territories with considerable autonomy; the samurai (some 5 to 6 percent of the population), a warrior class that performed military and civil duties; the peasant masses (80 percent of the population), whose labors supported the daimyo and samurai and who were forbidden to leave the land; and at the bottom of the hierarchy, reflecting Tokugawa contempt for commerce and trade, the artisans and the merchants (10 to 12 percent of the population). Below this hierarchy existed another class: perhaps half a million "outcasts" – Japan's "untouchables" – who were associated with butchery, tanning, and other occupations considered "unclean" in Confucian terms and who were unrecognized as legal entities. The Tokugawa bakufu took power following nearly three centuries of nearly constant warring among rival clans. It kept the peace from 1603 to 1868.

Viewed from the outside, it seemed that the bakufu's collapse in the 1860s came quickly and with little warning. Foreign powers won access to Japan, and in short order the bakufu were overthrown. As one 19th-century observer put it, "The Tokugawa shogunate had [given] way to the irresistible momentum of a higher civilization."

In fact, however, internal pressures for change had long been building. Merchants, though at the bottom of the social scale, were accumulating wealth and de facto power over the daimyo and samurai. Clans in the south and west of Japan – notably Satsuma, Choshu, and Tosa – flourished during the Tokugawa peace, outpacing the rest of Japan economically and building formidable clan armies. These outlying regions chafed under centralized rule and were suspicious of bakufu weakness in the face of a mounting Western threat. Throughout Japan, agriculture, the mainstay of the feudal economy, was growing slowly but steadily in productive power; the overall economy was diversifying as small-scale industry – in textiles, food products, local handicrafts – expanded in rural as well as urban areas. By the start of the 19th century, some 40 to 50 percent of the population was literate and reading not only Confucian tracts and haiku but also newly translated books from the West – about politics and philosophy as well as science and engineering.

The Western threat, too, had been present for decades. The United States, United Kingdom, and Russia had been pressuring Japan to open commercial trade from the beginning of the 19th century. 1853 marked a watershed, however, with the arrival of American naval gunships under the command of Commodore Matthew Perry. Ignoring protests from Japanese forces, Perry sailed into Edo (Tokyo) Bay, demanded an audience with the shogun, and called for the opening of trade between the two nations. Perry returned with his infamous "black ships" in the following year and won American access to two ports. In 1858, American diplomat Townsend Harris concluded a trade treaty between Japan and the United States, enabling further trade increases. The European powers quickly followed with their own treaties. Earlier that year, as Japanese officials knew well, Britain and France had won a second opium war in China and were preparing their own naval expeditions to Japan, doubtless accelerating the agreements.

The Western threat proved to be not only military but economic as well. Foreign capital quickly sank deep roots in Japan's port cities following the trade treaties. Commercial treaties enforced extraterritoriality in Japan until 1899. Tariff autonomy was not fully achieved until 1910. Japan was thus unable to use border protection for its fledgling industries. To protect them, it was forced to devise other means, more on which below.

In short, there were many changes taking place beneath the surface of regime continuity. In this sense, late-Tokugawa Japan might be compared to the last years of the Soviet Union, the collapse of which in 1991 so surprised outside observers, Soviet specialists not least. There, Gorbachev's reforms and political changes in Eastern Europe may have provided the catalyst, but the chief causes of collapse were more long term in nature (see Stephen Hanson's chapter on Russia).

Thus the Western threat combined with internal transformations to produce Tokugawa collapse. The bakufu, to be sure, responded in the 1860s with a series of last-ditch reforms – including a more moderate leadership, an alliance with the imperial court, a new Western-style political cabinet, and military reforms – but these proved too little, too late.

Dissident samurai, especially in Choshu, began to target Western ships, provoking fierce counterattacks and learning a hard lesson about the superiority of Western armaments. In 1864, Choshu samurai (and a growing number of commoners, now allowed to carry weapons) marched against the imperial court in Kyoto. In 1866, the alliance between the bakufu and the court broke down, and Satsuma, the second largest han, allied with Choshu. That same year, the bakufu attacked the Choshu rebels even after many daimyo had refused to support the attack. Better trained and better armed, Choshu and Satsuma routed the bakufu forces.

Henceforth, the bakufu's collapse came quickly. The Satsuma and Choshu leadership organized a military coup during 1867–8. As the bakufu had begun its own program of military modernization, the rebels decided to move swiftly. They joined with anti-bakufu nobles in the court to demand a peaceful transfer of power to the young Emperor Meiji, who had just ascended the throne. Bakufu leaders agreed to do so at the end of 1867, fearing that a civil war would invite Western intervention and foreseeing a place for themselves in the new government. During the negotiations, however, bakufu representatives became aware of rebel divisions and decided to mount a new attack. Nonetheless, the bakufu's forces were easily defeated. In April 1868, they surrendered Edo (Tokyo) without a fight and handed over power to the rebels.

In the beginning, the Meiji restoration amounted to little more than a palace coup, with few casualties and the participation of just a few thousand troops. The rebels' goals, however, were revolutionary – not in the sense of implanting some new political ideology, like democracy or socialism, but rather, in effecting thoroughgoing reforms in order to preserve Japan's national autonomy. The catchphrase that best captured Meiji objectives was *fukoku kyohei,* or "rich nation, strong defense." The slogan did not celebrate liberty, equality, or the proletariat. Instead, it celebrated the nation itself.

The rebel leadership came largely from the ranks of the junior samurai, part of the hereditary warrior class. In other words, the revolt was led by a disaffected segment of the old elite – a trait that would become so common in 20th-century social revolution. And while there were of course differences of opinion, by all accounts these paled in comparison to what the rebels held in common: a dissatisfaction with bakufu rule, an anti-Western sentiment, and a commitment to modernizing reforms. Overwhelmingly, these men came from the domains of Satsuma, Choshu, Tosa, and Mito, which lay outside the bakufu power bases. These outer domains had experienced the greatest development of commerce and staple industries under the clan monopoly system, and in them, too, Western capital was the most deeply implanted.

It was these junior samurai who became the leaders of the new regime. By 1869, only a very few daimyo remained in government posts, with all key positions held by the former samurai. But if the new leaders were ex-samurai, the samurai as a class would soon be destroyed. The former warriors were pensioned off, replaced by a professional, conscript army, and then their pensions, too, were commuted as the state concentrated its resources on industrial development and defense. By the mid-1870s, the samurai were stripped of their last privileges. Their dispossession provoked a number of bloody, local rebellions, but these proved little threat to the new regime.

Although merchants may have had the most to gain from the end of Tokugawa, they played virtually no active role in the rebellion. This was no bourgeois revolution. Merchant interests were too closely intertwined with the daimyo aristocracy – via trade and growing daimyo indebtedness – to attack it directly. Moreover, in the last decades of the Tokugawa era, many merchants bought or married their way into samurai families as their financial clout grew. But if the merchants were unwilling to mount a frontal attack, a number of them extended financial backing to the anti-bakufu movement. This assistance aside, the Meiji restoration involved little popular participation and was, again, primarily a palace coup carried out by an element of disaffected elites.

Why was the movement called a "restoration?" Simply put, the intent was to emphasize links to the past as a way of legitimizing present-day changes – in other words, by "restoring" the emperor to rule after having been displaced by the shogun centuries earlier. But in fact, the emperor would remain something of a figurehead, with the imperial advisors wielding the real power. Emperor Meiji was just sixteen years old in 1868, limiting his powers still further.

Though reforms were halting at first, the new regime soon committed to achieving two far-reaching objectives: first, the introduction of a range of Westernizing reforms, which were intended less to make Japan *like* the West than to repel the West. These reforms closely related to the second, and primary, objective: the preservation of national integrity and independence. The two Meiji goals were well captured in a slogan of the time: *wakon yosai,* which translates as "Japanese spirit, Western methods." The growing Western presence in East Asia, both military and economic, imparted a growing urgency to all these measures.

Specifically, the new leadership pursued three sets of reforms:

1. State building: the creation of a centralized nation-state, including a modern military and a professional civil service.
2. Rapid development: the pursuit of economic self-sufficiency, including investment in military-related heavy industry.
3. Social transformation: the molding, via education and national ideology, of those who lived on the Japanese islands into a single Japanese people, one supporting and identifying with the new Japanese nation-state (rather than, e.g., one's family or village alone).

Meiji elites hoped they could achieve these ends while avoiding the "evils" of industrialization that afflicted the West, including materialism, individualism, revolts by the underprivileged, and calls for democracy. Though such threats to the Meiji state were never eliminated completely, they were quite successfully channeled and contained. Peasant revolts peaked in 1873 but by 1877–8 were few and inconsequential. Samurai resistance proved a greater (and bloodier) challenge but was put down by 1877. Political challenges to the regime, too, were more or less successfully contained (until the 1930s, that is).

Disposing of the daimyo, a considerably more powerful group, called for gentler means. These feudal lords were not toppled via confiscation of their estates, as in post-revolutionary France. Instead, they were provided with generous pensions and ordered to live in Tokyo, the new capitol. Both measures were intended to reduce the likelihood of resistance. Daimyo pensions were commuted into government bonds in 1876, enabling the more prominent among them to enter the small financial oligarchy almost overnight.

Among the other Meiji achievements:

■ The new regime abolished the old clan districts (the *han*) in order to destroy the territorial bases of the daimyo. Daimyo powers devolved upward, to Tokyo. All clan lands were turned over to the Emperor by 1870. Local leaders were (from 1884) appointed by the central bureaucracy.

- ■ A professional civil service was created, where entrance depended on passing grueling exams, not heredity or personal ties. The civil service was patronage free for all but the highest posts. To train a new class of bureaucratic elites, Japan's first university, Tokyo Imperial University, was founded in 1888.
- ■ The new leadership introduced universal primary education. At first, just sixteen months over four years was mandatory, but this was extended with time, reaching six years in 1907. The objective was less to create free, independent-minded individuals than to create a singular, unique *Japanese* people and to propagate Japan's "ancient virtues" of obedience, filial piety, loyalty to the emperor, and discipline – to spread, in short, an ideology of commitment to the new Japanese nation-state.
- ■ The regime created a national conscript army where before there had been clan armies manned by the hereditary samurai. A conscription law was introduced in 1873 and samurai privileges were gradually eliminated.
- ■ The state gave farmers ownership of land they tilled but at the same time introduced a land tax that heavily penalized the countryside. The tax, set at 3 percent of the land's assessed value, was designed to squeeze the peasantry in order to subsidize industry.

Perhaps the greatest Meiji achievement was the introduction of state-led capitalism and industrial policy. For with Meiji, Japan entered into a headlong drive to catch up economically with the industrialized West. The country's very survival depended on the rapid acquisition of foreign technology and industrial development. For the Meiji leadership, the fundamental purpose of economic activity was to preserve national autonomy and integrity – to avoid the fate of China, which was being carved up by the Western powers before Japan's eyes. China had once been a model for emulation for Japan, but by the mid–19th century, it became a warning of the consequences of remaining weak and divided (see Yu-Shan Wu's chapter on China).

The state leadership alone possessed the will and the capacity to develop heavy industry. Private capital, such as it was, preferred to stay in trade, banking, and credit, especially in the safe and lucrative field of government loans. Small capital remained largely in the countryside, attracted by high farmland rents (averaging nearly 60 percent of the tenant's crop), as well as in usury and local trade. And although the new regime actively recruited foreign technology and advisors, it limited the role of foreign capital to just two loans. Instead, it was the state itself that financed heavy industry, providing over one-third of all capital to private industry in the first three decades of Meiji. It remained the single largest industrial investor until World War I.

The vast majority of this capital came from tax revenues, especially from the land tax. The early Meiji regime was hard-pressed for funds, having inherited huge debts from the bakufu and with onerous new obligations (including daimyo and samurai pensions) as well. The land tax supplied some 80 percent of Meiji tax revenues in the late 1870s and nearly 70 percent in the late 1880s. It appears that the cultivator's net share of output actually decreased under Meiji, despite steady gains in agricultural productivity. There is an old Japanese saying that goes: "Peasants are like sesame seeds; the more you squeeze, the more that comes out." The phrase is Tokugawa vintage, but it applies even better to Meiji.

The state established experimental factories to produce cotton, cement, tile, sugar, glass, chemicals, and so forth. From the 1880s, however, most nonstrategic industries were sold to private interests at prices well below market. This fire sale enabled the large banking houses of the day to enter into modern, capital-intensive industry almost overnight. These houses would soon become known as the *zaibatsu* (financial cliques), which dominated the Japanese economy until the end of World War II. Still, governmental policies of subsidies and support were maintained, if not strengthened, even after state ownership was abandoned. Japan's infant industries needed these supports to survive, as the country's "unequal treaties" with the West prohibited the use of protective tariffs.

## Political Developments

However much Meiji elites hoped to limit social-political change, they were unable to prevent it entirely. The first political parties (all of which opposed the Meiji leadership) made their appearance in the 1870s, and the oligarchs prepared a constitution in 1889 that severely restricted the parties' conduct. A parliament, known as the Diet, was reluctantly created in 1890 to channel party activity into an organized forum, one holding only consultative powers. The emperor – meaning, in practice, his advisors – continued to hold national sovereignty and ultimate authority. He alone could give sanction to laws and it was his power to dissolve the Diet and call new elections. Government cabinets and the military reported to him, not to the Diet. Japan's first elections were held in 1890 under these restrictions. From the first, government-placed members were outnumbered by their opponents.

Despite the limits set on Diet powers, the parties turned out to have certain resources of their own. One potent weapon derived from Article 71 of the Meiji constitution, requiring that the House of Representatives approve the annual state budget. If it did not, the budget from the preceding year was to be used. The article had been designed to limit party influence but it soon had the opposite effect. Since budgetary growth was extremely rapid amid inflation and Japan's military buildup, Article 71 became a powerful weapon for the parties – especially during the Sino-Japanese war (1894–5) and the Russo-Japanese war (1904–5).

Political parties gained in influence as the Diet became institutionalized, and as the chief imperial advisors, the *genro,* began dying off in the early 20th century. In the teens, party cabinets (rather than "transcendental cabinets" appointed by the emperor) became the norm, and Japan saw its first elected (rather than appointed) prime minister from 1918 to 1921. Big business, growing rapidly with military contracts and a boom in exports, began to see the parties as new means with which to advance its interests and bought its way into politics. The two largest zaibatsu, Mitsui and Mitsubishi, became closely tied to the two main parties, the Seiyukai and Kenseikai. For bureaucrats, too, the parties became an alternative vehicle by which to advance their careers and to resist manipulation by the genro. In short, although Japan's political parties had begun with the marginal "people's rights" movements in the 1880s, they were at the very center of the establishment by the early 20th century.

We should stress that big business did not pursue an anti-state agenda, in the Diet or anyplace else. Japanese capitalists did not develop in opposition to the state. To the contrary, the zaibatsu were virtually a creation of the state and industrial policy. The defining political quality of the Japanese bourgeoisie has been less revolution than dependence. In fact, what liberal movement there was – in the people's rights movements noted above – was predominantly rural in origin.

There was political change at the mass level, too. At first, in 1890, suffrage was extremely limited, extended to just 1 percent of the population. But as economic growth continued, more and more of the male population became eligible to vote. In 1925, suffrage became universal – universal, that is, for all males over twenty-five. Socialist and communist parties began to appear, as did labor and tenant unions. The upshot was that the decade was by far the most socially and politically liberal that Japan had yet experienced.

By the late 1920s, however, there were troubling signs of instability. By the early 1930s, Japan's military leaders pushed aside the Diet to seize the center stage of national politics. To be sure, the military never became all-dominant in Japan. It was never able to introduce anything like the penetrating totalitarianism of Nazi Germany (although many ultranationalists certainly tried). Even Prime Minister Tojo was forced to compromise with the bureaucracy, economic interests, and the Diet. Nonetheless, as one scholar has observed, the military in this period enjoyed "a degree of intervention that the armed forces of most countries could achieve only by means of a coup."

## MILITARISM AND WAR (1931–1945)

How do we account for the failure of democracy and the rise of militarism? The so-called "Taisho democracy" of the 1920s was riven with faults. Catch-up development had brought in its train a range of social dislocations – rapid urbanization, growing labor and tenant disputes, socialist and communist parties, and so forth. All such opposition movements, and "dangerous thoughts" more generally, were enthusiastically targeted for suppression by the police, but suppression was only partial and sometimes proved counterproductive. The era also witnessed cabinet instabilities and frequent government turnover, deep political corruption, and almost constant scandals. The two main parties, the Seiyukai and Kenseikai, were popularly regarded as differing little in ideology or stated policies, as in the pockets of the big economic groups, the zaibatsu, and as heavily dependent on landlord interests, who worked to mobilize the rural majority vote. The zaibatsu, for their part, had image problems of their own. By the late 1920s, a dozen zaibatsu controlled some 80 percent of all enterprises in Japan. "Monopoly capitalism" and its extreme concentration of wealth presented an easy target for critics on both left and right. The Great Depression from 1929 significantly worsened these tensions and instabilities.

But we should stress above all the institutional problem: the fractured lines of political authority, the ambiguity of the Meiji constitution on just who ruled. The cabinet was responsible not to the Diet but to the emperor, but as the emperor, sacred and inviolable, stood "above" day-to-day politics, it was his unelected advisors, especially the genro, who wielded real power. And as these advisors began to die off, they left a power vacuum that was filled by the bureaucracy, the parties (for a time), and, increasingly, the military. At the same time, the army and navy both reported to the emperor, not the Diet, and either service branch could topple the cabinet by refusing to appoint a war minister. Both were thus subject to only limited control from above and had their own problems in maintaining discipline within the ranks. In short, there were too many political competitors at the top without, as the genro disappeared, a single dominant power that could play the hegemon.

With post–Meiji Japan's overriding pursuit of *fukoku kyohei,* with rapid military expansion, and with dramatic and decisive military victories over China in 1895 and Russia in 1905, the military's power and prestige were much enhanced. Amid frequent scandals and corruption in the Diet, the military claimed that it alone possessed the vision, authority, and expertise to rule Japan effectively. All evidence suggests that the public was inclined, if anything, to agree.

Yet even as the military's public standing grew, problems of internal order mounted. Increasingly, the military leadership could not control its own. Renegade junior officers – often from rural areas hard hit by the depression and motivated by ultranationalist ideology – were taking matters into their own hands, setting state policy by fait accompli and creating an atmosphere of uncertainty and terror. Though we cannot "blame" Japan's turn toward militarism on them alone – the evidence of civilian complicity is too great – such officers certainly helped to accelerate it. Some of the more notorious incidents:

- In 1928, junior officers in the Manchuria-based Kwantung Army (charged with patrolling the Japan-owned South Manchurian railway) assassinated Chang Tso-lin, the warlord ruling over Manchuria. They did so hoping (but failing) to extend Japanese control over Manchuria as a whole.
- In September 1931, Kwantung Army officers tried again, this time blowing up a portion of the railway and blaming the Chinese military in order to provoke a conflict. The army moved to occupy one Manchurian city after another and controlled most of eastern Manchuria by the end of 1931. The act went unpunished by Japan's civilian government, which proceeded to establish the puppet regime of Manchukuo.
- In May 1932, young naval officers assassinated Prime Minister Inukai Tsuyoshi, marking the end of party government in Japan.
- In July 1935, Major General Nagata Tetsuzan, head of the army's military affairs bureau, was hacked to death by an army lieutenant colonel.
- In February 1936, a small group of young army officers and 1400 troops assassinated three high officials, attempted (in vain) to assassinate the prime minister, and seized the center of Tokyo to demand (again in vain) direct rule by the emperor and what they called the "Showa Restoration," an ill-defined sort of military-led state socialism.

## The Pacific War

Japan's turn toward militarism and expansionism culminated in the war on China, invasion and occupation of East and Southeast Asia all the way to Burma to the west and nearly to Australia to the south, and from 1941, war on the United States as well. As terrible as the costs were to Japan and its neighbors – perhaps 15 million were killed in China alone – we must stress that Japan's interests were above all *strategic*. The war was not driven primarily by profits, and certainly not by aggression for its own sake. Needless to say, this explanation cannot be taken as a justification for Japanese aggression, nor should it be used to mask or legitimize the jingoism and "war fever" among citizens and elites alike.

Specifically, the army argued that expansion into Manchuria and other parts of China would help resolve Japan's economic and security problems. These territories would provide the home islands with an abundance of mineral and agricultural resources, while control of Manchuria would help guard against any Soviet advance. The navy, long critical of army policy, advocated a push to the south while defending to the north. Japan basically compromised by choosing both.

The turning point of the war – that is, the beginning of the end for Japan – was the 1940 decision to move south, despite recognition that this would invite war with the United States and United Kingdom. The main attraction was the Dutch East Indies, rich in petroleum and other natural resources. With it, Japan hoped to break through the "ABCD encirclement" – the tightening economic blockade by America, Britain, China, and the Dutch – and to regain economic autonomy. In short, the military chose to widen the war rather than submit.

If resource access was central to Japanese expansion, however, it also proved central to Japan's defeat. At the onset of the war against the United States, Japan possessed stockpiles sufficient for only limited military engagement. To continue the war for more than two years, planners knew they had to win control of Southeast Asia and be able to transport its resources back to Japan. By 1943, the successes of American submarines meant that ten times as much Japanese shipping tonnage was being sunk as was replaced by new construction. Japan's resource stocks plummeted and the war economy entered its decline. In the end, the Japanese economy was (in the words of a Japanese scholar) "twice destroyed – first by the blockading of imports, and second by the air raids."

Although the attack on Pearl Harbor, like Japan's other early victories, may have been a brilliant opening strike, Japan's leaders underestimated both U.S. resolve to enter the war and its industrial capacity to sustain it. However great they imagined Japanese spiritual advantages, and however many lives they were prepared to sacrifice, it was U.S. industrial power that proved decisive in the end.

The Pacific War claimed the lives of some 2 million Japanese people, including 400,000 civilians – a full 3 percent of the population. The United States suffered 100,000 military deaths in the Pacific. For both countries, the great majority of these losses came in the last year of the war, when Japan's defeat was already inevitable.

## THE AMERICAN OCCUPATION (1945–1952)

With the loss of the war, Japan was occupied by a foreign military for the first time in its history. Though nominally overseen by the four Allied powers, the occupation was in fact an American show. The United States alone had significant forces in the Pacific and was determined (as were Britain and France) to keep the Soviet presence minimal. In practice, leadership came less from Washington than from the Supreme Commander for the Allied Powers, General Douglas MacArthur, whose brash, larger-than-life manner and missionary zeal dominated the era. Indeed, the acronym for his title, SCAP, came to stand for both MacArthur himself and the occupation forces as a whole.

In other ways, too, the occupation represented an utterly novel experience. First, despite the ferocity of the Pacific War, it was conceived as a primarily peaceful, not punitive exercise – as an effort, at once arrogant and idealistic, to remake Japan into a peaceful, democratic ally through what MacArthur called a "controlled revolution." Occupation planners had learned well the lessons of Versailles and were determined not to impose unduly harsh conditions on postwar Japan.

At the same time, we should not simply assume that the changes effected under SCAP owed entirely to American efforts. It is true that occasionally the occupation introduced new changes, but more often it revived existing Japanese initiatives that had been thwarted in the past.

The occupation era is typically divided into two periods: First was a liberal, "New Deal" phase, where the primary aim was, in effect, to remake Japan in the American image. The second period has become known as the "reverse course," where there was less concern for democratization than for rehabilitating Japan as an economically and politically stable junior partner of the United States in the new cold war. I briefly discuss each below.

The occupation's initial objectives were for demilitarization and demo-cratization. The first proved easier than one might suppose. As Japanese journal-ist Kazuo Kawai noted, the real demilitarization had already been accomplished with Japan's overwhelming defeat. All that was left for the occupation authorities, he added, was "to dispose of the debris." For any number of reasons – exhaustion, what remained of the military chain of command, the discovery that the foreign soldiers were not the demons that wartime propaganda had claimed – local resis-tance to the American forces was almost nonexistent. Some 200,000 wartime offi-cials – from the military, police, political parties, and the Home Affairs Ministry – were purged from office. Article 9, the famous "peace clause" expressly forbidding Japanese military forces, was written into the new Japanese constitution (drafted by a handful of Americans over seven days).

Democratization, however, called for considerably greater efforts, and SCAP reforms concentrated on two objectives: first, the clear establishment of popular sovereignty in the Japanese people, via a popularly elected national Diet, to which the cabinet and prime minister were now directly responsible. After protracted debate, the United States decided not to charge the emperor as a war criminal but forced him to renounce his divinity in a 1946 radio address. The hope behind this course was that, as a *New York Times* editorial put it, "a discredited god would be more useful [to the occupation effort] than a martyred god."

Second, SCAP introduced a set of reforms to broaden political participation: Women were at last granted suffrage (helping to elect thirty-nine women MPs [members of parliament] into the first postwar Diet), the voting age was lowered from twenty-five to twenty, and a range of civil liberties along U.S. and European lines were included in the new constitution.

Left-wing parties and labor unions were not only legalized but also positively encouraged as a force to counter-balance the right. Hundreds of political prison-ers were freed, many becoming the nucleus of the new opposition movements. By 1949, 7 million workers (of 15 million total) had joined the labor unions. Japan now had one of the largest labor movements in the world, with a higher unioniza-tion rate than in either the United States or Britain. In electoral politics, too, the left rapidly gained in strength. In the February 1947 elections, the combined vote for leftist parties reached 49 percent, with 36 percent of the vote going to the Socialist Party (JSP) alone. From April 1947 to February 1948, the Socialist Party led a multi-party governing coalition – the only time, as it happened, the party would participate in government until 1994.

SCAP also pursued economic democratization, starting with the zaibatsu-dissolution program. However, under attack by U.S. business groups (complaining of "Scapitalism"), Washington itself began to question the wisdom of breaking up what had been the mainstay of Japan's economic success. In the end, the reforms were drastically scaled back, but not before 83 zaibatsu holding companies had been broken up and approximately 5,000 companies had been forced through some financial reorganization. The two largest zaibatsu, Mitsui and Mitsubishi, were broken into about 240 companies. Nonetheless, most of the former zaibatsu were able to reconstitute themselves during the 1950s and are known in their new guise as *keiretsu* (literally, economic groupings).

The most impressive successes in economic democracy were in the land reforms. In 1945, 70 percent of Japan's farmers were full or partial tenants and rural poverty was held to have been a key cause of militarism. Under the reforms, a 2.5-acre ceiling was declared on individual landholdings (7.5 acres in Hokkaido), with excess holdings to be sold to the tenants. From 80 to 90 percent of tenanted land changed hands, benefiting about 4 million farm families. The reforms served at once to eliminate landlords as a political and economic force and to transform the politically volatile tenant farmers into small property holders with a stake in the (capitalist) status quo. The land reforms are often seen as the occupation's biggest success. They are also a good example of reforms that were already underway and would have occurred in some measure even without the American presence.

In attacking the bases of militarism, however, SCAP missed some big targets, the biggest of all being the bureaucracy. Excepting the breakup of the Ministry of Home Affairs (home of the notorious "Thought Police"), the bureaucracy emerged from the occupation virtually unscathed. Of 1,800 civil bureaucrats dismissed in the purges, 70 percent were police or other Home Affairs officials. Most bureaucrats continued to be drawn from the same social background and training as before 1945. Administrative discretion remained wide, and direct control by elected officials over administrators was, if anything, diminished. Indeed, the bureaucracy's powers were considerably enhanced under American rule. The military was disbanded, the Ministry of Home Affairs broken up, and the political leadership purged, creating a power vacuum that remaining ministries were quick to exploit. Their powers grew further as SCAP imposed economic controls that far exceeded those of the wartime era. The economic ministries were given virtual directive powers over the economy.

Why was the bureaucracy spared? Probably the most important reason is that the United States lacked the personnel and language ability to govern on its own.

Instead, it relied heavily on the support of the existing Japanese civil service, notwithstanding its complicity in the wartime regime. A second reason, stressed by T. J. Pempel, was the influence of 1940s-era public administration theory, which approached the civil service as essentially "power neutral" and focused instead on bureaucratic "efficiency" and how to increase it.

## The Reverse Course

What many have called Japan's New Deal gave way to a more conservative phase from 1947 or 1948, one dubbed by Japanese critics as the "reverse course." The chief causes for the shift came from outside Japan: the birth of the cold war between the United States and the Soviet Union, the victory of the Chinese Communists over the Kuomintang in 1949 (and seen as inevitable by 1948), and Republican gains in the U.S. Senate in the 1948 elections. Within Japan, too, there was growing concern over the sluggish pace of economic reconstruction and fear that the Left had outgrown its role as a useful counterweight to become a threat in its own right. Finally, the United States was beginning to strain at the heavy cost of supporting Japan and had no intention of mounting a Marshall Plan for Asia. In 1947 alone, the cost of American aid to Japan exceeded $400 million.

We should note that some analysts, and General MacArthur himself, objected to the division of the occupation into liberal and conservative halves. MacArthur claimed that the change was one of agenda, not direction. Indeed, in March 1947, he declared the occupation a resounding success and called for early withdrawal of U.S. troops.

Nonetheless, there is no denying the change in occupation priorities from reconstruction to rehabilitation, and, arguably, from Japan as an end in itself to Japan as a means in the war against communism. Three critical changes signaled the shift:

1. First, SCAP initiated a crackdown on labor with a ban on a Japan-wide general strike (scheduled for February 1, 1947). Now the purge directive, first used to remove from office those behind the war, was redirected to target activists on the Left. In the "Red purge" of 1950, more than 10,000 union activists were dismissed and effectively blacklisted from industrial employment. SCAP made removal of such activists from positions of influence a condition for receiving substantial U.S. aid. Henceforth, an accommodation for labor would be reached, one that rewarded a minority of full-time manufacturing workers with permanent employment and steady wage increases, but where a majority of workers – women, part-timers, and those in small enterprises – enjoyed less favorable conditions. This divide-and-conquer strategy crippled the independent, private-sector union movement. Those few radical unions which sur-

vived were concentrated in the public sector (e.g., education, transportation, and government offices), not in the sectors that drove postwar growth.

2. In early 1949, SCAP introduced an austerity program to stabilize the Japanese economy. It soon became known as the "Dodge line," taking its name from its chief architect, Joseph Dodge, a Detroit banker who had overseen banking reforms in occupied Germany. Specific goals were to cut government budget deficits, halt inflation, and reverse the zaibatsu-dissolution program. As an economic program, the Dodge Line proved a quick success, but the procurements boom during the Korean War (1950–2), which meant more than $2 billion in contracts for Japanese firms, was even more important in stimulating economic recovery.

3. In August 1950, MacArthur authorized the formation of a 75,000-strong National Police Reserve to fill the gap created by occupation troops reassigned to Korea. Its title notwithstanding, the Reserve was a barely disguised military force. Article 9 simply meant that it would have to be called something else. This about-face suggested possible rearmament for Japan – despite that MacArthur had spoken as late as March 1949 of Japan as a "Switzerland of the Pacific." More, it touched off a long and peculiar pattern of exchange in which the United States would pressure its former enemy to remilitarize while Japan, citing a constitution written by American officials, would resist. Yoshida Shigeru, the prime minister for most of the occupation period, was the chief architect of this resistance. His vision of postwar Japan constituted what scholars would later call the Yoshida Doctrine.

The Yoshida Doctrine is probably the single best way to characterize the postwar Japanese political economy. We can summarize it as threefold:

1. Japan's chief objective is economic recovery and development; political and economic cooperation with the United States is a necessary condition toward that end. Once preoccupied with the search for autonomy, Japan should now content itself with a "subordinate independence" with respect to the U.S.

2. Japan should pursue only limited rearmament and avoid involvement in international political/strategic issues. It should avoid divisive domestic struggles over foreign policy – again, focusing its efforts on economic recovery and development.

3. To provide for domestic security, Japan should rely on U.S. bases in Japan – which the United States valued both as outposts against the spread of Asian communism and as a "cap in the bottle" to block any resurgence of Japanese militarism.

In the next two sections of the chapter, we focus on the core of the Yoshida Doctrine: postwar industrial policy and the economic bureaucracy which was behind it.

## INDUSTRIAL POLICY AND POSTWAR ECONOMIC SUCCESS

For many contemporary observers, postwar Japan's economic "miracle" consti-tutes "one of history's most overdetermined outcomes." The country's highly skilled labor force, its powerful economic conglomerates, its single-minded state bureaucrats, and, perhaps most decisive, its track record as a successful late developer together made postwar recovery a virtual certainty. But if this assess-ment seems obvious today, it would have been regarded as wishful thinking in the early postwar years. For a decade or more after Japan's defeat, the problem (as phrased by one occupation official) seemed "less how to keep Japan down than how to prop it up." Japan's traditional markets in Asia were gone, and trade spe-cialists at the U.S. State Department judged the country's economic prospects to be "seriously weak and vulnerable." As late as 1957, noted Japan scholar Edwin Reischauer observed, "The economic situation in Japan may be so fundamentally unsound that no policies, no matter how wise, can save her from slow economic starvation and all the concomitant political and social ills that situation would produce." At this point, all eyes were on not Japan but mainland China, which was mounting a major campaign of economic modernization.

Even today, any visitor to Japan will hear the familiar litany: Japan is an over-crowded "small-island nation," it possesses few natural resources, and it depends on international trade for its very survival. Although these weaknesses are easily exaggerated, there is real basis for anxiety. Although the United States was poised to handle Japan's military concerns in the postwar era, its economic problems were another matter altogether. Postwar Japan's "GNP nationalism" has been dri-ven by what many have perceived as an enduring, pervasive "psychology of inse-curity." To the extent that the postwar Japanese leadership has been motivated by ideological concerns, this is perhaps their centerpiece. And in this respect, we may consider postwar strategy as but a new expression of the pursuit of security and national autonomy that has marked Japanese policy from Meiji onward. What is different about the postwar, of course, is that this strategy no longer contains a significant military component. Militarism had been totally discredited with the 1945 defeat. It was also totally out of the question in the context of postwar Ameri-can hegemony.

Faced with economic uncertainties of a new order, Japan was not about to leave reconstruction to the vagaries of the invisible hand (never mind the whims of American advisors). Instead, postwar economic planners dusted off the policies they had drawn up in the 1930s. In particular, they recommitted themselves to the prewar "Yoshino-Kishi" line, which stressed development via steel, auto, chemical, and other heavy industries, not (as U.S. officials sometimes counseled) bicycles, children's toys, and cocktail napkins. These industries were considered the "strategic sectors" of the modern economy, the development of which would cre-ate spillover effects benefiting the economy as a whole.

In sum, prewar and wartime economic policies were not abandoned but intensified. In his pioneering study *MITI and the Japanese Miracle,* Chalmers Johnson traces the striking continuities – in people, policies, and institutions – across the "divide" of the war. The prewar period signified far more than mere "heritage" for postwar MITI; those who led the Ministry in the 1950s and 1960s were already on the job in the 1920s and 1930s.

There are a number of misconceptions about industrial policy. Let me first clarify what it is not:

First, it is *not* a question of *whether* the state should intervene in the economy. Governments intervene in virtually every market. Scholars ranging from Ronald Coase and Douglass North to Karl Polanyi and Peter Evans have argued that it is state intervention that makes markets work in the first place. The real question, then, is not whether intervention but what kind and with what consequences?

Second, industrial policy does not imply state ownership of industry and is not in itself antimarket. State-owned enterprises were tried during the early Meiji period but were sold off to private interests as it became clear that they suffered the worst pitfalls of state ownership (e.g., corruption, bureaucratism, inefficiency). The Meiji leadership adopted a new policy of collaboration with select private interests that were capable of adopting the new technologies and were committed to the common objective of *fukoku kyohei.* Needless to say, state service and personal gain are hardly incompatible. As the protagonist of Natsume Soseki's *Sore Kara* (And Then) put it, "If one can make as much money as father has by serving the nation, I wouldn't mind serving it myself."

Nor, third, does industrial policy in Japan dictate a "national champions" strategy (as it has, say, in France), where the state backs a single firm. In Japan, industrial competition is limited but not eliminated. The state might permit the existence of ten firms in a given industry, but not a hundred. The state has used incentives and constraints to induce private economic interests to move in the direction of state-defined ends.

Fourth, the state is not (or not necessarily) captured by industry. We have seen the willingness of the Japanese state to discipline not only labor, but business as well. Programs for industrial support and promotion can be extremely generous, but in return, international competitiveness is expected. Poor performance is punished and good performance rewarded via a combination of carrots and sticks.

Fifth, industrial policy is not the product of an omniscient "super-state," nor is it read off some ready-made blueprint for growth. Industrial policy is a moving target; it represents what is learned from trial and error, from progress and regress, by fits and starts. Any theories or formulas for Japanese economic success (and failure) have been devised only in retrospect.

With these caveats and conditions in mind, we can define industrial policy as the government's development, nurturing, and guidance of industry in pursuit of national goals – most obviously and importantly, the pursuit of national security. Industrial policy means the development of strategic sectors that serve the national interest – as defined in a narrow military sense, in a broader economic sense, or preferably, in both.

Industrial policy is fundamentally motivated by *political* concerns. Economic activity does not reduce to the aggregation of millions of individual, self-interested producers and consumers acting in free, impersonal markets. It is also a matter of national security. And MITI bureaucrats have lacked the confidence that market forces alone will produce the desired results in a timely manner.

Chalmers Johnson describes Japanese industrial policy as "market-conforming." What he means is that industrial policy does not quash market incentives (as in Soviet-style economic planning, for instance) but rather manipulates them to promote desired ends. A steel firm, for instance, might be favored with interest-free loans, whereas a pachinko parlor has to borrow at market rates (or worse, from private moneylenders charging usurious rates). Markets are used as means to achieve state interests; they are not held up as an end in themselves (as in neoclassical economic theory). Johnson explains: "Industrial policy is not an alternative to the market but what the state does when it intentionally alters incentives within markets in order to influence the behavior of producers, consumers, and investors." Far from rejecting the market mechanism, then, the economic bureaucracy exploits it.

Another way of understanding industrial policy is as affirmative action on behalf of specific, targeted industries. In this case, the aim is not to effect redistribution as compensation for past wrongs, as in race-based affirmative action in the United States, but to foster future growth – the development of industries seen by the bureaucracy as essential to the nation's long-term economic prosperity.

So how do bureaucrats know which industries are strategic? In the 1860s, the answer was staring Japan in the face – in the form of big, ironclad gunships, the infamous "black ships" of Commodore Perry. The answer to this question, then, was steel, shipbuilding, heavy armaments, railroads, and so forth. In the postwar, it became autos, electronics, computers. So long as Japan was playing catch-up, the identification of strategic industries was a relatively simple matter. It may be less simple in later stages, however.

But having a model to copy, a goal to achieve, is obviously no guarantee of success. Many are called, few are chosen. Alexander Gerschenkron tells us that copying first-world means – that is, trying to behave like 18th-century England – will not suffice in late development. Gerschenkron argues that the desire to match first-world outcomes requires, for the would-be late developer, a qualitatively different strategy for getting there. In brief, what was attainable via slow, decentralized capital accumulation by private economic actors in England demanded powerful industrial banks in 19th-century Germany and action by the state itself in 20th-century Russia. In Gerschenkron's schema, Japan would probably lie somewhere near Russia at first, with success over time pushing it in the direction of Germany.

For Japan, as for Gerschenkron, the control of economic surplus – capital – is at the very center of economic development. Japanese industrial policy has centered around raising capital, deploying it in select industries, and imposing "performance standards" on its use. Because development is an ongoing process, not a one-shot deal, firms are less likely to "take the money and run" than to try to play well, stay in the game, and reap the long-term rewards of doing so.

Capital controls remained a key industrial-policy tool in the postwar era. During the 1950s, the state-created Japan Development Bank (JDB) alone provided 22 percent of new capital to industry. And while this share has declined rapidly over time, the size of a given loan mattered less than its "indicative" effect. That is, a state loan of any size has amounted to a MITI seal of approval for a given firm and/or sector. By contrast, the stock market has remained of limited significance, with the great majority of shares never traded but rather held as "mutual hostages" by closely related firms. In the 1950s, nearly 80 percent of all new capital came from banks, not the stock market.

In addition to capital controls, tax policy and border protection have also been central industrial-policy tools. Targeted firms have been favored with tax reductions and exemptions and accelerated depreciation on new investment. Again, MITI has used such perks to encourage rapid investment in targeted firms and industries. Naturally, under such "hothouse" conditions, any business would want to invest all the capital it could get. But while the bureaucracy created a condition of artificially low prices on investment (through subsidies, protection, and low interest rates), it provided these perks *on a discretionary basis* to select firms and sectors. Other firms were not necessarily blocked from making their own investments; instead, they faced considerably higher costs or red tape in doing so.

Many analysts argue that over time, with postwar Japan's developmental success, industrial policy has declined considerably in importance. By its very achievements, in this view, MITI has succeeded in putting itself out of a job. Japanese companies have become rich and increasingly able to rely on internal financing; they have internationalized their operations and moved beyond the reach of MITI; and international pressure, especially from the United States, has forced Japan to reduce its trade barriers.

All of these changes are real and important. They have reduced the coercive aspect of industrial policy and, no doubt, its overall importance as well. They have not eliminated it, however. A range of recent studies on topics as varied as declining industries, computers, telecommunications and financial services, Japanese foreign aid, and MITI-organized collective action confirm that the economic bureaucracy retains a variety of industrial-policy tools with which to shape economic development. To be sure, the bureaucracy is not always right and it certainly does not always win, but industrial policy has not disappeared. What has changed is the toolbox, which now has a few more carrots and a lot fewer sticks.

But even as the coercive powers of the state have declined, however, criticisms of industrial policy as outdated and counterproductive have only mounted, especially during the low-growth 1990s. The most damning charges come from economists, notably from the "public choice" school, who argue that industrial policy carries inherent risks. First, no single actor, let alone a state bureaucracy, can predict or control market behavior. Any such intervention is doomed to fail, especially as an economy grows in size and complexity. Second, industrial policy functions to socialize the risk of investment (where costs are borne by society, not the investor alone), thus encouraging overinvestment and excessively risky investment ("moral hazard"). Third, industrial policy is likely to devolve into subsidies that are "consumed" by recipients rather than invested for developmental purposes. These criticisms boil down to one thing: monies that are supposed to serve the public interest likely end up being used for someone's private interest. Leaving economic decisions to the free market is less risky and more efficient.

On all counts, the successful application of industrial policy stands or falls with bureaucratic excellence. It depends on bureaucratic commitment to serving the nation (rather than, e.g., lining its own pockets); bureaucratic insulation from election-minded politicians (who might prefer using industrial policy to reward their supporters rather than to promote growth); and the readiness to hold recipients of industrial policy accountable to performance standards. We address these concerns in the next section, in our review of the Japanese bureaucracy.

## THE JAPANESE BUREAUCRACY

The importance of industrial policy in modern Japan highlights the centrality of the bureaucracy as well. Japan's bureaucrats have provided guidance for the overall economy, drawn up most of the laws (notoriously vague, maximizing bureaucratic discretion), generated virtually all the information used in policy debates, and held considerable informal powers (known as "administrative guidance") over the private sector as well. Today, however, some claim that the bureaucracy has become the problem, not the solution, amid mounting charges of incompetence, irrelevance, and corruption.

As with industrial policy, we should first dispense with some misconceptions about the Japanese bureaucracy, the economic ministries in particular:

First, bureaucratic power is not raw, coercive power. At any time, there are perhaps 18,000 elite civil servants in the Japanese bureaucracy, far fewer than in other advanced countries. The picture is the same when we look at total numbers of all (including non-elite) civil servants. In 1990, the Japanese bureaucracy employed 8.8 workers per 100 citizens, one-third the figure for the United Kingdom and France and one-half that of the United States and (West) Germany. Japan is also the only advanced industrial country where this figure has appreciably decreased over time.

Nor, second, does bureaucratic power derive from massive budgets. MITI's budget, for instance, represents a tiny share of the economy and is indicative of what some have called Japan's "minimalist state." That share is minuscule compared to ministries in the West, and compared also to Japan's "distributional" ministries, such as the Ministry of Construction and Ministry of Agriculture, which wield great power in their own jurisdictions but are weak compared to MITI or the Ministry of Finance.

Rather than brute, coercive force, Chalmers Johnson and others stress the *selective* nature of state intervention. A good example is the "indicative planning" function noted above, where even a small MITI-arranged loan serves as a seal of approval for additional private investment. Indeed, recent scholarship stresses the coordination function of industrial policy (e.g., MITI organization of industry cartels and joint research and development projects), which is practically costless.

Why, then, is the bureaucracy so strong? First, we must stress the early institutionalization of the bureaucracy, well before the creation of the Diet in 1890 (which, as we have seen, was intentionally made weak to limit party powers). With it, the oligarchy hoped to create an additional power base through which it could retain control of government. The oligarchs got more than they bargained for, however, as bureaucratic elites began to take on powers and interests of their own. The bureaucracy's powers expanded further with the Pacific War and the introduction of national economic controls. They did so again with the occupation and the focus on economic reconstruction.

Even today, the bureaucrats remain among Japan's "best and the brightest," having passed extremely competitive entrance examinations (only 1 to 3 percent succeed) and having been educated, overwhelmingly, at the Department of Law of Tokyo University, the most prestigious faculty in Japan's top-ranked university. Ministry organization is Weberian, with merit-based recruitment and promotion, high social prestige and internal esprit de corps (bureaucrats work in the same ministry for their entire careers), and insulation from political meddling in internal ministry affairs. These "internal organization" characteristics constitute a second source of bureaucratic autonomy and strength.

A third source of bureaucratic power derives from state-society ties: the dense networks that connect the ministries to key societal interests, enabling information exchange, policy feedback, and consensus making. Examples of these ties include policy groups, industry associations, and the placement of bureaucrats in private companies upon their retirement from the civil service *(amakudari).* Amakudari postings are both lucrative for the ex-bureaucrats and useful as ministry conduits for the firms that hire them.

The importance of state-society cooperation is obvious. If the private sector ignores or resists bureaucratic planning and coordination, any plan for development, however brilliantly conceived, will be doomed from the start. The salience of these ties in Japan has provoked a spirited debate over the relative importance of private actors and state bureaucrats in driving growth and, analogously, the relative importance of politicians and bureaucrats in setting policy.

At the same time, it is precisely the importance of state-society ties that makes them so problematic. In short, how can we be sure that ties that are supposed to be developmental are not in fact predatory or rent-seeking? Scholarly progress on this front has been extremely limited. One recent survey confesses that there is "still little understanding of what distinguishes developmental from non-developmental networks." Given this confusion, it is no wonder that the 1990s – during which state-society ties seemed correlated with economic crisis, not growth – have sown such doubts. New stories of bureaucratic corruption have only exacerbated these doubts, as we shall see later.

## THE POLITICS OF CONSERVATIVE DOMINANCE

When we turn to electoral politics, the enormous literatures on industrial policy, the bureaucracy, and the developmental state do not, unfortunately, take us very far. Some political scientists argue that in Japan, electoral politics are practically irrelevant. As Chalmers Johnson puts it in his celebrated dictum, "politicians reign, but the bureaucracy rules." That is, politicians may be useful as figureheads, but the real business of government remains firmly in the hands of the bureaucratic elite. In a number of recent accounts, politicians go from being irrelevant to becoming a serious liability for the developmental state. Here, the "structural corruption" of electoral politics threatens not only to delegitimize Japanese democracy but also to undermine the developmental state itself.

Such accounts, however, understate the place of politics in postwar Japan. They discount both the importance of conservative political dominance for the bureaucracy and the economy and the difficulties and uncertainties in achieving and maintaining that dominance. Even granting that the bureaucracy is composed of the best and the brightest and that it dominates policy-making, there is one thing it can never do: win elections and control the Diet.

In the postwar era, winning elections became more essential than ever. Under U.S.-imposed occupation reforms, Japan became an electoral democracy, with popular sovereignty, universal suffrage, a secret ballot, and regular, competitive elections. However great the differences between reigning and ruling, stable, pro-business, conservative control of government was a *necessary condition* for development as conceived by big business and the bureaucracy. Government by the Left, in contrast, threatened redistributional policies (e.g., high corporate taxes, new welfare spending, support for labor unions) and nationalization of key industries, which would have undermined the bureaucracy's economic plans.

And while today, one might well imagine Japan's long-term conservative dominance (like rapid growth) to have been "overdetermined," few would have thought so in the early postwar years. As noted, support for leftist parties reached 49 percent in the February 1947 elections. Internationally, communist victory in China and the outbreak of the Korean War brought the cold war to Asia, adding credence to the Left's claims that history was on its side. Both developments raised fears of the spread of Asian communism to Japan in the near term, not in some distant future. Uncertainty and insecurity, not the complacency of unassailable dominance, marked conservative thinking of the day.

Further, the pursuit of rapid growth never sufficed to win votes for the conservatives (and the LDP platform had little else to distinguish itself). First, in the early postwar years, double-digit growth was only a fantasy; even recovery looked to be a long way off. But in the meantime, elections would have to be won somehow. Second, even when rapid growth was underway from the late 1950s, it carried its own political contradiction: Development spurred the growth of the urban middle classes, among the least likely of any social groups to vote conservative. In fact, the years of highest economic growth, the mid- and late 1960s, proved also to be the years of the LDP's most precipitous electoral declines. Faced with this social-structural dilemma, some party strategists predicted defeat by the Left within the decade.

Indeed, Japan's postwar conservatives faced fundamental difficulties from the very outset. Their core base, as for any conservative party, was but a small minority – society's upper strata, whether defined in terms of class or status. In order to win elections, their first task was to cultivate additional, mass-support bases.

Options for doing so were limited, however. Rural landlords, the mainstay of prewar conservative electoral politics, had been expropriated in the land reforms. Most of the labor movement was left-dominated and economic reconstruction depended in any event on low industrial wages. The urban middle classes were only inchoate and politically weak, and they too tended to vote left. Under these conditions, the farming communities and the small-business districts of the cities represented the conservatives' only hope.

Winning the farm vote was especially important. Following the land reforms, the new masses of smallholder farmers constituted a swing vote of huge proportion. Nearly 40 million people – almost half of the electorate and twice the size of the industrial labor force – lived on farms. To win power through elections and to pursue the policies of reconstruction, the conservatives had only one real option: winning the farmers first.

The conservatives' strategy for doing so was exactly what Samuel Huntington would advocate for developing countries a decade later: organize the farmers after conservatizing land reforms, marginalize and isolate urban interests and labor, and use the political space thus gained to consolidate the new regime and focus on development. By the mid-1950s, the bargain had been cast; henceforth, agricultural support for the conservatives would be significantly and consistently higher than the national average. The land reforms, significant increases in farm subsidies and the rice price in the early 1950s, and farm cooperative consolidation (aided by massive state subsidies) served as key instruments of incorporation. Through similar processes of organization, incorporation, and payoff, the LDP did much the same for small business. Together, the two sectors accounted for three-quarters of LDP support in the late 1950s and remained nearly half in the late 1980s. Throughout, they have served as the party's "social base" – its core of committed supporters.

Now, why have these social bases been so critical in Japanese politics? In brief, their importance owes to Japan's multi-member electoral district system; the chronically weak grassroots organization of political parties, especially the LDP; and the organizational strategies that have evolved to mobilize the vote.

Prior to the 1994 electoral reforms, Lower House representatives were elected in single, non-transferable vote (SNTV), multi-member districts. (Japan's Upper House wields considerably less power and is not discussed here.) In 1993, the last time the system was used, 129 districts elected 511 members. That is, each voter cast a single vote for a specified candidate, and each district elected between 2 to 6 candidates for terms of up to four years. Because each district elects 2 to 6 representatives, strong parties will run a plurality of party candidates in any given district. In order to win a Diet majority, a party needs to win at least 256 seats (of 511 total) across 129 districts. This means that it must not only defeat other parties, but also control intra-party competition in order to maximize the number of winnable seats per district.

Intra-party competition clearly lowers incentives for the individual candidate to campaign on party ideology and issues. Campaigning on the LDP platform, such as it is, may distinguish a candidate from other parties' candidates, but not from other LDP figures running in the same district. Thus LDP candidates seek other ways to distinguish themselves: constituency services, connections to local and Tokyo elites, and provision of such particularistic goods as public works and subsidies. This emphasis on material goods and connections significantly raises the costs of winning and staying in power. Although data relating to illegal expenditures are necessarily suspect, the cost of Japanese election campaigns appears to be orders of magnitude higher than in the United States.

In addition to maximizing the party vote, the party must also work to ensure that no single candidate gets too large a share of it. Because votes are non-transferable, a dominant candidate may attract more votes than necessary to win a seat, thus jeopardizing the chances of other party candidates running in the same district. To avoid this problem of "wasted votes," the party works to divide the vote among several candidates. In Japan, this is done via individual candidates' support networks, which the party leadership further supports through the generous provision of "pork."

These networks are known as *koenkai,* or personal political machines, organized by individual LDP members. Gerald Curtis defines the koenkai as "a mass membership organization with the function of organizing large numbers of the general electorate on behalf of the candidate." Koenkai are especially prevalent in districts with long-standing, close-knit, conservative-tending communities, most notably farming and fishing villages. They work less well in urban districts, where the electorate is too big, the economic structure and policy interests too diverse, and social intercourse too fragmented to sustain what is essentially a community-based social club.

To organize a koenkai, a politician starts close to home – organizing friends, relatives, local politicians, farm coop officials, and other "local notables." The typical MP spends much of his or her time in the home district, often returning from Tokyo each weekend to meet with constituency members. In the LDP, the average MP presides over 50 to 80 local constituent organizations, ranging from sports clubs and current-events discussion groups to women's clubs and elderly organizations. Maintaining these organizations is obviously time-consuming. It is also expensive, with koenkai expenses coming largely out of the MP's pocket.

The daily schedule of a typical Diet member revolves less around policy debates or Diet sessions than weddings, funerals, and coming-of-age ceremonies – what, in Japanese, are known collectively as *kankonsosai.* A 1989 *Asahi Shimbun* newspaper survey found that a politician attends an average of 9.6 weddings and 26.5 funerals each month. It is not unheard of for an MP to attend more than 100 funerals in a single month. And no one, least of all a national politician, goes to these events empty-handed. Keeping up with these day-to-day affairs, and keeping the all-important lists of local supporters, are perhaps the most important functions of the koenkai.

Probably the most famous koenkai of all was the *Etsuzankai,* Tanaka Kakuei's famed koenkai in Niigata Prefecture. In its prime, this massive organization had 92,000 members on the rolls, with all dues paid by Tanaka. And rather than, say, broadcasting Tanaka's views on the issues, the Etsuzankai devoted itself to good works: it hosted weddings, sponsored funerals, found jobs for its members, sponsored weekend trips to the spa, helped to settle local disputes, and served as an enormous *paipu* ("pipe") for pumping government subsidies into the local economy. In return for this political largesse, Etsuzankai members were expected to show their gratitude in appropriate ways – most appropriately of all, by support-ing their patron on election day.

This organizational strategy has worked brilliantly for the LDP, especially in rural areas and small cities. Its importance has increased dramatically over time. In 1976, just 14 percent of the electorate belonged to koenkai. By 1991, the share was 35 percent of the electorate and 44.6 percent of LDP supporters. Throughout, agriculture and small business have remained by far the most over-represented socioeconomic groups. The koenkai vote is the "hard vote" – the committed core of the LDP's support base.

But if koenkai have proved successful for individual politicians, they have also imposed costs on the party as a whole and the country as well. Most obviously, koenkai and the particularistic, pork-barrel politics on which they thrive cost a lot of money. A 1990 survey by Japan's National Diet Library found that Japan's per-capita election spending exceeded that in the United States by four to one. Consis-tent with these estimates, each LDP candidate spent $3 million to $12 million on his or her campaign in the elections that year.

Japan's "money politics" is fundamentally driven by political institutions: the electoral district system and the koenkai that have proliferated within it. In elec-toral systems that discourage campaigns based on issues or ideology and pit members of the same party against one another, money and connections move to the very center of political power. In other words, politicians behave this way less because they lack moral scruples or ideological principles than because that is what the system rewards. Whatever a politician's goals, he or she cannot pursue them without getting elected first.

## JAPAN IN THE 1990s: THE END OF THE DEVELOPMENTAL STATE?

It is not, or not only, Japan's poor economic performance that is so worrisome today. It is also that the very bases of the developmental state – the LDP and the bureaucracy – have experienced unprecedented problems of their own. For the LDP, these problems include loss of power in 1993 and a new electoral system that has, if anything, increased the costs and confusion of electoral campaigns. The bureaucracy, for its part, is reeling from unprecedented charges of corruption and growing public suspicion that bureaucratic self-interest may be eclipsing service to the nation.

### Electoral Reform

In July 1993, the LDP lost control of government for the first time in its history. Ozawa Ichiro and Hata Tsutomu, who had broken from the LDP with 42 followers earlier that year, put together an eight-party coalition (including the Japan Socialist Party [JSP], which jettisoned nearly all its ideological principles in order to join the government) with Hosokawa Morihiro as prime minister. It was the first government not led by the LDP since 1955. The new government advanced a reformist-conservative agenda and policies catering more to the "new middle classes" of urban Japan than to the old rural bases of the LDP.

In the end, however, most of what was billed as the "Hosokawa revolution" never really happened. Deregulation, market liberalization, pro-consumer policies, checks on bureaucratic power – much was promised and little delivered by the new coalition. The coalition collapsed and in June 1994, after ten months in the opposition, the LDP was back in power, now in coalition with the small Sakigake party and the conservatives' old nemesis, the JSP.

The Hosokawa government did succeed at one thing, however: It passed an electoral-reform package in January 1994, the first reforms to the electoral system since its 1947 introduction. Stated objectives behind the reforms were to reduce the role of money in politics and to encourage more issue-based campaigning – and ultimately, the emergence of two main parties, as in the United States and the United Kingdom. Main reform provisions included:

- 300 single-member districts and 200 proportional-representation seats in 11 regional districts.
- Substantially reduced malapportionment (which had favored rural districts).
- New limits on campaign contributions to individual politicians, with all other contributions going to political parties.
- $300 million in new public funds for political parties.

While it is likely to take several elections for the reforms' effects to become evident, at this point we have the results for just one: the Lower House election of October 18, 1996. Some preliminary observations may be in order:

First, and above all, we must stress the resurgence of the LDP. The party won 239 seats, going well beyond the 211 it had going into the election. Within a year, it would increase its share to a majority by wooing independents and poaching on other parties. Although the era of total LDP dominance may be over, no other party comes close to challenging it.

Second, the old conservative election strategies continue to work well under the new system. LDP candidates relied heavily on the tried-and-true methods of pork, the koenkai, and the farm vote. What is more, the cost of running election campaigns seems, if anything, to have increased.

Third, the election confirms the continued decline of the Left. The numbers of Socialist Party MPs were halved in the 1993 election and they were halved again in 1996. Once a serious threat to the LDP, the party was reduced to just 15 MPs in the Lower House and sat on the brink of extinction. Communist Party gains partly offset these losses, but overall, there are considerably more conservatives in the Diet today than at any other time in the postwar era.

Fourth, the election documents the eclipse of the "reformist conservative" threat. Ozawa Ichiro and his party lost four seats in the election after stressing the need to make big gains in order to mount a credible challenge to the LDP. Indeed, having failed to do so, Ozawa and his followers would choose in late 1998 to return to the fold – to enter into formal coalition with the LDP.

Fifth, we see the continued increase of the urban "floating vote." Despite extensive media coverage of the new election system, voter turnout was under 60 percent, the worst of the postwar. Turnout was lowest, around 50 percent, in large cities, a full eight points below previous lows. Disoriented by political instability and disgusted by chronic scandals, 35 percent of voters today say they do not support any political party. Faced with this crisis of confidence, the LDP has had little choice but to embrace its old constituents, especially the farmers, with new enthusiasm.

## Bureaucratic Corruption

Although the Japanese people have long been inured to corruption in party politics, corruption in the ministries is another matter. Even if bureaucrats are sometimes resented for their power, arrogance, and high-handedness, they have generally been accorded a grudging respect as a meritocratic elite and as guardians of the public interest. As we have seen, too, it is bureaucratic excellence and autonomy that have served as the foundation of industrial policy and the developmental state.

In the 1990s, however, troubling stories of bureaucratic corruption and incompetence emerged, undermining public confidence in government and, many fear, the developmental state itself. Some recent examples:

- Due to gross negligence by drug makers and the Ministry of Health and Welfare (MHW), nearly 400 hemophiliacs were treated with untreated blood and contracted AIDS. About 2000 more are HIV-positive. Though the blood transfusions took place in the 1980s, the cover-up was not exposed until 1997.
- Okamitsu Nobuharu, a former MHW vice minister, was charged with accepting a 60 million yen ($600,000) bribe and other gifts from a nursing-home contractor seeking ministry subsidies. Seven other MHW officials also came under investigation. Okamitsu is the highest-level bureaucrat to have been arrested in the postwar era.
- In 1995, a serious radiation leak occurred at the Monju nuclear reactor and was covered up by Science and Technology Agency officials.
- Media investigations have uncovered the ingrained practice of *kankan settai*, or the wining and dining of national bureaucrats by local officials hoping to win greater local budgets. In 1997 alone, it was estimated that some 30 billion yen of public monies was used in this manner.

Scandals have even surfaced involving the key economic ministries:

- In 1995, Yoshio Nakajima, the head of the Ministry of Finance's (MOF's) Institute of Fiscal and Monetary Policy, was dismissed for his ties to a leading player in a credit-union scandal.
- In 1996, six senior officials at MITI, including the vice minister, were given sanctions ranging from reprimands to salary cuts for breaking conflict-of-interest rules in their dealings with a shady oil trader.
- In Spring 1997, several bank inspectors at MOF were arrested for illegal entertaining by banks in return for advance notice of inspections.

These incidents, and the poor economic performance that has accompanied them, have brought unprecedented challenge to the bureaucracy and the bureaucratic-dominance thesis. Perhaps the best and the brightest have been getting greedy. Or maybe, some wonder, they have just started to get caught. In this context, proposals for wide-ranging administrative reforms have taken on a new urgency, and yet political commitment to the reforms is suspect and bureaucratic resistance remains severe. As of 1999, it appeared that with the important exception of MOF, which has lost exclusive jurisdiction over the banking and securities industries, administrative reform is likely to change bureaucratic practices by little.

## CONCLUSION

This chapter has attempted to put Japan's late development in its political and historical context. Economic growth neither began with the postwar nor is it "miraculous" in the sense of being beyond all explanation. Politically, Japan has undergone a long-term trend toward democratization, but this trend was interrupted rather significantly during the 1930s and 1940s. Even today, bureaucratic dominance and long-term, one-party rule pose serious questions regarding the depth and meaning of Japanese democracy.

None of this, however, made for any sort of "Japanese model" at the outset. The patterns and successes of Japan's late development have become clear only in retrospect, coming after what one scholar has described as "one of the most painful passages to modernity any nation has ever had to endure." More generally, as Gerschenkron has argued, "There are no four-lane highways through the parks of industrial progress. The road may lead from backwardness to dictatorship and from dictatorship to war." While Japan's troubles in the 1990s were not quite so dramatic as this, they too remind us of the contingency of development.

And yet, even if successful development was not foreordained and economic policies were not mapped out in advance, state interests have been clear and explicit: development as a political objective in order to catch up with and defend against Western powers. This goal has also been manifest in an enduring ideology of Japanese uniqueness and self-sufficiency, as well as in the dominance of a bureaucratic elite over state policy.

## BIBLIOGRAPHY

Curtis, Gerald L. *Election Campaigning Japanese Style.* New York: Columbia University Press, 1971.

Dower, John W. *Embracing Defeat: Japan in the Wake of World War II.* New York: Norton, 1999.

Duus, Peter. *The Rise of Modern Japan.* Boston: Houghton-Mifflin, 1976.

Gerschenkron, Alexander. *Economic Development in Historical Perspective.* Cambridge, Mass.: Harvard University Press, 1960, pp. 5–30.

Gluck, Carol. *Japan's Modern Myths: Ideology in the Late Meiji Period.* Princeton, N.J.: Princeton University Press, 1985.

Johnson, Chalmers. *MITI and the Japanese Miracle: The Growth of Industrial Policy, 1925–1975.* Stanford, Calif.: Stanford University Press, 1982.

Norman, E. H. *Japan's Emergence as a Modern State.* New York: Institute of Pacific Relations, 1940.

Pempel, T. J. *Regime Shift: Comparative Dynamics of the Japanese Political Economy.* Ithaca, N.Y.: Cornell University Press, 1998.

Scalapino, Robert A., and Junnosuke Masumi. *Parties and Politics in Contemporary Japan.* Calif.: 1962.

Waswo, Ann. *Modern Japanese Society, 1868–1914.* New York, Oxford, 1996.

## IMPORTANT TERMS

**ABCD encirclement**   the economic embargo of Japan by America, Britain, China, and the Dutch. The embargo significantly worsened Japan's access to natural resources and led Japan to widen the Pacific War beginning in the late 1930s.

*Amakudari*   literally meaning "descent from heaven," the phrase refers to the retirement of elite bureaucrats from the civil service into lucrative, private-sector positions.

**Article 9**   the "peace clause" of the Japanese constitution, in which Japan renounces war and prohibits the existence of armed forces. Nonetheless, ambiguous wording and cold war pressures led to the buildup of "self-defense forces," beginning in 1950.

**Commodore Matthew Perry**   the American navel officer who led the "black ships" into Edo (Tokyo) Bay in 1853 to present the U.S. demand for the opening of trade. The black ships have been a symbol of external pressure on Japan ever since.

*Daimyo*   the feudal lords of the Tokugawa era. The daimyo ruled their own territories *(han)* but owed allegiance and paid tribute to the central government.

**Diet**  Japan's parliament, created in 1890. The Diet's powers grew over the next four decades but remained limited by the Meiji constitution. Although Japan's postwar constitution mandates parliamentary sovereignty, the Diet's authority has remained overshadowed by the powerful state bureaucracy.

**Dodge Line**  the economic program introduced by Joseph Dodge in 1949 to cut Japan's budget deficits, halt inflation, and reverse the zaibatsu-dissolution program. It was part of the "reverse course."

*Etsuzankai*  the best-known of the koenkai. It was organized by Tanaka Kakuei, master of money politics and prime minister of Japan during 1972–4.

**floating vote**  voters, characteristically salaried workers from large cities, who do not support particular political parties or politicians. Their share has increased over time and has contributed to political instability.

*Fukoku kyohei*  translating as "rich nation, strong army," the slogan is a good summary of overall Meiji-era policy.

**General Douglas MacArthur**  a leading U.S. general in the Pacific and Korean Wars, he served as Supreme Commander for the Allied Powers in occupied Japan. Such were his powers and influence that the acronym for his title, SCAP, came to stand for the occupation forces in general.

*Genro*  the unelected senior advisors to the emperor, former leaders of the Meiji rebellion. As they began to die off early in the 20th century, a power vacuum emerged in Japanese politics, ultimately enabling the military's rise to power.

**industrial policy**  the government's development, nurturing, and guidance of industry in the pursuit of national security.

**Japan Socialist Party (JSP)**  the most powerful of Japan's left-wing parties. It led coalition governments in 1947–8 and 1994–6 but has been in long-term electoral decline.

*Kankan settai*  literally, "bureaucrat-bureaucrat entertaining," the wining and dining of national bureaucrats by local officials hoping to increase their share of budget subsidies provided by Tokyo.

*Koenkai*  personal political machines, used extensively by LDP politicians to organize their supporters.

**Kwantung Army**  the Japanese army stationed in Manchuria (northeast China) to patrol the Japan-held South Manchuria Railway. Acting on its own, the army provoked conflicts with the Chinese military in order to seize Manchuria and widen the war with China.

**Liberal Democratic Party (LDP)**  formed in 1955 via the merger of the two main conservative parties, the party that held power continuously until July 1993. It returned to power in April 1994, though in coalition with other parties.

**Meiji restoration**  the revolt led by Satsuma and Choshu rebel domains against the Tokugawa bakufu to "restore" the emperor to power and implement a program of crash modernization for Japan. The rebels seized power in 1868.

**MITI**   Ministry of International Trade and Industry. Along with Japan's Ministry of Finance, it was the core of postwar Japan's economic bureaucracy and the chief architect of industrial policy.

**Multi-member election districts**   the electoral system used for the Lower House from 1925 until electoral reforms in 1994. Each voter cast a single vote for a specified candidate, and each district elected 2 to 6 candidates.

**Reverse course**   the second, more conservative phase of the occupation, during which policy emphasis shifted from demilitarization and democratization to economic reconstruction and partial remilitarization of Japan as a junior partner to the United States in the new cold war.

*Samurai*   the hereditary warrior class of the Tokugawa era. Samurai rebels led the Meiji rebellion in the 1860s and defeated the shogunate in 1868. Destroyed as a class in early Meiji, they were replaced by a conscript army.

**Shogun**   the military leader of the Tokugawa bakufu (1603–1868).

**Taisho democracy**   though named for the reign of Emperor Taisho (1912–25), the phrase refers to the period of party government in Japan between 1918 and 1932.

**Townsend Harris**   U.S. diplomat who concluded the trade agreement between the United States and Japan in 1858.

*Wakon yosai*   translating as "Japanese essence, Western learning," the phrase refers to Meiji Japan's effort to modernize by using Western tools and technologies, but with the aim of preserving Japanese national integrity.

**Yoshida Shigeru**   prime minister during 1946–7 and 1949–54. Yoshida was the chief political figure behind Japan's postwar policy of limited rearmament, low-posture diplomacy, and a focus on economic reconstruction.

**Yoshino-Kishi line**   the line that guided economic policy from the 1930s through the early postwar years by stressing development via steel, auto, chemical, and other heavy industries.

*Zaibatsu*   translating literally as "financial cliques," the merchant houses that rapidly became economic/industrial powers from mid-Meiji onward. They became known as *keiretsu* (economic groupings) in the postwar era.

## STUDY QUESTIONS

1.   What were the main causes of the Tokugawa bakufu's collapse? Why did part of the samurai class – part of Japan's elite – break from the old order to lead the Meiji rebellion?

2.   Why did the Meiji leadership choose to pursue a policy of "state capitalism"? How did subsequent economic/industrial policy evolve?

3.   Why were the Meiji oligarchs opposed to political parties? What constraints did the Meiji constitution impose on them? How were the parties able to overcome these restrictions?

4.  What is meant by the "institutional problem" of prewar democracy in Japan? How do you think this experience relates to the more successful experience of democracy in the postwar era?

5.  Why did Japan enter the Pacific War? Why did it lose?

6.  Why was the bureaucracy not targeted for reform during the occupation? What were the consequences? What does it mean to speak of postwar Japan as a democracy if some of its most powerful actors are unelected civil servants?

7.  What led to the reverse course? What were its consequences? Did it "reverse" all earlier reforms?

8.  If Yoshida Shigeru is considered – as he usually is – to be an old-guard conservative and a Japanese nationalist, why did he resist Japanese rearmament so strongly?

9.  What is industrial policy? Why do you think it is so often misunderstood? Do you think it could work in the United States?

10. What does it mean to call corruption in electoral politics "structural"? If Japanese politics are so corrupt, is it surprising that corruption has become more common in the ministries as well?

# ⪻ Stop and Compare

## EARLY DEVELOPERS AND MIDDLE DEVELOPERS

Once Great Britain and France developed, all other countries were forced to respond. Germany and Japan were among the first to do so. By the middle of the 19th century, Germany was not yet unified and Japan was facing Western imperialism. German and Japanese variations on the grand strategies of development found in the early developers are the direct result of international competition – military, economic, and cultural – between early and middle developers.

If Great Britain's and France's historical experiences are models of development and revolution from below, Germany and Japan represent instances of development and revolution from above. Compared to their predecessors, the middle and lower classes in Germany and Japan were weaker, and the upper classes stronger. The state, in alliance with the upper classes, helped initiate economic development. The military component of the developmental strategy was more prominent.

This developmental pedigree had fateful consequences for liberal democracy and ultimately for world peace. After abortive attempts at representative democracy, both Germany and Japan thus went through a period of fascism before they could participate in the world economy on an equal basis with the developed West.

## MIDDLE DEVELOPERS: GERMANY AND JAPAN

French power on the European continent had guaranteed throughout the first seventy years of the 19th century that Germany would remain a fragmented group of kingdoms and principalities. Among these separate states, however, some were more powerful than others. The most militarily capable was Prussia, which, under the leadership of Chancellor Bismarck, succeeded in defeating the French in the Franco-Prussian War of 1870 and unifying the German states under Prussian leadership in 1871. From the outset, German economic and political development reflected the fact that it came in response to French and British advancement. The fact that the need for military power came in anticipation of, rather than in response to, economic development meant that the path taken by Britain and France, which was largely a story of rising middle classes gradually securing power over monarchs and nobilities, would not be a historical possibility for Germany. Unable to rely on an economically ingenious and politically assertive rising middle class, Germany industrialized by allowing capital to concentrate in relatively few large banks, permitting industrialists to reduce risk through the creation of cartels, and creating a modern military officer corps and state apparatus on the basis of premodern agrarian elites. The coalition on which power rested was constituted of an alliance of "iron and rye" that had little interest in genuine parliamentary rule. The parliament, known as the Reichstag, was not fairly elected, nor did it have sovereignty over the kaiser, whose governmental ministers continued to be appointed from the ranks of the noble elite.

Although this pattern of development forestalled democracy, it succeeded quite spectacularly in military competition and economic development. By the beginning of the 20th century, Germany could field land armies superior to those of the French and could float ships on par with those of the British. German chemical, machine building, and metal industries were as advanced as those of its competitors. Such rapid development, occurring really in less than forty years, had a price. German craftsmen and especially industrial workers, who were often first-generation city dwellers, lived mostly in very difficult circumstances. Radical working-class parties, such as the Social Democrats could easily recruit the disaffected and the poor into mass politics. The ruling elite responded two ways: first, by banning the Social Democrats, and when that could not be sustained, second, by relying on a kind of militaristic German nationalist appeal for solidarity among classes against other nations. Unfortunately, this latter strategy did work. Perceiving the balance of forces to be temporarily on their side, and, by tradition, inclined to military solutions to social and diplomatic problems, the kaiser and his advisors exploited a crisis in European security relations in 1914 to launch a continent-wide war, which ultimately became known as World War I.

Defeat in this war forced the kaiser to abdicate and led to a fundamental democratization of German politics. This first try at parliamentary democracy, known as the Weimar Republic (1920–33), suffered from innumerable handicaps. The old elites had not been decisively replaced, either in the economy or in the state bureaucracy; the victory of democracy was associated in many people's minds with a humiliating loss in war (in a country that lived by the cult of war) and an equally humiliating peace treaty signed at Versailles; the country was saddled with heavy reparations payments to the victors; and the political institutions led to a fragmented party system and the temptation to rule by emergency presidential decree. This last factor became the fateful one when Adolf Hitler's Nazi Party managed to gain a plurality of seats in the Reichstag in the 1932 elections. Hitler had revived much of the older militaristic thinking of the pre-Weimar era, but he now laced the new ideology with large doses of revenge and racism. After having spent the middle half of the 1930s preparing for war, in 1939 Germany initiated, for the second time in the 20th century, a European-wide conflict that cost the lives of millions.

Since war had emanated from Germany twice in the century, the Allied victors decided that this would not happen again. The ultimate price that Germany paid for defeat was, in some sense, to return to the situation from which it had started: national division. The Soviet Zone of occupation became communist East Germany, or what was called the German Democratic Republic, and the three Western zones of occupation (those of Britain, the United States, and France) became West Germany, or the Federal Republic of Germany.

Apart from division, the Western allies and democratically minded Germans were also determined to remake Germany from the inside in order to ensure that democracy would genuinely take root there. To that end, Germany developed a set of policies, as well as constitutional and institutional innovations, designed to foster democratic stability and prevent extremist politics from ever returning. For example, although Germany continues to have a multiparty system, there are constitutional features to guarantee that it does not become too fragmented, unstable, or gridlocked in indecision. Another such arrangement is corporatism. Most Germans are organized into trade unions or employer associations. The German government, through its public offices, assists these two groups in hammering out agreements that will ensure just wages, low unemployment, and high growth rates. In turn, the government attempts to soften out many of the rougher edges of capitalist economics by means of a comprehensive welfare state. The net impact of these policies is designed to ensure that economic downturns do not occur often and, when they do occur, that they do not turn public opinion against democracy. Perhaps more crucially, corporatist policies are supposed to prevent the most rancorous debates over wages, prices, and welfare and move them off the parliamentary floor and out of politics in general.

Such policies helped secure the Federal Republic quite remarkable growth rates throughout the postwar era, and they also created a society which, for the first time in Germany's history, genuinely values liberal democracy for its own sake. Recently, however, the challenges of reunification, European unity, and global capitalist competition have induced slower growth rates, much higher unemployment, and a new domestic debate on whether the German model can be sustained into the future. Such questioning is indeed troubling to most Germans, precisely because it was this model that brought the country affluence and, after 1989, national unity – two things that had eluded Germany for the previous century.

Although Japan lies thousands of miles away from the European continent, grouping it together with Germany makes a great deal of sense to comparativists. For one thing, like Germany, Japan confronted external challenges to its sovereignty that forced it into rapid economic development in order to compete militarily. For another, the responses to these challenges were remarkably similar. Finally, the long-term path on which these responses set Japan led it to a similar form of militarism that could only be overcome by fundamental restructuring after World War II.

Japan entered the early modern period a fragmented country dominated by alliances of local feudal lords who each tried for more than a century to gain control over the country. Under the leadership of the Tokugawa regime (1603–1868), however, Japan at the start of the 17th century overcame its feudal fragmentation. By the concentration of power in the hands of the emperor (through the shogun), the institution of a rigid class system in which the warrior samurai nobility were given the lion's share of privileges, and the isolation of the island through a prohibition on foreign travel and a ban on the practice of Christianity, successive Tokugawa rulers succeeded in crafting a distinctive Japanese identity and a unified Japanese state.

As effective as this system was in solving the problems of political unification – and the fact that it lasted for 250 years suggests that it was effective – the arrival of U.S. Commodore Perry's "black ships" in 1853, with the purpose of forcing Japan to open its borders to trade and foreign influence, posed challenges that the Tokugawa order was not equipped to confront. In the mid-1860s, a series of rebellions among low-level samurai, who incorporated nonprofessional soldiers and even peasants into their army under a nationalist banner of expelling the foreign "barbarians," succeeded in overthrowing the last Tokugawa shogun from office and replacing him in 1868 with an emperor whom the samurai considered to be the true emperor of Japan, the fifteen-year-old Meiji.

The Meiji restoration, as historians have subsequently dubbed it, set Japan down a course of economic and military modernization with the purpose of securing the country from foreign control. The slogan of the time, "rich country, strong army," captured the essence of what the Meiji restoration was about. As in Germany, our other middle developer, industrial modernization occurred primarily in the form of a "revolution from above." A modern army and navy were created, feudal-style control over localities was replaced with a modern local government, and class privileges were formally abolished, thus reducing the power of the old samurai class, in theory, to that of the commoners. As in Germany, industrialization was accomplished at breakneck speed under the guidance of a national bureaucracy and with capital controlled by large, family-owned industrial conglomerates called zaibatsu. Also as in Germany, the Japanese Meiji elite sought a political model that could accommodate the kinds of changes that were taking place. The constitutional model they settled on, not surprisingly, was that of imperial Germany, with its parliamentary electoral rules that favored the landed elite and a government that remained dominated by military institutions and values.

Fundamental democratization occurred in Japan for the first time only in 1925 with a series of electoral reforms. Unfortunately, the old Meiji ruling elites who remained on the political scene, especially within the officer corps, never fully supported democracy. When the political and economic crises of the 1930s hit, consistent pressure from right-wing extremists and the military high command constrained the actions of civilian government. The ideas of the far Right and the military about what Japan needed were somewhat diffuse, but they can be summarized relatively easily: Solve Japan's economic and domestic problems by the colonization and economic domination of continental Asia. To achieve these goals, starting in 1936 Japan engaged in a series of wars in China that yielded even more power to the military. The military viewed the United States as the main obstacle to Japan's plans for Asia, and it finally pushed Japan to attack Pearl Harbor in 1941 as a preemptive strike against American might.

The devastating end of the war followed the U.S. decision to drop the atomic bomb twice on Japan, after which the American occupation inaugurated a series of political and economic reforms that changed life in Japan. A new constitution that forbade foreign military involvement, the removal of the emperor completely from political life, and a series of new institutions and political rules designed to bring constitutional democracy all brought about a fundamental change. Japan lives with the result to this very day.

Despite these changes, the nature of the Japanese political and economic model shows considerable continuities, or at least influences, from the past that remain a constant source of fascination for comparativists. Government and business continue to work closely together (although Japan's government is the "smallest" in the industrialized world), and capital remains far more concentrated than in the Anglo-American model. Furthermore, Japan continues to utilize the combination of a hierarchy in political and social culture with a remarkable degree of equality in salaries and living standards. Japanese workers are highly unionized but almost never go on strike. Japan's trade tariffs are among the lowest in the world, but it continues to be a country that foreign businesses have trouble penetrating. Finally, Japan's parliament, while democratically elected, continues in many ways to reign rather than rule. The latest round of globalization, however, has brought about considerable rethinking among the Japanese, who have started to question seriously whether these long-term characteristics of the Japanese model will be able to continue on into the future. As in Germany, where the fundamental democratization of the postwar period was accompanied by a selective retention of important aspects of the earlier model that had seemed to work, the need to rethink the postwar political-economic model has led to considerable unease within Japan.

# PART THREE

# Late Developers

## Cases

# 5

# Russia

## ❧ Stephen E. Hanson

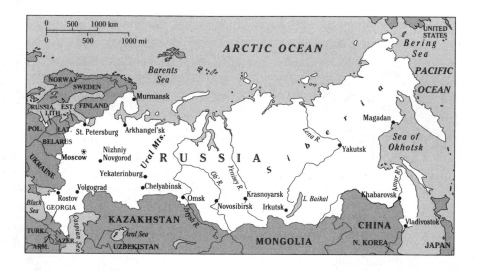

# INTRODUCTION

Russia has long puzzled and surprised observers of international politics. For seven decades Russia was at the center of a communist regime – the Union of Soviet Socialist Republics, or USSR – that competed with the United States for global supremacy. Now the country has fallen into a prolonged period of political, military, and economic decay. There is no consensus among specialists about how this one-time superpower became so weak, so quickly. Indeed, it seems that Russia simply doesn't fit conventional analytic categories.

Geographically, Russia is the biggest country in the world, spanning eleven time zones. Most of its population is in Europe; most of its territory is in Asia. Although about four-fifths of its population is ethnically Russian, the Russian Federation contains hundreds of other ethnic groups, some of which are now struggling for greater autonomy or full independence. Should we call Russia a European, an Asian, or a "Eurasian" state? Is Russia a nation or an empire? Or will Russia eventually break up into smaller regional units?

Economically, Russia is largely industrialized and urbanized, with only about a fifth of its population living in rural areas. Its population is highly educated. Yet most of its factories are inefficient, technologically backward, and environmentally unsafe; its villages still often lack paved roads, sewage systems, and basic services; and its gross domestic product is tiny in comparison with most countries in Western Europe. Should we call Russia an advanced, a developing, or an underdeveloped state? Or does Russia's misdeveloped economy deserve some new theoretical category of its own?

Culturally, Russia has played a key role in European intellectual and artistic

history, producing such well-known writers and composers as Tolstoy, Dosto-
evsky, and Tchaikovsky. Yet for centuries – and even today – prominent Russian
thinkers have claimed that their country can never be truly "Westernized," due to
what they claim is the essential mysticism, communalism, and idealism of the
Russian "soul." Should we call Russia's culture Western, non-Western, or something else entirely?

Neither Western analysts nor Russians themselves have come up with consistent answers to these questions. Indeed, since the collapse of the communist
empire in 1991, life in Russia has become even more unpredictable and confusing.
As the twenty-first century dawns, Russians are engaged in a seemingly endless
debate about their country's identity. Meanwhile, Russia's economy has suffered
through a severe depression. Early hopes for a rapid transition to democracy and
capitalism have been dashed, replaced by a pervasive anxiety that the future will
be even worse than the present.

Faced with the paradoxical nature of Russia's geography, economy, politics,
and culture, many political scientists have been tempted to agree with Winston
Churchill that Russia is "a riddle wrapped in a mystery inside an enigma." Detailed
descriptions of Russian institutions seem to become outdated almost as soon as
they are written. However, the comparative and theoretical approach to political
analysis presented in this book can help us explain Russia's unfortunate history.

This chapter argues that contemporary Russian interest groups have been
decisively shaped by the ideological identity and distinctive institutions imposed
on the country by Vladimir I. Lenin and his followers from 1917 to 1991 in an effort
to catch up to and overtake the West. Ironically, the collapse of Soviet institutions
has left Russia once again on the periphery of the global capitalist system, facing
similar challenges of economic backwardness, ethnic conflict, and international
insecurity. Thus, an analysis of the rise and fall of the Soviet Union is crucial for
understanding Russian politics today.

## THE RISE AND FALL OF THE USSR

### From Marx to Lenin

What did "communism" mean to the founders of the Soviet regime and their heirs?
To answer this question, we must begin with an examination of the Western European theorist who originally invented the idea of communism – Karl Marx. To be
clear: Marx himself did not provide a "blueprint" for the Soviet system. Indeed, he
died thirty-four years before the Russian Revolution of 1917. Those who wish to
blame Marx for Soviet tyranny forget how little control philosophers and theorists
have over the ways in which their ideas are interpreted decades or centuries later.

Still, the Soviet leaders all considered themselves Marx's faithful disciples. We therefore need to understand Marx's ideas in order to make sense of the rise and fall of the Soviet empire.

Karl Marx was born in 1818 in what is now Germany. When Marx was growing up, the vast majority of German speakers, like the vast majority of human beings elsewhere, lived in small peasant villages governed by various local lords and princes. The Industrial Revolution that had already transformed England and the United States had yet to reach Germany, where merchant activity was largely confined to the larger cities and towns. Thus, Marx wrote about capitalism as it was being first developed on the European continent.

When Marx was just twenty-nine years old, he and his best friend Friedrich Engels composed the most influential revolutionary essay ever written: the *Communist Manifesto*. The starting point for the analysis contained in the *Manifesto* – and indeed for all of Marx's later works – is a theoretical approach that later became known as historical materialism, which asserts that economic forces have ultimately determined the course of human social history. Politicians and philosophers may think that they are battling over principles, but in Marx's view they are really always fighting over the question of which groups get which shares of a society's overall wealth. The ruling ideas in each historical period, according to Marx, are always the ideas of a particular society's ruling class.

Marx argued that every stage of history has been marked by class struggle. Society has always been divided into two main classes: those who own property, and those who are forced to work to survive. The ruling class, Marx claimed, takes all the wealth that is left over once people's basic survival needs are met – what Marx called surplus value. However, the oppressed class always struggles to regain this surplus, which, after all, the workers themselves produced. Eventually, class struggle ignites a full-scale social revolution against the old order, leading to the emergence of a new and more advanced form of economic organization.

According to Marx, three main types of class society have shaped human history to date: slavery, feudalism, and capitalism. Slavery was the dominant "mode of production" in the earliest human civilizations, such as ancient Greece, Egypt, and Rome. After the fall of the Roman Empire, slavery in Europe gave way to feudalism, in which the main class struggle was between the ruling aristocracy and the oppressed peasantry. After 1500 or so, this mode of production also began to weaken and finally disintegrate.

The third and final type of class society, capitalism, emerged in its full-fledged form in England and the United States in the 1700s. In the *Communist Manifesto,* Marx predicted – correctly, as we now know – that it would eventually encompass the entire globe. Capitalists themselves naturally argue that this new mode of production promotes individual freedom and wealth. In reality, Marx insisted, capitalism is simply another form of class exploitation with its own distinct type of class struggle. The ruling class under capitalism, the bourgeoisie, consists of those who hire workers for wages and/or own the factories, banks, and housing upon which workers are dependent. The oppressed class, the proletariat, consists of all those who own nothing more than their own labor power and are therefore forced to compete for a job in order to survive – that is, the vast majority of people. Surplus value, in the form of capitalist profits, goes straight into the pockets of the ruling class, while the proletariat must continually struggle to raise their wages above a very low level.

Marx was convinced that the capitalist system, like slavery and feudalism before it, would eventually be destroyed in a social revolution – this time eliminating class divisions among human beings altogether and ushering in an era of global human harmony and abundance. Marx argued that the experience of working together under the dehumanizing conditions of capitalism would serve to strip the proletariat of all forms of identity that had previously divided it. Subjected to the same forms of underpaid, repetitive, mechanized labor, workers would stop caring about one another's race, ethnicity, religion, or nationality and recognize their common humanity. The proletarian revolution, then, would be a revolution of the vast majority of human beings, united as one, to take control over the global economic system. Freed from the tyranny of wage slavery and the terror of unemployment, workers would henceforth work together in conditions of free, creative cooperation. The *Communist Manifesto* concludes: "The proletarians have nothing to lose but their chains! They have a world to win! Working men of all countries, unite!"

Yet there was a central paradox in Marx's thinking. On the one hand, Marx called for workers to unite and struggle for better conditions and wages, in order to build proletarian solidarity and learn to exploit the vulnerabilities of the bourgeois system. On the other hand, Marx expected that workers under capitalism would become increasingly miserable over time, making revolution inevitable. What should communists do, then, if every successful workers' struggle against the bosses made them less miserable and more satisfied with capitalism? Should communists support change within the existing system? Or should they continue to promote global revolution regardless of how capitalism reformed itself? Marx himself never quite resolved this strategic paradox.

In fact, no Marxist revolution has ever taken place in a developed capitalist country. Instead, communist revolution occurred first in 1917 in Russia – a country that had then only barely entered the capitalist age, with over 80 percent of its population consisting of peasants and only around 8 percent workers. Why? Ironically, precisely because of Russia's underdevelopment, Marx's ideas were relatively more consistent with the interests of Russian workers and intellectuals. Although reforms had moderated the worst abuses of Western European capitalism, Russia in the early 20th century was still suffering through the early period of industrialization, with its characteristic disregard for worker health and safety and its total lack of legal channels for worker representation. The Russian proletariat, small as it was, was thus much more revolutionary than were the better-off workers of the West. Meanwhile, many Russian intellectuals saw in Marxism a way to escape their country's economic and military backwardness without having to adopt the Western capitalist system. By achieving "socialism," it seemed, Russia could miraculously leap ahead of countries like England and France in historical development. Finally, Marx's inspiring vision of communism proved especially powerful in a tsarist empire that had become embarrassingly weak, poor, and corrupt. Such factors help to explain the rapid spread of Marxist ideas in a feudal country – and the political evolution of the man who eventually founded a Marxist regime there, Vladimir Il'ich Lenin.

Vladimir Ulyanov – Lenin's real name – was born in the provincial town of Simbirsk, Russia, in 1870. When Lenin was fourteen years old, his older brother Alexander was arrested for participating in a plot to assassinate the tsar, and later executed. This event placed the entire Ulyanov family under a cloud of suspicion. Lenin was allowed to attend law school in the capital city of St. Petersburg, but shortly after he began his legal studies, he was expelled for participating in student demonstrations against the regime. He began to read radical literature, and at the young age of eighteen, he became a convinced Marxist. By 1900, he had become prominent enough within Russian Marxist circles to be invited to join the leading Russian Marxists in exile in Switzerland, where they lived and worked in order to avoid harassment and arrest by the tsarist police.

In 1902, Lenin published his most famous essay, entitled *What Is To Be Done?*. Lenin's ideas on party organization in this work ultimately inspired revolutionaries in China, Vietnam, Cuba, and elsewhere to create one-party regimes modeled on the "Leninist" example. Lenin's essay contained three main arguments, all of which became quite controversial among Marxists. First, Lenin bluntly insisted that the working class by itself could never make a successful anticapitalist revolution. More than fifty years after the publication of the *Communist Manifesto,* it had become clear that workers would always be satisfied with gains in local wages, benefits, and representation; in this sense, Lenin argued, workers had a kind of "trade-union consciousness," instead of the revolutionary consciousness needed for the successful overthrow of global capitalism. Second, Lenin argued that the movement must be led instead by Marxist intellectuals devoted at all times to revolutionary activity. A special organization of these intellectuals – a "party of professional revolutionaries" – was needed to guide the proletariat toward its eventual and inevitable victory over the bourgeoisie. Finally, Lenin insisted that the party of professional revolutionaries itself be organized as a strictly hierarchical, disciplined, and unified body. Attempts to introduce "bourgeois" forms of voting or legal procedure into the communist camp would only turn it into an ineffective debating society. Instead, the party should practice what Lenin would later term "democratic centralism" – meaning that debate within the party should end the moment the party's Central Committee had made a decision on any given issue.

It would be a long time, however, before Lenin and his followers built a party that in reality looked anything like his original institutional proposal. Indeed, Lenin's insistence on his model of organization at a congress of Russian Marxists in 1903 led to a split between two different factions: the Bolsheviks, or majority – so named because of Lenin's success in getting a bare majority of delegates present to vote to prohibit part-time party membership – and the Mensheviks, or minority, who argued for a more decentralized and inclusive organization of Marxists and workers. By 1904, even many of those Russian Marxists who had originally supported Lenin joined the Mensheviks to protest what they saw as his increasingly dictatorial behavior – ironically leaving the Bolsheviks very much a minority among Russian Marxists until 1917.

Indeed, had it not been for dramatic changes in Russia's global environment, Lenin's party might have faded into historical insignificance. However, the outbreak of World War I in 1914 revived the Bolsheviks' fortunes. The tsarist regime found itself hopelessly outgunned, and began to disintegrate quickly. In addition, the war's unprecedented bloodshed discredited the capitalist system. Finally, the war divided the Western European Marxist parties, each of which voted to support its own capitalist government in a war against their fellow proletarians.

Lenin was outraged by what he saw as the spinelessness of German, French, and other Western socialists. He argued in his essay *Imperialism* that European Marxists had become hopelessly corrupted by payoffs from capitalist imperial expansion. The proletarian revolution, he concluded, was therefore more likely to begin in Russia, in the periphery of the global capitalist system, than in the developed countries of the West. Lenin made it clear, too, that his own Bolshevik Party was ready to lead the Russian proletariat in its revolutionary struggle. Once Russia proved to the workers of the world that socialist revolution was possible, Lenin argued, communism would spread like wildfire throughout the West and beyond.

The opportunity to act on this theory soon arose when the tsar, Nicholas II, suddenly abdicated in March 1917, in response to mounting losses on the battlefield, peasant uprisings in the countryside, and bread riots in the cities. This "February revolution" – so named because the old Russian calendar was then about two weeks behind the modern Western calendar – left Russia in a state of near anarchy. A provisional government made up of former members of the tsarist parliament tried, with the support of the United States, Britain, and France, to revive the Russian economy and to continue the war against Germany. But this government had very little real authority, and in the cities, actual power devolved to what were called soviets, or councils, of workers and soldiers. Meanwhile, in the countryside, peasant revolts spread; many of the old nobility were killed or forced to flee.

Lenin did not, in any way, cause the collapse of tsarism; he had been in Switzerland for most of the war. He returned to the capital city of Petrograd (formerly St. Petersburg) in April 1917, advocating the overthrow of the provisional government, the establishment of a socialist republic based upon the soviets, and the immediate cessation of the war. Although the radicalism of these proposals at first stunned many of his own closest supporters, by the summer, mounting war casualties and the disintegrating economy rapidly turned the tide of public opinion among workers and soldiers in the Bolsheviks' favor.

On November 7 – the so-called October Revolution – Lenin and his supporters successfully seized power in Petrograd. Within a year they had wiped out all other organized political forces within the territory they controlled. Not only were tsarist and capitalist parties banned, but socialists who disagreed with Lenin were also suppressed. A new secret police force, the Cheka – later to become the KGB – was set up to hunt down "enemies of the revolution." Even the soviets, the spontaneous organizations of the workers themselves, were reduced to little more than rubber stamps for the party's central decrees. Party organizations were set up in every factory, every school, and every public organization to help "guide" the proletariat to communism.

Lenin's theoretical expectation that Bolshevik victory would spark communist revolutions throughout the capitalist world turned out to be unfounded, however. From 1918 to 1920, Lenin and Leon Trotsky directed an enormously destructive and bloody civil war against various supporters of tsarism, liberalism, anarchism, and anti-Bolshevik socialism. But after having reconquered most of the territory of the former Russian empire, Lenin began to realize that the final global victory of the proletariat might be delayed indefinitely. Global capitalism, apparently, had stabilized.

To survive in power, then, the Bolsheviks had to revive the ruined Russian economy. In March 1921, Lenin introduced the New Economic Policy, which freed grain markets and allowed small-scale capitalism in the cities. Trade and agriculture began to recover soon afterward. Simultaneously, however, Lenin further strengthened one-party rule by implementing a "ban on factions" within the party's ranks. In 1922, he promoted a young disciple by the name of Joseph Stalin to the new position of General Secretary of the Communist Party, entrusting him with the task of ensuring party discipline by control over personnel decisions.

Another vexing problem was that the new Soviet state occupied a territory containing hundreds of different religions and ethnic groups. According to Marx, of course, such identities were supposed to disappear entirely with the victory of communism over capitalism. In reality, such groups as the Ukrainians, the Georgians, and the Muslim peoples of Central Asia tended to perceive the new regime in Moscow as a continuation of the former Russian empire. Lenin appointed Stalin to be the new Commissar for Nationalities, expecting him to find a reasonable balance between the need for the party's central control and the concerns of non-Russians – after all, Stalin himself was an ethnic Georgian. To Lenin's dismay, Stalin immediately tried to eliminate all forms of national autonomy, even using physical violence to intimidate ethnic leaders who resisted his will. Ultimately, the new "Soviet Union" formed in 1923 did include several "national republics" for the largest and most powerful nationalities of the regime. Real political power, however, was concentrated in the Kremlin in Moscow (where the Soviet capital had been relocated from Petrograd in 1918).

Shortly after having promoted Stalin to these important positions, Lenin suffered a series of strokes that ultimately left him incapacitated. As Lenin lay on his deathbed in 1923, a fierce struggle for power broke out. In the last letter he was able to dictate, Lenin warned that such internecine battles could fatally weaken the party. In particular, his protege Stalin had concentrated "immense power in his hands," and was "too rude" to occupy the post of General Secretary. Lenin's warnings were ignored. Lenin died in January 1924. Within five years, Stalin emerged as the sole leader of the Soviet regime.

## From Lenin to Stalin

How did Iosef Djugashvili, the son of a poor cobbler in the small, mountainous country of Georgia, eventually become one of the most powerful and brutal tyrants in history? This question is of immense historical importance, since Stalin, even more than Lenin, shaped the playing field upon which Russian and other post-Soviet politicians now struggle for power. Moreover, by forging a communist bloc extending from Asia to Europe, Stalin also helped to create the basic contours of international politics in the second half of the 20th century.

From the comparative point of view, however, the two main arguments that have been advanced to explain Stalin and Stalinism are rather unsatisfying. Some analysts argue that Stalin defeated his rivals for power, then established a tyranny, simply because he was the most power hungry, the most brutal, and the most opportunistic of any of Lenin's heirs. While Stalin obviously wanted power and was willing to use violent means to get it, it makes little sense to accuse Stalin of simple opportunism. In order to rise within Lenin's Bolshevik Party in the first place, Stalin had to fight for fourteen years for an illegal organization that until 1917 had few resources, only a few thousand loyal supporters, and a leader who lived in exile in Switzerland. During this period the tsarist police arrested him a half-dozen times. If this was a strategy to attain future political power, it was one we can only recognize as such in retrospect. Certainly no ordinary rational politician would have chosen Stalin's early career path!

The second argument often made to explain Stalin's behavior is a psychological one: in short, that Stalin was a paranoid schizophrenic who thought that hidden enemies were always plotting against him. Again, this analysis may be clinically accurate. But this hardly explains how Stalin rose to the leadership of the world's largest state. Somehow, Stalin's personal psychology did not prevent him from convincing many intelligent men and women that he was a socialist genius, and not a lunatic. How he did so must be explained in terms of the larger political, social, and global environment in which Stalin's personality was situated.

An alternative point of view, which will be defended here, is that Stalin rose to power and remained in control of the USSR until his death because he, like Lenin, was an institutional innovator within the Marxist ideological tradition. In short, Stalin was a convinced communist, as well as a staunch supporter of Lenin's ideas about party organization. Stalin was in a position to gain unprecedented political power at the head of the Leninist party only because he had identified enough with it early in life to have faith in its eventual triumph. This is why Lenin gave Stalin the crucial post of party General Secretary: Stalin had proven his loyalty in times of trial, and so Lenin thought he could be counted on to defend the party's interests.

Certainly, Stalin did his best to enforce Leninist norms of strict party discipline and control over a potentially hostile society, using his position to attack and purge any party member who dared disagree with the "general line" of the party leadership – within which, of course, he himself was a key figure. In this respect, however – despite Lenin's complaints about Stalin's "rude" behavior – he was only following Lenin's own principles of "democratic centralism." Shortly after Lenin's death, Stalin promoted thousands of young workers to party membership in a mass campaign called the "Lenin levy," creating an even larger base of personal supporters within the Leninist regime. None of Stalin's opponents possessed either the institutional levers or the organizational skills possessed by the future dictator – a factor that cannot be ignored in accounting for his rise to power.

Stalin's victory was not only institutional, however; it was ideological. Stalin, in fact, proposed a very distinct set of answers to the most troubling issue confronting Marxists in the Soviet Union in the wake of their revolutionary victory: namely, how to build "socialism" in a largely peasant country without the support of proletarian revolutions in more advanced capitalist countries. The policies that flowed from Stalin's analysis ultimately annihilated millions of people and left a burdensome economic legacy for post-Soviet Russia. Yet Stalinism was arguably the most consistent ideological response to the question of "what was to be done" after Lenin's death.

In order to see this, we must briefly examine the views of Stalin's main opponents. There were three main positions in the debate: the left, the right, and the orthodox center. The left was led by the famous revolutionary Leon Trotsky, who had played a crucial role in the Bolshevik takeover, almost single-handedly building up the new Red Army and leading it to victory during the civil war. But after Lenin's incapacitation, Trotsky became disillusioned with what he saw as the gradual "bureaucratization" of the party and the loss of the Soviet Union's revolutionary momentum. Trotsky exhorted Soviet workers to redouble their efforts to build a strong industrial infrastructure as rapidly as possible and argued that the Bolsheviks should strive to foment revolutions throughout Western Europe. Unfortunately for Trotsky, after three years of world war, a year of revolution, and three years of civil war, most party members and ordinary workers were tired of revolutionary appeals. Some thought Trotsky might be harboring designs to take power for himself through a military coup. In the fall of 1923, the "left opposition" was overwhelmingly outvoted in the party's Central Committee, and by 1924 Trotsky's power and influence began to decline rapidly.

The "right opposition" in the 1920s was led by Nikolai Bukharin, a well-known Marxist theorist who edited the party's newspaper *Pravda* (meaning "truth"). After an early alliance with Trotsky, Bukharin became convinced that the left's proposals for continuous revolutionary advance were not feasible. Instead, Bukharin advocated a slow, evolutionary path to socialism in the USSR. Specifically, he argued that Lenin's New Economic Policy allowing small-scale capitalism should be continued "seriously and for a long time." The peasantry should be encouraged to get rich. Within factories, efficient management should be promoted – even if that meant keeping the same capitalist bosses as before the revolution. Eventually, Bukharin claimed, this policy would allow the Soviet people gradually to "grow into socialism." Such a policy was certainly more realistic than Trotsky's romantic leftism. Yet it failed to appeal to those who genuinely believed in the ideals of 1917. Why did we fight for communism, asked many party members, workers, and intellectuals, if the end result was simply to establish a "New Economic Policy" that looked more like a "New Exploitation of the Proletariat"?

The "center" or orthodox Leninist position in the 1920s was advocated by Grigorii Zinoviev, who had been one of Lenin's most loyal supporters in the pre-1917 period. Zinoviev led the Bolshevik Party in the newly renamed city of Leningrad (formerly St. Petersburg and Petrograd). He also directed the Comintern, a global organization of communist parties loyal to Moscow, which Lenin had founded in 1919. Zinoviev argued that both the left and the right had gone too far: One side called for revolution without rational analysis or professionalism; the other side called for rational economic policies without any revolutionary vision. Surely, true "Leninism" – as he now began to refer to the regime's ideology – required both revolution and professionalism simultaneously! Unfortunately, Zinoviev himself had little idea of how to bring about a "Leninist" synthesis of these two concepts. His most original idea – enthusiastically supported by Stalin – was to place Lenin's mummified body on display in Moscow's Red Square, so that generations of grateful proletarians could line up to see the founder of Soviet communism.

None of these men proposed any practical policies for dealing with Russia's severe economic backwardness in a way that seemed consistent with the Soviet regime's socialist identity. Stalin did. In December 1924, Stalin proposed an alternative vision that appeared far more realistic in the context of the international isolation of the Soviet regime: "socialism in one country." The basic idea behind "socialism in one country" was simple: It was time to stop waiting for revolutions in other capitalist countries and start building socialism at home. This theoretical position contradicted Trotsky's calls for continuous revolutionary advance in Western Europe, as well as Zinoviev's hopes to inspire the world communist movement from Moscow without actually risking revolutionary changes. Bukharin, assuming that Stalin's idea of "socialism in one country" was identical to his own evolutionary socialism, threw his support behind Stalin in the power struggle against Trotsky and Zinoviev. By 1928, however, having defeated his latter two opponents, Stalin began to attack Bukharin as well, accusing him of being an opportunist who had sold out to the "bourgeois" rich peasants and industrialists. Stalin lined up large majorities to vote against the right opposition in the Central Committee, and in 1929 he expelled Bukharin and his supporters from the party leadership.

Now the unchallenged leader of the regime, Stalin revealed that his vision of "socialism in one country" required a new revolutionary assault on Soviet society. Like Lenin, Stalin proposed to translate Marxist identity into concrete institutions that would structure the incentives of millions of ordinary people – this time, in the economic and not just the political realm. Marx himself had said very little about how economic institutions should be organized in the postrevolutionary period; certainly, he had provided no guidance concerning how a single socialist state surrounded by capitalist ones could transform a largely peasant economy into an industrial power. However, Marx had indicated that he expected the "dictatorship of the proletariat" to organize state control over both the industrial and agricultural sectors of the economy, to eliminate private property wherever possible, and to organize production according to a common plan. Stalin now expanded on these principles to propose the revolutionary restructuring of the entire Soviet economy on the basis of "Five-Year Plans" drawn up by the state and enforced by the Communist Party. Stalin insisted that although the Soviet economy was a century behind the West in developmental terms, that distance had to be made up in a decade – or the capitalists would "crush us."

The Stalinist planning system contained three key elements: collectivization of agriculture, a novel form of "planned heroism" in industry, and the creation of a huge system of prison labor camps known as gulags. The first of these, collectivization of agriculture, represented Stalin's "solution" to the dilemma of how to deal with the huge peasant population in forging a socialist Soviet Union: Basically, he decided to enslave or kill the entire peasantry. Again, Stalin put his argument in clear Marxist terms. The peasantry as a class, Marx had argued, was a left-over from feudalism. Capitalism was destined to destroy the peasantry and the aristocracy alike; there would be no place for peasant villages in the socialist future. Those who benefited from private property in agricultural production, Stalin reasoned, formed a sort of peasant bourgeoisie – "kulaks," meaning "the tight-fisted ones" – while the poor peasants who worked for them were essentially part of the proletariat. Proletarian revolution in the countryside required class struggle against the kulaks and eventually, as Stalin put it, "the liquidation of the kulaks as a class." In place of the old system of private peasant farming, Stalin proposed the creation of new "collective farms" (*kolkhozy*) and "state farms" (*sovkhozy*), where peasants would work for the greater good of the proletariat – under strict party supervision.

In reality, the drive to create collective farms amounted to an all-out assault on the countryside by Stalin's party supporters, by the army, and by various thugs and brigands who took advantage of the chaos to loot, steal, and rape. All over the Soviet Union, peasants battled to preserve their autonomy, even killing their own livestock rather than letting their pigs, cows, and chickens fall under party control. By 1932, the collectivization drive had generated a famine throughout the agricultural regions of the USSR during which millions of people starved to death. Even so, Stalin's goal of gaining party control over the production of food was realized. Indeed, even at the height of the famine, Stalin continued to export grain to Europe in order to earn hard currency for the regime. By the mid-1930s, most of the land in the country had been collectivized, excluding only tiny private plots where peasants were allowed to work for themselves and their families.

The second key element of Stalin's socioeconomic system was the imposition of centrally planned production targets for every manager and worker within the Soviet Union. The State Committee on Planning, or Gosplan, had been formed in the mid-1920s to provide general projections for future economic development in the USSR; in this respect, the organization acted in ways similar to planning bureaucracies in Western capitalist countries, such as France. But in 1929, Stalin gave Gosplan officials the unprecedented task of supervising the rapid industrialization of an enormous nation. The specific institutional mechanisms used to ensure this result were designed to elicit a sort of "professional revolutionary" economic activity, comparable to that expected of good Leninist party members. Specifically, monthly and yearly production targets, calculated in terms of gross output, were issued for workers and state managers of every factory and collective farm in the USSR. However, the party did not promote workers or managers who simply attained these targets – in fact, just "fulfilling" the plan was held to be a "bourgeois," unrevolutionary sort of behavior, and those who never did better than this were sometimes even arrested. Only those who consistently overfulfilled their plan targets, thus supposedly demonstrating their superior revolutionary enthusiasm and dedication, were rewarded. Such "shock workers" and "heroic managers" were given monetary bonuses, special housing, better food, and even trips to Moscow to visit the dictator himself.

This system of incentives encouraged an atmosphere of constant, chaotic activity, as workers and managers struggled to produce higher and higher volumes of cement, coal, and steel, urged on by the state planners and party leadership. However, Soviet citizens soon learned that overfulfillment of plans by too great an amount could also sometimes get them into trouble. According to a principle known as "planning from the achieved level," Gosplan was instructed to raise plan targets to the point attained in the previous planning period. Thus, if a worker somehow produced double his or her required amount of coal in one year, he or she might be required to attain the same absurd amount of production the next – and failure to do so, again, could lead to arrest and imprisonment. Thus, Stalinist institutions encouraged individuals to overfulfill their plans, but not by too much. Managers and workers were given incentives to be "revolutionary," but in a manner that was simultaneously "disciplined and professional."

During the First Five-Year Plan, an industrial infrastructure was built in the Soviet Union in an incredibly short period of time; this result looked all the more impressive against the backdrop of the Great Depression then enveloping the capitalist West. Over time, though, the constant demands to "fulfill and overfulfill the plan" in the 1930s alienated even those groups who most benefited from Stalin's policies – the proletariat and party officials. A "final-exam economy," in which constant "cramming" to complete plan assignments before the final deadline was followed by the imposition of even greater work demands, could not but produce exhausted and exasperated managers and workers.

Thus, the third key component of Stalin's economic system, the creation of the gulag system, was vital to its overall functioning. The "gulags" – short for "state camps" – were originally set up during the civil war to incarcerate those who opposed Lenin's plans for Communist Party rule. Under Stalin, however, their scope expanded rapidly; tens of millions of people were arrested as "class enemies" of the "proletarian dictatorship." Gulag inmates were put to work building canals, paving roads, digging coal, and constructing monuments to Lenin and Stalin, often in the most brutal conditions imaginable. The contribution of the gulag system to overall Soviet production under Stalin is hard to estimate, but it clearly played a crucial role in the attainment of the ambitious industrialization targets of the 1930s. Moreover, the constant threat of the gulag undoubtedly did much to inspire ordinary people's continued efforts to overfulfill the plan.

However, the types of economic activity encouraged by Stalin's incentive structure were not conducive to the long-run performance of the system. Already in the 1930s, all sorts of dysfunctional behaviors emerged within Soviet enterprises. First, since plan targets were formulated in terms of gross quantities of output, the quality of Soviet production often suffered greatly; as a result, the basic infrastructure of Soviet industry began to crumble and decay almost as soon as it was built. The problem of quality control was even more severe in such sectors of economic production as consumer goods and services, which were given low priority by Stalin. Second, the system was poorly equipped to handle technological change. Shutting down assembly lines in order to introduce new, up-to-date machinery meant failing to meet one's monthly and annual production targets, and so Soviet managers tended to rely on their existing equipment. Third, Stalinist industrialization was an environmental disaster; to fulfill and overfulfill plans mattered more than long-term concerns with people's health or the preservation of nature. Today, former Soviet factory towns are some of the most polluted places on earth. Fourth, collectivized agriculture was enormously inefficient and wasteful. Indeed, by the late Soviet era, approximately 65 percent of all vegetables and 90 percent of all fresh fruit was produced on the mere 2 to 3 percent of the land given to peasants' private plots!

Finally, the Stalinist system was prone to rapid institutional corruption. The official banning of most forms of private property and markets meant that all kinds of buying, selling, and stealing of state resources went on in black markets and within personal networks. Managers often colluded with local party officials to lower plan targets, falsify production reports, or otherwise protect enterprises from the demands of central planners. Given the absence of either unemployment or bankruptcy procedures, the only way to curtail such behavior was to arrest the perpetrators – but since almost everyone was involved in some form of informal evasion of their official responsibilities, rooting out corruption completely was impossible.

Stalin knew full well that his vision of socioeconomic socialism was, despite its external successes, falling victim to such forms of corrosion from within. But having sacrificed decades of his life – and millions of other people's lives – to establish this system, he was not about to rethink his policies. Instead, he tried to explain the corruption of the planning system as the work of "hidden class enemies" within the USSR and "survivals of capitalist psychology" within people's minds. In 1936, Stalin began a massive blood purge of everyone he thought was conspiring with the global bourgeoisie against socialism. In Stalin's mind, this supposed conspiracy included the right, left, and center oppositions of the 1920s, economists and plant managers, independent artists and intellectuals, and the entire general staff of the Red Army. Between 1936 and 1938 – the period known as the Great Terror – Stalin killed about 75 percent of the Communist Party's Central Committee, including Zinoviev and Bukharin, who were tortured and forced to testify that they were agents of capitalist intelligence services, then executed. In 1940, one of Stalin's agents assassinated Trotsky, then living in exile in Mexico City. Meanwhile, millions more Soviet citizens were imprisoned or killed.

How did such a coercive system maintain itself? Every institutional order, no matter how oppressive, requires the allegiance of some social group whose interests it advances, and the Stalinist system is no exception. In fact, one small group did quite well within the framework of Stalinist industrialization – namely, blue-collar workers in their 20s and early 30s who had joined the party during Stalin's rise to power. Many of these men (and women, although this group was predominantly male) found themselves promoted extremely rapidly during the period of the First Five-Year Plan to positions of management and within the party hierarchy. They rose even further when their immediate supervisors were killed during the Great Terror. Some of these people ultimately became members of the post-Stalin Soviet Politburo, including such future leaders as Khrushchev and Brezhnev. For these men, who had started their careers as ordinary workers, the Soviet Union was truly a "dictatorship of the proletariat"!

Even with the support of the communist worker elite, however, Stalin's system of planned heroism and mass terror might well have disintegrated had it not been for the enormous changes in the international environment wrought by World War II. When Adolf Hitler invaded the USSR in June 1941, Soviet forces were hardly able to resist; within months, the Nazis were at the gates of both Leningrad and Moscow. However, before the conquest of the Soviet Union was complete, the Russian winter began to set in, and the German soldiers found themselves quite unprepared for the extreme cold. Soon fresh troops from the east came to reinforce Moscow. By December, when the United States entered the war after the Japanese attack on Pearl Harbor, the pressure on the fascists was increasing. Fighting between Soviet and Nazi troops continued for three more years, and ultimately the USSR lost more than 20 million people in the conflict. However, by the end of 1943, the tide had turned decisively against Hitler, and by 1945, Red Army troops met Allied troops in Berlin in triumph.

After the Soviet victory in World War II, Stalin insisted that his policies of the 1930s had been vindicated. After all, the giant steel mills, cement plants, and weapons factories set up in the First Five-Year plan had played a crucial role in the Soviet war effort; without rapid industrialization, the Nazis might actually have conquered Russia. Stalin could now claim – despite his genocidal policies – that he was a great Russian patriot who had defeated an alien invader of the motherland. Finally, at the conclusion of the war, Soviet troops occupied most of Eastern and Central Europe, including the eastern portion of Germany. Within three years, Stalin had imposed both Leninist one-party rule and Stalinist collectivization and planning on these unfortunate nations. If one accepted Stalin's definition of "socialism," then, it followed that Stalin was the first person who had successfully created an "international socialist revolution," one that even included part of Marx's homeland. World War II – or, as the Russians still refer to it, the "Great Patriotic War" – thus greatly solidified the legitimacy of Stalin's regime and led many ordinary citizens to embrace a "Soviet" identity for the first time.

Until his death in 1953, Stalin continued to defend the system he had created – and to use terror to silence his real and imagined opponents. Entire peoples whom Stalin accused of being disloyal during the war, such as the Crimean Tatars, the Volga Germans, and the Chechens, were deported to Siberia and Central Asia. The arrest of supposed capitalist spies continued; even the relatives of prominent Politburo members were sent to the gulag. Meanwhile, Stalin promoted a "cult of personality" in the Soviet media and arts that constantly trumpeted the dictator's supposed genius as an architect, as a poet, as a military commander, as a linguist, and so on. Shortly before his death, Stalin proposed to launch a new terror campaign against supposed "enemies of the people" – this time including Politburo doctors, whom he accused of plotting to poison the leadership, and, even more ominously, Soviet Jews, who he claimed were part of a global Zionist conspiracy against him. Fortunately, Stalin died in March 1953 before he could act on these ideas.

## From Stalin to Gorbachev

Stalin's successors were faced with a dual legacy. On the one hand, by 1953 the USSR was a global superpower. Its industrial production had become sufficiently large to allow it to compete militarily with the capitalist West; by 1949 it had also built its first nuclear bomb. Newly decolonized and developing countries looked to the Soviet Union as a counterweight to the power of the West, and in some cases as an ally whose institutions should be emulated. The Western powers themselves had just emerged from decades of world war and global depression – phenomena Marx had predicted would result from capitalism's "inner contradictions" – and it would be some time before analysts were sure that democratic capitalism in Europe could be revived and sustained.

On the other hand, the fundamental problems of Leninist party politics and Stalinist planned economics remained. Years of dictatorship and terror had killed off whatever popular enthusiasm had once existed for heroic efforts to "build socialism." Bribe taking and black-market activity on the part of Soviet officials had already become a way of life. Problems with economic waste and inefficiency, worker absenteeism and alcoholism, and poor-quality production had become more severe. Clearly, something had to be done to address the growing cracks in the foundation of the Soviet superpower.

Again, the post-Stalin leadership analyzed and responded to these problems in a way they thought was consistent not only with their own personal interests but also with the basic outlines of the Soviet socialist identity. First, every Soviet leader after Stalin's death in 1953 agreed that the days of mass, indiscriminate terror in Soviet society must end. Stalin's last secret-police chief, Lavrenti Beria, was himself executed by the end of the year; millions of people were freed from the gulag; and the most extreme forms of Stalin worship ceased. The post-Stalin leadership also agreed that the next stage in building socialism somehow had to involve the creation of a truly socialist culture that would inspire ordinary workers and peasants to contribute their energies to the further development of Soviet institutions voluntarily. Concerning how to do this, however, there was no clear consensus.

From 1953 until 1985, leadership struggles again centered on debates among what we can now recognize as right, left, and centrist orthodox strategies concerning how to create a "socialist way of life" without Stalinist terror. Supporters of the "right-wing" strategy in this period, such as Georgii Malenkov, the first post-Stalin prime minister, argued that Soviet socialism must abandon revolutionary crusades in economic and foreign policy, and instead promote efficiency within enterprises and high-quality production for ordinary consumers. This advice, however sensible from our perspective, struck most party officials and Stalinist planners as a direct attack on their interests and as a departure from the revolutionary ideals of Marxism and Leninism.

By 1954, Malenkov's authority had been eclipsed by Communist Party leader Nikita Khrushchev. Khrushchev advocated the opposite of Malenkov's policies, calling for revolutionary advance toward communism as rapidly as possible; indeed, he revised the party program to include a timetable according to which Marx's original vision of "full communism" would be attained in the USSR by 1980! Khrushchev sought to inspire mass revolutionary sentiments by exposing the abuses of the Stalin period as "deformations" of socialism that would never be permitted again. He called on the Soviet people to participate in a whole series of economic campaigns to set records in corn planting, milk and meat production, and chemical manufacture. He also pursued a risky and often reckless foreign policy, threatening the West with nuclear missile attacks if it did not agree to Soviet demands. Such "leftist" policies led to administrative chaos at home and military embarrassments, such as the Cuban missile crisis, abroad. In 1964 Khrushchev was ousted in a Politburo coup.

From 1964 until 1982, Leonid Brezhnev presided over an orthodox Marxist-Leninist Politburo that resisted any reform of Soviet institutions – and, besides supporting various pro-Soviet regimes in the Third World, did very little else. Brezhnev's leadership arrested vocal dissidents and censored open criticism of the regime, but largely turned a blind eye to private disaffection, corruption and black-market activity. Party officials and state bureaucrats were rarely fired, and the Soviet elite began to age, and ultimately to die, in office. The planning system, now lacking either mass enthusiasm or fear as incentives for the fulfillment of production targets, sank into stagnation and decline. By the mid-1970s, the Soviet economy became dangerously dependent upon energy exports and sales of vodka. The disastrous Soviet military intervention in Afghanistan in 1979, combined with the declaration of martial law to suppress the independent Solidarity trade union in Poland in 1981, exposed the growing vulnerabilities of the Soviet army and the Warsaw Pact alliance of Leninist regimes in Eastern Europe. Meanwhile, such leaders as Margaret Thatcher in Britain and Ronald Reagan in the United States were calling for a much more aggressive foreign policy to attack the Soviet "evil empire." Finally, from 1982 until 1985, a veritable parade of dying General Secretaries – Brezhnev, Yuri Andropov, and Konstantin Chernenko – made the USSR an international joke.

It was under these dire global and domestic circumstances that the party elite decided to entrust the key position of General Secretary to the 54-year-old Mikhail Gorbachev. Upon his promotion to the leadership in March 1985, a furious debate ensued among Western Sovietologists. The "totalitarian" school, which insisted that the Soviet system was still in essence a regime based on terror, tended to see Gorbachev as merely a more polished representative of Soviet tyranny and warned the West to remain vigilant. "Modernization" theorists, who claimed that the USSR had become a developed, modern society not unlike the United States, saw Gorbachev's leadership as a final break with the Stalinist past, and hoped for a new era of peace and cooperation between his regime and the West.

In effect, each side assumed that Gorbachev knew what he was doing, but didn't believe what he was saying. The totalitarian interpretation of Gorbachev assumed that he knew how to revitalize the Soviet economy in order to produce a more technologically advanced and efficient communist challenge to the West, but didn't believe his own promises of reform and democratization of the Soviet system. The modernization interpretation of Gorbachev assumed that he knew how to eliminate the corruption, mismanagement, and ideological rigidity of the Brezhnev period, but didn't believe his own constant assurances that he was a "Leninist" who hoped to revive the ideals of the October Revolution. In fact, we now know that Gorbachev believed what he was saying, but didn't know what he was doing. When he told the world that he was a "Leninist reformer," he meant exactly that. As to what a reformed Leninism in the Soviet Union would eventually look like in practice, however, he had no concrete idea.

How could Gorbachev really believe in Leninism as late as the 1980s? Gorbachev had been promoted his whole life for espousing this ideology. He had come of age politically during the successful and painful struggle against the Nazis, and had been a teenager during the triumphant emergence of the Soviet Union as a global superpower. As a young man he was given the Order of the Red Banner of Labor for his "heroic" work as a combine operator on a collective farm. Largely as a result of this award, he was admitted to the prestigious Moscow State University Law School. In his twenties he became a party official, and by his thirties he had been appointed the first party secretary in Stavropol, an agricultural region in southern Russia. Owing to Stavropol's strategic location on the way to various Black Sea and Caucasian mountain resorts, Gorbachev got to know almost every significant Soviet leader, including Brezhnev, Andropov, and Chernenko. By 1978, at the age of 47, he had been promoted to the Politburo as secretary of agriculture, in part because his sincere enthusiasm for Leninism and socialism had impressed his somewhat more jaded elders.

Thus, by the time he became General Secretary, Gorbachev was one of the few people in the USSR who still truly believed in Leninist ideology. People's enthusiasm for participation in the Communist Party and for heroic plan fulfillment, Gorbachev insisted, could be rekindled – but only if he found some way to eliminate the corrupt, petty bureaucracy that had blocked popular initiative during the "years of stagnation" under Brezhnev. His first step was to purge hundreds of old party bureaucrats. By 1986, Gorbachev had already dismissed or retired almost 40 percent of the Central Committee, and felt strong enough to launch his dramatic campaign for "perestroika," or restructuring.

Perestroika consisted of three basic elements: *glasnost'*, democratization, and "new thinking" in foreign policy. "Glasnost," or openness, meant greater disclosure of people's criticisms of the Soviet past and present in newspapers, television, and films. This campaign got off to a rather ambiguous start when, in April 1986, the Chernobyl nuclear power plant in Ukraine exploded and the Soviet government hid this information from its citizens for a full three days after the event. However, by the fall of 1986, the quantity and quality of published revelations about Soviet history and current Soviet society began to increase markedly. The release in December 1986 of the famous Soviet nuclear physicist and dissident Andrei Sakharov, who had been sent into internal exile for his public denouncement of the Soviet invasion of Afghanistan, demonstrated the seriousness of Gorbachev's break with Brezhnevite forms of censorship. After 1987, the scope of glasnost widened to include every conceivable topic, including Lenin's terror during the civil war, the horrors of collectivization, and even the dictatorial nature of Communist Party rule itself.

Democratization, too, began slowly, with vague calls to reinvigorate the system of soviets that had been subordinated to the party hierarchy since the Russian civil war. By 1988, however, at the Nineteenth Party Conference, Gorbachev announced that genuine multicandidate elections would be held for a new Soviet Congress of People's Deputies, to replace the old rubber-stamp Supreme Soviet. To be sure, Gorbachev attempted to guarantee the continued "leading role" of the Communist Party, reserving a third of the seats in the new 2,250-seat congress for "public organizations" under direct party control. Moreover, in many electoral districts, local party bosses still ran unopposed, as in the times of Stalin and Brezhnev. Nevertheless, the national elections held in the spring of 1989 led to serious, competitive races between "reformers" and party "conservatives" that galvanized Soviet society.

Finally, Gorbachev's campaign for "new thinking" in foreign policy announced a turn away from attempts to build client regimes in the Third World, a campaign to reduce tensions with the capitalist West, and, most significantly, an end to the Stalinist subordination of countries in the communist bloc. Since the end of World War II, Soviet leaders had been able to preserve Leninist rule in Eastern Europe only through repeated military intervention, including Khrushchev's invasion of Hungary in 1956, Brezhnev's invasion of Czechoslovakia in 1968, and the Soviet-supported declaration of martial law in Poland in 1981. Now, one of Gorbachev's spokesmen announced that the old "Brezhnev doctrine" of military intervention had been replaced by the "Sinatra doctrine": the former communist satellite states would be allowed to "do it their way." Again, early reaction to this announcement was skeptical, both in the West and in Eastern Europe. In 1989, the seriousness of new thinking was tested when Solidarity candidates won every possible seat in new elections for the Polish parliament. When Gorbachev did nothing to prevent the creation of the first non-Leninist government in the communist bloc, liberal democrats and nationalists throughout the region moved to gain their own independence. By the end of the year, revolutions against Communist Party rule had succeeded in every single country of the former Warsaw Pact.

Gorbachev's perestroika, then, was every bit as revolutionary as its author had intended – but not with the results he had expected. Within three years of the launching of the campaign for restructuring, both the identity and the institutions at the core of Leninism had disintegrated. Instead of inspiring a new faith in socialist ideas as Gorbachev had hoped, glasnost made the history of communism appear to be a long and bloody tragedy. Democratization, designed to remove corrupt Brezhnevite bureaucrats in order to make space in the system for more enthusiastic socialists, instead destroyed Lenin's "party of professional revolutionaries" altogether. New thinking, which was supposed to allow the USSR to compete with capitalism more effectively by discarding the coercive methods of past foreign policy, resulted in the rapid disintegration of the Soviet empire.

By 1990, the spiraling loss of party control produced two further unanticipated results: an economic crisis and a nationalist resurgence. Economically, Gorbachev's perestroika had done surprisingly little to change the fundamental elements of the Stalinist planning system, other than to permit small-scale "cooperatives" in the service sector and limited "joint ventures" with foreign capitalists. The breakdown of party authority by 1990 meant that producers no longer had any reason to obey the orders of the planning bureaucracy. Those who simply hoarded raw materials or manufactured goods, then sold or traded them on the black market, could not be punished in the absence of an effective central-party dictatorship. As soon as some people stopped deliveries of goods to Gosplan, however, other enterprises found themselves without necessary supplies; they were also then forced to hoard whatever they had and barter with their former suppliers. Outright theft of enterprise resources, too, became commonplace; in some cases, corrupt party officials even shipped valuable minerals out of the country for hard currency and had the proceeds placed in Swiss bank accounts. As a result of the breakdown of the planning system, goods began to disappear from store shelves all over the country.

At the same time, nationalism began to fill the gap left by the discrediting of Marxism-Leninism. In many ways, it is ironic that the system of "Soviet Republics" created by Lenin and Stalin to deal with the multiethnic nature of Soviet territory had actually reinforced national identity in the USSR. Peoples living in the republics had been allowed to preserve schools, museums, and cultural institutes promoting their native traditions and languages, but had been ruthlessly subordinated to Moscow politically and economically. The Baltic republics of Estonia, Latvia, and Lithuania had even been independent countries until 1940, when Stalin annexed them to the USSR after having made a secret deal with Hitler. After the revolutions of 1989 in East-Central Europe, people in the republics began to demand greater autonomy, and in the case of the Baltics, outright independence. These trends were further fueled by elections to the Supreme Soviets of the fifteen republics in 1990. In each of these campaigns, nationalists outpolled representatives of the Soviet communist center; even those who didn't really want full republican independence often voted for the nationalists as a way of protesting Gorbachev's ineffective leadership. By the end of the year, however, the disintegration of the USSR had become a very real possibility.

That possibility became a reality due to Boris Yeltsin's mobilization of a powerful movement for national independence within Russia itself. Yeltsin had originally been brought to Moscow by Gorbachev in 1986 to be the city's party boss and a candidate member of the Politburo. Yeltsin, born the same year as Gorbachev, shared the latter's belief that Soviet socialism had grown stagnant and corrupt. He won the hearts of Muscovites by criticizing party conservatives, making surprise televised visits to shops suspected of profiting on the black market, and talking with ordinary people on the streets wherever he went. In October 1987, however, Yeltsin made the mistake of attacking conservative Politburo members in a party meeting – thus violating Lenin's decades-old prohibition of "factions" within the party. He was drummed out of the Politburo and given the dead-end job of USSR deputy minister of construction.

The elections for the Soviet Congress of People's Deputies in the spring of 1989, however, revitalized Yeltsin's political career. Running on a platform of greater democracy and marketization, Yeltsin gained 90 percent of the votes in his Moscow electoral district. Together with Sakharov he formed a movement of Congress deputies committed to the end of one-party rule and reintegration with the West. Such a reintegration, Yeltsin argued, could be achieved only if Russia attained greater autonomy from the Soviet Union and took control over its own political and economic life. Yeltsin's embrace of this distinctive anti-Soviet Russian nationalism attracted even some conservatives to his side, including the Afghan war hero Alexander Rutskoi. By the summer of 1990, Yeltsin had quit the Communist Party, and in February 1991 he called on Gorbachev to resign. In June 1991, Yeltsin, with Rutskoi as his vice-presidential candidate, easily won election to the new post of President of the Russian Federation – the first time in history a Russian leader had been democratically elected.

Faced with the potential secession of the Soviet republics, the disintegration of the Soviet economy, and the emergence of a powerful Yeltsin-led opposition in Russia itself, Gorbachev tried desperately to hold the regime together. In May, he negotiated a new "Union Treaty" with the newly elected leaders of those republics – or at least the nine still willing to talk to him. But on August 19, the day before the treaty was to take effect, conservative Leninists within the leadership mounted a coup against Gorbachev as he vacationed on the Black Sea. The heads of the KGB, the Defense Ministry, and the Interior Ministry announced that Gorbachev was "too sick to continue" in office, and proclaimed the formation of a "State Committee for the Emergency Situation" that would lead the country for an unspecified period. However, the coup attempt was ineptly planned and executed. Gorbachev refused to cooperate with the coup plotters, as they had apparently hoped he would. Meanwhile, Yeltsin made his way to the Russian "White House," the building housing the Russian Congress, where hundreds of thousands of Muscovites had gathered to protest the coup. He climbed on top of a tank and declared his uncompromising opposition to the coup plotters. At that moment, he became, in essence, the new leader of Russia.

Key units of the KGB and military defected to Yeltsin's camp. The coup unraveled shortly thereafter. Interior Minister Boris Pugo committed suicide; the other leaders of the coup were arrested. Yeltsin announced Russia's recognition of the independence of the Baltic states; he also banned the Communist Party of the Soviet Union, branding it a criminal organization. Gorbachev returned to Moscow on August 22, but he appeared to be totally out of touch with the changed situation in the country, defending Lenin and the Communist Party at a televised press conference. Gorbachev continued to try to preserve what was left of the Soviet Union, but Yeltsin and other leaders of the national republics soon committed themselves to full independence. In December, the leaders of Russia, Ukraine, and Belarus announced the formation of a new, decentralized Commonwealth of Independent States to replace the USSR; a few days later, over 90 percent of the Ukrainian population voted for national independence in a referendum. On December 26, 1991, Gorbachev, bowing to the inevitable, resigned as leader of the Soviet Union, thus ending the seventy-four year history of the Leninist regime.

# INTERESTS, IDENTITIES, AND INSTITUTIONS IN POST-COMMUNIST RUSSIA

## The Leninist Legacy and Post-Soviet Interests

When the Soviet Union was officially declared dead on December 31, 1991, most Western governments and many analysts understandably greeted the news with euphoria, predicting that Russia would join the prosperous, democratic West in short order. Unfortunately, Westerners tended at the time to underestimate the enormous structural problems that would inevitably face new democratic and market-oriented governments in Russia and other former Soviet republics. As we emphasize throughout this textbook, institutions inherited from the past can exert a powerful influence on politics in the present. This was especially true in the postcommunist world, which was saddled with the legacy of a particularly brutal ideological, political, and socioeconomic tyranny that had endured for decades. Moreover, former communist countries now found themselves exposed to competition from technologically advanced capitalist countries. The economic gap between Russia and the West in 1991 was, if anything, even greater than it had been in 1917.

It was extremely unlikely, then, that a rapid "transition to democracy and markets" in Russia would take place without reversals, inasmuch as the elimination of Soviet institutions often contradicted the interests of the people who had previously lived under them. It is unsurprising that those institutions most costly for individuals to abandon proved the most difficult to destroy. For this reason, Soviet institutions decayed in the same order as they were originally created: first Marxist ideology, then Leninist party politics, and, only very slowly, Stalin's planned economy.

Marxist ideology was the easiest to abandon, and died soon after the collapse of the regime. Indeed, in the immediate aftermath of the August coup, popular disgust with the ideological language of the old regime was so widespread that labeling oneself a "Leninist" or even a "socialist" was tantamount to committing political suicide – as Gorbachev soon discovered. Mainstream Russian politicians strove to outdo one another with professions of opposition to communism. Even those who still called themselves "communists" largely stopped referring to Marx, Engels, and the global proletarian revolution. Perhaps the most significant legacy of Marxism-Leninism, therefore, was a negative one: In the short run, its sudden disappearance left an almost total ideological vacuum.

In response to this situation, Yeltsin and his advisors became convinced that there was no alternative to adopting liberal capitalist ideology. However, whereas liberals in other postcommunist countries could claim – with some justification – to be returning to national traditions suppressed under Soviet rule, liberalism in post-Soviet Russia appeared to many as a capitulation to the West. As the post-Soviet crisis continued, anti-Western sentiments in Russian society understandably strengthened, and those in search of a consistent ideological vision often gravitated toward radically antiliberal figures.

This brings us to the second legacy of Leninism, that of one-party rule. Again, the initial effect of Yeltsin's banning of the Communist Party of the Soviet Union in the days after the August coup was to encourage widespread formal defection from that organization. However, leaving the party was potentially far more costly than disavowing Marxist-Leninist ideology. Since Communist Party officials had monopolized every significant position of power in society, right down to the shop-floor level, membership in alternative political organizations could hardly deliver comparable benefits in the short run. For this reason, formal withdrawal from the CPSU was, in most cases, followed by a scramble to cement key personal ties and to maintain access to economic resources inherited from one's days as a communist functionary.

It was, therefore, somewhat comical to see post-Soviet Russian politicians accuse their opponents of being "communists," since almost all of them had been members of the CPSU in the recent past. This is not to deny that a very real degree of political pluralism has emerged since 1991, especially compared to Soviet times. However, the legacy of one-party rule continues to be a serious obstacle to the formation of genuine, alternative grassroots organizations and mass political parties in the Russian Federation. In the rural regions and smaller towns, in particular, one often finds the same officials ruling over their local fiefdoms as they did under Leninist rule.

A final political legacy of Leninism was the inheritance of administrative boundaries that tended to worsen, rather than ameliorate, ethnic conflicts. The borders of the Russian Federation, like those of the other Soviet republics, had been drawn up by Stalin with little concern for nationalist sensibilities. More than 20 million ethnic Russians lived outside the new Russian state – now suddenly inhabitants of foreign countries. Meanwhile, the Russian Federation itself contained dozens of "ethnic republics" and "autonomous districts" formally set aside for regional non-Russian ethnic groups, and although most of these regions seemed content to remain part of Russia, others, like Chechnya, mounted their own drives for national independence. As a result, popular acceptance of the existing boundaries of the state was weak, and several prominent opposition figures called for restoration of at least part of the old Soviet empire.

The most burdensome institutional legacy of the Soviet system, however, was the residue of the Stalinist planned economy. All over Russia and the other former Soviet republics – indeed, all over the postcommunist region – an enormous "rust belt" of outdated factories continued to produce goods that few consumers wanted, to poison the surrounding environment, and to waste scarce energy and other resources. Enterprises that had for decades been judged solely according to their ability to overfulfill plan targets – or at least fake it – were poorly prepared to compete in a market economy, especially in the global high-tech environment of the 1990s. Unfortunately, Stalinist factories employed tens of millions of people, and under the Soviet system had distributed a whole range of welfare benefits, including child care, recreational facilities, housing, and even food. The loss of one's factory job meant the loss not only of one's salary but also of one's social safety net. Blue-collar workers, former Soviet managers, and the local party officials who had formerly supervised them thus formed a natural lobby against any rapid transition to competitive capitalism.

The legacy of Stalinist collectivization of agriculture reinforced this antimarket lobby. The brutal methods used to create *kolkhozy* and *sovkhozy* in the 1930s had drained the countryside of its most knowledgeable and productive farmers; the poor services and supplies found in rural regions had inspired most young people to leave the villages for the cities. The remaining 30 million Russians living in rural areas were primarily elderly, poorly skilled, and culturally conservative. They, too, were hardly prepared for the establishment of a capitalist farming system.

Along with the sheer weight of inefficient agricultural and industrial sectors in the post-Soviet Russian economy came a more subtle problem: namely, the absence of most of the market institutions now taken for granted in advanced capitalist societies. The USSR, for example, had never created a functioning real estate market, since private ownership of land was banned; years after the Soviet collapse, there was still no consistent legal basis for land ownership in Russia. Nor did the Soviet economy possess anything like a capitalist financial system. The Soviet ruble was never freely tradable for currencies like the U.S. dollar or German mark; its value was set artificially by state bureaucrats. Soviet banks, instead of making careful investment and loan decisions based upon calculations of profit and loss, simply funneled resources to those enterprises the planners directed them to support. Stock and bond markets were also nonexistent under Soviet rule, and those operating in the Russian Federation have been prone to wild speculative swings. Finally, the Soviet judiciary was not trained in the enforcement of legal property rights, and it has been difficult to get post-Soviet Russian courts to uphold business contracts in a consistent manner.

Thus, decades of Leninism had generated enormous institutional obstacles to a smooth reentry into the Western capitalist world. Nonetheless, Yeltsin and his supporters chose what might be termed a revolutionary, rather than evolutionary, approach to Westernizing Russia. With the support of Western political leaders and economic advisors, they launched an all-out drive to reintegrate Russia into the global economy. Predictably, the results have fallen far short of expectations.

## Yeltsin and the Design of Post-Soviet Institutions

During the autumn of 1991, Boris Yeltsin fought successfully against conservative nationalists and supporters of Gorbachev who wished to preserve the USSR. In this struggle, he maintained the enthusiastic support of the Russian Congress of People's Deputies that had been elected in 1990. The Congress voted in November to grant Yeltsin special "emergency powers" for one year in order to deal with the extraordinary political and economic crisis resulting from the Soviet Union's collapse. On New Year's Day, 1992, the Russian Federation became, along with the rest of the former Soviet republics, an internationally recognized independent state; Yeltsin declared himself Russia's first prime minister.

Immediately, Yeltsin used his emergency powers to implement a policy of rapid marketization popularly known as "shock therapy." To administer this policy he named a thirty-five-year-old economist, Yegor Gaidar, as his deputy. The theoretical assumption behind shock therapy was that unless Russia made immediate moves toward capitalism, it would remain stuck in a hopeless halfway house between the old Stalinist system and the new global economy. In theory, shock therapy would be painful in the short run, but better for Russian society in the long run. The shock therapy plan, drawn up in close consultation with Western advisors and the International Monetary Fund (IMF), contained three key elements: price liberalization, monetary stabilization, and privatization of state property.

The argument for freeing prices was hard to refute. For decades, the Soviet planners had kept prices for energy, housing, consumer goods, and basic foodstuffs artificially low in order to prevent public protest. Such low prices made it unprofitable for anyone to produce these goods, except on the black market. Letting prices rise was arguably the only way to induce entrepreneurs to deliver food and basic goods to markets in time to prevent starvation during the cold Russian winter. But the end of price controls was bound to cause social unrest.

Price liberalization was announced on January 2, 1992. Within days, prices had doubled and even tripled; by the end of the year, they were thirteen times higher. The effect was to wipe out most people's savings. An elderly person who had painstakingly saved 10,000 rubles, for example, now found that her fortune was worth approximately $10. On the positive side, goods did reappear in shops throughout the country; the old Soviet phenomenon of people lining up for blocks to buy scarce consumer goods was now a thing of the past.

To fight inflation required attention to the second key element of shock therapy, monetary stabilization – controlling the money supply in order to make the ruble a strong, convertible currency like the dollar. This turned out to be easier to do in principle than in practice. By the spring of 1992, Soviet factories and collective farms everywhere were struggling to pay for supplies at vastly higher prices than before. Russian managers called up their old friends in the Congress of People's Deputies in Moscow to demand that money be sent to help enterprises pay their bills. By May, the Central Bank of Russia had begun to print new rubles day and night to subsidize failing enterprises. Instead of achieving monetary stabilization, Russia was flooded with paper money; as a result, inflation remained extremely high. The alternative, however, was to shut down an enormous number of huge factories and farms and to fire the millions of workers who worked in them.

In theory, of course, unemployed workers should have been able to find new jobs at more efficient start-up companies generated by capitalist competition. But new companies could not easily emerge in a country still owned almost entirely by the state. Thus, the third element of shock therapy, privatization of property, was seen as crucial to the entire reform effort. The privatization drive was led by Gaidar's close ally and friend, Anatoly Chubais. In late 1992, privatization "vouchers" were issued to every man, woman, and child in Russia; they could either use them to bid on state enterprises put up for sale at privatization auctions or sell them for cash. The idea was to build a mass base of support for the new capitalist economy by giving everyone at least a small share of the proceeds of the sale of Soviet properties. Unfortunately, few ordinary Russians had much of an idea of what to do with their vouchers. Many people invested them in bogus "voucher funds," the organizers of which simply cashed in all their vouchers and fled the country. An even greater problem was that much of Soviet state property was doomed to produce at a loss under market conditions – so why bid on it? After a few showcase privatization auctions, the voucher campaign bogged down.

Chubais now engineered a compromise proposal. According to a "second variant" of privatization worked out with leaders of the Russian Congress, 51 percent of the shares of a company could simply be handed over to its existing management and workers, with the rest being divided between the state and any interested outside investors. More than two-thirds of Russian enterprises chose this form of privatization – which, in effect, amounted to a simple declaration that former Stalinist factories were now "private property," although they were run by the same people, and with the same workforce, as before. In this way Yeltsin, Chubais, and Gaidar could claim that within two years, two-thirds of the Russian economy had been privatized; underneath the surface, however, inefficient Soviet production methods remained largely in place.

The inconsistencies and mounting social unrest associated with the shock-therapy program quickly turned a majority of Congress deputies against Yeltsin's Westernization drive. Yeltsin's own vice president, Alexander Rutskoi, now forged an alliance with the parliament's leader, Ruslan Khasbulatov, in opposition to Yeltsin and Gaidar. At the Sixth Congress of People's Deputies in December 1992, a majority refused to confirm Gaidar's reappointment as prime minister. Yeltsin's emergency powers had by then expired, and so he was forced to appoint a compromise candidate, Viktor Chernomyrdin. Chernomyrdin was the former head of the natural gas monopoly, Gazprom, and shared the basic economic views of the factory managers clamoring for an end to shock therapy. At the same time, Chernomyrdin was rumored to have become a millionaire through profits from exports of gas to Western Europe. In practice, Chernomyrdin tried to be a "centrist," calling for an "end to market romanticism," but not a reversal of market reforms.

Chernomyrdin's appointment as prime minister did not end the growing tensions between Yeltsin and the Congress. Rutskoi and Khasbulatov now openly called for the creation of a new government led by the Congress itself. In April, Yeltsin turned to the public, sponsoring a nationwide referendum on his leadership and economic policies, and asking whether early elections should be held for the president and/or the parliament. The results showed that Yeltsin's public support remained, at this stage, remarkably strong, with a majority even supporting the basic economic policies of the past year. The opposition in the Congress, however, continued to press for Yeltsin's ouster.

During the summer of 1993, a form of "dual power" emerged. Both the president and the Congress issued contradictory laws and decrees; both sides drew up new constitutions for the Russian state. Given the administrative chaos in Moscow, Russia's 89 regions and ethnic republics began to push for even greater autonomy, withholding taxes and resources and often insisting on the primacy of regional over central laws. Fears that Russia would disintegrate like the Soviet Union became increasingly widespread. In September, Yeltsin brought the crisis to a head by announcing the dismissal of the Congress of People's Deputies. The Congress responded by declaring Yeltsin's presidency null and void, and declaring Rutskoi as the new Russian leader. The possibility of civil war loomed. On October 3, extremist supporters of the Congress tried to take over the main television station and mayor's office in Moscow. Yeltsin then decided to order a military assault on his enemies.

More than 150 people were killed in the attack on the Russian White House in October 1993. There was a sad symbolism in watching Yeltsin order the shelling of the very building where he had courageously defied the Soviet coup plotters just two years earlier. After October 1993, the impression that "democracy" was merely a disguise for naked presidential power became widespread among disaffected groups in Russian society.

The destruction of the Russian Congress did, however, allow Yeltsin to design and implement a new constitution in December 1993 (just barely approved by Russian voters – at least officially). The Russian constitution, like democratic constitutions elsewhere, formally divides political power among the legislative, judicial, and executive branches. The legislature is bicameral. The lower house, the State Duma, consists of 450 deputies, half of whom are representatives of national parties selected on the basis of proportional representation, and half of whom are representatives of local electoral districts. The 178 members of the upper house, the Federation Council, are the governors and heads of regional legislatures from each of Russia's 89 federal regions. The judicial branch is led by the Constitutional Court, empowered to rule on basic constitutional issues, and the Supreme Court, the country's highest court of appeal. However, Yeltsin's constitution gives by far the greatest share of political power to the president. The Russian president is the commander in chief of the armed forces, appoints the prime minister, and even has the right to issue presidential decrees with the force of law. Moreover, if the State Duma refuses to confirm the president's choice for prime minister three times or votes no confidence in the government twice, he can dissolve the lower house and call new elections.

Notwithstanding the enormous powers of the presidency, elections since 1993 have had genuine political significance. Even in the first elections to the State Duma in December 1993, Russian voters were able to express their alienation from those responsible for the shock-therapy reforms of the preceding two years. Despite highly visible state support, Gaidar's political party, Russia's Choice, attained only 15.5 percent of the party-list vote. Meanwhile, the other two most successful parties were led by antiliberal ideologues. A full 23 percent of the electorate chose the farcically named Liberal Democratic Party of Russia (LDPR) led by Vladimir Zhirinovsky, a flamboyant ultranationalist who promised to lower the price of vodka, shoot criminals on the spot, and invade the Baltic states and the Middle East. An additional 12 percent of the voting public chose Gennady Zyuganov's Communist Party of the Russian Federation (CPRF), which called for the resuscitation of the Soviet Union – not because of any lingering faith in Marx's communist workers' utopia, but in order to rebuild Russia as a "great power." The remainder of the Duma was split among smaller parties that managed to surpass the 5 percent barrier to party-list representation, such as the more moderate pro-market party "Yabloko" (Apple), led by economist Grigory Yavlinsky, the Agrarian Party representing collective farms, and the "Women of Russia" party, which emphasized problems of unemployment and abuse facing many Russian women.

A new constitution and elections did not eliminate Russia's continuing economic problems, however. The government did gradually manage to get inflation under control, primarily by stopping the printing of rubles. But factory managers throughout the country responded to the cutoff of subsidies by resorting to barter and by ceasing to pay their workers for months at a time. Eventually, mounting "wage arrears" to Russian workers, state employees, and soldiers grew into an intractable social problem. Small businesses, meanwhile, continued to be strangled by a combination of overzealous state taxation and interference by local "mafias" demanding protection money. Foreign and domestic investment remained at a very low level, and the overall gross domestic product (GDP) continued to decline. Taxation to cover government expenditure became increasingly difficult, since many people (understandably) did their best to hide their incomes. The government began to rely on revenues from the privatization drive, which continued to favor well-connected elites. By 1995 a handful of multimillionaires – popularly known as the "oligarchs" – had gained control of most of the country's mass media, energy and mineral resources, and banks.

Moreover, although the new constitution contributed to a temporary stabilization in relations between Moscow and the various regional governments of the Russian Federation, the danger of state disintegration remained. Yeltsin was soon forced to conclude a series of separate treaties with restive regions, such as oil-rich Tatarstan and the diamond-producing republic of Sakha in the Far East. Then in December 1994, hard-line advisers persuaded Yeltsin to reassert Moscow's authority over the regions by invading the rebellious republic of Chechnya. The invasion quickly escalated into a full-scale war that killed tens of thousands of ordinary citizens – many of them elderly ethnic Russians who could not escape the Chechen capital of Grozny in time. But the war only succeeded in further stiffening Chechen resistance to Russian rule. The utter failure of the campaign in Chechnya demonstrated clearly that the Russian military, like the rest of the government, was in a state of near-total demoralization and ineffectiveness.

Given Russia's continuing decline – and Yeltsin's growing health problems and increasingly erratic behavior – it is perhaps unsurprising that parliamentary elections in 1995 once again favored antiliberal forces. That voters were confronted with a long, confusing ballot listing forty-three competing parties did not help matters. This time Zyuganov's CPRF was the biggest vote getter, attaining 22 percent of the vote. Zhirinovsky's LDPR still polled a disturbing 11 percent. The only other two parties to exceed the 5 percent barrier were Yavlinsky's Yabloko, with 7 percent, and a new pro-government party called "Our Home Is Russia," led by Prime Minister Chernomyrdin, which managed to attain only 10 percent of the party-list vote despite an expensive government-sponsored media campaign. Gaidar's party dropped below the 5 percent barrier and won just a few single-member district seats. Meanwhile, a majority of Russian voters voted for parties that didn't get any Duma seats at all.

The first post-Soviet presidential campaign in Russia in 1996 thus began with Yeltsin's political future in grave doubt. In February, polls showed that only 6 percent of Russians supported the Russian president, while over a quarter supported his communist challenger, Zyuganov. With the fate of Russia's weak democratic-capitalist regime hanging in the balance, however, Yeltsin mounted a remarkable comeback. He traveled throughout the country, energetically shaking hands, handing out money to pay late pensions and wages, and even dancing to a rock band. Yeltsin's campaign was financed by a huge infusion of cash from the IMF, which delivered the first installment of a $10 billion loan to Yeltsin's government, and by the oligarchs, who were terrified that their newly privatized companies would be renationalized in the event of a communist victory. The oligarchs also flooded Russian newspapers and television with political advertising portraying Zyuganov as a tyrant who would reimpose totalitarian rule. Zyuganov, meanwhile, made such fears seem realistic by praising Stalin as a great Russian leader and declaring that the USSR still legally existed.

In the first round of the presidential elections in June 1996, Yeltsin got 35 percent of the vote to Zyuganov's 32 percent. In third place with 15 percent was General Alexander Lebed, who called himself a "semidemocrat" and promised to restore "truth and order." Yavlinsky managed fourth place with 7 percent of the vote, while Zhirinovsky came in fifth with 5 percent. Five other minor candidates polled less than 2 percent each – including Mikhail Gorbachev, supported by a minuscule 0.5 percent of the electorate.

Russian electoral rules require a runoff between the top two vote getters in the first round of presidential elections if no candidate attains a majority. Thus, voters now faced a stark choice between Yeltsin and Zyuganov. The oligarchs continued their media campaign, portraying the election as a decision between freedom and totalitarianism. Lebed decided to support Yeltsin in return for an important government post. Zyuganov himself repeated his standard themes, blaming the IMF, the West, and Yeltsin for the ruin of Russia and calling for the restoration of Soviet power. In early July, Yeltsin completed his comeback, gaining 54 percent of the vote versus 40 percent for Zyuganov (5 percent of voters declared themselves "against both").

Yeltsin's reelection meant that the flawed democratic-capitalist institutions he had established after 1991 in Russia would endure at least a while longer. However, powerful postcommunist interest groups, including many blue-collar workers, collective farmers, pensioners, military men, and anti-Western intellectuals, continued to oppose Yeltsin's regime. Moreover, the perpetual crises, violence, and economic decline of the early post-Soviet period had alienated even Yeltsin's own supporters among the urban, educated middle class, most of whom had voted in 1996 *against* Zyuganov and a return to communism, rather than *for* the aging and erratic president. Indeed, a few days before his reelection, Yeltsin had suffered a severe heart attack; he was barely able to attend his own inauguration ceremony, and was only sporadically active afterward. The president's incapacitation set the government adrift while its political, economic, and regional challenges mounted. Elections for regional governors in 1997 – though marking an important extension of Russian democracy – tended further to strengthen the power of Russia's regions as the capacity of the central government decayed.

In the spring of 1998, during one of his infrequent periods of political activity, Yeltsin made one last effort to rejuvenate market reforms. He unexpectedly fired Chernomyrdin as prime minister, replacing him with Sergei Kiriyenko, a thirty-five-year-old ally of Gaidar, Chubais, and other liberal "young reformers." However, the underlying structural problems in the Russian economy were by this point too severe to fix. Given continued economic stagnation, decreasing confidence on the part of foreign investors, poor tax collection, declining world oil prices and an increasingly unmanageable debt burden, Russia's budget deficit became unsustainable. The IMF tried to help Kiriyenko's government, delivering almost $5 billion in late July, but within a few weeks this loan had been exhausted in a vain attempt to prop up the weakening ruble.

On August 17, Kiriyenko suddenly announced a devaluation of the ruble and a ninety-day moratorium on government debt payments. A deep financial crisis ensued. Inflation soared to almost 40 percent for the month of September alone; dozens of banks failed; and foreign investors left in droves. Yeltsin fired Kiriyenko, but then inexplicably proposed to replace him once again with Chernomyrdin. Besides Chernomyrdin's own party, no major faction in the Russian parliament would go along. After tense negotiations, all sides agreed to support the compromise candidacy of Foreign Minister Yevgeny Primakov, a Soviet academic specialist on the Middle East and former chief of the Russian successor to the KGB. On September 11, Primakov was overwhelmingly confirmed as Russia's new prime minister. The constitutional order had been preserved.

Unfortunately, the endemic uncertainties of Russian politics continued. Only seven months after Primakov's promotion, another nearly disastrous battle between the president and the parliament erupted when Zyuganov's Communist Party initiated impeachment proceedings against Yeltsin. Although more moderate political forces seemed unlikely to support some of Zyuganov's most extreme claims – for example, that Yeltsin had committed "genocide" against the Russian people by launching the shock-therapy program – the vote to impeach the president for unconstitutional actions in launching the war in Chechnya looked too close to call.

But on May 12, 1999, just three days before the impeachment vote in the Duma, Yeltsin suddenly dismissed Primakov as prime minister, proposing to replace him with Interior Minister Sergei Stepashin. Now a full-scale constitutional crisis loomed. According to the text of the 1993 Russian constitution, the Duma would be disbanded if it failed to confirm Stepashin as the new prime minister on a third vote; yet at the same time, the constitution also *forbade* the president from dissolving the Duma if it voted for impeachment. Faced with the very real possibility that Yeltsin would take advantage of the constitution's ambiguity to declare a state of emergency rule – and worried that they would lose their parliamentary perks and priviliges as a result – the Duma majority backed down. The vote to impeach Yeltsin failed, and Stepashin was later easily confirmed as prime minister.

Even this was not sufficient to make the increasingly isolated president feel secure, however. In early August, two new threats to Yeltsin's regime emerged. First, Primakov and the powerful mayor of Moscow, Yuri Luzhkov, announced the formation of a new political party supported by many of Russia's most powerful regional governors, the "Fatherland-All Russia Bloc," which would compete against parties supported by the Kremlin in the December 1999 Duma elections. Then, Chechen extremists led by Shamil Basaev and the Islamic fundamentalist Khattab invaded the neighboring ethnic republic of Dagestan, proclaiming their goal to be the creation of an Islamic state in southern Russia. Yeltsin fired Stepashin, who appeared to have been taken by surprise by these events, and replaced him with the dour, forty-six-year-old former KGB spy Vladmir Putin. Yeltsin also announced that he considered Putin to be his "heir," and that he hoped that Russians would rally around him as the 2000 presidential elections neared. Remarkably, despite Putin's almost total political obscurity at the time of his appointment, this is exactly what happened.

The key event propelling Putin into the top position in Russian politics was the outbreak of the second war in Chechnya in the fall of 1999. Although rumors of a renewed Russian assault on the breakaway republic had been swirling for some time, the final decision to launch a second invasion was propelled by shocking events in September: terrorist bombings of apartment buildings in the suburbs of Moscow and in the southern Russian city of Volgodonsk that killed nearly 300 Russian citizens. Putin's government immediately blamed these attacks on the Chechen rebels led by Basaev and Khattab, whipping up an understandable public outcry for revenge – although no one has yet been convicted of these bombings, and suspicions about who is really responsible for them remain.

The Russian military counterattack on the Chechen rebels soon escalated into an all-out invasion of the Chechen republic. Putin now declared his intention to wipe out the Chechen "bandits" once and for all. The resulting conflict, like the first Chechen war, resulted in the deaths of thousands of innocent Russian and Chechen civilians and the near-total destruction of much of the region, including the capital city of Grozny, which was finally taken by Russian troops in February 2000.

The emotionally charged political environment generated by the new Chechen war could not but affect the outcome of the 1999 Duma elections. A new pro-Putin party known as "Unity" (also sometimes called the "Bear" party), made up of various regional leaders and state bureaucrats, was hastily thrown together in October; it ended up gaining 23 percent of the party-list vote. Zyuganov's nationalist KPRF did very well, attaining 24 percent of the party-list vote and 46 seats in single-member districts. The "Union of Right-Wing Forces," including famous "young reformers" such as Gaidar, Nemtsov, Kiriyenko, and Chubais, also received an endorsement from Putin; as a result they too did surprisingly well, attaining 8.5 percent of the party vote. Meanwhile, pro-Kremlin television mounted a sustained mudslinging campaign against Primakov and Luzhkov; as a result, the Fatherland-All Russia party performed well below early expectations, with just over 13 percent of the vote. Finally, Yavlinsky's Yabloko party – the one political force publicly critical of the war in Chechnya – barely squeaked past the 5 percent barrier, as did Zhirinovsky's LDPR.

This popular endorsement of Putin and his policies reassured Yeltsin that he could now leave the political stage with no fear that he or his circle of intimates would later be investigated or prosecuted, as had been continually threatened by the communists and their allies. On New Year's Eve, 1999, Yeltsin stunned the world with the sudden announcement of his early resignation as Russia's president. As specified in the Russian constitution, Prime Minister Putin now became Acting President as well, and early elections for the presidency were scheduled for March 26. Given Putin's war-driven popularity and the limited time available for campaigning, his election in the spring of 2000 looked very likely indeed. It was not at all clear, however, just what sorts of policies the inexperienced and secretive Putin might adopt after the elections. The Yeltsin era in Russian politics had drawn to a close – but the country's political and economic future remained as murky as it had been a decade before.

## Institutions, Interests, and the Search for a New Russian Identity

By the end of the 1990s, it was clear to everyone that the dream of a rapid transformation of post-Communist Russia into a liberal capitalist country like the United States was just that – a dream. From the perspective adopted in this textbook, which emphasizes the long-term impact of institutions created at critical junctures in a country's history and the specific social interests these institutions generate, the failure of capitalism in Russia should not have been surprising. After all, the political and economic institutions of the Soviet Union were designed by men committed to destroying global capitalism. The all-powerful Communist Party was supposed to train new "professional revolutionaries" to conquer the world bourgeoisie, but it degenerated into a giant, corrupt bureaucracy entangled with a vast network of secret police. Those who had benefited from their positions in the party hierarchy were thus rarely interested in establishing new institutions that would strictly enforce norms of democratic citizenship and the rule of law. Soviet industrial cities were supposed to be heroic sites for revolutionary production, but decayed into polluting, outmoded factory towns. They were thus ill suited to the task of producing consumer goods according to Western standards of efficiency.

Despite the burdensome legacy of the communist past, the collapse of the Soviet Union in 1991 – like the collapse of tsarism at the beginning of the century – marked another critical juncture in Russia's history during which new institutions promoting new interests could be established (see Table 1). Indeed, despite all of the country's well-publicized problems, Russia did manage during the 1990s to

TABLE 1. KEY PHASES IN RUSSIAN DEVELOPMENT

| Date | Regime | Global Context | Interests, Identities, Institutions | Development Path |
|------|--------|----------------|-------------------------------------|------------------|
| 1690–1917 | Tsarist empire | Great power on periphery of capitalist West | Landowning aristocracy, "divine right" monarchy, feudal state | Autocratic modernization |
| 1917–1928 | Soviet Russia/ USSR | World War I, collapse of tsarist empire, civil war, postwar isolation | Revolutionary intellectuals and workers, Marxist ideology, Leninist one-party rule | Party control over key industries, toleration of market production |
| 1929–1945 | USSR | Great Depression, rise of Nazism in Germany, World War II | Stalinist secret police and "heroic" workers, Marxism-Leninism, planned economy | Rapid industrialization, brutal collectivization, prison labor, military build-up |
| 1945–1984 | USSR | Cold war with United States, anti-Soviet rebellions in Poland and Afghanistan | Corrupt party and state elites, "superpower" socialism, stagnating planned economy | Enforcement of status quo, military expansion in Third World |
| 1985–1991 | USSR | Military buildup in West, disintegration of Soviet bloc and USSR | Reformist intellectuals, "socialist renewal," institutional disintegration | "Perestroika" (unintended self-destruction of Leninism) |
| 1991– present | Russian Federation | Fading power on periphery of triumphant capitalist global system | Former party and state elites and local "mafias," search for new Russian identity, weak democracy | "Shock therapy," corrupt capitalism |

establish the first democratic regime in its long history. Even if Russia's democracy remained rife with state corruption, undermined by abysmal economic performance, and threatened by vocal antiliberal movements, this accomplishment should not be dismissed.

Where is Russia headed now? The future of Russia depends not only upon the nature of its institutions and interests. It depends also upon the outcome of Russia's search for a new state identity, now that both Marxism-Leninism and revolutionary capitalism have failed. Indeed, with the military underpaid and underfed, with ethnic and Russian regions alike pressing for greater autonomy, and with widespread popular distrust of all political parties and movements, some fear the country will collapse altogether – a terrifying prospect because of Russia's substantial stockpiles of chemical, biological, and nuclear weapons. This extreme scenario, however, appears unlikely given the strong sense among almost all citizens of the Russian Federation that "Russia," in some form, must be preserved.

But which Russia? The liberal capitalist Russia originally envisioned by Gaidar and his allies has been largely discredited by the economic crisis. Zyuganov's nostalgic communist version, which includes the entire former Soviet Union, has little appeal for younger, educated Russians. The neoimperialist nationalism of Zhirinovsky has also lost much of its support. More explicitly pro-Nazi and anti-Semitic politicians are trying to convert disgruntled youth and soldiers to their cause – but ever since Hitler's invasion in World War II, "fascism" has been deeply unpopular in Russia. Nor do any of Russia's other leading political figures – including Yury Luzhkov, the powerful mayor of Moscow, General Lebed, who is now the governor of the mineral-rich Krasnoyarsk region in Siberia, former prime minister Primakov, and Putin himself – have a clearly developed new definition of "Russia."

The one thing that can be predicted with confidence, then, is that we have not seen the final chapter in Russia's painful transition from Soviet rule. On the one hand, this implies that the potential for a total collapse of state authority in post-Soviet Russia is still real. On the other hand, it means that the possibility of procedural, democratic compromise remains open.

## BIBLIOGRAPHY

Breslauer, George. *Khrushchev and Brezhnev as Leaders: Building Authority in Soviet Politics.* London and Boston: Allen and Unwin, 1982.

Brown, Archie. *The Gorbachev Factor.* Oxford and New York: Oxford University Press, 1997

Conquest, Robert. *The Great Terror: A Reassessment.* New York: Oxford University Press, 1991.
  *The Harvest of Sorrow: Soviet Collectivization and the Terror Famine.* New York: Oxford University Press, 1987.

Dunlop, John B. *The Rise of Russia and the Fall of the Soviet Empire.* Princeton, N.J.: Princeton University Press, 1993.

Fish, M. Steven. *Democracy From Scratch: Opposition and Regime in the New Russian Revolution.* Princeton, N.J.: Princeton University Press, 1995.

Fitzpatrick, Sheila. *The Russian Revolution.* 2d ed. Oxford and New York: Oxford University Press, 1994.

Handelman, Stephen. *Comrade Criminal: Russia's New Mafiya.* New Haven, Conn.: Yale University Press, 1995.

Hanson, Stephen E. *Time and Revolution: Marxism and the Design of Soviet Institutions.* Chapel Hill, N.C.: University of North Carolina Press, 1997.

Jowitt, Ken. *New World Disorder: The Leninist Extinction.* Berkeley: University of California Press, 1992.

Kotkin, Stephen. *Steeltown, USSR: A Soviet Society in the Gorbachev Era.* Berleley: University of California Press, 1992.

McAuley, Mary. *Russia's Politics of Uncertainty.* Cambridge and New York: Cambridge University Press, 1997.

Solnick, Steven. *Stealing the State: Control and Collapse in Soviet Institutions.* Cambridge, Mass.: Harvard University Press, 1998.

Stoner-Weiss, Katherine. *Local Heroes: The Political Economy of Russian Regional Governance.* Princeton, N.J.: Princeton University Press, 1997.

Remnick, David. *Resurrection: The Struggle for a New Russia.* New York: Random House, 1998.

Yeltsin, Boris. *The Struggle for Russia.* New York: Random House, 1994.

Zaslavsky, Viktor. *The Neo-Stalinist State: Class, Ethnicity, and Consensus in Soviet Society.* Armonk, N.Y.: M. E. Sharpe, 1994.

## IMPORTANT TERMS

**Alexander Lebed**   popular general who came in third in the 1996 presidential elections, after which he became the head of the Security Council. After having settled the first war in Chechnya, Lebed was fired by Yeltsin. In 1997 he was elected governor of the vast Krasnoyarsk region in Siberia.

**Alexander Rutskoi**   general during the Soviet war in Afghanistan, and Yeltsin's vice president from 1991 to 1993. He originally supported Yeltsin's Russian nationalism against Gorbachev's conception of "socialist reform," but later broke with Yeltsin when the president agreed to break up the USSR and tried to implement capitalism in the Russian Federation. Rutskoi was a leader of the opposition in the Russian Congress in 1993.

**Boris Yeltsin**   the first democratically elected president of Russia. He organized the movement to declare the "Russian Federation" an independent country, and thus to destroy the USSR; in 1993 he violently disbanded the Russian Congress of People's Deputies and introduced the new Russian constitution. After winning reelection in 1996, Yeltsin experienced increasing health problems and his power gradually diminished. He resigned on December 31, 1999.

**Chechnya**   an ethnic republic that declared its independence from the Russian Federation in September 1991. In December 1994, Yeltsin launched a disastrous full-scale military attack on Chechnya in which tens of thousands of Chechens and Russians were killed. This first war was settled in the summer of 1996, but the political status of the republic remained unresolved. A second Chechen war broke out in the fall of 1999.

**collectivization**   Stalin's policy of creating "collective farms" (*kolkhozy*) and "state farms" (*sovkhozy*) throughout the Soviet countryside, supposedly in order to build socialist agriculture. This policy led to the deaths of tens of millions of peasants through political violence and famine and the creation of an enormously inefficient agricultural system.

**Commonwealth of Independent States** the loose association of former Soviet republics formed in December 1991 to replace the USSR. It was officially created at the Belovezh forest meeting of Boris Yeltsin, president of the Russian Federation, and the presidents of Ukraine, Belorussia (Belarus), and Kazakhstan. The CIS has been largely ineffective since the collapse of the Soviet Union.

**democratic centralism** the central institutional principle of Leninist political organization. According to this principle, "democratic" debates among party members are allowed only until the party leadership makes a final decision, at which point all members are obliged to implement the orders of their superiors without question.

**Federation Council** the upper house of the Federal Assembly. The Federation Council has 178 members and includes the governors and heads of regional legislatures in all 89 of Russia's federal regions and republics.

**Five-Year Plan** the basic organizing framework of Stalinist economic institutions. Beginning with the First Five-Year Plan of 1928–32, all industrial and agricultural production in the USSR was regulated by monthly and yearly output targets given to each manager and worker. Bonuses went to those managers and workers who overfulfilled their plan targets enough to demonstrate their revolutionary zeal.

**Gennady Zyuganov** leader of the Communist Party of the Russian Federation (CPRF). Zyuganov and his party argue for the restoration of "Soviet power," including the reconstitution of the USSR and the renationalization of much of the property privatized since 1992. The ideology of the party, however, is much more oriented toward great-power nationalism than toward original Marxism or Leninism.

**Grigory Yavlinsky** leader of the "Yabloko" (Apple) movement, so named after the initials of its three founders. He argues that capitalism in Russia must be implemented by means of strong and uncorrupted state institutions, rather than via shock therapy.

**gulag** the Russian abbreviation for "state camp." The gulags were a vast network of labor camps set up by Lenin and greatly expanded by Stalin, used to imprison millions of people who were suspected of opposing the Communist Party and its policies.

**Joseph Stalin** the unrivaled leader of the Communist Party of the Soviet Union from 1928 to 1953. Stalin rose to power in a bitter and prolonged struggle with Trotsky, Bukharin, and Zinoviev after Lenin's death. He then implemented a policy of rapid industrialization and mass terror designed to build "socialism" in peasant Russia as quickly as possible – at the cost of tens of millions of lives.

**Karl Marx** 19th-century German intellectual, the coauthor (with Friedrich Engels) of the *Communist Manifesto* and the author of *Capital*. Marx provided the main theoretical inspiration for the later movement to create a socialist society in Europe.

**Leonid Brezhnev**  leader of the Communist Party of the Soviet Union from 1964 until his death in 1982. He presided over an "orthodox" Marxist-Leninist regime that became more and more politically corrupt and economically stagnant over time.

**Mikhail Gorbachev**  leader of the Communist Party of the Soviet Union from 1985 to 1991. Gorbachev tried to reverse the stagnation of the Brezhnev era by launching a policy of "revolutionary restructuring" (*perestroika*) that called for open criticism of the past, greater democracy, and "new thinking" in foreign policy. The result was the wholesale disintegration of Leninist political institutions and Stalinist economic organizations, leading to the collapse of the USSR.

**New Economic Policy**  often abbreviated NEP, the economic program adopted by Lenin in 1921 in the wake of the social devastation caused by the Russian civil war, which he saw as a "strategic retreat" from the ultimate goal of building socialism. The NEP allowed for the reestablishment of markets for agricultural products and legalized small-scale trade in the cities, but the Soviet state retained control over the major industries, and one-party rule was strengthened.

**Nikita Khrushchev**  leader of the Communist Party of the Soviet Union from shortly after Stalin's death until 1964. Khrushchev endeavored to reinvigorate Soviet socialism by means of a series of "revolutionary" economic campaigns in agriculture and industry; he also attacked Stalin's terror. This "leftist" strategy, however, only produced general administrative chaos, and Khrushchev was ousted in a Politburo coup.

**oligarchs**  the group of a half dozen or so bankers and industrialists who took advantage of the rapid privatization of Soviet property to amass huge personal fortunes. This group controls most of Russia's most powerful media, banks, and raw-material companies.

**provisional government**  the temporary government of former parliamentarians that ruled Russia after the fall of the tsarist empire in February 1917. This ineffective body failed to stabilize the revolutionary situation in the country, and was overthrown by Lenin's Bolshevik party in October.

**shock therapy**  policy of rapid transition to capitalism officially adopted by Boris Yeltsin in January 1992. In theory, shock therapy was supposed to involve the simultaneous liberalization of all prices, privatization of state property, and stabilization of the Russian currency. In reality, the program was implemented only haphazardly, generating disastrous economic and social results.

**soviets**  a word that means "councils" in Russian. It refers to the spontaneous groups of workers and soldiers that formed in the chaotic social situation under the provisional government. Lenin saw these bodies as the seeds of the future communist society, and for this reason he declared the country a "soviet regime" after his party seized power. Until Gorbachev, however, these councils remained politically powerless and wholly subordinate to the party.

**State Duma**  the lower house of the Federal Assembly, the Russian parliament created in the Constitution of 1993. The Duma has 450 members, half of whom are selected by proportional representation on party lists, and half of whom are elected in single-member districts.

**Viktor Chernomyrdin**   prime minister of the Russian Federation from December 1992 until March 1998. Chernomyrdin, the former head of the Soviet natural gas ministry, was originally promoted as a compromise candidate after the refusal of the conservative Russian Congress of People's Deputies to reconfirm arch-marketizer Yegor Gaidar as prime minister. Later he became the leader of the pro-regime "Our Home Is Russia" Party.

**Vladimir I. Lenin**   Russian revolutionary and the author of *What Is To Be Done?*, Lenin insisted on strict "professional revolutionary" discipline among Marxists. In 1917 Lenin led the October Revolution and founded the Soviet regime in Russia.

**Vladimir Putin**   appointed prime minister by Yeltsin in August 1999; also designated Yeltsin's "heir" as Russia's president. Putin attained high popularity among Russians for his prosecution of the war in Chechnya and his promises to restore the power of the Russian state.

**Vladimir Zhirinovsky**   leader of the so-called Liberal Democratic Party of Russia (LDPR). Zhirinovsky and his party argue for an ultranationalist solution to Russia's postcommunist problems, envisioning an eventual expansion of Russia to the Indian Ocean. In practice, however, Zhirinovsky has often voted in support of the government in return for political and financial support.

**Yevgeny Primakov**   former academic advisor to Gorbachev, later head of the Foreign Intelligence Service and foreign minister. Primakov was appointed prime minister in a compromise between Yeltsin and the communist-led Duma after the financial crisis of August 1998; he was then fired as the communists tried to impeach Yeltsin in the spring of 1999.

**Yuri Luzhkov**   mayor of Moscow and leader of the Fatherland Party. Luzhkov has built a mini-empire through his control over business activities in Russia's capital city, and has become one of the country's most influential politicians.


## STUDY QUESTIONS

1.  Should Russia today be classified as a "developed" industrial society comparable to Britain, France or Germany? Why or why not?

2.  Was Lenin's conception of a "revolutionary" one-party regime consistent with Marx's vision of communism, or was it a betrayal of Marx's dream of worker liberation?

3.  What were the main reasons for the rise of Stalin and his policies of mass terror? Would you blame primarily the ideals of communism, the institutions of Leninism, the interests of Stalin and his supporters, or the global context in which the Soviet Union was situated?

4.  Does the failure of Gorbachev's perestroika demonstrate that the Soviet system in the 1980s was unreformable? Or could some alternative strategy for reforming communism have succeeded in revitalizing the institutions of the USSR? What is the relevance, if any, of Deng Xiaoping's reforms in China to the Soviet case?

5.  Should social scientists have been able to predict the disintegration of the Soviet

bloc? What explains the remarkably poor track record of Western scholars making predictions about the future of the Soviet Union and Russia?

6. Compare and contrast the problem of ethnic conflict in the Soviet Union and in the Russian Federation. Do you think that the Russian Federation will eventually break up into smaller countries as the Soviet Union did? Why or why not?

7. Does the failure of Yeltsin's shock-therapy program demonstrate that capitalism in Russia is simply impossible? Or might some alternative political strategy have been more successful in creating the institutions typical of Western liberal-capitalist countries in the post-Soviet context?

8. Are capitalism and democracy in conflict in post-Communist Russia? Or do they instead reinforce each other?

9. In 1917, the tsarist empire collapsed; soon Lenin's radical Bolshevik party came to power. In 1918, the German empire collapsed; within fifteen years the Nazi party came to power. Is there any chance that a radically antiliberal party like Lenin's or Hitler's will eventually triumph in post-Soviet Russia as well? Why or why not?

10. Would you expect the next generation of Russian politicians to be more successful at institution building than was the generation reared under communism? Why or why not?

# 6

# China

≋ **Yu Shan Wu**

# INTRODUCTION

China has one of the world's most ancient civilizations, dating back to more than 3,000 years. It is easy for political scientists studying China to emphasize its uniqueness, as the Chinese culture, language, political thought, and history appear quite different from those of any of the major Western countries. Modern Chinese history was obviously punctuated with decisive Western impacts, but the way China responded to those impacts is often considered to be uniquely Chinese. Furthermore, Chinese political leaders themselves frequently stress that they represent movements that carry unique "Chinese characteristics." China, it seems, can only be understood in its own light.

When put in a global and comparative context, however, China loses many of its unique features. Imperial China, or the Qing dynasty, was an agricultural empire when it met the first serious wave of challenges from the West in the middle of the 19th century. The emperor and the mandarins were forced to give up their treasured institutions grudgingly after a series of humiliating defeats at the hands of the Westerners. The pattern resembled what occurred in many traditional political systems when confronted with aggression from the West. From that time on, the momentum for political development in China was driven by the need for national survival and global competition. China differed from other cases in the developing world mainly in the immense dimensions of the country, not in the nature of its response.

Like in other developing countries, different political forces in China competed for power as the country faced international challenges. Those different political forces represented distinct interests, developed alternative identities, and pro-

TABLE 1. INTERESTS, IDENTITIES, AND INSTITUTIONS IN CHINESE POLITICAL
DEVELOPMENT

| Model of Development | Interest | Identity | Institution | Reference |
|---|---|---|---|---|
| Liberal | Urban intellectuals | Liberalism | Democracy | Britain |
| Statist | KMT | Nationalism | Authoritarianism | Japan |
| Communist | CCP | Communism | Totalitarianism | Soviet Union |

posed competing institutions (see Table 1). The outcome of their competition shaped the developmental route of China, and that outcome was, in turn, contingent on the international environment in which China found itself.

As previous chapters have noted, late developers tended to put more emphasis on the state's role in development. Thus from Britain to France, Germany, and ultimately Russia, one finds an increasingly coercive state accumulating sparse capital to fuel economic growth. British liberalism was translated into strategic investment in France and state sponsorship in Germany, and total state control under the name of communism in Russia. Following this logic, one could safely predict that China would follow a development strategy that puts a much stronger emphasis on a "developmental state" than would a typical Western liberal model.

"Developmental state" in the German (and Japanese), or in the Russian sense? This is the major difference between the Kuomintang (KMT or Nationalist) regime that ruled China from 1928 to 1949, and the Communist regime that established the People's Republic of China in 1949 and has ruled the country since then. The global European and Japanese challenge forced the Chinese to adopt new institutions with greater governing capacity and, at the same time, offered models for the Chinese to emulate. The KMT opted for the German model, whereas the Chinese Communist Party (CCP) chose the Soviet model. The KMT and the CCP represent two different interests, upheld nationalism and communism as their respective identities, and established an authoritarian and totalitarian regime respectively. In short, the international challenge to China brought about two distinctively different developmental models, as represented by the KMT and the CCP, and the interests, identities, and institutions of these two dominant political forces.

The post-1949 political division between mainland China and Taiwan witnessed the deployment of the Soviet model in the hands of Mao Zedong, followed by a convergence toward the world market under Deng Xiaoping. On the island of Taiwan, to which the KMT and its followers had fled after 1949, the KMT experienced a less turbulent and more linear development toward Western liberal capitalism and an increasing attenuation of its statist model. Viewed from a historical perspective, irresistible forces have compelled both the CCP and the KMT to adapt to the world market and "play by the rules." Global competition first compelled the Chinese to establish a strong state for the initial push of industrialization, and then pressured them to tinker with the market when state planning proved ineffective in sustaining growth. Markets and private property then nurtured social demands for pluralism and a shift of political culture away from the collectivism that had been vital in sustaining authoritarian rule in both mainland China and Taiwan. Taiwan has already conformed to that pressure for democracy, owing partly to the strong influence of the United States on which Taiwan has been totally dependent, while mainland China is still opposed, but with increasing difficulty.

In short, global challenges, foreign examples, and reliance on outside sponsors (in the case of Taiwan) shaped the political institutions of China. It is impossible to recognize or understand Chinese political development without first grasping the fundamental forces that influence China from outside its borders. Chinese responses to the world do carry certain characteristics that one does not easily find in other developing countries. However, the impetus and momentum for those responses and the general directions they took are quite understandable in a global and historical context. In the following discussion, we will trace the political development of China in modern times from the Qing dynasty to the Dengist reform. Our focus will be on mainland China, but we will also make comparative references to Taiwan, an alternative Chinese society that has taken on a different developmental route.

## HISTORICAL BACKGROUND

Imperial China was as a static system. Dynasties came and went, but the basic outlines of China's patriarchal social structure and absolutist-monarchical political institutions remained unchanged from the Han dynasty (206 B.C. to A.D. 226) until its collapse at the beginning of the 20th century. Confucianism was enshrined as the state ideology that emphasized filial piety and loyalty to the emperor as the ultimate virtues. A sophisticated examination system recruited intellectuals into the government based on their mastery of Confucian classics. Technological innovations and successful human organizations made it possible for the Chinese dynasties to expand into great empires that oftentimes dominated neighboring tribes and nations in East Asia. Up until the Yuan dynasty when China had Mongol rulers, the Middle Kingdom was the envy of many Europeans.

Its ancient civilization, however, proved to be a mixed blessing for the Chinese

people when the real challenge came. Equipped with guns and steamers, Westerners began their exploitation of China's vast markets on a mass scale in mid–19th
century, pioneered by British opium dealers. This could not have come at a worse
time. China was then in the middle of the Qing (also known as the Manchu)
dynasty. Following the pattern of all established dynasties, the Qing emperors during that period were not great rulers, but neither were they weak enough to be
overthrown easily. Had the Qing emperors at the time been as ambitious and
capable as their forefathers, China would have had a much better chance of reju-
venating itself in confrontation with the Western powers. Had they been totally
weak, then the dynasty might have fallen and a new one come to power, as had
happened in Chinese history more than two dozen times. Since the Manchu
dynasty was in the middle point of its dynastic cycle, it was able to drag on in
decline for yet another half century before it was buried amid lost wars, unequal
treaties, depleted national wealth, and a disintegrated social fabric. During this
agonizing period of national humiliation and attrition, the deep-rooted sense of
superiority by the Chinese elite gradually gave way to a realization that China was
actually inferior to the West, not only in military might but also in institutions, and
even in culture.

The Manchu dynasty was ultimately overthrown in 1912 by a revolutionary
movement led by Dr. Sun Yat-sen, an America-trained doctor from the Guangdong
province. The Republic of China (ROC) was then founded. Dr. Sun's ideal was to
transform China into a modern, democratic, and affluent country, one that could
repel foreign invasion and offer the Chinese people a decent life. Dr. Sun and his
colleagues were at the time mainly inspired by the Western model, and hoped
China could evolve into a liberal democracy. However, political turmoil ensued, as
no political-military force was able to prevail in China's postimperial era. Yuan
Shikai, a Qing general-turned-ROC president, attempted to restore imperial rule
and make himself emperor. He was forced to curtail his ambition when belea-
guered by defecting generals and Sun's comrades who swore to protect the new
republic.

After Yuan's death in 1916, China split into warring territories controlled by
warlords of various kinds. Foremost were Zhang Zuolin in Manchuria and northern China, Wu Peifu in the Yangtzu area, and Sun Quanfang in the southeast
provinces. For his part, Dr. Sun established the KMT in 1919, expecting to rely on
the support of China's urban intellectuals. He then sought Soviet support from his
base in the southern province of Guangdong, and accepted Moscow's advice to
establish the Whampoa Military Academy for the training of an officer corps loyal
to his ideas, foremost of which were the "Three Principles of the People": nationalism, democracy, and people's livelihood, a kind of democratic socialism with distinct Chinese charateristics. General Chiang Kai-shek was then appointed commander of the academy and charged with producing a highly indoctrinated

revolutionary army for the KMT. Though still holding the liberal model as the ultimate goal, Dr. Sun now envisioned a strong state to fulfill his ideal. This change of mind is important in that the KMT had opted for a nonliberal strategy in state building. However, whether the KMT would choose a German-style statist model or a communist model was unclear at the time, for the two tendencies were competing for dominance in the party.

General Chiang succeeded in building a revolutionary army committed to Sun's ideas, but only with heavy infiltration by the communists, who followed an order from Moscow to join Dr. Sun's KMT and develop the CCP's influence inside the KMT apparatus and military establishment. Sun died of liver cancer in 1925, leaving a heavily divided KMT. Chiang then launched a northern expedition to expand the KMT's territory and shed communist influence. The initial thrust north was successful, and in early 1926 the KMT army was able to control the provinces south of the Yangtze River. Chiang established his power base in Nanjing and Shanghai, on the east coast of China, while the KMT Left and their communist allies set up a separate center in Wuhan in central China. Chiang then purged the communists in territories under his control, while the left-wing elements of the KMT and the communists were finding their relations strained because they could not agree on how to deal with Chiang. Finally, the communists were forced out of the KMT and began organizing riots against the KMT government and the gentry class that dominated China's rural areas.

The communists became rebels in China's mountainous areas, which they called the "Soviet regions." A Chinese Soviet Republic was established there, becoming a target for Chiang's "annihilation campaigns." In 1934 the communists' main base in Jiangxi was attacked, and they were chased across the south and southwest provinces of China by the pursuing KMT army. This strategic retreat was what the communists would call in their folklore the "Long March." Ultimately, the retreating communist forces founded a base in Yan'an, a remote town in the north of China. There the KMT offensive was finally thwarted, for the KMT government faced a much more serious challenge from Japan's military conquest. During the Long March, Mao Zedong was able to grasp first military and then political leadership of the CCP by criticizing and ousting those Chinese communists trained in Moscow. In Yan'an Mao firmly established his personal leadership.

The period of 1928 through 1936 is considered the golden years of the KMT's rule in China. Industry grew, commerce expanded, and foreign trade surged. China might have taken a different route than what it actually did, had it not been for an all-out Japanese invasion and the ensuing Sino-Japanese war that totally devastated the country. As it turned out, the communists were able to appeal to nationalism and generate strong support among Chinese intellectuals, who grew increasingly critical of Chiang's concentration on crushing the communist insurgency. In December 1936, Chiang was kidnapped by the son of a Manchurian warlord and although he was finally released, the KMT was forced to shift its priority from mopping up the communists to preparing for war with Japan.

On July 7, 1937, Japan launched an all-out attack on the Chinese army guarding Beijing. China and Japan entered into a protracted and devastating eight-year war. The Japanese had built a powerful war machine that dwarfed China's fragmented and poorly equipped army. Chiang's strategy was to "trade space for time," and the KMT troops went into a large-scale retreat. As the war dragged on and the Japanese military was spread thin in China's vast territory, the KMT army was able to hold its defense line, while the CCP found great opportunities to expand in rural China. As it turned out, the Sino-Japanese war decisively altered the balance of power between the KMT and the CCP, so that at the end of the war the communists were in control of north China and, with the help of the Soviets, Manchuria.

The Nationalist government was not prepared to fight a civil war with the communists after eight years of fighting with the Japanese. Most people simply wanted peace and were unwilling to support the KMT's war effort. Corruption and inflation cost the Nationalists their traditional urban support, while communists were successful in mobilizing peasants with their land-reform programs. In the end, the Nationalist troops were demolished in several decisive campaigns, and Chiang Kai-shek led millions of KMT loyalists to the island of Taiwan. On October 1, 1949, the People's Republic of China (PRC) was formally established in Beijing, while the ROC migrated to Taiwan. There has been no peace treaty between mainland China and Taiwan since then, and the Chinese civil war technically has not ended.

The civil war was significant in shifting China's developmental strategy. During the republican period, the KMT basically pursued a statist development model, which had bureaucratic capitalism, authoritarian political control, and exultation of nationalism as its major components. Even though one finds traditional elements and emphasis on Confucian teachings in the KMT's ideology, the system established by Chiang was modeled on Germany and Japan. It was not totalitarian, as the KMT lacked the capacity to penetrate deeply into the rural grass roots, and had to share power with the gentry class, urban bourgeoisie, and international capital. Religious leaders, intellectuals, and underworld gangs also exercised great influence. The KMT attempted to monopolize the mass media but was unable to do so. Those weaknesses were fully exploited by the communists. With the defeat of the KMT, China moved into a new developmental stage, one characterized by Soviet-style institutions and, later on, Maoist frenetic movements.

The reason the KMT opted for the German or Japanese model was simple. China was facing a crisis of national survival. It was only natural for the ruling elite to emphasize the importance of concentrating power in the hands of the leadership and guiding national development from the top. However, as the Nationalist leaders came primarily from the middle and upper classes of Chinese society, they had no appetite for radical social revolutions as championed by the communists. The

Nationalists appealed to Chinese nationalism to gain legitimacy and criticized the communist notion of a "class struggle." This strategy proved successful in their initial competition with the communists, inasmuch as the latter's radical land-redistribution program antagonized the landowning class while failing to mobilize genuine peasant support. Also, it can be argued that the rise of communist power during the Sino-Japanese war was a direct result of the CCP's shifting from blatant class struggle to peasant nationalism. The Nationalists' social background further suggests a deep commitment to many traditional values, such as filial piety, and the rich cultural legacies of China. For the communists, however, those values were dispensable so long as they stood in the way of rapid modernization.

In the first half of the 20th century, international competition and national survival forced the Chinese elite to choose an effective modernization model. The liberal, statist, and communist models, as exemplified by Britain, Japan, and the Soviet Union, were particularly appealing to the urban intellectuals, the KMT, and the CCP, respectively. These were the interests on which the identities of liberalism, nationalism, and communism were formed. Three distinctively different institutions would flow naturally from the three interests and identities: The triumph of the urban intellectuals would bring about a Western-style democracy. The victory of the KMT would install an authoritarian regime. The success of the CCP would establish a totalitarian party-state. As it turned out, the liberal intellectuals lacked the organizational means to realize their ideas. The British model never had a real chance.

China's choice, then, was narrowed down to two models: authoritarian statist or communist. When the CCP won the civil war in 1949, China's fate was sealed. There was going to be a series of stormy movements aimed at thoroughly transforming the society based on the communist model. The CCP's interest was reflected in the communist identity and a totalitarian institution – the Communist Party. On the separate island of Taiwan, however, the KMT kept the statist model alive and managed to produce an economic miracle based on private enterprise and government control of the market. The identity on Taiwan was nationalism, and the institution was an authoritarian state. In later years, Taiwan's statist model was attenuated by the rise of an affluent middle-class society and the hegemonic influence exercised by the United States that preferred the liberal democratic model.

As Taiwan gradually moved to liberalism, mainland China experienced a shift from the communist model to the statist model that Taiwan had exemplified in the past. The inner drive for such a fundamental change was derived from the inherent defects of the communist, and particularly the Maoist, developmental model, in the context of intensive international competition. As we will see, the destructive Cultural Revolution transformed the minds of the party cadres and turned them into modernizing bureaucrats. They became keenly aware of the deficiencies and atrocities of the old model. The CCP regime began moving toward the KMT's statist model. Communism is gradually being replaced by nationalism as the national identity, and the totalitarian regime is being transformed into an authoritarian state. With the relaxation of political control, the adoption of an "open-door policy" to the outside world, and the introduction of the market and private property, reform in China has even rekindled a liberal tendency rooted in the republican period, as demonstrated in the Tiananmen Square protests in June 1989 when Beijing's college students allied themselves with workers and citizens in order to stage a massive, one-month sit-in for political freedoms in the heart of the capital. During that month, there were several massive demonstrations that involved more than a million participants. This is unprecedented in Communist China. However, the ease with which this pro-democracy movement was suppressed shows that liberal roots have not been thoroughly established in China. The current economic reform, however, may ultimately bring about an affluent middle-class society heavily influenced by international liberalism and eventually turn China institutionally towards liberalism, as happened earlier in Taiwan.

## DEVELOPMENTAL STAGES OF THE COMMUNIST REGIME

Since political power in the PRC is highly concentrated in the hands of a small group of communist leaders, and particularly in the hands of the paramount leader (Mao Zedong from 1949 to 1976 and Deng Xiaoping from 1978 to 1997), China's post-1949 political development can best be understood in terms of the ideas and policies of its top leaders. However, this does not mean that individuals determined China's political development by dint of their personalities and particular political inclinations. Strong as Mao's and Deng's influence on the political process may have been, they nevertheless reflected underlying forces that propelled a communist regime through the kinds of different developmental stages that one can also find in the Soviet Union. In this sense, both Mao and Deng (and Jiang Zemin who succeeded Deng) were more representatives of the underlying trend than they were creators of such a trend.

As we have seen in the Russian example from Lenin to Brezhnev, the developmental stages of a Leninist regime can be characterized as 1) the initial transformation aimed at remaking the society; 2) the reform backlash; and 3) the conservative consolidation. The logic behind these stages is simple. The communists as true believers of their utopian ideas tended to act on the ideology when they seized political power. This was the period of great transformation and revolutionary politics: Private property was confiscated; markets were abolished; a centrally planned economy was erected; and a forced draft industrialization drive was launched. At this stage, one usually finds a tyrannical despot concentrating all political power in his hands, and terrorizing his subjects into total subservience.

Elaborate party networks, an all-powerful secret police apparatus, and gigantic state enterprises were created. A totalitarian party-state came into existence. However, after years of traumatic totalitarian rule, a reform period was bound to emerge. Thus, one finds a relaxation of state control over the economy in the form of "perfecting the planning system" or "market socialism," a withdrawal of secret police from their most blatant intrusion into citizens' private life, and a diminution of the party's omnipresent control of cultural expressions of the society. A more benign ruler replaced the despot, but usually not until the despot died a natural death, as in the case of Khrushchev's succeeding Stalin and Deng's succeeding Mao. The party-state then came to a truce with the society.

The reform backlash did not last long, however, as the very "liberal" policies characterizing this period bred further social expectations and threatened to undermine the communist regime. What followed then was usually a conservative bureaucratic regime that did not embark on any major institutional initiatives or structural reform, but clung to the status quo and gave it a conservative twist. The mission was no longer radical transformation of the society or desperate redressing of the excesses of totalitarianism but, rather, entrenchment and consolidation. The consolidational leader may keep certain aspects of the reform stage, but the overall mentality is conservative. In the Soviet Union and most of Eastern Europe, this period was embodied in the rule of Leonid Brezhnev and like-minded communist leaders, such as Gustav Husak of Czechoslovakia. In the following analysis, we see that China moved into the consolidation stage with the death of Deng Xiaoping and the political ascendancy of the bureaucrat par excellence, Jiang Zemin, as the new top leader of the CCP (see Figure 1 at the end of the chapter).

## THE MAOIST PERIOD: HIGH TOTALITARIANISM

We begin our analysis with Mao, the totalitarian despot. Mao rose to power when he assumed command of the Red Army at the Zunyi conference in 1935 on the Long March. Prior to that meeting, Mao had been dominated by a group of Moscow-trained communists. Mao understood that there was no hope for the communists to establish power bases in China's cities. The size of the working class there was too small and their revolutionary consciousness too underdeveloped. Instead, the Chinese communists had to rely on the peasants. This meant that the CCP had to adopt a strategy of "encircling the cities from the countryside" and tailor their programs to the needs of the peasants, that is, redistributing land instead of creating communes. Mao's idea was in serious conflict with the Soviet experience, which relied heavily on the workers in the cities for vital support. It was not until the KMT's fifth annihilation campaign, which swept the communists from their Jiangxi base, that Mao grasped a golden opportunity to unseat his Moscow-trained rivals and assume military leadership. He then put his strategy into practice. This realistic shift of strategy, when combined with the Japanese invasion, contributed greatly to the CCP's resurgence as a serious contender for power in the post–World War II period.

Mao's greatest contribution to the communist movement was, of course, leading the party to the defeat of Chiang Kai-shek in the civil war and establishing the People's Republic in 1949. In 1950 Mao paid a tribute to Stalin in Moscow when he made his first visit to a foreign country and signed a treaty of friendship between China and the Soviet Union. To the outside observer, especially to politicians in the United States, it appeared as if there was now one large, unified communist bloc that extended from Berlin to Beijing.

It was only a matter of time, however, before the Chinese and the Soviets would compete for influence in the world communist movement. Mao was, after all, the leader of China, one of the five permanent members of the UN Security Council (though the seat was at that time still held by the Republic of China in Taipei), the world's most populous nation, and a country proud of its ancient civilization. It would be difficult to imagine a subservient China bowing to the interests of the Soviet Union in the name of a world communist movement. During the 1950s, Mao developed his own ideas about how to govern China and conduct Beijing's relations with other countries in the world.

The disagreement with Russia led to an outright acrimonious split after Stalin's death and the criticism of Stalin in the Soviet Union under Khrushchev's rule. Mao launched a series of verbal attacks on Soviet "revisionism," seeing in Nikita Khrushchev a weak, willing traitor who flirted with the world's archcapitalist nation, the United States. Determined to shed Soviet influence, Mao in the late 1950s urged the party to adopt a uniquely Chinese modernization strategy that would prove disastrous for the nation.

Mao's experience with the Chinese civil war, in which the ill-equipped communist fighters had overpowered the KMT's huge army, convinced him that spiritual mobilization was the key to success. As China was short of capital, Mao found the abundant Chinese labor a ready substitute. Mao believed that people could be mobilized through political campaigns modeled on revolutionary action. This idea was a natural extension of Mao's wartime strategy that had relied on China's huge peasantry. The result was a policy that Mao called the "Great Leap Forward." As compelling as the political logic was to this campaign, it had little economic rationality and ended in an unprecedented man-made famine during which some 30,000,000 Chinese people died. Mao was forced to the "second line" by his pragmatic colleagues, such as Liu Shaoqi, Deng Xiaoping and Chen Yun, but the "great Helmsman" refused to accept his political downfall, and made a revengeful comeback by launching the Great Proletariat Cultural Revolution that ravaged the nation for a whole decade (1966–76).

Mao's comeback tilted the balance between the party and the state to. Prior to 1949, the CCP had an extensive party organization that performed regular government functions in the communist-controlled areas. The party was initially led by a general secretary, then by a chairman. It practiced the "democratic centralism" of a typical Leninist party, which meant, in practice, the concentration of power at the hands of a supreme party leader. After the establishment of the People's Republic, the communists began to build a set of state institutions and gradually shifted administrative power to the newly founded government bureaucracies. This process of "normalization" coincided with Beijing's "leaning toward the Soviet Union" and demonstrated, at the time, China's earnest effort to build a society modeled on the well-established Soviet system.

In September 1949, the party began to set up a Central People's Government as the highest organ of state power. Mao was elected as its chairman. Under it was the Government Administrative Council headed by Zhou Enlai. After the 1954 constitution was promulgated, a National People's Congress was created to serve as the parliament. The Government Administrative Council became the State Council and remained responsible to the people's deputies. Zhou Enlai continued to serve as the premier. This arrangement resembled the governing structure of a typical communist country. The Communist Party remained the ultimate source of power and legitimacy. The leader of the party, Chairman Mao in the Chinese case, ruled supreme. The head of government was usually the second-most-powerful figure in the party-state, so long as that position was not taken by the party leader himself.

There was an ill-defined division of labor between the party and the government, with the party initiating policies and guaranteeing their political correctness, and the government implementing those policies. The military also played an important role at this initial stage of the People's Republic. From 1949 to 1952, military administrative committees directly controlled twenty provinces. The power of the generals, however, was curbed by Mao when the political and economic situation of China stabilized. Mao himself headed the party's Central Military Commission (CMC), and directed the People's Liberation Army in that capacity. The government's control of the military (both the People's Revolutionary Military Commission and the National Defense Council) was totally overwhelmed by the party CMC. A firmly established tradition in the PRC is for the party to "command the guns" and for the leader of the party to head the party CMC. The party's control over the military was also guaranteed by recruitment into the party of all officers above the rank of platoon commander, setting up political commissars and political departments in the army, and establishing party committees at the regiment level and above.

The party, the government, and the army are the three power pillars in the PRC. In Table 2 we find it is not always easy to figure out the real paramount leader simply by taking a look at the official positions held by China's top politicians. The general rule seems to be that the paramount leader always controls the party CMC. This held true until Deng formally gave that position to Jiang in the

## TABLE 2. CHINA'S TOP LEADERS AND THEIR POSITIONS

|  | President* | Prime Minister | Communist Party Leader | Chairman of Party CMC | Paramount Leader |
|---|---|---|---|---|---|
| 1949 Oct. | Mao Zedong | Zhou Enlai | Mao Zedong | Mao Zedong | Mao Zedong |
| 1959 Apr. | Liu Shaoqi |  |  |  |  |
| 1968 Oct. | Dong Biwu |  |  |  |  |
| 1975 Jan. | Zhu De |  |  |  |  |
| 1976 Feb. |  | Hua Guofeng (acting Feb.–Apr. 1976) |  |  |  |
| 1976 July | Song Qinglin (acting) |  |  |  |  |
| 1976 Oct. |  |  | Hua Guofeng | Hua Guofeng | Hua Guofeng |
| 1978 Mar. | Ye Jianyig |  |  |  |  |
| 1978 Dec. |  |  |  |  | Deng Xiaoping |
| 1980 Sept. |  | Zhao Ziyang |  |  |  |
| 1981 June |  |  | Hu Yaobang (Party Chairman) | Den Xiaoping |  |
| 1982 Sept. |  |  | Hu Yaobang (General Secretary) |  |  |
| 1983 June | Lia Xiannian |  |  |  |  |
| 1987 Jan. |  |  | Zhao Ziyang |  |  |
| 1987 Nov. |  | Li Peng |  |  |  |
| 1988 Mar. | Yang Shangkun |  |  |  |  |
| 1989 June |  |  | Jiang Zemin |  |  |
| 1989 Nov. |  |  |  | Jiang Zemin |  |
| 1993 Mar. | Jiang Zemin |  |  |  |  |
| 1997 Feb. |  |  |  |  | Jiang Zemin |
| 1998 May |  | Zhu Rongji |  |  |  |

* The PRC's president is the state chairman when that position exists, i.e., from 1954 to 1966, and from 1983 on. In the absence of state chairman, it was the chairman of the National People's Congress who took the function of head of state.

end of 1989, while still running the show from behind the scenes. That anomaly did not occur during Mao's reign from 1949 to 1976, however, when he concurrently held chairmanship of both the CCP's Central Committee and its Central Military Commission. That is to say, Mao directly controlled the party and the military. The government was left in the hands of Zhou Enlai, who had risen to the CCP's top leadership earlier than Mao. The 1959 promotion of Liu Shaoqi to state chairman was not an insignificant move, for even though the PRC's head of state was a titular position, Liu's advancement was widely considered to be a sign that Liu was Mao's successor in the context of the de-Stalinization campaign in the Soviet Union. However, Liu's assumption of the state chairmanship proved ominous in view of Mao's vengeful rearguard actions that followed his blunders in the Great Leap Forward. These kinds of power struggles, inherent in communist leadership succession, became entangled with international competition and ideological dispute within China.

Mao's rupture with Khrushchev proved fatal to China's state-building efforts, as he began to whip up local support for his Great Leap Forward and People's Communes. Mao abhorred Soviet-style bureaucratism and overconcentrated state planning. In 1958 Mao began to delegate very significant power to party cadres in running the economy, which set China apart from the Soviet Union and East European countries that had a more centrally controlled economy under communist rule. Even though China underwent several rounds of "decentralization-recentralization" in the following years, it never went back to the original planned-economy model that the Soviet advisors had helped China to build during the 1950s. This historical legacy of a decentralized system was later hailed as a unique Chinese advantage for implementing market reform in the 1980s. However, institutionally, the most important development in the 1958 decentralization was the shift of power from state bureaucrats to party cadres, reminiscent of the revolutionary years when they had had an important mission.

Mao's experiment proved disastrous and temporarily diminished his power. As a result, the short interlude between the Great Leap Forward and the launching of the Cultural Revolution saw a temporary revival of state institutions. The stormy politics of the Cultural Revolution, however, again dampened the vitality of government agencies and again returned power to party cadres. Mao launched campaigns against the "small clique of capitalist-roaders in power" who were oftentimes found in government institutions. Revolutionary committees took the place of the local governments, and direct military control was instituted to curb the excessive infighting among "Red Guard" zealots whom Mao had unleashing during the Cultural Revolution. The normal politics of the 1950s was replaced by the stormy movements of the 1960s. State institutions were attacked, government officials were purged and officials sent to reeducation camps in China's remote provinces, and millions of intellectuals were humiliated and condemned to forced labor. For Mao, this was "class struggle." The simple fact remained that Mao did his best to undermine the very institutions that he helped establish in the first decade of the People's Republic.

Even though Mao vehemently attacked the Soviet Union in the ideological battle between the two communist giants, his position and policies did not deviate from orthodox Stalinism. As a matter of fact, he based his attacks on Khrushchev's lead-

TABLE 3. SHARE OF INVESTMENT BY INDUSTRIES, 1953–1976

| Years | Agriculture | Light Industry | Heavy Industry | Other Industries |
|---|---|---|---|---|
| First Five-Year Plan (1953–7) | 7.1 | 6.4 | 36.2 | 50.3 |
| Second Five-Year Plan (1958–62) | 11.3 | 6.4 | 54.0 | 28.3 |
| 1963–5 | 17.6 | 3.9 | 45.9 | 32.6 |
| Third Five-Year Plan (1966–70) | 10.7 | 4.4 | 51.1 | 33.8 |
| Fourth Five-Year Plan (1971–5) | 9.8 | 5.8 | 49.6 | 34.8 |
| 1976–8 | 10.8 | 5.9 | 49.6 | 33.7 |

Source: Lin Yifu, Cai Fang, Li Zhou, *Zhongguo de qiji: Fazhan zhanlue yu jinglji gaige* (China's miracle: Developmental strategy and economic reform) (Hong Kong: Chinese University Press, 1995), p. 56.

ership on its betrayal of the original ideals of communism. During the decade of the Cultural Revolution, the personality cult of Mao was carried to absurd lengths. Mao ruled by terror, exercising it even against his chief lieutenants (most notably State Chairman Liu Shaoqi and Party General Secretary Deng Xiaoping). Public denunciations and beatings at mass rallies were substituted for Soviet-style show trials with equally fatal consequences for the accused. The Red Guards were Mao's invention, for he lacked organizational means, such as the Stalin's secret police, to defeat his opponents in the party-state hierarchy. As a result, the chairman was able to unleash abundant social anger at the regime after the traumatic Great Leap Forward campaign and the resulting famine, directing it toward his enemies. The devastation was greater than in the Soviet Union, where purges and power struggles were conducted in a more "orderly" manner. Mao mercilessly mobilized China's resources to pursue heavy industrialization, and both agriculture and light industry that directly affected the livelihood of the population were severely neglected (Table 3). The development priorities were thus the same as in the Soviet Union, although Mao's strategy of spiritual mobilization and absolute egalitarianism were quite counterproductive in the long run. In short, Mao's rule in China was a classical case of high totalitarianism.

## DENG UNLEASHES REFORM

The political conflict between Mao and perceived enemies in the leadership was a fight between the leftist radicals and the pro-stability bureaucrats, between the movement-oriented party and order-conscious state. Here one finds the conflict between two interests (cadres vs. bureaucrats), two identities (revolution vs. development), and two institutions (party vs. state). With the death of the charismatic despot Mao, a new force emerged that advocated market reform and political relaxation. This was a force for which one easily finds counterparts in the post-Stalinist Soviet Union and Eastern Europe. However, because of the artificial suppression of the reform momentum during Mao's years, the reform in China came with a vengeance.

The pro-stability bureaucrats constituted a significant political force in the PRC after the 1950s. However, throughout the Maoist era, they were suppressed by the leftists. Their early leader was Liu Shaoqi, Mao's designated successor. Liu was an organizational man who favored orderly development of the country's economy in the manner of Soviet-style five-year plans. He abhorred the anarchy that Mao's endless campaigns brought about. Concerning basic economic policy, Mao's "red" line insisted on breathtaking growth through ideological movements, whereas the "expert" line of Liu's bureaucrats emphasized the need for balanced development and allowed modifications of the system in order to improve performance. This "line struggle" was elevated by Mao to the height of "class struggle," and repeated movements were launched from above to ensure that Mao's line was in command.

As the Soviet and East European experiences demonstrate, "totalitarianism" is but a stage in the development of Leninist regimes. Routinization of politics and economic reform seem to be a natural tendency. In the PRC, however, Mao's political genius and his overwhelming prestige in the party-state artificially delayed the advent of "mature communism." In the 1960s and 1970s, Mao mustered all his vigilance to guard against the CCP's slipping into Soviet-style bureaucratic communism as in the Khrushchev and Brezhnev eras. As a result, the Chinese communist regime delayed its reform stage until the death of its despotic ruler.

Reform was inevitable, however. The very fact that mainland China resisted it longer than most other socialist countries foretold the vengeance with which reform would ultimately come. As it turned out, Deng Xiaoping transformed the Chinese economic system much more thoroughly than did Nikita Khrushchev in the Soviet Union. In terms of politics, the personality cult and ruthless persecution of comrades were denounced in reform-era China, very much like in its Soviet and East European predecessors. Obviously this is not democratization but relaxation in a post-totalitarian society, as witnessed by Deng's continued insistence on the leading role of the Communist Party. Stability now hinged on material benefits that the communist regime delivered and on a widespread sense of improvement on the previous decades of impoverishment and rule by terror.

China's reform after Mao's death was based on domestic and international grounds. The very trauma that both the elite and the ordinary Chinese people suffered at the hands of the despot Mao convinced them that they had to put an end to stormy movements and revolutionary politics. Persistent poverty seriously undermined the regime's legitimacy, particularly when the population compared China's economic plight with the high-speed growth of neighboring countries in East Asia. Even more ominous was the realization by Beijing's communist leaders that a backward economy and a predominantly rural society could not support China's ambition to compete on the world stage with the Soviet Union and the West. In order to survive both domestically and internationally, China had to restructure its system and shed the debilitating aspects of Mao's totalitarianism.

Mao's legacy was dismantled bit by bit. One month after Mao's death in September 1976, the Gang of Four (including Mao's wife Jiang Qing and three other ultraleftist leaders) were arrested. Two years later, at the historic Third Plenum of the CCP's Eleventh Central Committee held in December 1978, the interregnum leader Hua Guofeng was defeated by Deng Xiaoping, and the reform era was ushered in. However, the pro-stability bureaucrats still found themselves subject to the movement mentality of the new paramount leader. The radical economic reformers, led by Deng and his handpicked lieutenants Hu Yaobang (general secretary of the party) and Zhao Ziyang (premier), did not see eye to eye with the bureaucrats, led by Chen Yun. Although Deng's reform project was a reaction to totalitarian excesses, one can nevertheless find a similar mentality among ultraleftists and radical reformers. They all took a pro-growth stance as opposed to the bureaucrats' pro-stability line. Mao, Hua, and Deng were all proponents of growth, though they resorted to different means for achieving that same goal: Mao with his Great Leap Forward, Hua with his Great Leap Westward, and Deng with his market reform. The determination of those Chinese communist leaders to achieve supergrowth had a lot to do with their realization that China was backward and that extraordinary means were necessary for the country to compete in the world effectively. It was under this "surpassing mentality" that the strategic goal of doubling the PRC's industrial and agricultural production by the year 2000 was set at the Twelfth Party Congress in 1982, when the era of reform formally began.

The bureaucrats thought otherwise. For them, stability of the system was a paramount consideration. Led by Chen Yun in the post-Mao era, the bureaucrats stressed the need for balanced development, limited spending, and measured growth. After the death of Mao and the short interlude of Hua Guofeng, the bureaucrats' line temporarily gained dominance in Chen Yun's "adjustment" policy, designed to curb the rash and unbalanced investment surge under Hua's Ten-Year Plan. But Chen's line was in command for only five years (1979–83). It was then swiftly replaced by Deng's pro-growth marketization drive, implemented by the new prime minister, Zhao Ziyang. With the country on the road to reform, that is, with Deng in command, the bureaucrats found themselves circumvented, though struggles between the reformers and bureaucrats testified to the resilience of the latter.

Several economic cycles in the 1980s shaped the balance of power between the pro-growth reformers and the pro-stability bureaucrats. As a rule, the reformers fueled the economy with expansionary monetary policies and liberalization. High growth was pursued at the expense of macrostability. Under Deng, one saw the notorious People's Communes farming system abolished and a realistic household-responsibility system instituted that combines compulsory state procurements with peasant discretion over above-quota produce. Prices of agricultural products increased. Rural markets revived. Township and village enterprises mushroomed. In the cities one first saw the emergence of millions of small individual businesses *(getihu),* then the rapid development of hitherto unthinkable private enterprises. The state enterprises were also reformed, first by raising the profit-retention ratio, then by a contract scheme that resembled the household-responsibility system in the countryside. A tax-for-profit reform was launched in 1983–4, designed to provide a level ground for healthy competition. Various kinds of ownership reforms were tested after 1986, culminating in the introduction of stock shares and their free trade in newly opened stock markets. An open-door policy invited huge inflow of foreign capital that provided timely funding for the rapid growth of the Chinese economy. Indirect foreign investment also surged, as international lenders designated China as a promising market. According to the World Bank, China's annual per capita GDP (growth domestic product) growth reached an average of 8 percent between 1978 and 1995. Only South Korea and Taiwan have grown at comparable rates (at 6.9 percent and 6.3 percent, respectively).

It is unsurprising that high growth brought about inflation and a trade imbalance, as happened in 1985, 1988, and 1993–4. After the eruption of serious social disturbance (such as the student unrest in the winter of 1986–7 and the pro-democracy demonstrations in the spring of 1989), and the political demise of top reformers (Hu Yaobang in January 1987 and Zhao Ziyang in June 1989), the bureaucrats regained some power, reducing investment and tightening monetary policies. Further reform measures were put on hold. In this way, stabilization was restored but only at the expense of growth. With Deng's active intervention, the reformers then resurged and snatched power from the bureaucrats. The economy entered a high-growth phase, starting a new cycle.

Deng's strong reaction to Mao's line was, arguably, comparable to Khrushchev's reform after the death of Stalin. Both carried a movement mentality and focused on institutional innovations. Even though the economic reform of Dengist China went far beyond the scope of the limited market experiments of the Soviet Union under Khrushchev, the prevalent ethos and the impact of radical reform were similar in the two cases. Both the Soviet Union and the PRC were plunged into constant institutional flux by their reform leaders, and powerful bureaucratic interests were violated.

In the Soviet Union, Khrushchev was ultimately deposed by a rebelling bureaucracy led by Leonid Brezhnev, the bureaucrat par excellence, who then ruled with his colleagues in a self-perpetuating Politburo for eighteen years during the most stable and immobile period of Soviet history. In mainland China, on the other hand, Deng was able to sustain the reform's momentum through his prestige and masterful maneuvering among central and provincial interests. However, bureaucratization was a natural tendency for a mature communist regime, just as reform was inevitable after the rule of a revolutionary tyrant, hence the conservative triumph during the retrenchment period of 1988–91. And yet, the advent of the bureaucratic age in China was artificially thwarted by Deng, who, in his famous southern tour of 1992, single-handedly relaunched the hypergrowth reform and brought mainland China out of its conservative retrenchment at one stroke, despite opposition by most of his bureaucratic lieutenants. That phenomenal achievement of Deng, however, should be viewed as the last gasp of radical reform, rather than the beginning of a new reform era.

During the course of relaunching the reform, Premier Li Peng was reprimanded by Deng for his overconservative goal of 6 percent annual growth for the Eighth Five-Year Plan period (1991–5). After a southern tour, Deng was temporarily triumphant, and the Chinese economy registered double-digit growth rates for four consecutive years. Soon, however, the economy overheated and a new policy of "macroadjustment" came into vogue. The person in charge of this limited austerity program was Zhu Rongji. Zhu was for a while widely considered Deng's favorite for succeeding Li Peng as the prime minister. In Zhu's stern attitude toward the state-owned enterprises heavily in debt, however, one finds no substantial difference between him and Li Peng or Jiang Zemin. Jiang, Li, and Zhu are all bureaucrats with a technocratic background, and they all consider stability a paramount goal at the PRC's current stage of development. They may belong to different power blocs and may compete vehemently for ascendancy in the post-Deng period, but they are no pro-growth zealots in the mold of the old patriarch. The desperate, extraordinary, period of supergrowth has come to an end with the phasing out and, ultimately, the death of Deng.

## JIANG ZEMIN AND NEOCONSERVATISM

In China, new developmental stages seem to await the physical death of the leader who dominated the earlier stage. For a while, Jiang was considered an opportunist, one who shifted his opinions to suit the political needs of the time. Thus, his various speeches made in the immediate post-Tiananmen period of 1989–91 were characterized by the themes of "anti–peaceful evolution" and "socialism or capitalism?" These were ideological themes and in tune with the conservative backlash of the moment. Within a few years, however, Jiang suddenly became a champion of pro-growth economic reform and stressed repeatedly the need to "prevent the resurgence of the left line." The contrast is sharp but can be explained. After Deng had been disabled by poor health (particularly after 1994), Jiang began to show his true colors. "Stability in command" became the regime's motto. Through various administrative and macroeconomic policy instruments, the overheated growth and the accompanying inflation of 1993–4 were effectively curbed, and the leadership engineered, in 1996, a "soft landing" of the economy with an annual growth rate of 9.7 percent and inflation down to 6.1 percent (from 21.7 percent in 1994 and 14.8 percent in 1995). Economic imbalances were redressed without undue austerity and loss of growth. And yet with all the good news, Jiang still insisted on stability in early 1997, not succumbing to the temptation of raising the economic growth rate in the year of a party congress. This cautious approach suggests that stability is indeed a paramount consideration for Jiang.

Jiang's commitment to stability is also reflected in his speech on being "mindful of politics." Initially launched in September 1995, this slogan became a nationwide campaign in 1996, embraced first by an ardent People's Liberation Army. The purpose of this old-style "politics-in-command" campaign is to raise party cadres' communist political consciousness, something that has become increasingly difficult as economic reform progresses. While the idea of soft landing is to pursue economic stability, the campaign "mindful of politics" is designed to ensure political stability. Both themes testify to the important role that stability plays in Jiang's mind.

Jiang should be viewed less as a unique personality than as representative of a new generation of bureaucrats who rose to positions of leadership after the rule of revolutionaries (the Maoists) and radical reformers (the Dengists). The new bureaucratic rulers wield much less power than their predecessors. As shown in Table 4, Deng was less powerful than Mao because he mustered fewer power resources, but in many respects these two men were still comparable. The difference between Deng and his successors is much more striking. Except in the area of education, the third generation of leaders are dwarfed by Deng in terms of all forms of power resources. As a result, Deng's successor(s) will definitely wield much less power than he did, and the personal imprint of Jiang or any other third-generation leader on Chinese politics and society will be markedly lighter than that of Mao or Deng.

Declining personal authority and increasingly bureaucratic rule seem to be an evolutionary regularity for communist regimes. From a comparative point of view, communist regimes naturally evolve from the stage of high totalitarianism, through reform, to bureaucratic rule. The totalitarian ruler (Stalin, Mao) launched political and economic campaigns to transform the society. The horrendous human costs that such transformation entailed forced the second-generation rulers to seek a truce with the society and terminate the rule of terror. Material

TABLE 4. POWER RESOURCES OF THREE GENERATIONS OF LEADERS IN THE PRC

| Mao | Deng | Jiang (or Other Successor) |
|---|---|---|
| Experience (broad and deep) | Experience | Limited experience |
| History | Some history | Limited history |
| Military support | Military support | Limited military support |
| Charisma | Slight charisma | No charisma |
| Will to power/ruthlessness | Will to power | Questionable |
| Vision/ideology | Vision | Questionable |
| Self-confidence | Self-confidence | Questionable |
| Transformative leader | Brokerage leader | Brokers, reactors? |
| Superiority recognized by Politburo | First among equals on Politburo | Questionable |
|  |  | Education |
|  |  | Vigor |
|  |  | Pragmatism |
| Creator of the People's Republic of China, Chinese Communist Party, People's Liberation Army | Helped build PRC/CCP/PLA | Product of the system |

*Source:* David Bachman, "The Limits on Leadership in China," *Asian Survey* 32, no. 11 (November 1992): 1048.

improvements and political relaxation ensued. However, the reformers, in their zeal to redress the excesses of high totalitarianism, often went too far, creating instability with their institutional restructuring, and risking the regime's political control over the society. The cadres' huge vested interest was also undermined. All this prompted reactions from the bureaucrats.

Just as the reformers naturally acted against the extremes of revolutionary enthusiasm, the bureaucrats by their nature sought to bring about stability (on both the individual and regime levels), which had been undermined by radical reform measures. Thus, economic experiments were circumvented and political control was tightened. In form, this seemed like a partial return to totalitarianism, but in essence the emergent bureaucratic rule was a conservative backlash against both revolution (the first stage) and reform (the second stage). The purpose of the regime was no longer to remold the society, or to redress the atrocities of the past and catch up with the world, but simply to keep things as they stood, particularly to keep the communist regime in power. This was what the Brezhnevite era meant in the Soviet Union.

The same development is now dawning on mainland China. The death of Deng Xiaoping and the political ascendancy of Jiang Zemin signify the advent of the bureaucratic era. Jiang and his colleagues of the "third-echelon leadership" have more formal and technical education than their predecessors had. They are all products of an established bureaucratic system and not its creators or builders. Their experience is typically concentrated on one functional area, and that usually is not military affairs. As a bureaucrat, Jiang and his associates sitting on the CCP's Politburo are intrinsically more interested in preserving the status quo and pursuing stability than exploring new reform frontiers. In this sense, whether it was Jiang or any other bureaucrat to succeed Deng is not really important, as communist bureaucratic rulers basically behave in similar ways. They have a realistic understanding of the popular desire for material betterment, they loathe destruction in the name of revolution and the institutional flux brought about by reform, they want to absorb Western technology and capital, but they abhor pluralistic ideas and democracy. When faced with a choice between economic development and political stability, they overwhelmingly opt for the latter. Jiang Zemin or not, the new bureaucratic rulers of mainland China will probably not deviate from those basic postulates.

The advent of a bureaucratic era has been fostered by the country's economic development. The urgency under which Deng pursued his reform programs has diminished over time. Mainland China's annual economic growth rate averaged 9.5 percent for 18 years (1979–96), and the size of its economy is predicted to surpass that of the United States in the early 21st century. The desperate need to grow at a breathtaking speed has been reduced. At the same time, the anxiety over the grave costs accompanying rapid growth has increased. Since growth is more or less taken for granted, the paramount consideration is naturally stability, both economic and political. This developmental feature plays into the hands of the bureaucrats, who treasure stability as the primary policy goal of the regime. Thus, when Jiang outlined his blueprint for governing China, he treated stability as a precondition for development and reform, a lesson he said he had gained only with painful experience.

Besides evolutionary necessity and economic prosperity, there is a third major reason that links the Jiang regime to stability. As has been mentioned, the new leaders are much weaker than their predecessors. This means that their ability to initiate and implement new policies against the entrenched interests – ministerial, military, regional, and others – will be much smaller than when Mao or Deng ruled. Stability, then, will be the default outcome, the result of inaction.

The post-Deng era will be characterized by a bureaucratic rule and stability. Power struggles will increasingly take a purely factional form, in which political leaders clash not over pro-growth or pro-stability strategy, but over personal power and prestige. Very much like Brezhnev, Jiang will be *primus inter pares,* rather than a strongman like Mao or Deng. Certainly the PRC's economy will grow much faster than its erstwhile Soviet or East European counterparts, and China's political control will probably be a bit looser, but the pro-stability bureaucratic mentality will be the same in post-Deng China as in the Soviet Union under Brezhnev. Nothing appeals to party cadres, state officials, and managers of state enterprises more than job security, and nothing attracts communist leaders in a postideological age better than a secured political career. Here lies the appeal of stability. Communist bureaucrats were suppressed in both the revolutionary and reform periods, for Mao and Deng were committed to transformation of the society, albeit in opposite directions. With Jiang, a bureaucrat par excellence, acting as the core of the leadership, pro-stability bureaucrats in the PRC finally are having their way.

## WILL CHINA BECOME DEMOCRATIC?

Although the communist regimes developed through concrete stages within the basic one-party structure, this does not mean that democratization is impossible in the long run. However, academic discussion on this issue is usually shaped by the current situation, thus projecting into the future a fixed picture of the present.

Most discussion on China's political future after the Tiananmen Square protests of 1989 has shifted focus with the apparent increased stability of the communist regime. Although in the immediate wake of the Tiananmen crisis a complete breakdown of the system was predicted, with the consolidation of the post-1989 power structure, less-dramatic scenarios have been presented. Among the latter one finds a revival of the "neoauthoritarianism" theme, which depicts mainland China's future in the light of the East Asian capitalist-authoritarian model, Taiwan and South Korea in particular. Some scholars argue that, although direct democratization is unlikely and even undesirable, a two-step transition through an intermediary phase of enlightened authoritarianism toward the ultimate destination of democracy should be welcomed. China's introduction of competitive (though not multiparty) elections at the local level is seen, from this perspective, as a particularly encouraging sign, which shows mainland China gradually evolving toward political pluralism following Taiwan's model. This is actually a variant on the theme of the time-honored modernization theory, which predicts a universal pluralistic outcome for authoritarian systems undergoing rapid economic development. Also among the less-dramatic scenarios is the "neoconservatism" theme that popped up in the "retrenchment" period. In the more rigid political and economic atmosphere after the Tiananmen protests, especially in light of the difficulties facing Russia after its democratic transition, this "neoconservative" theme emphasizes order and stability and harks back to traditional values, as opposed to the radical reform of the previous decade.

From systemic breakdown to "neoauthoritarianism," to "neoconservatism," one finds a gradual acceptance of the post-Tiananmen regime. Parallel to this shift in regime characterization, many students of China have begun to predict a greater chance for political survival to Jiang Zemin as the successor to Deng Xiaoping. Jiang was first treated as a transitional figure overshadowed by the imminent prospect of a democratic resurgence in the aftermath of the Tiananmen suppression. Then he was considered to be threatened by the reform wing in the party, and his fate contingent on the play-off between the reformers and conservatives after Deng's death. Most recently, however, Jiang has been seen as irreplaceable but still lacking the necessary legitimacy to buttress his rule. Underlying the different predictions of the CCP regime's fate and the different images of Jiang Zemin is the ostensible, increasing stability of communist rule in mainland China. The lasting power of the post-Tiananmen regime and Jiang as its leader forced observers to alter their views. Jiang's succession to Deng is increasingly viewed as a leadership change that does not entail either a reorientation shift or a systemic transformation. Now that Deng has finally passed away, discussion on China's political future has narrowed down to Beijingology, that is, the study of who gets what position in the top echelon of the party-state, without bringing in the theme of reorientation or transformation.

This perspective, however, is too narrow. China's political development has always been heavily influenced by the global context in which the country finds itself. The emergence of the Nationalists and Communists as the competing political forces in China was embedded in the country's desire to regain its power and rightful place in a challenging international environment. The KMT and the CCP adopted different development models from abroad to revive China. Because the KMT regime lost the civil war and has been highly dependent on the United States, its development on Taiwan witnessed a gradual shedding of the statist system, and an adoption of liberal-democratic institutions. The mainland moved into a comparable point in Taiwan's past when it realized that the Soviet/Maoist system was totally ineffective for China to compete in the world and for the communist regime to hold on to power. It has decisively shifted to a statist model, with authoritarian politics and developmental economic policies, and this new model has specific implications that favor the growth of liberalism.

Global competition will force China to maintain its openness to the world and sustain its market reform. But China will not soon become a democracy. In the short run, the legitimacy of the regime will be buttressed by superb economic performance. In the long run, rapid economic development may nurture social forces that are difficult to contain in an authoritarian political environment. When China reaches a stage at which economic growth inevitably slows down, while at the same time the structural changes go deep enough to arouse strong political participation for liberalization, then the pressure for democracy will greatly increase. As China is not as dependent on a liberal hegemon as Taiwan is, the route toward democratization will take much longer and will encounter greater difficulties. Nevertheless, the possibility of China's becoming a liberal, democratic system should not be dismissed under its current image of a successful, authoritarian, developmental state.

China (including Taiwan) has made a historical detour away from the original pursuit of liberal democracy in the early days of the Republic of China, through the choice of statist authoritarianism (ROC to the mid-1980s) or communist totalitarianism (post-1949 PRC) as the major development strategy, and finally to the adoption of the liberal formula (Taiwan) or a gradual approach to it (mainland China). China's developmental trajectory has been, to a large extent, determined by a challenging international environment that forces different political actors representing different interests to respond. Urban intellectuals, the KMT, and the CCP speak for different class interests, opt for different identities, and develop different institutional preferences. The lack of organization and power by the urban intellectuals doomed their effort to bring about a liberal democracy in China in the early years of the republican period. The authoritarian model that the KMT chose was imposed on the country before 1949 but then was transplanted to Taiwan when the KMT lost the civil war to the Communists. American pressure and international competition later persuaded the KMT to embrace liberal democracy and abandon its authoritarian past. On the Chinese mainland, the CCP's victory foretold the inauguration of a communist-totalitarian regime modeled on the Soviet system. Ensuing economic disasters and the pressure of international competition prompted the leadership to embrace the authoritarian model, but not until the death of Mao Zedong. The natural tendency toward pluralism inherent in market reform has already planted seeds of political liberalization in China, even though that tendency is now being resisted by a bureaucratic regime that treasures stability more than anything else and holds fast to its vested interests.

In short, as in other developing countries, different political forces in China competed for ascendancy as the country was facing international challenges. Those different political forces represented distinct interests, developed alternative identities, and proposed competing institutions. The outcome of their competition shaped the developmental route of China, and that outcome was, in turn, contingent on the international environment in which China found itself. The momentum for political development in China has been derived from the need for national survival and global competition. China differed from other cases in the developing world mainly in the immense dimensions of the country, not in the nature of its response. As such, China's political development can be best understood in a global and comparative perspective.

## BIBLIOGRAPHY

Bachman, David. "The Limits on Leadership in China." *Asian Survey,* 32, no. 11 (1992): 1048.

Baum, Richard. "China After Deng: Ten Scenarios in Search of Reality." *China Quarterly* 145 (1996): 153–75.

Bialer, Seweryn. *The Soviet Paradox.* New York: Alfred A. Knoff, 1987.

Blondel, Jean. "Dual Leadership in the Contemporary World." In Arend Lijphart, ed. *Parliamentary versus Presidential Government.* Oxford: Oxford University Press, 1992.

Chen Yun. "Guanyu diyige wunianjihua de jidian shuoming" (Some explanations on the first Five-Year Plan). In *Chen Yun wenxuan* (Selected works of Chen Yun). Vol. 2. Beijing: Renminchubanshe, 1984.

*China 2020: Development Challenges in the New Century.* Washington, D.C.: The World Bank.

Cohen, Stephen F. *Rethinking the Soviet Experience: Politics and History Since 1917.* New York: Oxford University Press, 1985.

Deng Xiaoping. "Deng Xiaoping tongzhi zai Wuchang, Shenzhen, Zhuhai, Shanghai dengdi de tanhua yaodian" (The main points of Comrade Deng Xiaoping's talks in Wuchang, Shenzhen, Zhuhai, and Shanghai). In Zhonggong Shenzhen shiwei xuanchuanbu, ed. *Yijiujiuer nian chun: Deng Xiaoping yu Shenzhen* (The spring of 1992: Deng Xiaoping and Shenzhen). Shenzhen: Haitian chubanshe, 1992.

Dittmer, Lowell. *China's Continuous Revolution: The Post-Liberation Epoch, 1949–1981.* Berkeley: University of California Press, 1987.

Dittmer, Lowell, and Yu-Shan Wu. "The Modernization of Factionalism in Chinese Politics." *World Politics* 47, no. 4 (1995); 467–94.

Duan Jiafeng. "Zhonggong lijie 'quanguo daibiao dahui' jianxi" (A brief analysis of the CCP's national congresses). In Zhang Huanqing, Duan Jiafeng, and Zhou Yushan, eds. *Zhongguo dalu yanjiu* (Mainland China studies). Taipei: San-min, 1991.

Fewsmith, Joseph. *Dilemmas of Reform in China.* Armonk, N.Y.: M. E. Sharpe, 1994.

Friedrich, Carl J., and Zbigniew K. Brzezinski. *Totalitarian Dictatorship and Autocracy.* New York: Praeger, 1963.

Gerschenkron, Alexander. *Economic Backwardness in Historical Perspective.* Cambridge, Mass.: The Belkap Press of Harvard University Press, 1962.

Gold, Thomas. *State and Society in the Taiwan Miracle.* Armonk, N.Y.: M. E. Sharpe, 1986.

Hicks, George. *The Broken Mirror.* Essex, Eng.: Longman, 1990.

Hu Angang. *Zhongguo jingji bodong baogao* (A report on economic fluctuations in China). Shenyang: Liaoning renminchubanshe, 1994.

Hu Sheng, ed. *Zhongguo gongchandang de qishinian* (The CCP's seventy years). Beijing: Zhonggong dangshi chubanshe, 1991.

Jennings, M. Kent. "Political Participation in the Chinese Countryside." *American Political Science Review* 91, no. 2 (1997): 370.

Jiang Zemin. "Zhengque chuli shehuizhuyi xiandaihua jianshe zhongde ruogan zhongda guanxi" (Properly manage certain major relations in the modernization construction of socialism). In Weng Jieming et al., eds. *Yu zongshuji tanxin* (To have an intimate talk with the general secretary). Beijing: Zhongguo shehuikexue chubanshe, 1996.

Johnson, Chalmers. *Peasant Nationalism and Communist Power*. Stanford, Calif.: Stanford University Press, 1962.

Jowitt, Ken. "Inclusion and Mobilization in European Leninist Regimes." *World Politics* 28, no. 1 (1975): 69–96.

"Soviet Neotraditionalism: The Political Corruption of a Leninist Regime." *Soviet Studies* 35, no. 3 (1983): 275–97.

Lee, Hong Yung. *From Revolutionary Cadres to Party Bureaucrats in Socialist China*. Berkeley: University of California Press, 1991.

Lin Yifu, Cai Fang, and Li Zhou. *Zhongguo de qiji: Fazhan zhanlue yu jingji gaige* (China's miracle: Developmental strategy and economic reform). Hong Kong: Chinese University Press, 1995.

Lowenthal, Richard. "Development Versus Utopia in Communist Policy." In Chalmers Johnson, ed. *Change in Communist Systems*. Stanford, Calif.: Stanford University Press, 1970.

"The Post-Revolutionary Phase in China and Russia." *Studies in Comparative Communism* 16, no. 3 (1983): 191–201.

Meaney, Constance Squires. "Is the Soviet Present China's Future." *World Politics* 39, no. 2 (1987): 203–30.

Montias, John. "Types of Communist Economic Systems." In Chalmers Johnson, ed. *Change in Communist Systems*. Stanford, Calif.: Stanford University Press, 1970.

Montinola, Gabriella, Yingyi Qian, and Barry R. Weingast. "Federalism, Chinese Style: The Political Basis for Economic Success in China." *World Politics* 48, no. 1 (1995): 50–81.

Nathan, Andrew. "A Factionalism Model for CCP Politics." *China Quarterly* 53 (1973): 34–66.

Niou, Emerson M. S. and Tianjian Shi. "An Introduction and Evaluation of the Electoral Systems Used in Chinese Village Elections." Paper delivered at the 26th annual Sino-American Conference on contemporary China, College Park, 1997, June 9–10.

Overholt, William H. "China after Deng." *Foreign Affairs* 75, no. 3 (1996): 63–78.

Perry, Elizabeth. "Intellectuals and Tiananmen: Historical Perspective on an Aborted Revolution." In Daniel Chirot, ed. *The Crisis of Leninism and the Decline of the Left*. Seattle: University of Washington Press, 1991.

Qi Mo, ed. *Xinquanweizhuyi* (Neoauthoritarianism). Taipei: T'ang-shan, 1991.

Shirk, Susan. *The Political Logic of Economic Reform in China*. Berkeley: University of California Press, 1993.

Wang Shan. *Disanzhi yanjing kan zhongguo* (Viewing China through a third eye). Hong Kong: Mingbaochubanshe, 1995.

White, Gordon. "Democratization and Economic Reform in China." *Australian Journal of Chinese Affairs* 31 (1994): 73–92.

*Riding the Tiger: The Politics of Economic Reform in Post-Mao China*. Stanford, Calif.: Stanford University Press, 1993.

Wu, Yu-Shan. *Comparative Economic Transformations: Mainland China, Hungary, the Soviet Union, and Taiwan*. Stanford, Calif.: Stanford University Press, 1994.

Zheng, Shiping. *Party vs. State in Post-1949 China: The Institutional Dilemma*. Cambridge: Cambridge University Press, 1997.

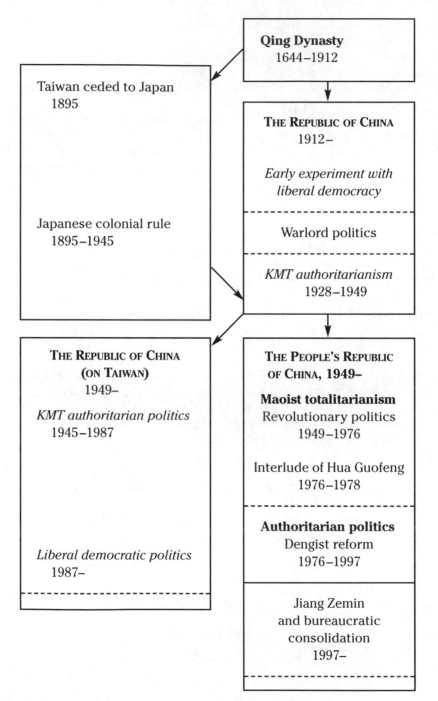

**FIGURE 1.** Key phases in Chinese development.

## IMPORTANT TERMS

**CCP** the Chinese Communist Party, founded in 1921 as a part of the international communist movement. From the very beginning, the CCP was heavily influenced by the Communist International. Its organization, guidelines, and leadership were to a great extent determined by Moscow. In 1922 the CCP members were instructed by the Soviets to join Dr. Sun Yet-san's KMT, to form a united front against the warlords. This KMT–CCP collaboration was short-lived, as the death of Sun and the launch of the Northern Expedition caused an open split between Chiang Kai-shek and the Communists over leadership in the revolutionary movement. The Communists then organized riots in the rural areas and saw their bases annihilated by the KMT army one by one. The incoming Japanese invasion saved the CCP as Chiang was not able to concentrate on mopping up the Communists. Under the leadership of Mao Zedong, the CCP was able to mobilize peasant nationalism and defeated the KMT after the surrender of Japan. The CCP then founded the People's Republic of China in 1949, and is still now the ruling party in China.

**Chairman of the Central Committee of the Chinese Communist Party** the paramount leader of the CCP from the Seventh Party Congress of April 1945, when that position was instituted, to September 1982, when that position was abolished. Three persons have assumed that position: Mao Zedong, from April 1945 to his death in September 1976; Hua Guofeng, from October 1976 to June 1981, when he resigned at the Six Plenum of the Eleventh Central Committee; and Hu Yaobang, from June 1981 to September 1982, when the Twelfth Party Congress abolished the chairmanship.

**Chen Yun** an important leader in the Chinese Communist Party who was particularly powerful during the First Five-Year Plan period (1953–7) and in the "adjustment" period that followed Mao's disastrous Great Leap Forward. Chen was a worker when he joined the communist movement. After the founding of the People's Republic of China, Chen's became the most important cadre in charge of economic construction. He was purged during the Cultural Revolution but was rehabilitated when Deng Xiaoping came to power in 1979. He then resumed the leading role in directing China's economic reconstruction in 1979–83. After 1983 he quarreled seriously with Deng and the radical market reformers, insisting on "birdcage economy," by which he meant that the market should be given somewhat of a free hand. Chen represented the pro-stability bureaucrats.

**Chiang Ching-kuo** son of Chiang Kai-shek and his successor. He was sympathetic to the communist cause when he was young and spent twelve years in the Soviet Union. Because of his father's anticommunist policy, Ching-kuo was kept as a hostage by Stalin and prevented from returning to China. After his eventual return in 1937, Ching-kuo became an able lieutenant to his father. After the ROC's displacement to Taiwan, Ching-kuo headed the China Youth Corps, the Political Department in the National Army, and the Defense Ministry. He finally became the premier in 1971 and succeeded his father as the KMT chairman in 1975 and ROC president in 1978. Ching-kuo led Taiwan through the turbulent 1970s when the ROC faced international isolation and global economic recession. Toward the end of his rule, Ching-kuo initiated political reform and lifted martial law in 1987. He died in 1988.

**Chiang Kai-shek**    the KMT's supreme leader, who succeeded Dr. Sun Yat-sen in 1926. Chinag led the Northern Expedition to unify China in 1928 and purged the communists from the KMT. He was forced to stop his annihilation campaign against the communists after the Xi'an incident of December 25, 1926. Chiang then led China's resistance war against the Japanese to victory, but was defeated by the communists in the civil war that followed. He then led the Nationalist government to Taiwan and ruled the displaced ROC on the island country until his death in 1975.

**Cultural Revolution**    Great Proletarian Cultural Revolution, the great political upheaval in the PRC that lasted for a decade (1966–76). Touched off by Mao's effort to regain political influence after the disastrous Great Leap Forward, the Cultural Revolution was ostensibly aimed at uprooting the traditional Chinese culture that was accused of undermining the communist revolution. The concrete targets were party cadres, state officials, and intellectuals whom Mao and the radicals found threatening to their power. Liu Shaoqi, Mao's designated heir and state chairman, Deng Xiaoping, the CCP's secretary general, and many other prominent leaders were purged. During the revolution, the state was paralyzed, educational system destroyed, and production seriously disrupted. Young students were recruited into the "Red Guards" brigades and dubbed "rightful rebels" by Chairman Mao. They finally came into serious conflict with the army and were expelled to the countryside for correction. The Cultural Revolution brought unimaginable damage to China, but paradoxically, it also laid a solid background for the post-Mao reform.

**Deng Xiaoping**    paramount leader of the Chinese Communist Party from 1979 to 1997. Deng was originally a lieutenant to Mao and was appointed the CCP's general secretary in 1956. He was purged during the Cultural Revolution but rehabilitated in 1973, purged again in 1976, and rehabilitated again in 1977. Deng was a pragmatist; thus he opposed Mao's ultraleft line, which caused his downfalls. However, with the death of Mao, Deng was able to gain political ascendancy and directed China toward a fundamental economic reform. The inefficient People's Communes were abolished, the market was introduced, foreign capital was invited, stock markets were opened, special economic zones were set up, industrial ownership rights were restructured, and people's living standards were significantly improved. Deng's economic liberalism, however, does not mean he was a democrat, as witnessed by his order to crush the pro-democracy movement in Tiananmen Square in 1989. Deng died in 1997.

**Gang of Four**    four ultraleftist leaders who were most prominent under Mao Zedong during the Cultural Revolution period. The four were Jiang Qing, Mao's wife and Politburo member; Yao Wenyuan, Mao's son-in-law and Politburo member; Vice Chairman of the CCP Wang Hongwen; and Vice Premier Zhang Chunqiao. They formed a faction against the old cadres, such as Liu Shaoqi, Zhou Enlai, Deng Xiaoping, and Chen Yun. After Mao's death in September 1976, the Gang of Four attempted to seize party leadership but was thwarted by Hua Guofeng. They were arrested in October and put on trial for high treason.

**General Secretary**   the top leader of the Chinese Communist Party. From the Fourth (January 1925) to the Fifth Party Congress (April 1927), Chen Duxiu was the general secretary of the CCP. After the KMT purged the Communists, Qu Qiubai, Xiang Zhongfa, Chin Bangxian, and Zhang Wentian assumed that position successively before Mao Zedong discarded it at the Seventh Party Congress in 1945 and led the CCP as chairman of its Central Committee. However, the Eighth Party Congress reinstituted the title of general secretary and elected Deng Xiaoping to fill the position, which was reduced to that of chief lieutenant to the party chairman and in charge of the secretariat, rather than that of the party's paramount leader. After Deng's purge during the Cultural Revolution, the position was again abolished. At the Twelfth Party Congress of 1982, Hu Yaobang was elected general secretary, but he was obviously beholden to Deng, the then-paramount leader of the CCP. Finally, Zhao Ziyang (October 1987) and Jiang Zemin (June 1989) were elected general secretary under Deng's auspices. With the death of Deng, general secretary again became the most important position in the party, a situation that may change if Jiang retires at the Sixteenth Party Congress in 2002 but manages to exercise the kind of influence that Deng had over Hu, Zhao, and himself. If that happens, then the new general secretary will be beholden to Jiang, who may or may not keep any formal position.

**Great Leap Forward**   Mao's greatest economic adventure. During the First Five-Year Plan period (1953–7), the PRC adopted the Soviet model and built a centrally planned economy to boost economic growth. Toward the end of that period, serious bottlenecks developed and Mao was impatient. His solution was to mobilize human labor through ideological agitation and plunge the whole population into production campaigns. The goal was to surpass Europe and the United States in industrial production. The Great Leap Forward brought unprecedented famine and the death of 3 million Chinese people.

**Hu Yaobang**   one of Deng Xiaoping's major lieutenants in the reform era whose death in 1989 touched off unprecedented massive demonstrations for political reform in Tiananmen Square. Hu first succeeded Hua Guofeng as the CCP's Chairman in 1981; then at the Twelfth Party Congress in 1982, he was elected secretary general of the party. From 1982 to 1986, Hu faithfully executed Deng's reform policies and earned himself a liberal reputation. However, Hu was considered too soft toward dissident intellectuals by Deng, and in January 1987 Hu was removed from the position of general secretary.

**Jiang Zemin**   the current CCP secretary general and PRC president. Jiang was the CCP's Shanghai party secretary when the Tiananmen incident broke out in June 1989. He was chosen to replace Zhao Ziyang because he had been successful in combining economic reform with a tough political stance against "bourgeois liberalism" in both December 1986 and June 1989 without resorting to force. Jiang's strengths also included his being an outsider and not beholden to any of Beijing's entrenched factions. He took the position of chairman of the party's military commission in November 1989, and he was elected president of the PRC in 1993. Since the death of Deng Xiaoping in February 1997, Jiang's leading position in the CCP has become indisputable.

**KMT**    Kuomintang, or Chinese Nationalist Party, the ruling party in the Republic of China. The KMT has its precedents in *Xingzhonghui* (Society for Regenerating China) and *Tongmenghui* (Society of Common Cause), the two revolutionary organizations aimed at overthrowing the Qing dynasty. After the founding of the ROC, Dr. Sun first transformed *Tongmenghui* into a parliamentary party, the Nationalist Party, and then remade it into the Chinese Revolutionary Party when he saw no hope of practicing democracy in a China plagued by warlord politics. In 1919, Dr. Sun again transformed the Chinese Revolutionary Party into the Chinese Nationalist Party (Kuomintang, KMT) and then in 1924 reorganized it on the Soviet model. The new KMT was equipped with a centralized party organization, special departments targeting particular groups in the population, and the National Revolutionary Army. After the death of Dr. Sun, Chiang Kai-shek became the paramount leader of the KMT and, in that capacity, dictated politics in the ROC. When the ROC was displaced to Taiwan in 1949, Chiang continued to lead the KMT-ROC party-state until his death in 1975, after which his son Ching-kuo assumed the party's leadership. In 1988, Ching-kuo died and Lee Teng-hui took over. Lee Taiwanized the KMT and led the party to victory in all the major elections on the national level after having successfully democratized the ROC. Lee is the current (2000) chairman of the KMT.

**Long March**    the retreat of the communist forces of Mao Zedong from the Nationalist army after the annihilation campaign of 1934. After the communists had been purged from the KMT in 1925, the CCP organized riots and set up many "Soviet regions." The KMT then launched five annihilation campaigns against them. In 1934 the largest Soviet region in Jiangxi was overrun by the KMT troops, and the communists were forced to flee from their base with the Nationalist army in hot pursuit across southwest China over the most difficult terrain with the most hostile environment. After this Long March, Mao's forces ultimately settled in Shan'xi Province.

**Mao Zedong**    leader of the Chinese Communist Party from 1935 until his death in 1976. Mao espoused an unorthodox strategy of revolution in China that emphasized the importance of the peasants and land reform, and the need to "encircle the cities from the countryside." That strategy at first found no favor with the party leaders, but after the Moscow-sponsored leadership had failed to thwart the KMT's onslaught in 1934 and the whole party had been forced to flee, Mao captured the military leadership at the Zunyi Conference in 1935 and gradually moved to the top position. Mao's strategy brought about the CCP's victory over the KMT, and he became the party chairman. After the founding of the People's Republic of China, Mao continued to apply his guerrilla-warfare strategy to economic development, causing the famine and destruction of the Great Leap Forward. His refusal to give up power was followed by his launching of the Cultural Revolution, which threw China into a decade of political chaos.

**People's Communes**   political and production organizations that Mao Zedong set up during his economic adventure in the late 1950s. People's Communes were characterized by their large size and collective ownership. They were designed to increase agricultural production and realize the ideological goal of the Communist Party. A People's Commune is composed of several production brigades, which are subdivided into production teams. Communes organize production activities, distribute revenues, perform governmental functions, and take care of social welfare. In the heyday of communization, rural markets were abolished, prices were set by the state, and private property was eliminated in the countryside. The result of this experience was total disruption of agricultural production and unprecedented famine. The communes were sustained during the Cultural Revolution period but were ultimately abolished in 1983 when Deng's reform was in full swing.

**Politburo**   the organ in the Chinese Communist Party where the real power resides. The CCP follows the Soviet model in its power structure. Ostensibly, the Party Congress is the source of ultimate power in the party. However, under the practice of Lenin's "democratic centralism," the real power migrates to the Central Committee, which the Congress elects, and then to the Politburo, which the Central Committee elects. The Politburo is headed by the general secretary and composed of the highest-ranking officials from the party and the government. The Politburo has a Standing Commission, which assumes the power of the Politburo when it is not in session. The current (July 2000) Standing Commission of the CCP's Politburo is composed of seven members: Jiang Zemin, Li Peng, Zhu Rongji, Li Ruihuan, Hu Jintao, Wei Jianxing, and Li Lanqing. These seven persons are the most powerful leaders in the PRC.

**PRC**   People's Republic of China, the socialist country founded in 1949 and ruled by the Chinese Communist Party. The PRC has had four paramount leaders of the country and CCP since its fouding: Mao Zedong (1949–76), Hua Guofeng (1977–8), Deng Xiaoping (1979–97), and Jiang Zemin (1998–). During Mao's rule, the PRC had a totalitarian regime. Since Deng, however, the country has gradually shifted to an authoritarian system.

**Qing dynasty**   the last imperial dynasty in China (1644 to 1911). The Qing dynasty was founded by the Manchus who originally lived in the northeastern part of China outside the Great Wall (Manchuria). In the middle of the 17th century they invaded the Ming Empire to the south, captured the capital city of Beijing, and established their own rule all over China. The original emperors of the Qing dynasty – Kangxi, Yongzheng, and Qianlong – were able rulers who contributed greatly to the consolidation of the Manchu reign in China. When the Western powers arrival, however, the Qing dynasty was already showing signs of decline, but was able to survive military defeats at the hands of foreigners, unequal treaties, domestic rebellions, and a bankrupting economy for the next eighty years. In 1911 the Qing dynasty was overthrown by a revolutionary movement led by Dr. Sun Yet-san.

**ROC**   Republic of China, the country founded in 1912 by Dr. Sun Yat-sen. The ROC suffered from warlord politics and did not reach genuine political unification until after the Northern Expedition (1925–8) led by Chiang Kai-shek. After the Communists defeated the Nationalists in the Chinese civil war, the ROC retreated to Taiwan, an island province off the eastern coast of China. From the 1950s to 1980s, Taiwan was an authoritarian country with a thriving market economy. Since the late 1980s, its political system has been democratized.

**State Council**   the central government of the People's Republic of China. The State Council's predecessor was the Government Administrative Council headed by Zhou Enlai that was set up in 1949. After the 1954 constitution was promulgated, the Government Administrative Council became the State Council, and Zhou remained the premier until his death in 1976. The State Council is headed by the premier, who is usually the second most important person in the PRC.

**Sun Yat-sen**   the founding father of the Republic of China, who led a revolutionary movement to overthrow the Manchu (Qing) dynasty in 1912. When the ROC disintegrated into warring regions, Dr. Sun founded the Kuomintang (KMT) and built a power base in the southern province of Guangdong, and began inviting Soviet advisors to his camp. He died in 1925 before China was unified under the KMT.

**Third Plenum of the CCP's Eleventh Central Committee**   the historic party meeting held in December 1978 that ushered in the reform era in post-Mao China. At the meeting, Deng Xiaoping saw his political influence greatly expand as his lieutenants were elected to the Central Committee, and his line, the "Four Modernizations," was substituted for Mao's "treating class struggle as the major link." Hua Guofeng's authority as paramount leader was undermined with the institution of a collective leadership. The CCP's historians treat the Third Plenum as the turning point in the party's development. It signifies the shift from the totalitarian stage to the reform stage in China's post-1949 political development.

**Three Principles of the People**   Dr. Sun Yet-san's political philosophy of nationalism, democracy, and people's livelihood, with the last principle denoting a pragmatic program that emphasizes the combination of private entrepreneurship and active state involvement in economic development. This doctrine is by nature a liberal program for reconstructing China. It is enshrined in the Constitution of the Republic of China.

**Tiananmen Incident**   the massive student pro-democracy movement of June 1989 and its brutal suppression. Deng Xiaoping's reform during the 1980s opened up China to the world, but rapid economic growth was accompanied by omnipresent corruption and rising expectations for greater political liberties. Fluctuations in the economy fueled public dissatisfaction, and students became inspired by Western, especially American, democracy. Hu Yaobang's death and the visits to China by U.S. President George Bush and the Soviet Communist leader Mikhail Gorbachev also came into play. The convergence of these factors in the summer of 1989 brought Beijing's college students to the streets and to Tiananmen Square, demanding fundamental political reform. After a protracted stalemate between the students and the authorities that lasted for a month, martial law was declared and the troops moved in on June 4. Great casualties running in the thousands were reported.

**Zhao Ziyang**   one of Deng Xiaoping's major lieutenants, who from 1983 to 1989 was mainly in charge of economic reform. Zhao succeeded Hua Guofeng as premier in 1980. After the purge of Hu Yaobang in 1987, he was promoted to general secretary of the CCP. His "soft" attitude towards the students in the summer of 1989 cost him his job. After the June 4 suppression of the pro-democracy movement, Zhao was replaced by Jiang Zemin.

**Zhou Enlai**   China's prime minister from 1949 to January 1976. Zhou was a senior CCP leader who directed the director of the political department at Whompoa Military Academy in 1924–5, that is, during the first KMT–CCP collaboration. Zhou was very close to the Communist International but was wise enough to side with Mao Zedong at the Zunyi conference at which Mao took military leadership of the party. After 1949, Zhou became prime minister of the new government, a position he held until his death. Zhou is remembered for his restraining influence on Mao during the Cultural Revolution period, and for his diplomatic sophistication outside China. In 1973 Zhou rehabilitated Deng Xiaoping, a move that later proved critical in bringing the totalitarian phase of China to an end after the death of Mao.

**Zhu Rongji**   Chinese prime minister since March 1998. Zhu is a technocrat by training, who rose in Beijing's state hierarchy until his critical tendency got him into trouble during the 1957 antirightist campaign, after which he was purged. Deng Xiaoping's political ascendancy brought Zhu back to the official arena, and he advanced rapidly until he was mayor of Shanghai. There he executed Deng's plan to build China's most important window to the world. He was promoted to vice premier during Deng's famous Tour to the South that relaunched economic reform following the conservative retrenchment period of 1988–91. In March 1988 he was elected premier to replace Li Peng.

## STUDY QUESTIONS

1. What was the kind of developmental strategy that the Kuomintang took on the Chinese mainland? Was it an effective response to the international challenge that China faced at that time?

2. Dr. Sun Yat-sen originally attempted to build China on the liberal model. Why and how did he abandon that model?

3. How was the first KMT-CCP collaboration formed and dissolved?

4. How did the Japanese invasion and the Chinese civil war alter China's developmental strategy?

5. Discuss the similarities and dissimilarities between political development in the PRC and in the Soviet Union.

6. Explain China's post-1949 political turbulence in terms of the conflict between the party and the state, and in terms of the shift from transformation to reform.

7. How did Deng Xiaoping's reform agenda conflict with Chen Yun's emphasis on stability in the post-Mao period?

8. How do you place Taiwan's democratization in the general framework of China's political development?

9. Discuss the possibility of China's democratization.

10. Is China unique in its response to international challenge in the 20th century?

# ⇜ Stop and Compare

## EARLY, MIDDLE, AND LATE DEVELOPERS

If it makes sense to group Britain and France as early developers and Japan and Germany together as middle developers, comparativists think that it makes even more sense to group Russia and China together as late developers. Not only did both countries industrialize only in the 20th century, but both also experienced communist revolutions and have lived with the long-term burdens of communist economic and institutional development. Although Russia cast off its communist political institutions and ideology in 1991, it continues to search for a viable path into the capitalist world. China, on the other hand, has retained its communist political structures but has done so while rapidly introducing capitalist economic institutions in important parts of the economy. These are the ironies that we examine in the case of the late developers.

## LATE DEVELOPERS: RUSSIA AND CHINA

Compared with its European neighbors, Russia entered the 20th century as a politically and economically backward country. As the core region of the tsarist empire, Russia had neither a constitution nor a working national parliament. Instead, Russia's tsar, Nicholas II, ruled as his father and grandfather had – as an autocrat unchecked by the power of law or political opposition. The privileged nobility served the tsar and lived in a moral and political universe separate from that of the masses of powerless and impoverished peasants. Nor did Russia have a consolidated sense of its own nationhood; one look at a map was enough to see that the empire consisted of well over a hundred different ethnic groups and languages. Its economy was still primarily agricultural, despite some serious efforts to modernize agriculture and initiate industrialization in the latter part of the 19th century.

In fact, several of Russia's earlier rulers had attempted modernizing reforms. Peter the Great (1680–1725) had introduced modern technologies acquired in the West and had even built a new capital city, St. Petersburg, on the Gulf of Finland, replete with the best Italian and French architecture of the day, as a tangible symbol of Russia's Western orientation. Catherine the Great (1762–96) had welcomed significant elements of Enlightenment rationalism and European thinking into imperial administration. Alexander II had freed the peasant serfs in 1861 with the intention of unleashing the social energies of ordinary Russians in order to harness them for economic development and military competitiveness.

The problem with all of these reforms, however, was the deep ambivalence Russia's rulers felt toward them. The tsars wanted the military and technological advances that reforms and economic development might bring, but they feared the kinds of social and psychological changes in the population that had occurred in France and ultimately led to revolution. Over time, as the rest of Europe was democratizing, this contradiction grew more intense: Military competitiveness required economic development; economic development entailed adopting Western technologies, methods, and ideas; but Westernization appeared to lead inexorably toward some kind of political liberalization – something that all tsars resisted until the very end.

Even within Russian society, there was an ambivalence about embracing the experience of the West. During the 19th century, some parts of the intelligentsia wanted to preserve distinctive Slavic traditions and were thus dubbed "Slavophiles." Others looked to the West and hoped one day to force a rupture with the nobility, who dominated political life, and the Orthodox Church, which dominated the spiritual life of Russia – and were thus labeled "Westernizers." The Westernizers themselves were split between those who wanted liberal democracy and those who wanted a distinctively socialist form of industrial modernity. Yet even among the socialists, there was a further split. The Mensheviks wanted to come to power democratically and the Bolsheviks wanted a revolution and to construct a communist society. Which path Russia would ultimately take became the burning question of the 19th and early 20th centuries.

The Russian Revolution of November 1917 led by Lenin and his Bolsheviks answered this question for the better part of the 20th century. Although the Bolsheviks wanted to build a new kind of society, they still had to build this society in a world of hostile countries, and they were thus confronted with some of the same challenges that had faced their tsarist predecessors. How could a first-rate military be built on the resources of a less-than-second-rate economy? Unlike their tsarist forebears, however, the Bolsheviks faced a further dilemma. How could all of this be done without capitalist markets and be made into something called "socialism" or "communism"? Lenin died too early to deal with these questions, but his successors were forced to deal with little else.

Lenin's successor, Stalin, undertook what some comparativists have called a second revolution and created distinctive communist economic and political institutions in the successor to the Russian empire, the Soviet Union. The Communist Party became the sole ruler of the country, agriculture was collectivized, and the economy was transformed into a command economy planned and administered from Moscow (which, perhaps tellingly, had become the new capital after the revolution). The net result of the revolution was to create a totalitarian dictatorship that succeeded in rapidly industrializing the country and creating a huge military-industrial complex. As we now know, this could only have been accomplished at a tremendous price in terms of lost lives and wasted resources. After Stalin's death, successive Soviet leaders, once again like the Russian tsars of earlier eras, sought ways to improve the economy and compete with the West without dismantling the distinctive communist political and social order.

The last Soviet leader, Mikhail Gorbachev, undertook what was perhaps the most important set of communist reforms. He too failed, but he implemented important political changes (his economic programs were utter nonstarters) that permitted society to mobilize against the Communist Party. In 1991, the Soviet Union broke up and Russia emerged as a smaller but formally democratic state. Once again, however, in some respects Russia finds itself in the position it was in before it embarked on the failed communist experiment – a country that is trying to catch up to the West by using institutions, methods, and ideas not of its own design. The added burden, however, is that the legacy of the Lenin-Stalin system has made democratic and capitalist transformation exceedingly difficult for Russia's postcommunist leaders.

Like Russia, China also experienced a communist revolution. But China continues to be ruled by a Communist Party that has overseen a stop-and-go series of economic reforms during the last fifteen years that have led to spectacular rates of economic growth accompanied by new social tensions. The reasons for the divergence in experience between the two countries are to be found in the very different legacies of the global past.

Comparativists are quick to point out that unlike Russia, which had always viewed itself as embedded within the broader European culture, China has always understood itself as culturally distinct from Europe. And for good reason, too. Chinese culture is far older than Europe's, and for centuries, China remained isolated from the outside world. Under successive Confucian rulers, China had managed to create an impressive form of bureaucratic rule based on an educated elite. These rulers were not subject to democratic control, but they did face the threat of overthrow if the mandarin and gentry elite felt that they had lost the "mandate of heaven" to govern their country.

The imperial order had lasted for centuries but was ultimately destabilized by its encounters with the industrialized West. Over the course of the 19th century, the Western powers had forced China to open an increasing number of its port cities to foreign merchants and trade. Chinese imperial bureaucrats brought this access into question in 1842, when the British were forbidden to market opium to the population. In response, the British successfully waged war and secured, for the next century, foreign domination of China's economically important coastal regions. British imperialism in the region ultimately paved the way for Japanese imperialism, which culminated in the Japanese invasions and atrocities of the 1930s.

Military pressures and internal fragmentation brought down the final Chinese emperor in 1911. Initially, after the emperor's departure, China was united under an alliance of the Nationalist Party (the Kuomintang) and the Chinese Communist Party (CCP), but the alliance collapsed in 1927 in a bloody rupture between the two partners. The CCP, although it was nominally a Marxist party and thus could be expected to look for support among the urban proletariat, fled to the countryside where it worked closely with the peasant masses and perfected its unique contribution to revolutionary theory: the conduct of a guerrilla war. The leader of the CCP, Mao Zedong, established his base in the countryside among the disaffected and the outlawed. Faced with increased military pressure from the Kuomintang, in 1933 thousands of communists abandoned their base in Jiangxi to begin their Long March of 7,000, a forced retreat that decimated the ranks of the party (only 8,000 of the original 100,000 arrived at the end) but also provided a formative, steeling experience for the Communist Party elite.

At the end of World War II in 1945, the Japanese fled the country and the civil war between the Nationalists and the Communists resumed. With the support of the majority of the peasants, who in fact constituted the vast majority of all Chinese, the CCP won the war in 1949 and the Nationalists were forced to flee to the island of Taiwan. The People's Republic of China was proclaimed on October 1, 1949. The CCP could look to the Soviet Union for a model to emulate, but they could easily look to their own "heroic" past to justify carving out their own path. Although important aspects of the Soviet model were adopted, the CCP under Mao's leadership pursued policies that were at times much more radical than in the Soviet Union (the Great Leap Forward and the Cultural Revolution). After Mao's death in 1976, the reformist-direction branch of the party emerged dominant, and under Deng Xiaoping's leadership, the CCP ushered in several waves of successful marketizing by instituting economic reforms and a broad opening to international market forces. At the same time, the party has retained tight control over political life and has forestalled any move toward democracy. Thus, whereas the Soviet Communist Party appeared to fall because it democratized before it marketized, part of the secret of the Chinese Communists' capacity to retain control has been their willingness to marketize their economy without democratizing their politics.

# PART FOUR

# Experimental Developers

## Cases

# 7

# Mexico

## ❧ Anthony Gill

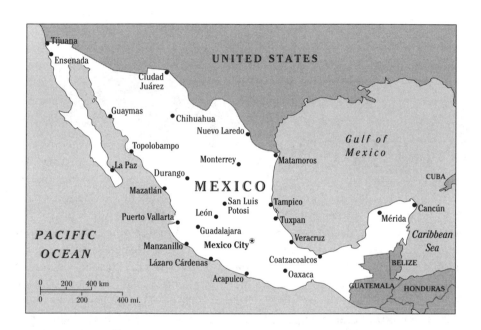

# INTRODUCTION

January 1, 1994, will be remembered as an important date in Mexican history. As Mexicans celebrated the beginning of the new year, two events occurred that marked profound changes in the country's political development. First, the North American Free Trade Agreement (NAFTA) took effect. This treaty integrated Mexico's economy more closely with those of the United States and Canada, marking the end of a nearly seven-decade strategy of sheltering Mexico from the vagaries of global markets. Pressures from international investors and trading partners to create greater economic openness dramatically affected (and continue to affect) Mexico's domestic institutions and day-to-day politics. The day's second memorable event made this readily apparent. As Mexico's President Carlos Salinas de Gotari was celebrating the new year and the implementation of NAFTA at a cocktail party, he received word that a major guerrilla insurgency had erupted in the southern Mexican state of Chiapas. A revolutionary organization known as the Zapatista National Liberation Front (or Zapatistas) was demanding greater political participation and a solution to the dire economic plight of poor rural farmers.

That the guerrillas attacked on the same day NAFTA took effect was no accident: The Zapatistas considered Mexico's increased integration into the world economy a threat to the economic well-being of the majority of Mexico's rural population, most of whom are of indigenous origin. Once considered to be part of Mexico's national identity – a blend of pre-Columbian and Spanish heritage – the majority of Zapatista supporters asserted their ancient cultural origins as part of a subnational identity that divided Mexico along racial and ethnic lines.

The insurgency also shook the foundation of Mexico's political institutions, long considered one of the developing world's most stable polities. The Zapatista

272

rebellion highlighted a growing trend in contemporary Mexican politics – the rise of political instability and the breakdown of one-party rule. Throughout 1994, Mexico witnessed a rash of political assassinations, including that of the ruling party's presidential candidate. Protests against the government, rare before 1980 but on the increase since the mid-1980s, became almost daily occurrences. Social turmoil alarmed many international and domestic investors, who began withdrawing their money from the country. By the end of the year, Mexico had undergone a major economic crisis that further exacerbated social tensions. The impact of this conflict was felt internationally. Fearing that other countries in Latin America would experience similar socioeconomic problems, foreign businesses scaled back their economic connections to the region, increasing unemployment and affecting the economic policies in such countries as Argentina, Brazil, and Colombia. As many Mexicans fled to the United States in hopes of finding better economic opportunities, anti-immigration pressure influenced election results in California, Texas, and other states. Clearly, the international environment has played an important role in shaping the domestic political identities, institutions, and interests of Mexico. Likewise, Mexico's developmental path has equally affected the politics of countries abroad.

To many comparative political scientists, the events of 1994 indicated a profound change in Mexican politics. Throughout most of the 20th century, a single party – the Institutional Revolutionary Party (PRI) – dominated Mexican politics. Although technically a representative democracy with regular elections, the PRI has dominated nearly all elected offices, tightly regulated social organizations, and dampened real political competition. To the extent that the PRI was able to promote rapid economic growth and rising standards of living, the party retained popular support among the citizenry. This popular support translated into an unprecedented level of political stability. While most other countries in Latin America were experiencing turbulent oscillations between democratic and authoritarian rule, or facing serious revolutionary challenges, Mexico has maintained a peaceful transfer of power among national and local rulers since 1920, longer than a number of European countries, such as Germany and Italy. However, as the 21st century begins, one-party rule and political stability can no longer be taken for granted.

How was Mexico able to maintain such a high degree of political stability over the past century? Why did this political stability come under such intense pressure during the 1990s? What does the future hold for Mexico's political development? Will the country become more democratically open via the peaceful transfer of power to opposition parties, or will we witness a breakdown of the social and political order and the rise of an authoritarian regime? Answers to these questions will tell us more about Mexico's political history and help us to understand how the global context shapes domestic interests, identities, and institutions and how these give rise to varying types of developmental paths.

## HISTORICAL, SOCIAL, AND IDEOLOGICAL ORIGINS

As seen in the introductory chapter to this text, political systems evolve from the choices and actions of earlier political actors. Previous institutional arrangements, entrenched interests, philosophical mind-sets, and the international environment all fashion a country's contemporary political institutions and social identity. Reflecting on the past is thus crucial for understanding the present. For Mexico, the obvious point of historical departure starts with the Spanish Conquest in 1521 (see Table 1 at the end of the chapter). This does not imply that indigenous societies had no role in shaping political and social arrangements in the Western Hemisphere. Several pre-Columbian social and political structures were adopted by the conquistadors to subjugate the indigenous populations. Indigenous cultures also play a complex role in shaping Mexican political identities (for example, in the way they view themselves in relations to the polity). In part, Mexicans pride themselves on a general identity that blends the country's Spanish and indigenous heritage. Yet, indigenous populations have not been fully incorporated into national life. The difficult economic problems facing these communities, particularly in southern Mexico, continue to promote social tensions. Nonetheless, when tracing the history of Mexico's contemporary political landscape, one can see that the forceful imposition and near-total dominance of Spanish institutions make the conquest a conventional starting point.

## THE COLONIAL PERIOD

The roots of the contemporary Mexican political system date back to the 16th-century invasion by Spanish conquistador Hernán Cortés. With his defeat of Aztec emperor Montezuma in 1521, Spain's distinct style of colonial governance prevailed over the territory of New Spain for exactly three centuries. The colonial period had three important effects on modern Mexican political life. First, it laid the ideological bedrock of corporatism, the core philosophical framework guiding Mexican political life. Second, the centralized and top-heavy political structures established by the Spanish monarchy provided comparatively little opportunity for self-governance in the colonies, resulting in political instability and all-out war for power following independence in 1821. Third, labor relations and landholding patterns established during the colonial era set the stage for future economic and political problems.

The cultural framework that came to dominate Mexico's national political identity emanated from the intersection of a strong religious tradition, Catholicism, and a political philosophy, corporatism. This line of thinking viewed society as an organic whole: Individuals belonged naturally to a variety of functional social groups (e.g., craft guilds, clergy, aristocracy). While each of these groups may have dissimilar interests, they all are needed for the harmonious operation of society. It stands to reason that the interests of the entire "body politic" should come before the interests of any particular component. Politically speaking, the needs of the state take precedence over the specific desires of any single group or individual within the state; groups exist to serve the state, not vice versa.

The institutional impact of this worldview was a statist, patrimonial style of government. For the body politic to function properly, so the argument ran, a centralized entity needs to mediate any potential conflict between social groups. The most effective way to do this is to have the state determine which interest groups are socially vital and then regulate their operation. Rather than allowing for the autonomous, grassroots organization of individuals with distinct interests, the state itself organizes, grants legitimacy to, and absorbs these groups into the decision-making apparatus of society. It also has a tendency to promote rigid class distinctions while downplaying the possibility of social mobility.

Corporatism, in the Mexican context, reflects a "top-down" strategy of interest aggregation, in contrast to the "bottom-up" approach of classic liberalism. This latter philosophy, a product of the English Enlightenment, emphasizes individual (not group) rights and views competition among autonomously organized interests as healthy for the economy and polity. The fact that Spain tried to keep its colonies isolated from such ideological influences had a long-term impact on Mexico's political identity and institutional design. Yet despite the hegemonic influence of corporatist thought, liberal ideas eventually found their way into the political fabric of Mexican life by the end of the colonial era. The struggle between the corporatist and liberal worldviews is an ongoing theme in Mexican political history, still playing itself out today.

In terms of social interests, the primary motivation driving colonization was the enrichment of Spain, particularly in relation to its European rivals. Although mineral wealth (e.g., silver) was highly prized, the Spanish crown also taxed other economic production (e.g., cotton, sugar) with the goal of increasing royal wealth. Given the distance between the crown and the colonies, ensuring the proper amount of revenue flow back to Madrid was a difficult task. Colonists had a competing interest in keeping as much wealth as possible for themselves, and thus tried to hide their wealth from royal tax agents. The political institutions established to govern the colonies reflected an attempt to minimize the problem of wealth extraction for Spain.

The colonies were governed with an eye toward ensuring that local officials remained strictly loyal to the crown. Only individuals born in Spain were appointed to the highest levels of colonial government. Each official served a specified term and then returned to Spain. Inasmuch as poor administration was punished on return, the rotation of colonial officials in this manner ensured a high degree of loyalty. To enhance it further, the monarchy conducted regular audits of colonial administrators. The Catholic Church was also under control of the king and was used to keep watch over both colonial officials and citizens (specifically by the Holy Office of the Inquisition). Though relatively complex in nature, the system of colonial administration was far from perfect. The immediacy of their living situation often dictated that even high-ranking officials cull the favor of the colonists. Because it was difficult to supervise the behavior of colonial officials completely, corruption was common and, up to a point, even tolerated by Spain.

Despite tight control by Spain, colonists were granted a limited degree of self-governance. Municipal councils *(cabildos),* staffed primarily by individuals born in the colonies, administered the day-to-day activities of town life (e.g., issuing building permits). These local councils later became the locus for the independence movement. However, it is important to note that the cabildos were relatively isolated from one another and were in no position to provide unified national leadership. Therefore, when Spain eventually did retreat, no strong centralized institutions existed to replace the colonial administration. The inevitable result was that the postindependence period would be one of substantial political uncertainty and instability.

The final consequence of the colonial period for the contemporary era relates to the pattern of land tenure and the resulting social-class relations. To encourage the conquest and settlement of New Spain in the mid-1500s, the Spanish monarchy had granted large tracts of land to conquistadors and the Catholic Church. These land grants typically included access to the labor and tribute of indigenous communities. The result of this pattern of land tenure and labor relations was the creation of a rigid class structure and a serious maldistribution of wealth that closely paralleled racial cleavages: *criollos* (individuals of pure-blooded Spanish descent) typically have occupied the upper classes; indigena, the lowest classes; and *mestizos* (mixed blood), in between. As the indigenous population has tended to be concentrated in southern Mexico, economic and political tension has had a strong geographic component to it. Under such conditions, trying to construct a fair and just governmental system, representing the interests of all Mexicans and creating a common national identity, has proven an enormous challenge. With criollos claiming higher economic status than the indigena, interest-based conflict has frequently inspired clashes over cultural identity.

## INDEPENDENCE AND THE ERA OF THE CAUDILLOS

Comparative political scientists understand that seemingly distant international events can have very important effects on domestic political arrangements. Mexican decolonization is a prime example. Both material interests and ideological influences emanating from abroad provoked the separation of Mexico from Spain. The seeds of Mexican independence were sown during the 17th-century decline of Spain. With the Spanish fleet unable to seal off New Spain from foreign ships (primarily French and British), contraband trade increased. Colonists began to get a taste for economic life beyond Spain's exploitative system. In 1700, a new royal dynasty (the Bourbons) attempted to reverse Spain's imperial decline. The central goal of the Bourbon Restoration was to rebuild Spain's influence in European affairs. Achieving this meant extracting greater amounts of revenue from the Americas. To this end, Charles III (1759–88), the most influential Bourbon monarch, initiated a series of economic and political reforms. He promoted intra-colonial trade, which spurred economic activity and increased Spain's colonial tax revenue. The king also tightened administrative control over the colonies by introducing a more rigorous bureaucratic arrangement borrowed from France. The plan was an overall success. The colonial economy boomed. Despite their resentment over the effective collection of higher taxes, most colonists benefited economically from the reforms. Nonetheless, political tensions erupted as many of the Spanish bureaucrats sent to administer the king's affairs replaced or marginalized local administrators. Just as in the U.S. War of Independence, "taxation without representation" stirred discontent with Spain among the populace.

The final series of events that sparked the drive toward independence had their origins in Europe. In 1808 French troops invaded Spain and imprisoned Charles IV. Confusion reigned as to who had final authority in the colonies: The deposed king? The king's colonial administration? The local cabildos? A small number of criollos influenced by European liberalism and the U.S. and French revolutions declared independence. Colonists loyal to the crown immediately quashed this liberationist movement and arrested all involved. A more significant challenge came in 1810 from two renegade Catholic priests – Padres Miguel Hidalgo and José María Morelos. Following a severe economic crisis in 1809, they rallied a significant peasant army around the symbolic banner of the Virgin of Guadalupe – an apparition of the Virgin Mary seen by an indigenous man in 1531. Given the dark, indigenous complexion of the Virgin, this apparition became one of the most important symbols of Mexican nationalism, reflecting the country's unique blending of European (Catholic) and indigenous cultures. The lower-class rebellion inspired by Hidalgo and Morelos, who were eventually captured and executed, lasted nearly five years. Many landholders and urban criollos, fearing a radical peasant rebellion, allied with the royalists. This caused independence to be delayed a decade.

The path toward independence followed a circuitous route. Once French troops had withdrawn from Spain, Ferdinand VII took the throne and increased military assistance to New Spain in a relatively successful effort to extinguish lingering separatist forces. However, just when it appeared that the independence movement had been defeated, events in Spain intervened to turn the tide. Under pressure from the Spanish parliament, Ferdinand VII endorsed a liberal-inspired constitution in 1820. Frightened that similar liberalizing tendencies would infect New Spain, many conservative, pro-royalist forces abandoned their support of the king and opted for Mexican sovereignty. Mexico's independence thus had a decidedly conservative, antiliberal tinge. Instead of a liberationist movement promoting the democratic ideal, the newly separated Mexican state declared itself a constitutional monarchy under the reign of Emperor Augustín de Iturbide.

The monarchy did not last long. Several events conspired to bring it to an end in 1824. First and foremost was a serious economic crisis facing the new nation. Eleven years of war had destroyed most of the revenue-producing assets in Mexico, including mines, livestock, and cropland. The financial capital and entrepreneurial skill needed to restart the economy had fled to safer haven in Spain. War casualties had depleted the source of skilled labor. Lacking a strong economy and tax base, the government found itself bankrupt. Even had the economy been able to jump-start itself, the state lacked the institutional capacity to collect taxes. Because central administrative authority was largely in the hands of Spaniards at the turn of the 19th century, this bureaucratic capacity vanished when those officials fled. The paucity of internal transportation networks further meant that centralizing control over an expansive territory would be an impossible task. Attempts to reign in autonomous localities met with fierce resistance. Unable to raise revenue, the new regime could not finance basic governmental functions, including the salaries of military officers and troops. Criticism of the monarch grew rapidly, forcing him to resign in 1823 under the threat of a military coup and civil war.

Iturbide's abdication marked the beginning of a cycle of political instability known as the "era of the caudillos." (*Caudillos* refer to independent military leaders who commanded localized armies.) The most famous (perhaps notorious) was Antonio López de Santa Anna, who ruled Mexico directly nine times and manipulated the choice of the presidency on numerous other occasions. The pattern of political instability during this period followed a typical cycle: A sitting president would discover the government bankrupt and be forced to cut back on military expenditures, including salaries and troop levels. With a stagnant economy, unemployed soldiers and officers were unable to find work. Discontent spread rapidly among the military, provoking a coup d'état. The new president would find himself in the exact same situation as the previous one and the cycle repeated.

All told, there were roughly fifty separate administrations from 1821 to 1860. This was hardly the environment for any single model of government, let alone democracy, to flourish. Nor was this a suitable context for the forging of a national identity, though the long-term effect of this chaos was a preference for more corporatist (in contrast to liberal) forms of government. The anarchic nature of this period allowed for the rise of local political bosses *(caciques),* who firmly resisted attempts to centralize national authority in any meaningful sense. To this day, the "culture" of the caciques persists, as current administrations have difficulty implementing policies without first considering the interests of local power brokers.

International pressures aggravated Mexico's political chaos. Foreign powers could easily take advantage of the country's weakened domestic position. Primary among these foreign interlopers was a young, expansionist United States. U.S. settlers began occupying the Texas region in 1821, the year of Mexico's independence. Although Texans were technically citizens of Mexico, efforts by Mexican authorities to make them accountable to central rule led the settlers to call for secession. Tensions escalated as U.S. settlers quickly outnumbered native Mexicans. Domestic U.S. pressure to annex Texas eventually provoked a war in 1846. With Mexico in political disorder, the United States won the war and roughly half of Mexico's national territory (extending from present-day Texas to California and Washington State).

The United States was not the only foreign power to play a role in complicating Mexico's political development. Several European powers, most notably France, also intervened. Financial interests were at the heart of the conflict. With the national treasury essentially empty from the first days of independence, various Mexican administrations had found it difficult to make restitution for damage done to foreign property during the wars of independence. Nor could the government repay foreign loans used to fund day-to-day administrative operations. In 1861, the Mexican government, facing a serious fiscal crisis, suspended payment on foreign debts owed to Britain, France, and Spain. These three powers responded by occupying Mexican ports to collect customs duties as repayment. French ambitions, however, extended beyond this action. Emperor Louis Napoleon Bonaparte opted for an all-out invasion of the country and installed an Austrian aristocrat, Ferdinand Maximilian Joseph, as president. The French intervention lasted three years (1864–7) until Mexican armed forces prevailed in ousting Maximilian. Such intervention only aggravated the country's political instability, retarding the creation of viable political institutions.

## THE ASCENDANCY OF LIBERALISM

Foreign occupation and war were not the only international influences to shape the Mexican polity. An ideological "invasion" also proved decisive in Mexico's political history. Along with increased contraband trade in material goods during the latter half of the 18th century, new ideas began to filter into the region. Increased contact with Britain, France, and the United States following independence further exposed many Mexican elite to new streams of political thought.

The philosophies of the English Enlightenment and French Revolution, with their emphasis on citizens' liberties and rights, contrasted with conservative, corporatist thought that gave primacy to the state over the individual. Throughout the 19th century and for the first several decades of the 20th, the struggle for a national political identity involved the efforts of liberals to graft their ideological beliefs onto a culture heavily influenced by medieval Catholicism.

The conflict between liberalism and corporatism resulted, during the 1800s, in a bloody contest between two factions – Liberals and Conservatives. The former sought to build a political system based upon many of the same precepts as the U.S. Constitution. Mexico's first constitution (1824) divided national government among three branches – legislative, executive, and judicial. A bicameral legislature further balanced the geographical interests of states (two senators per state), with representation based on population (one deputy per 8,000 people). The document also promoted a federalist system that distributed power away from the capital, Mexico City, and toward local governments. Subsequent constitutions of 1836, 1857, and 1917 were based on this earlier document and kept a preference for liberal political institutions. Liberals also favored moving Mexico toward a more secular society and pursued anticlerical reforms to restrict the Catholic Church's cultural, political, and economic power. Conservatives, alternatively, preferred centralized government based upon a strong executive. Their philosophical identity owed more to the corporatist thought of medieval Catholicism than to the English Enlightenment. It was their defense of the Catholic Church that most differentiated Conservatives from their Liberal counterparts.

Although the political instability of the 1800s took on the veneer of a great battle between competing worldviews, the ideological basis for conflict during this period should not be overestimated. Interest-based struggles over personal power prompted constant turnover in presidential administrations. Politics became a "winner-take-all" game; daily survival in office took precedence over achieving long-term philosophical goals. Over time, Liberals and Conservatives became virtually indistinguishable in their economic policy preferences, both favoring export-oriented growth and trade relations with Europe and the United States. Politically, Liberals abandoned their federalist pretensions and opted for centralized government, which allowed them to rule a large territory more effectively. This was most evident during *La Reforma* (1855–76), when Liberals finally dominated their Conservative rivals. Dominance did not imply political stability, though. This period included a major civil war (1858–61) and the French occupation of 1864 to 1867. The most prominent politician during this period was Benito Juárez, a pure-blooded Zapotec Indian who demonstrated that while upward mobility was very difficult for the indigenous, it was not entirely impossible. (Juárez's heritage is often championed as evidence of the strong indigenous influence in Mexico's cultural identity.) Juárez, a Liberal, realized that Mexico needed a strong, centralized government to end the internecine warfare that had torn the country apart since independence. He concentrated power in the presidency against his own liberal principles calling for a strong legislature. In doing this, Juárez became the first president to complete a constitutionally prescribed term in office (1867–71) and provided the country with its most stable governance to date. This lesson was not lost on future leaders. Ruling Mexico meant maintaining centralized political institutions. Under Juárez's presidency, business investment became a reasonably safe activity and the economy began to show signs of growth.

## The Porfiriato

President Juárez's successful completion of his presidential term raised the hope that a stable rule of law had finally arrived in Mexico. Unfortunately, personal hostilities erupted during Juárez's next term in office, which ended prematurely with his natural death. The resulting succession crisis gave way to a harsh dictatorship under Porfirio Díaz (1876–1911), a period known as the *Porfiriato.* Although ruthless, the dictatorship did have a beneficial side. For thirty-five years, Mexico experienced unprecedented political stability and economic growth, bolstered by a favorable global context. Industrial growth in Europe and the United States fueled demand for raw materials. Rising commodity prices boosted Mexico's domestic economy and helped fill state coffers. Government tax revenue, along with U.S. and British foreign investment, was used to build Mexico's infrastructure. Railroads were built, ports modernized and the national bureaucracy expanded. Since Britain had no interest in expanding its empire into the Americas, and the United States was pursuing a policy of relative isolation, direct foreign intervention in Mexican affairs was minimal. Expansionary desires of other countries were kept in check by the Monroe Doctrine, a U.S. policy designed to prevent European encroachment into the Americas.

Porfirio Díaz also left his mark on Mexico's political landscape. He was the first of Mexico's rulers to unify Mexico effectively under central authority for any extended period. He accomplished this by means of shrewd manipulation of military appointments, the buying off of local political bosses *(caciques),* and the creation of a separate police force directly loyal to his authority. Despite ideological loyalty to the liberal constitution of 1857, which provided for a strong legislative branch, Díaz further concentrated institutional power in the executive. Since this time, the Mexican president has enjoyed political power above and beyond what is legally prescribed.

The Porfiriato's final legacy was to establish a style of rule that has been used to guarantee political stability to the present day – *pan o palo,* the rule by "bread or club" – meaning the dual use of patronage and coercion. With increased revenues flowing into the treasury during the economic boom, Díaz bought the loyalty of various towns and constituencies. Important members of the elite received lucrative positions in the governmental bureaucracy in exchange for their support. Hence, Díaz earned his legitimacy not by appealing to the will of the majority but, rather, by being able to "deliver the goods." The liberal goal of popular sovereignty gave way to the corporatist manipulation of political support. Alternatively, those individuals or groups not willing to cooperate with the policy directives of the president were dealt the heavy hand of the police.

Although dissent was not permitted, it could not be entirely prevented. The economic prosperity of the late 1800s gave rise to a new set of middle-class interests. While generally pleased with the economic management of the country, middle-class professionals began demanding greater political participation, something that their brethren in other Latin American countries were enjoying at this time. With Díaz nearing his 80th birthday, many anticipated that the dictatorship would soon end and lead to a liberalization of Mexican politics. Díaz himself heightened these expectations by announcing in 1908 that he would not run for office in 1910. Positioning began in earnest for the upcoming presidential campaign, with Francisco Ignacio Madero as an early favorite. As the election neared, Díaz changed his mind and Madero found himself in prison for mounting an effective opposition campaign. Díaz's rigged electoral victory in 1910 unleashed the Mexican Revolution.

## THE MEXICAN REVOLUTION

The Mexican Revolution began as another conflict over presidential succession, something that Mexicans had grown accustomed to. The ideological rhetoric of the initial rebellion mirrored the liberal leanings of the previous century, with a call for representative democracy coupled with checks and balances on executive power. Early on, revolutionary leaders attempted to institutionalize the classic liberal tenets contained in the 1857 constitution. However, the Mexico of 1910 was much different from what it was just thirty years prior. New social classes such as urban labor had arisen, and existing ones (especially the rural peasantry) had grown politicized. These groups brought to the political arena a new set of interests – a desire for higher wages, better working conditions, social welfare, and access to arable farmland – that political institutions needed to capture. A new global ideological climate also shaped the course of the revolution; in Europe, socialist ideals began challenging the underlying logic of liberal capitalism. The Russian revolutions of 1905 and 1917 provided further examples that the peasantry and urban labor were becoming a major force for social change and could not be ignored in any new political arrangements. Many of those participating in the revolution not only wanted liberal political institutions but also major social reforms aimed at bringing the lower classes into a ruling coalition. Such demands radicalized the revolution and gave form to the resulting Constitution of 1917 and the corporatist institutions it would spawn.

With the disappearance of Díaz's effective system for holding the country together, internal chaos again reigned. The initial coalition that brought Madero to power began unraveling. Accusing Madero of failing to carry out his promised social reforms, a rebel from southern-central Mexico, Emiliano Zapata, declared war on the Liberal administration. An attempt to suppress this rebellion by relying on one of Díaz's former generals backfired, and Madero was overthrown in a counter-revolution supported by the Catholic Church and the U.S. government. Another faction led by Venustiano Carranza (northern Mexican governor and landholder) toppled this counterrevolutionary regime with the help of Zapata. Unhappy with Carranza's reluctance to implement progressive policies, Zapata's forces marched on Mexico City and forced a number of radical reforms that resulted in the drafting of a constitution in 1917. This new constitution included provisions for workers' rights to unionize, exclusive national ownership of mineral wealth, and communal land redistribution. These provisions represented a step beyond classical liberalism's preference for individual rights and established a basis for a modern corporatist system that gave the state enhanced powers in regulating social conflict. Much of the contemporary political strife in Mexico relates to efforts by recent presidents to rescind these social duties and move the country back to a more liberal framework.

The consolidation of the modern Mexican state began in 1920, the year typically viewed as the end of the revolutionary transition. That year marked the beginning of the peaceful transfer of power between presidential administrations and the return of political stability. The decade running from 1924 to 1934 saw the emergence of another presidential strongman, Plutarco Calles. Calles became the first president to implement the revolution's most radical promises, including the distribution of nearly 8 million acres of land to communal farms *(ejidos)* and the organization of labor into government-sponsored unions. Other social policies, including increased wages, better sanitation, and health programs, were also implemented. All of this was made possible by a relatively strong global economy that allowed Mexico to increase its export of raw materials and attract foreign investment.

Despite the progressive social policies undertaken by Calles, the actual political working order that emerged was far from the liberal democratic ideals contained in the 1917 constitution. Dissidents were jailed and the press censored. Calles's governing strategy closely resembled the *pan o palo* methods of Porfirio Díaz. Indeed, the heavy reliance on patronage networks by a centralized presidency to win social support and legitimacy is one of the main reasons Mexico's political system remained stable and free from military intervention from the

1920s to the present. Coercion *(palo)* became less needed as time wore on, since rapid economic growth guaranteed that the patronage strategy *(pan)* would work effectively. In effect, the legacy of the revolutionary era was the forging of a new mode of governance for Mexico – one that synthesized the basic political elements of liberalism (e.g., elections, popular sovereignty) with the corporatist mode of operation (i.e., top-down social organization, increased political centralization). While corporatism came to dominate liberalism, the blend of these two forms of government represented a political system uniquely Mexican.

## THE REVOLUTION INSTITUTIONALIZED

The figure most credited with shaping the Mexican political system into what it is today is Lázaro Cárdenas. As president from 1934 to 1940, he institutionalized the corporatist philosophy of government. However, the revolutionary process had radically transformed the philosophic basis of corporatism. The corporatism of the 19th century was inherently conservative and exclusionary, seeking to preserve the socioeconomic organization of a bygone colonial era. Political participation by those other than the landed elite was strictly forbidden, and class relations remained static. The corporatist philosophy underlying Cárdenas's political arrangements, on the other hand, was progressive and inclusionary. It sought to transform Mexico into a modern industrial nation by organizing, coordinating, and controlling the social groups that would build the nation. Government would be pro-worker and pro-peasant. The state would try to tame the ravaging effects of "raw capitalism" and build a nation free from foreign influence. Under Cárdenas, Mexico had finally achieved a strong, national identity based on a unique blend of liberalism, corporatism, and socialist ideas.

Economically, Mexico's international position prescribed a more state-centric approach to development. Being an industrial latecomer placed several constraints on the country's ability to achieve a modern economy. Most of what Mexico wanted to produce domestically was already being produced more efficiently in the United States and Europe. Mexican entrepreneurs were at an inherent disadvantage since domestic consumers would invariably prefer less-costly, higher-quality goods manufactured abroad. No incentive existed to engage in entrepreneurial activity unless the state stepped in to guarantee businessmen domestic markets (via protective tariffs) or to subsidize their production costs. It is ironic that providing business with domestic markets meant creating a consumer base for manufactured goods. This, in turn, meant promoting higher wages for urban and rural workers.

The political tumult that ravaged the country for nearly a century meant that there was little private capital to provide the impetus to build factories. Given the high start-up costs of building heavy industry in the mid-20th century, few Mexican citizens had the financial capacity to invest in large-scale industry. As in other cases of late development, the state would become the main vehicle for raising and investing capital. Mexico's industrialization was promoted extensively by a combination of state-owned enterprises and state subsidization of preferred industries. Overall, this general economic strategy was known as import-substituting industrialization (ISI). The component parts of ISI included high import tariffs on manufactured consumer goods, financial subsidies to private business, overvalued exchange rates (to reduce the costs of producer imports), and state ownership of industries with high capital costs (e.g., electrical power, steel). Unionization and higher wages were promoted and a welfare system created to provide a consumer base for domestically produced goods. ISI policies were common throughout Latin America and other parts of the developing world (e.g., Iran) during the mid-20th century and were largely a reaction to the Great Depression and World War II when these countries were cut off from the manufactured goods traditionally provided by Europe and the United States. Although ISI policies were designed essentially to promote autarkic development, the lack of domestic capital inevitably meant courting foreign investment.

The revolutionary party, created under President Calles, became Cárdenas's institutional vehicle for achieving political stability and industrialization. The Mexican Revolutionary Party – later renamed the Institutional Revolutionary Party (known by its Spanish acronym, PRI) – was created as an autonomous entity to mobilize the population in support of his reformist agenda. Cárdenas structured the party around three organizational pillars, each representing an important social sector: 1) the Mexican Workers' Confederation (CTM) representing urban, industrial labor; 2) the National Peasant Confederation (CNC) representing rural workers and the ejidos; and 3) the National Confederation of Popular Organizations (CNOP) composed of white-collar professionals, government bureaucrats, and small entrepreneurs. Each of these organizations was given representation in the policy-making apparatus of the party and, hence, the government. (The PRI has been the only party to hold national office since 1934). However, since the party's top leaders chose the officials of these organizations, the PRI became the epitome of inclusionary corporatism. The ruling party organized societal interest groups from the top down, and political loyalties were based on "corporate," not geographic, identities. Autonomous groups that arose over the years were absorbed into the corporatist structure, ensuring that the government maintained tight regulatory control over popular interests.

A fourth organizational body representing the armed forces was also created. Cárdenas's early incorporation of the military into the party proved crucial to ensuring his immediate political survival. By currying the favor of officers and troops with substantial pay raises, educational opportunities, and other benefits, he prevented his rivals from using the army to plot against him. More importantly, these actions institutionalized civilian control over the armed forces, something historically rare in Latin America. In large part, Cárdenas's actions in the 1930s prevented Mexico from falling prey to the intermittent coups and military dictatorships that plagued South America for most of the 1960s and 1970s. The military reforms proved so successful that when the party disbanded the official organization representing the military in 1940, no military revolt ensued.

The institutionalization of labor, the peasantry, and the middle class into the ruling party became the crucial defining feature of Mexican politics for the next six decades. By connecting each social sector to the party, Cárdenas ensured enormous popular support for the PRI and set the stage for a single-party state. Relying more on "pan" (patronage) than "palo" (coercion), Cárdenas won the long-term loyalty of the Mexican lower classes. He dramatically improved urban working conditions and promoted the unionization of more than a million workers. During his presidency, roughly one in three Mexicans benefited from land reform involving nearly 50 million acres. The majority of land went to communal ejidos, which received privileged loans and technology from the government, further ensuring their political support. Finally, the incorporation of government bureaucrats, teachers, and lawyers into the PRI meant that the state and revolutionary party would become virtually indistinguishable.

Cárdenas also instituted many of the political practices that became standard fare over the next several decades: He extended the presidential term to six years. The president, as head of the PRI, would nominate his successor. Patronage benefits to privileged groups, controlled almost exclusively by PRI officials, increased in the months preceding a national election. Government-organized labor received higher wages; business groups were granted subsidies; and public works projects sprang up in rural communities. This increased spending prompted a period of inflation leading up to the election. Following national elections, the outgoing president would undertake deflationary policies so that the new president could begin his term with the task of rebuilding the economy. In many respects, this pattern represented a classic "political business cycle" of inflation and recession, determined by the electoral calendar.

Cárdenas also institutionalized a number of other political practices that made the Mexican system uniquely stable. Retiring presidents left office quietly and avoided interference in political matters. Power continued to be concentrated in the presidency; the Senate and House of Deputies served as a rubber stamp for the policies of the executive. Although the CNOP, CTM, and CNC were supposed to be involved in the policy-making process, they fell under the increasing dictate of party leaders. Government and party officials decided when and where labor could strike or make demands on employers. Assistance to rural communities was conditioned on unswerving support of the PRI. Reasonably fair elections were held, but real political competition was minimized. All of this combined to ensure the electoral dominance of the PRI, and gave the state a "quasi-authoritarian" flavor. While outsiders may be quick to criticize the lack of effective democracy in Mexico, it should be remembered that the institutionalization of one-party rule in Mexico gave the country something it had long lacked – political stability. This in turn provided the basis for rapid and sustained economic growth until the 1980s.

The final legacy of the Cárdenas era was his reaction to the international environment. Mexico had always been at the mercy of foreign powers, either militarily or economically. This changed in the 1930s. The 1938 nationalization of twelve foreign-owned oil companies not only signaled a country seeking to control its own economic development, but also was a high point in the creation of a Mexican national identity. Antiforeign (particularly anti-U.S.) sentiment increased noticeably. The economic policies of ISI were a natural extension of this growing nationalism as Mexico sought to become industrially self-sufficient. Despite being located adjacent to the world's foremost superpower, the Mexican government exercised a substantial degree of autonomy in its economic and foreign policy. Mexico became a leading member of the nonaligned, developing nations during the cold war and frequently criticized U.S. foreign policy in Latin America.

The reforms of the Cárdenas era were politically and economically successful, and they benefited from a favorable international climate. When manufactured imports from Europe and the United States slowed to a trickle during the Great Depression and World War II, Mexican industry developed to fill the supply gap. The war also created a high demand for oil and other primary commodities in the world market. Political stability further boosted the domestic economy, and the country entered an era of unprecedented growth known as the "Mexican Miracle" (ca. 1940–80). Gross domestic product grew at an average annual rate over 6 percent, an unprecedented feat in Latin America. Accounting for population growth, per capita income increased approximately 3 percent per year. Within two short decades (1950–70), living standards doubled.

Presidential succession continued peacefully for the next six decades, and the PRI held on to the major institutions of power. Although much of the PRI's dominance can be attributed to its control over important government resources and manipulation of patronage to loyal constituents, the party's popularity was also due to the nation's strong economic performance. The Mexican single-party system maintained a high degree of popular legitimacy. This is not to say that economic gains were distributed evenly. Over time, the actual policies of the government began to deviate from its revolutionary rhetoric and the redistributive legacy of Cárdenas. Large, private industries not included in the 1930s corporatist arrangement gained an increasingly privileged position among policy makers. Contrary to the nationalist intentions of ISI, Mexico increasingly depended on foreign investment to fuel economic growth. Nonetheless, economic growth and political stability became mutually reinforcing. So long as the economy stayed healthy, the PRI was able to "buy" the support of most major social groups. And a politically dominant PRI ensured a stable social environment that was attractive to domestic and foreign investors. Despite outward appearances of durability, though, the corporatist system built under Cárdenas was fragile. Should either the economy or the PRI falter, the political system as a whole would become vulnerable to serious crisis. This is exactly what happened in the 1980s and 1990s.

## THE CONTEMPORARY POLITICAL LANDSCAPE: THE END OF CORPORATISM?

Mexico's recent political development, defined by the historical tension between liberalism and corporatism, has been a battle of interests as well as identity. Following decades of social turmoil, top-down corporatist institutions proved best at reducing political conflict and promoting rapid industrialization. In turn, the Mexican Miracle provided financing for the corporatist system. But miracles rarely last forever. Political stability and economic growth gave rise to new social interests and demands for a liberalized political system. Addressing these demands was easy when the economy was strong and government resources plentiful. However, changes in the world economy during the 1970s seriously limited state access to the resources needed to keep patronage-based corporatist arrangements intact. With the PRI finding it financially difficult to fulfill its corporatist obligations, groups that were once loyal constituents began organizing independently and seeking help from new political parties. The ruling party's rule is no longer guaranteed, and corporatism is giving way to demands for political liberalization. How Mexico negotiates its transition from a single-party, corporatist state to a liberal-pluralist democracy, if at all, is the central problem facing the country today.

### Origins of the Crisis

Mexico's political foundation began to show cracks in the late 1960s. Just as economic growth in the late 1800s gave rise to new social interests that prompted the Mexican Revolution, the Mexican Miracle created new social interests that demanded reform of the country's corporatist institutions. Among these new demands were greater autonomy for local governments, the ability to organize groups independent of government ties, and alternative (non-PRI) political representation. Such demands appeared first in the wealthy industrial and ranching states of northern Mexico. The central government's corporatist policies worked against northern interests by directing patronage resources away from them and toward the more populous central and southern regions. Defending their economic interests meant promoting electoral competition; should PRI power be challenged in the region, the central government would be required to respond to northern interests. In 1965, candidates from the center-right National Action Party (PAN) won two mayoral elections in the prosperous state of Baja California, Norte. The ruling PRI, unfamiliar with such a challenge, nullified the elections, marking the first time fraudulent tactics were used openly to retain power. Political liberalization might favor the industrial north, but it was not in the interests of the ruling party. Corporatism still trumped liberalism.

University students also began calling for political change. A booming economy created an expanding middle class; more youth were attending college and expected professional careers. However, the closed political and economic system of the time could not adapt to meet these heightened expectations of a rapidly expanding population. Frustration among students ensued. Inspired by campus unrest in the United States and Europe, they began agitating for expanded civil liberties. These protests boiled over just before the opening of the 1968 Olympic Games in Mexico City. The spark was a brawl among high school students that prompted local government officials to call riot police in a massive show of force. Police overreaction enraged students, who then demanded police reform and expanded civil liberties. The well-organized student protesters eventually mobilized the largest antigovernment rally in Mexican history, involving some 500,000 people. Unfortunately, a two-monthlong series of protests ended with government troops firing on demonstrators in the Tlatelolco district of Mexico City, killing more than 100 civilians (and perhaps upwards of 400). The Tlatelolco massacre showed that popular support for the corporatist political system was waning.

By the early 1970s, the economy also began showing signs of stress. ISI policies encouraged inflation, currency overvaluation, and a serious balance-of-payments crisis. Inflation ate away at the real wages of most Mexicans. More important, the corporatist institutions designed to give workers and small farmers a voice in government (e.g., the CTM, ejidos) increasingly became a way to repress their demands. The government discouraged workers from striking and implemented policies favoring business interests. The government also promoted large-scale, capital-intensive farming for export, which markedly slowed the pace of land redistribution between 1940 and 1970. Disaffected peasants responded by invading private lands. Contrary to nationalist rhetoric, foreign investment gained a noticeable presence in the economy, causing resentment among local workers and small businesses.

The social unrest of the late 1960s challenged Mexico's corporatist system, but did not break it. President Luis Echeverría (1970–6) responded to this discontent by increasing wages, distributing more land to the rural poor, and permitting the autonomous organization of labor. His administration also allowed limited civil protests. Bowing to pressure for increased political representation, Echeverría's successor enacted legislation in 1977 that guaranteed opposition parties 100 seats in the Chamber of Deputies, based on proportional representation. These reforms represented a limited "democratic opening" and raised expectations for future liberalization.

The corporatist system survived due in large part to the oil crisis of the 1970s. Mexico, an oil-exporting nation, benefited from the dramatic rise in petroleum prices beginning in 1973. Revenue from the state-owned petroleum industry flowed into the national treasury where it was used to alleviate economic hardship caused by a global economic slowdown. Additionally, the flood of Middle East "petrodollars" on world financial markets allowed the Mexican government to borrow abroad. Increased government revenue prompted more state intervention in the economy as the state began nationalizing hundreds of firms. In turn, the expansive economic reach of the government provided more avenues for distributing patronage in the form of jobs, preferential loans for favored businesses, and subsidies to important rural clientele. Because Mexico's political stability was built upon the PRI's extensive patronage networks, oil revenue and foreign loans bolstered the survival of the corporatist system in a time of growing popular discontent.

The same global economic system that provided the financial liquidity to keep corporatism afloat in the 1970s served to undo the system in the 1980s and 1990s. Relying upon oil revenue and foreign loans to buy domestic political support was at best a temporary solution for Mexico's socioeconomic ills. Loans required repayment, and reliance on petroleum for the bulk of government revenue was an inherently risky strategy. Two international events in the late 1970s/early 1980s made this strategy unworkable and sent shock waves through Mexico's political system. First, to combat soaring inflation at home, the U.S. Federal Reserve raised interest rates between 1979 and 1982. Rates on international loans followed suit, dramatically increasing Mexico's debt obligation. Concurrently, the world market experienced an unexpected oil glut and prices dropped precipitously. With roughly two-thirds of Mexico's foreign revenue coming from petroleum exports, government income fell sharply just as international financial obligations increased. Facing a massive outflow of economic resources, Mexico devalued its currency, announced it was suspending payment on its international debt, and nationalized the country's banking system.

Business and consumer confidence disintegrated rapidly. International loans dried up and domestic investment slowed to a standstill. Mexico, like many countries in the developing world, entered its worst economic recession in more than a century. Total domestic production declined by 4.2 percent in the year following the devaluation and debt moratorium. Real wages tumbled by over 25 percent between 1980 and 1987. Unemployment and underemployment soared. With the economy in decline, government revenue (collected from taxes as well as oil) shrank noticeably. While halting payment on international loans would seem a reasonable response to such a crisis in government revenue, this solution was not feasible. Defaulting on its loans would have entailed severe economic sanctions from the world community, including the denial of loans in the future. Over the next several years, Mexico renegotiated repayment of its foreign debt, thus averting a major default and restoring partial confidence in the economy.

Part of the debt-negotiation agreement required the implementation of a series of "austerity measures" designed to control inflation and reduce the fiscal deficit. A radical reduction in government spending ensued. Jobs and wages in the government bureaucracy were trimmed. The government privatized hundreds of state-owned enterprises, which were used in the past to reward union supporters with high-paying jobs. Making these firms competitive meant slashing salaries and positions. Privatization thus struck at the heart of one of the central institutional pillars of corporatism – industrial labor. The peasantry felt the pinch of austerity as well. In order to generate foreign exchange with which to pay back foreign loans, the PRI began promoting agricultural exports. Government policy favored the most efficient, export-oriented farmers, typically those with large, capital-intensive plantations. Ejidos typically did not meet this need, and policy turned against their interests. Again, a traditional clientele of the corporatist system felt the brunt of the international economic crisis. A Mexico that had once tried to gain independence from the vagaries of the world market was now more than ever at its mercy.

Events in the economy profoundly affected the political sphere. The loss of government revenue placed severe restrictions on government spending. This undermined the ability of the PRI to manipulate patronage networks to ensure popular support. Discontent that had been brewing since the late 1960s erupted in the mid-1980s. A strong civil society began emerging at the grass roots, a trend contrary to the corporatist philosophy of "top-down" organization. The growth of civil society received an unlikely push from a series of major earthquakes in 1985 that killed more than 10,000 residents of Mexico City. The massive destruction left a cash-strapped government paralyzed. Foreign assistance poured in, but what really mattered most was the autonomous creation of thousands of small, community organizations that assisted in rescue and clean-up efforts. These organizations sowed the seeds from which independent political-action groups took root. For the first time since the modern corporatist system was constructed, a complex network of nongovernmental social groups emerged to challenge the hegemonic authority of the PRI.

The self-assertion of an autonomous civil society affected electoral politics. In 1983, members of the opposition National Action Party (PAN) won a significant number of municipal posts in the northern states of Chihuahua and Sonora. It is interesting to note that while one would expect leftist parties to make the greatest gains due to labor discontent, PAN occupied the center-right and advocated an economic platform similar to the PRI's current neoliberal policies. PAN candidates won these elections because they were the only opposition party with significant organizational strength to mount an independent attack aimed at loosening the PRI's hold over the government. Most left-wing parties had been previously co-opted by the PRI through links to labor unions. Officials in those parties accepted this situation in exchange for token positions at various levels of administration. In other words, the leftist leadership owed its existence to the PRI and thus had little incentive to challenge the ruling party's authority. Only PAN had sufficient leadership that remained independent of the PRI.

The PAN's electoral success went beyond organizational strength. It also signaled growing dissatisfaction with the PRI. As northern Mexico is more industrially developed and wealthier than the central and southern states, it was apparent that business interests were becoming increasingly unhappy with a PRI-dominated government. Furthermore, the preference for PAN indicated that there was more to the electoral discontent than strictly pocketbook matters; the electorate wanted real political choice and a greater say in government. The top-heavy corporatist model was facing a serious challenge from the grass roots.

The extent of popular unhappiness became clear during the presidential election of 1988. The handpicked PRI candidate, Carlos Salinas de Gotari, won the presidency with only 50.5 percent of the vote, the slimmest margin of any previous PRI candidate. Cuauhtémoc Cárdenas, son of the former president and the representative of a loose coalition of left-wing parties, came in second with 30.9 percent. The PAN candidate finished third with 16.7 percent. This in itself signified a substantial defeat for the one-party state. In reality, Salinas may have actually lost the election. Electoral irregularities marred the election, including a power outage that affected the computerized ballot counts. As political competition grew throughout the 1980s, the PRI increasingly resorted to electoral fraud to retain important seats. While the true totals from the 1988 election may never be known, it is enough to say that this election had a lasting impact on the Mexican polity. The Mexican corporatist framework that had brought an era of unprecedented political stability for Latin America could no longer be sustained in its present form. The 1990s thus initiated a transitional period for the Mexican state. While the outcome is still uncertain, a conflict-ridden move toward liberal democracy appears to be in the works.

## POST-1988 MEXICO: INTERESTS, IDENTITIES, AND INSTITUTIONS

At the beginning of the 21st century, Mexico finds itself struggling with one of the central political themes of its past – the tension between liberal and corporatist forms of government. While this conflict was resolved for most of the century in favor of a corporatist one-party state, the crises of the 1980s and the rise of an

autonomous civil society makes liberal-pluralism a viable contender as the organizing principle of Mexican political life. Economic globalization and the collapse
of the socialist model of development have pushed economic policy in the direction of laissez-faire policies. President Carlos Salinas (1988–94) stepped up the
pace of privatization begun by his predecessor, Miguel de la Madrid (1982–8).
Under pressure to attract foreign capital and cultivate new export markets, Salinas
also gave the central bank greater autonomy and entered into an expansive free
trade agreement (NAFTA) with the United States and Canada. His successor,
Ernesto Zedillo, has continued on the same path. Salinas's policy of economic liberalization under a one-party state was reminiscent, in some ways, of similar
reforms undertaken by Mikhail Gorbachev in the Soviet Union – so much so that
the Mexican reforms were given the name "Salinastroika." But as Gorbachev found
out, economic liberalization unleashes powerful forces in society. New interests
are created, institutions transformed, and identities reshaped.

The economic crises of the 1980s and the resulting laissez-faire (neoliberal)
policies remade political interests in ways not seen since the Mexican Revolution.
Definite winners and losers emerged. The most extreme example has been in the
southern state of Chiapas where a guerrilla insurgency burst onto the scene in
1994. With land becoming increasingly concentrated in the hands of a few large-
scale farmers, ejidos found it exceedingly difficult to sustain a living, and grievances against the government grew. In 1992, President Salinas revised Article 27 of
the 1917 constitution, which was the cornerstone for earlier land-redistribution
programs. The new article made privatizing ejido lands easier. Peasants seeking to
have their concerns addressed were frequent targets of violent attacks by the
state police and private paramilitary groups supported by large landholders. The
implementation of NAFTA in 1994 further threatened the interests of ejido farmers,
as it favored large-scale agricultural exporters over small-scale communal farms.
With their economic livelihood at risk, many peasants found it worthwhile to join
the Zapatista National Liberation Army (EZLN). As of this writing, the EZLN and
the Mexican government remain deadlocked over a variety of issues affecting the
peasant interests, including land redistribution, human rights, effective political
representation, and electoral fraud.

The Zapatista movement is not only about economic interests. Because many
of the peasants in Chiapas are of direct Mayan ancestry, the movement has
asserted strong indigenous claims. Mexican nationalism plays little, if any, role. In
fact, the insurgency in Chiapas has demonstrated the difficulty in forging a single
Mexican identity. In societies where economic class divisions map closely onto
racial and ethnic cleavages, ethnic identity is bound to be closely associated with
interest-based politics. How the central government treats the descendents of pre-
Columbian inhabitants has become a central policy issue in a country that has
largely ignored such concerns for nearly five centuries. Indigenous communities

are now identifying themselves as distinct groups within the Mexican polity and demanding to have their voices heard in the central government. This implies a greater respect for civil liberties (e.g., freedom of association) and the ability to freely elect government officials representing their interests. The rise of a strong indigenous identity thus creates pressures for political liberalization.

The political legacy of the 1990s may very well be the emergence of real electoral competition, one of the central features of a liberal democratic polity. With the PRI losing its ability to deliver patronage to its core constituencies because of fiscal restraints on state spending and an ambitious program of privatization and government downsizing, many of those interests tied tightly to the party in the past have sought new avenues of representation. Nongovernmental organizations have appeared as a new force in society. Political participation also has been channeled into two major opposition parties – the National Action Party (PAN) and the Democratic Revolutionary Party (PRD). The latter was forged from a coalition of leftist parties and disaffected members of the PRI in the early 1990s. It has attracted mostly members of the urban and rural working class and poor, although significant portions of lower-income voters remain tied to the traditional patronage networks of the PRI. Political infighting has also weakened the PRD. During the 1994 presidential elections, the PRD candidate – Cuauhtémoc Cárdenas (a former member of the PRI) – won only 17 percent of the vote in a reasonably clean election. Nonetheless, by the late 1990s, the PRD had scored a number of important victories at the local level, including winning the mayoral seat of the nation's capital.

The PAN has been the most consistent threat to the PRI's political hegemony. Representing upper-income interests, the PAN has tapped into domestic business disapprobation with many of Salinas's and Zedillo's economic policies. While it seems odd that domestic businesses would be dissatisfied with laissez-faire policies, it must be remembered that many of these businesses benefited from the high tariffs and government subsidies of the 1960s and 1970s. They were not prepared to compete internationally. Neoliberal policies took many of these benefits away, although overall they have helped to create a friendlier environment for foreign investment. It is ironic that the PAN champions many of the same policies as the PRI's neoliberal agenda. In this respect, much of the support for the PAN can be viewed more as a search for an alternative political voice than as a desire to shift the economic policies of the state. This voice has found a forum, as PAN candidates have won numerous local offices and captured key gubernatorial positions in several northern states.

The increase in electoral competition has affected two of the country's primary political institutions – the national legislature and the PRI. Power still remains highly concentrated in the presidency, and the executive remains under the control of the PRI. However, in 1997 the PRI lost control of the Chamber of

Deputies (equivalent to the U.S. House of Representatives). Previously, the PRI had enjoyed majority representation in both the Chamber of Deputies and the Senate, making the Congress a "rubber stamp" for executive decisions. This pattern was reinforced by the fact that PRI party leadership chose each legislator, which meant that the president had a strong influence over the career paths of politicians. In some respects, this resembled "parliamentarianism in reverse" – the leading party executive chose legislators rather than vice versa. Results from the 1997 midterm elections earned opposition parties a combined majority in the Chamber of Deputies for the first time during the 20th century. Although the PRI still controls the Senate and can play "divide and conquer" among the deputies to ensure a winning legislative coalition, the presence of a majority opposition in the lower house has forced the PRI to engage in negotiation and compromise, both steps toward more pluralistic interest representation. With opposition parties in general agreement on the need for further electoral reforms, this environment bodes well for continued political liberalization. Political liberalization, in turn, raises the prospects for greater representation for opposition parties in the Congress and for a stronger legislative branch. Though still too early to tell, the classic liberal notion of checks and balances may become a reality in the near future.

Increased political competition and social pluralism have shaken the dominant party itself. Within the party elite, a debate rages over how to manage the economic and political turmoil currently engulfing Mexico. The faction that emerged dominant in the past two decades represents a more reformist line of thinking. Known as the *técnicos* (technocrats), they hearken from the bureaucratic side of the party. Presidents Salinas and Zedillo are members of this faction. Both were educated in U.S. universities and earned their political stripes by working their way through the Mexican bureaucracy, rather than by winning seats in local and regional government. The técnicos began occupying high-level offices during the 1980s when economic crisis called for policy makers with specific expertise in managing domestic and international macroeconomic affairs. The ascendance of técnicos gave rise to a competing faction within the PRI called the *dinosaurios* for their hard-line, traditional corporatist stance.

The split within the PRI created an interesting and fluid constellation of alliances. The primary intraparty cleavage related to economic policy. While the técnicos favored neoliberal economic reforms to modernize Mexico's economy, the dinosaurios preferred the old formula of state-directed growth and opposed the privatization of industries and NAFTA. This put the latter group in policy agreement with the PRD. The técnicos found policy allies among the center-right PAN. Despite their differences, both the técnicos and dinosaurios strongly desired the PRI to hold onto political power. Political survival tended to take precedence over economic policy disagreements, and both factions were involved significantly in vote tampering during the 1980s. The transparency of electoral fraud, especially at the local level, only fueled further dissatisfaction with the ruling party and intensified public cries for electoral reform.

Whereas President de la Madrid (1982–8) represented a transition between the hard-line dinosaurios and the técnicos, Carlos Salinas firmly identified himself with the latter. Following his narrow electoral victory in 1988, Salinas surprised many analysts by charting a course independent of the dinosaurios. It was believed that this would be a dangerous strategy for a man who needed as much internal party support as he could muster. Nonetheless, his institutional reengineering had a lasting impact on the Mexican polity, and he most likely will be remembered as a pivotal character in Mexico's political history. Salinas was credited with disassembling many of the PRI's traditional patronage networks. Realizing that dinosaurio power rested in those channels, he cut funds to favored programs and dismissed important union officials. Still needing social support for his presidency, though, Salinas created the Solidarity Program, a new set of patronage networks that circumvented many of the local political bosses who remained loyal to the dinosaurios. President Zedillo continued this tradition through a similar set of programs. The end result was nearly to destroy the traditional pillars of support holding up Mexico's corporatist system, which had ensured political stability in the past.

Constitutional reforms undertaken in 1992 further changed Mexico's political landscape by removing some of the most radical elements of the revolutionary constitution. Without recourse to the revolutionary ideals of the past, a new legitimating formula needed to be found. While Salinas and the técnicos hoped that economic growth would boost support for the PRI, they realized that economic restructuring would pay dividends too far off in the future. Discontent with the country's economic situation was increasing, especially among the traditional, corporatist allies of the PRI – labor, the peasantry, and middle-class bureaucrats. Both presidents Salinas and Zedillo have sought to restore the PRI's legitimacy by championing political reform. Salinas began the process of promoting electoral reforms that would allow opposition parties a fair chance at winning office. Secret balloting was guaranteed to prevent voter intimidation, and ballot counts came under greater scrutiny. Salinas further cracked down on local PRI officials who engaged in electoral fraud, although enforcement of this policy typically favored the PAN, not the PRD. Given that the técnicos and PANistas shared a similar economic policy agenda, capitulating to their electoral victories was a more palatable solution than allowing PRD victories. Fraud continued against PRD candidates, leading to violent clashes between protesters and police. Despite ideological disagreements, however, leaders of the PAN and PRD found it in their mutual interest to cooperate and press for more electoral reform. The PRI still controlled access to state financial resources and public media outlets, giving it a significant electoral advantage.

Political reform was put to the test in 1994. The growing rift within the PRI erupted in violence. In March, Luis Donaldo Colosio, a técnico and Salinas's hand-picked presidential successor, was assassinated on the campaign trail. Although the crime was pinned on a young garage mechanic, it was widely suspected that members of the PRI's dinosaurio faction had masterminded the plot. Several months later, the secretary-general of the PRI (and brother-in-law to the president) was gunned down. Salinas's own brother was arrested as the prime suspect. Such high-level political violence had a profound effect on Mexican politics. To ensure free and fair elections and deflect further accusations of fraud, an independent electoral commission was established to monitor voting practices. International observers also were invited to oversee national balloting. As a result, Mexico's 1994 presidential elections were the most honest in nearly two decades, a triumph for liberal-pluralism.

The PRI's Ernesto Zedillo, another young técnico, won the election with a plurality of the vote (48.8 percent), and the ruling party hung onto a narrow majority in the Chamber of Deputies. The victory came at a severe cost for the country, though. To win popular support amid growing political turmoil, the PRI inflated the Mexican economy throughout most of 1994, making it easier to pay off needed constituents with government projects and providing a general feeling of economic prosperity in the country. The government also issued a large quantity of short-term government bonds to boost the confidence of foreign investors who were growing increasingly nervous about the spreading political violence (including the Zapatista uprising). However, faced with rapidly declining foreign currency reserves, the incoming Zedillo administration was forced to devalue the Mexican peso. Traditionally, hard economic choices had been made by the *outgoing* president, thereby allowing the incoming president to avoid public hostility. Former President Carlos Salinas, however, was pursuing a bid to become the president of the newly created World Trade Organization, based on his success in negotiating NAFTA. He refused to devalue the peso, knowing that such action would reveal weakness in his administration's monetary policy. When Zedillo finally attempted a controlled devaluation, speculator pressure pushed the currency into a spiraling free fall. Inflation soared and government actions to stem rising prices plunged the economy into another major recession, just as it had a decade earlier. Salinas further challenged the informal norms of Mexican political life by criticizing the Zedillo administration's handling of the economic crisis. Zedillo countered by investigating the former president's financial dealings. In a unique turn of fate for a former Mexican president, Salinas exiled himself abroad, fearing arrest should he return to Mexico. Such an unprecedented situation clearly signals that the Mexican political system is no longer operating as it has in the past, though the future shape of the polity is still unclear.

Pressured by a severe recession, a stalemated guerrilla insurrection, and growing international skepticism about Mexico's business climate, Zedillo was forced to speed up the political reforms begun under Salinas. The centerpiece of these reforms was an electoral reform package implemented in 1996. Among its many provisions, the new laws provided for greater public financing of campaigns and media access for all parties. The plan also eliminated party membership based upon group ("corporate") affiliation. This measure effectively eliminated the basis for corporatist interest representation that had been the bedrock of Mexico's political system for most of the 20th century. Implementing these reforms has not been easy. Regional PRI *caciques* continue to manipulate local politics, subverting the implementation of the new laws. A once-hegemonic party facing real political competition for the first time can be expected to bend or break rules in order to stay in power. Nonetheless, the reforms have shown some success in guaranteeing a more open political process. The 1997 midterm elections for the national legislature gave opposition parties their first combined majority in the Chamber of Deputies. Both the PAN and PRD have made substantial gains in local elections, and the Zedillo administration has abided by the results. Though still too early to tell, corporatism appears to be yielding to liberal democracy. For the most part, the transition has been smoother than expected, though not completely free of conflict. The presidential elections of 2000 will test whether Mexico will continue to march toward political liberalization or not. There has already been talk of the PRI holding a presidential primary similar to that in the United States, thus bringing down one of the last vestiges of Lázaro Cárdenas's corporatist legacy – the direct nomination of the party's presidential candidate by the sitting president.

## CONCLUSION

The Mexico we see today is an artifact of its past. The legacy of political violence in the 1800s and early 1900s paved the way for a quasi-authoritarian, corporatist regime. Foreign intervention in Mexican affairs complicated the country's search for political stability and gave the country's policies a decidedly nationalist and autarkic tone. But the world economy could not be ignored. Despite attempts to free itself from dependency on the world economy, Mexico found itself more dependent upon the good graces of the international financial community by the late 1970s. The economic crisis of the 1980s prompted Mexicans to rethink not only their economic development strategy but also their political system. Grass-roots demands for greater political representation prompted a movement away from a one-party corporatist state and toward a multiparty pluralist democracy.

All of this historical activity has shaped the interests and identities found within Mexico today. Moreover, Mexico's position in the international arena has combined with these interests and identities to shape its current political landscape. Mexico's long-standing tradition of corporatism has created strong interests in society that expect government patronage. Unionized labor has come to expect job security and wages that support an increasing standard of living. Rural *campesinos,* particularly in the South, have come to expect a certain level of stability that the constitutionally mandated ejido system provided. And both small and big businesses (in both the industrial and agricultural sectors) have demanded subsidies and tariff protection to shield them from international competitors. Meeting these basic economic interests was possible when the Mexican economy was growing by leaps and bounds.

Those days ended in the early 1980s when Mexico was saddled with an expanding international debt and a sharp loss in export revenues. While the international economy changed, societal interests in Mexico did not. The PRI could no longer meet the societal demands that had become part of the institutional and ideological fabric of Mexican society. With a shrinking economy, the various sectors (labor, agriculture, and industry) found their demands in direct competition with one another. Mexico's corporatist identity – the ability to develop economically based on the harmonious balance of competing social interests – was also torn apart. Recognizing that the PRI could no longer deliver upon past corporatist privileges, citizens began demanding more organizational autonomy from the government and a greater say in political decision making.

This conflict of interests also appeared to tear at another aspect of Mexico's national identity. While Mexican heritage had often been presented as a distinct mix of two cultures – Spanish and indigenous (Aztec and Mayan) – it became increasingly apparent during the past two decades that economic inequity closely mirrored racial and ethnic divisions within society. Criollos maintained their historic position at the top of the socioeconomic ladder, while indigenous populations languished at the bottom. As noted at the beginning of this chapter, this long-standing problem became evident to the world on January 1, 1994, when a guerrilla insurgency composed mainly of impoverished, indigenous farmers placed a damper on the festivities of a New Year's eve party attended mostly by criollos and well-to-do mestizos. These insurgents proudly identified themselves as of Mayan ancestry, and far from simply demanding reintegration into past corporatist arrangements, they announced their desire for greater political independence and the ability to freely choose their political representatives. It is interesting to note that these demands demonstrated that the struggle between corporatism and liberalism was not just a historical artifact, but a present reality.

At the dawn of the 21st century, Mexico finds itself at a critical juncture not unlike many it has faced in the past. Demands for greater political participation in the early 1800s resulted in independence from Spain, though many among the governing elite sought to keep the top-down political arrangements of the colonial era. Similar cries for political reform were heard during the Mexican Revolution a century later. Although significant changes did result in a general rise in economic

well-being, governing structures continued to leave little room for popular participation at the grass roots of society. The changes taking place today are reminiscent of those earlier eras. However, the contemporary world in which Mexico
operates is, in many ways, smaller than it was before. With international investors
demanding a liberalized economy, and with labor and capital mobility more fluid
than ever, the Mexican government has less leeway in determining its economic
policy. Yet the urgency to rekindle economic growth will affect the country's social
stability. The new neoliberal course that the PRI charted in the 1990s will
undoubtedly affect the interests of important political players and reshape the
national character of Mexican society. As in previous centuries, the new shape of
politics will play out over time. Interests and identities are not set in stone. While
it is too early to predict what the political outcomes will be, this ever-shifting environment offers a wonderful opportunity to understand the complexities of comparative politics.

## BIBLIOGRAPHY

Bulmer-Thomas, Victor. *The Economic History of Latin America Since Independence.*
    Cambridge: Cambridge University Press, 1994.
Camp, Roderic Ai. *Politics in Mexico.* 2nd ed. New York: Oxford University Press, 1996.
Cardoso, Eliana, and Ann Helwege. *Latin America's Economy: Diversity Trends and Con-
    flicts.* Cambridge, MA: MIT Press, 1992.
Cothran, Dan A. *Political Stability and Democracy in Mexico: The "Prefect Dictatorship"?*
    Westport, CT: Praeger, 1994.
Eckstein, Susan. *The Poverty of Revolution.* Princeton, NJ: Princeton University Press,
    1988.
Fuentes, Carlos. *A New Time for Mexico.* Berkeley: University of California Press, 1997.
Grayson, George W. *Mexico: From Corporatism to Pluralism?* Fort Worth, TX: Harcourt
    Brace, 1998.
Hamilton, Nora. *The Limits of State Autonomy.* Princeton, NJ: Princeton University
    Press, 1982.
Hansen, Roger D. *The Politics of Mexican Development.* Baltimore, MD: Johns Hopkins
    University Press, 1971.
Meyer, Michael C., and William L. Sherman. *The Course of Mexican History.* 4th ed. New
    York: Oxford University Press, 1991.
Middlebrook, Kevin J. *The Paradox of Revolution: Labor, the State, and Authoritarianism
    in Mexico.* Baltimore, MD: Johns Hopkins University Press, 1995.
Morris, Stephen D. *Political Reformism in Mexico: An Overview of Contemporary Mexi-
    can Politics.* Boulder, CO: Lynne Rienner Publishers, 1995.
Skidmore, Thomas E., and Peter H. Smith. *Modern Latin America.* 4th ed. Oxford:
    Oxford University Press, 1995.
Wiarda, Howard J. "Toward a Framework for the Study of Political Change in the Iberic-
    Latin Tradition: The Corporative Model." *World Politics* 25(1973): 206–35.
Womack, John, Jr. *Zapata and the Mexican Revolution.* New York: Vintage Books, 1970.

**TABLE 1. KEY PHASES IN MEXICAN DEVELOPMENT**

| Date | Global context | Political regime | Economic regime |
|------|----------------|------------------|-----------------|
| 1521–1821 | Rise and decline of the Spanish empire. Napoleonic Wars and occupation of Spain, combined with growth of liberalism in Spain, prompt independence movement. | *Colonialism* – strict control of Spanish America by crown. Spain discourages autonomous government in colonies, though some local control granted. | *Mercantilism* – raw-material exports from colonies to Spain; finished goods imported to colonies from Spain. Tight regulation over domestic colonial economy. Colonial manufacturing discouraged. |
| 1820s–1876 | Growth in European economic influence (primarily British and French). U.S. territorial expansion leads to war and loss of Mexican territory. | *Era of the caudillos* – period of political uncertainty, instability, and internecine warfare, punctuated by foreign economic and military intervention. Battles between Liberals and Conservatives. | *Economic chaos* – political instability discourages economic investment and fosters government fiscal crises. Export-led growth based on primary goods in latter period. |
| 1876–1911 | Direct foreign economic and military interference wanes. | *Porfiriato* – "Liberal dictatorship" of Porfirio Díaz. Expansion of middle class. | *Export-led growth* – Economic stability and growth prompts initial industrialization. |
| 1910–1920 | General noninterference in Mexican affairs. U.S. maintains isolationism, and Britain's presence in Western hemisphere wanes. | *Mexican Revolution* – begins as succession crisis, but radicalized by lower-class social movements and leftist political ideologies. General political chaos. | *Economic chaos* – Economic activity severely limited by political chaos caused by revolutionary fighting. |
| 1920–1982 | Growing U.S. influence in Latin America; Great Depression and movement toward economic openness among industrialized nations. | *State-led corporatism* – one-party rule based on incorporation of social groups into government structure. Creation of extensive patronage networks. | *"Mexican Miracle" and import-substitution industrialization (ISI)* – restriction of imports of manufactured finished goods; increasing government intervention in economy. |
| 1982–present | Third World debt crisis and end of cold war. | *Decline of corporatism* – movement toward greater political openness and party competition. Rise of civil society. New model of governance still uncertain. | *Neoliberalism* – promotion of free trade (NAFTA) and less government regulation of economy. |

## IMPORTANT TERMS

**cabildos**  town councils established during the colonial periods that served as the basis for the independence movement.

**caciques**  political bosses who control local government and are relatively autonomous from the federal government. Co-opting these individuals has been a main concern in the centralizing of political authority in Mexico.

**Cárdenas, Lázaro**  president of Mexico from 1934 to 1940. He was responsible for institutionalizing the corporatist form of government and bringing labor, agricultural workers, and industry under the control of the state.

**caudillos**  political strongmen during the 1800s who frequently controlled their own army and dominated local politics. Their presence made centralized political authority difficult to establish during the 19th century and led to decades of political instability.

**Conservatives**  loose-knit political party during the 1800s that represented the interests of the agricultural sector, while opposed to industrialization and democratic reforms.

**Constitution of 1917**  constitution of the Mexican Revolution that promoted radical agrarian reform and worker's rights. It would become the legal basis for Lázaro Cárdenas to redistribute land and nationalize Mexico's oil industry.

**corporatism (Mexican)**  an ideology derived from medieval Catholic thought that sees the polity as an organic whole and seeks to minimize social conflict via central government organization of competing interests in society. In its institutionalized form, the government organizes and directs urban and rural labor unions, as well as professional organizations.

**criollos**  individuals of pure-blooded Spanish heritage born in Mexico. The economic and political elite tend to be from this racial class.

**Democratic Revolutionary Party (PRD)**  a leftist political party formed after the 1988 presidential elections by defectors from the PRI in order to offer an electoral alternative to the dominant party.

**dinosaurios**  a faction of the ruling PRI party in the last two decades of the 20th century. Its members want to maintain corporatist forms of economic and political organization.

**ejidos**  communal farms that originated in pre-Columbian indigenous societies and were promoted in the 1917 constitution. Lázaro Cárdenas established a number of them in the late 1930s as a way of distributing land among indigenous populations and poor farmers (found mostly in southern Mexico).

**Import-Substituting Industrialization (ISI)**  the dominant economic policy of Mexico from the 1930s to the early 1980s, designed to industrialize the nation. According to this general economic strategy, high import tariffs are imposed to stimulate domestic production of consumer goods.

**Institutional Revolutionary Party (PRI)**  the dominant ruling party of Mexico since the 1920s. Although it originated as a center-left party, it has drifted toward the center-right in recent decades.

**Juárez, Benito**   a liberal reformer in the mid-1800s who sought to promote land reform, centralize political authority, and modernize Mexico.

**La Reforma**   a period in Mexican political history (ca. 1855–76) during which liberal political forces predominated over their conservative rivals and began implementing economic and political reforms designed to bring Mexico closer to the policies and forms of government of the United States and northern Europe. This represented the first time since the end of colonialism that a consistent governmental plan appeared, even though this era was beset by civil war and a foreign occupation.

**Liberals**   a loose-knit political party in the 1800s that represented urban interests and promoted increased trade ties with northern Europe and the United States.

**López de Santa Anna, Antonio**   the most important caudillo in Mexico during the 19th century, who intermittently served as president.

**mestizos**   individuals of mixed Spanish and indigenous heritage. They represent the mingling of two different cultures into a distinct Mexican identity.

**Mexican Miracle**   a period from the 1940s to the 1970s (with the apogee from 1950 to 1970) wherein rapid industrialization promoted high levels of economic growth and improved living standards. This era gave rise to a new middle class with rising expectations that were restricted by the government's inability to satisfy these demands in the last two decades of the 20th century.

**Mexican Revolution**   the period from 1910 to 1920 wherein a major civil war among various factions eventually led to a set of radical social programs, namely labor rights and land reform, included in the Constitution of 1917 and eventually implemented under Lázaro Cárdenas in the 1930s.

**National Action Party (PAN)**   a center-right party established in the mid-1900s as a challenge to PRI dominance. It won some critical local elections in the 1980s and 1990s that pushed Mexico toward greater political liberalization.

**neoliberalism**   a policy that emphasizes free trade, privatization of industry, and a reduction in government intervention in the economy. This strategy was pursued by Presidents Salinas and Zedillo during the 1980s and 1990s.

**North American Free Trade Agreement (NAFTA)**   an international treaty that lowered trade barriers among Mexico, the United States, and Canada. The centerpiece of President Salinas's neoliberal economic strategy, it was implemented on January 1, 1994, the same day the Zapatista National Liberation Army initiated its guerrilla insurgency.

**pan o palo**   literally meaning "bread or club," the phrase that refers to two common forms of political power in Mexico. *Pan* (bread) denotes the use of political patronage to buy political support, while *palo* (club) implies the use of coercion.

**Porfiriato**   the period from 1876 to 1910 during which caudillo and dictatorial president Porfirio Díaz ruled Mexico. This was the first time since colonial days that

Mexico was unified under central rule for a significant period; it was also a time of strong economic growth that gave rise to new social classes and, eventually, the Mexican Revolution.

**Salinas de Gotari, Carlos**   Mexican president from 1988 to 1994. He reversed decades of corporatist and ISI policies in favor of a neoliberal economic agenda. His economic liberalization prompted calls for political liberalization at the end of the 20th century.

**técnicos**   a faction within the ruling PRI that rose to prominence in the 1980s by promoting neoliberal economic reforms. Typically trained in U.S. and European universities, the members are in conflict with the dinosaurios, who favor corporatist policies.

**Tlatelolco**   site of a massacre in 1968 where more than 100 protesters were killed by state police. The protest signaled that the long-standing legitimacy of the PRI's corporatist rule was wearing thin, especially among students and the middle class.

**Virgin of Guadalupe**   a symbol of Mexico's unique national identity that blends European Catholicism with indigenous images. It represents the appearance of the Virgin Mary before an indigenous boy during the colonial period and has since been used as a rallying point for Mexican nationalism.

**Zapata, Emiliano**   the leader of a revolutionary army during the Mexican Revolution. He demanded greater rights for indigenous rural workers in southern Mexico, including a substantial land reform that eventually became a centerpiece of the 1917 constitution.

**Zapatista National Liberation Army (EZLN)**   a guerrilla army that appeared in the southern Mexican state of Chiapas in 1994, following the implementation of NAFTA. Like their earlier revolutionary namesake, the Zapatistas, as they are known, demanded land reform, economic justice, and freer political representation for the poor indigenous communities.

**Zedillo, Ernesto**   president of Mexico from 1994 to 2000. He oversaw an extension of neoliberal reforms and promoted greater political liberalization, including the first-ever presidential primary election in Mexican history.

## STUDY QUESTIONS

1.  Mexico has prided itself on its unique blend of Spanish and indigenous heritage. Not only did the Spanish conquistadors adopt a number of indigenous traditions and symbols, but Spaniards and indigenous people also physically intermingled, forming a mestizo (mixed-blood) ethnic group. Nonetheless, economic and political power remains highly stratified along class lines, with criollos holding the most powerful positions, the indigenous population inhabiting the lowest economic classes, and the mestizos falling in between these two groups. Tensions between these groups spilled over most recently in the Zapatista uprising in

southern Mexico, with the guerrillas being composed mostly of indigenous, non-Spanish-speaking individuals. How might this ethnic/racial stratification affect the ability of Mexicans to craft a single national identity? So long as this stratification exists, is it possible to speak of "one Mexico"? What actions might the government take to alleviate the problems created by these socioeconomic and ethnic divisions?

2.  Political instability was one of the main features of Mexico during the 1800s. What factors led to and exacerbated this political instability? (Consider a comparison with the United States, which won its independence from colonial powers four decades earlier.) What were the short- and long-term consequences of this era of political instability? Consider how this era both shaped the interests of various actors in society and affected the nation's political consciousness.

3.  A common problem faced by political rulers during the colonial and postcolonial periods was how to govern distant geographic regions that had incentives not to obey central authority. Even today, the Mexican president has difficulty implementing policies in isolated regions, such as the state of Chiapas. Local political bosses (caciques) retain a great deal of power over local populations. How have political leaders dealt with this problem throughout Mexican history? What types of policies could the current Mexican government develop to bring local caciques in line with national policy?

4.  The revolutionary Constitution of 1917 promised radical changes in land tenure and workers' rights. Many of these proposals were implemented by Lázaro Cárdenas in the late 1930s, but enthusiasm for continuing these programs has since waned. Why has this been the case? Are policies that support communal farms (ejidos) and government-sponsored labor unions possible to maintain in an increasingly globalized world economy?

5.  Consider the name of the Institutional Revolutionary Party. Looking at Mexico's history, why do you think this name was chosen? To what extent can a revolution be institutionalized? To what extent has the PRI remained a revolutionary force in Mexican society? Now consider the name of the Democratic Revolutionary Party. Why do you suppose this name was chosen? Should the PRD gain power, do you expect to see it evolve similarly to the PRI? Discuss.

6.  Mexican corporatism brings various social actors (e.g., labor, business professionals) into an officially sanctioned ruling coalition. While guaranteeing certain privileges for these groups (e.g., job security for unionized labor, subsidies for businesses), it also limits such freedom as choosing when to strike or how to allocated capital. Discuss the advantages and disadvantages of such arrangements. In recent years, there has been a move by some groups to obtain greater autonomy from the government. Why? Consider the role of the economic crisis in the 1980s and its effects on government revenue.

7.  Mexico's general economic strategy from the 1930s to the 1980s (known as import-substituting industrialization) was to isolate itself from the world economy by imposing high tariffs on imported consumer goods and limiting foreign

investment in the economy. While successful in generating rapid economic growth in the short term, this plan has created some long-term problems. Discuss. To what extent is it possible for Mexico to isolate itself from the world economy today? What possible effects might increased economic integration (e.g., NAFTA) have on domestic politics?

8. There is a popular saying in Mexico that describes the country as follows: "So far from God; so close to the United States." What role has the United States (and other foreign countries) played in shaping Mexican politics? How has this role changed over the past 200 years? What does NAFTA have to say about changing relationships among the countries of North America? Is the relationship between the United States and Mexico only a "one-way street," or has Mexico influenced the domestic politics of its northern neighbor?

9. Both Presidents Salinas and Zedillo faced the difficult task of promoting economic growth and political democracy while maintaining the PRI in political power. What are some of the difficulties in balancing these competing interests? How has the pursuit of these different goals affected the PRI itself? To what extent does the pursuit of economic liberalization and liberal democracy conflict with the nation's long-standing identification with a corporatist philosophy?

10. Many observers of Mexican politics argue that Mexico's transition to a liberal democracy will not be complete until there is a new party in charge of the executive branch. Do you agree with this statement? Why or why not? Consider that the 1994 presidential elections was determined to be relatively free and competitive by outside observers. Even though the PRI's Ernesto Zedillo defeated candidates from the rival PAN and PRD parties by a plurality (i.e., less than 50 percent) of the popular vote, would this qualify Mexico as a liberal democracy in your opinion? If yes, explain. If not, discuss what other reforms must be made before Mexico can be considered a liberal democracy?

# 8

# India

≋ **Rudra Sil**

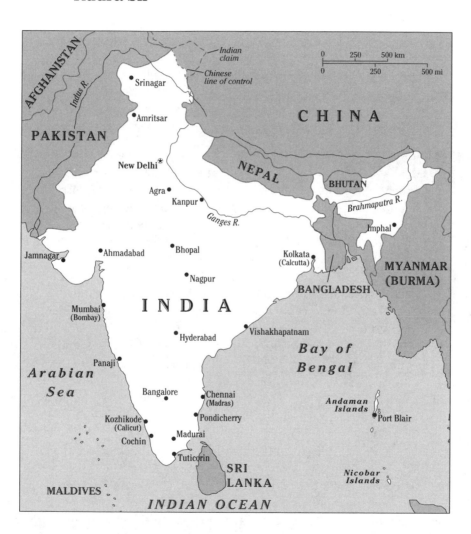

# INTRODUCTION

In 1998–9, several events occurred that could potentially alter the course of India's political development since the achievement of independence in 1947. First, in March of 1998, hundreds of millions of Indians went to the polls in what many call the "world's largest democracy" to elect a new parliament. Elections were nothing new to Indians; what was striking about this election was its outcome. The 1998 elections led to the formation of the first government in independent India's history to be dominated by a party – the Bharatiya Janata Party (Indian People's Party, or BJP) – that explicitly seeks to redefine Indian national identity in terms of "Hinduttva" (Hindu culture and civilization). Every other government, whatever their other differences over policy or ideology, had remained committed to the vision of a modern, secular India embraced by the nation's founders. Although new elections were called for 1999, the BJP was again able to form the new government. These election results raise new questions about the very definition of India's national identity and about the ability of India's secular political institutions to reconcile the cross-cutting interests of a billion people belonging to different religions, castes, regions, and socioeconomic classes.

Only a few weeks after the BJP had first assumed power, on May 13 and May 15, 1998, India held five underground nuclear tests and proclaimed itself a "nuclear power." India had already conducted a "peaceful" nuclear explosion in 1974, but since that time had made no overt attempts to acquire a nuclear arsenal. Thus, the underground tests came as a surprise to the rest of the world, leaving the United States and several other nations to denounce the tests and issue economic sanctions, while prompting neighboring rival Pakistan to launch its own nuclear tests two weeks later. This was followed in the summer of 1999 by a military conflict in Kargil in Indian-held Kashmir (the Himalayan region claimed by both countries) as Indian troops ousted Pakistani-backed insurgents, spurring joyous celebrations as well as tributes to the "Kargil martyrs" throughout India. Whether these events will lead to further tensions or to a rapprochement in Indo-Pak relations in the long run, the reaction to the nuclear tests and to the Kargil conflict show that Indians – whatever religion, caste, language, or class they identify with in the domestic realm – have a strong sense of national pride linked to a common desire for international status and influence.

What implications do these events have for the future of India as a secular, democratic nation-state and as an actor on the international stage? How are they significant in terms of our understanding of identities, interests, and institutions in postcolonial settings? This chapter is designed to help you make more sense of these questions in the course of introducing you to India's postcolonial development within a changing global context. The chapter is divided into three sections, each divided into several subsections. The first section discusses the formation of a precolonial South Asian civilization, the encounter with British colonial rule, and the rise of Indian nationalism. The following sections trace the shifts in political and economic development in relation to the leadership of particular parties and individuals: The second section discusses the 1947–84 period, when the Congress Party dominated Indian politics under the leadership of Jawaharlal Nehru and his daughter, Indira Gandhi. This section incorporates an overview of the Indian political system as well as the statist program of economic development. The third section examines the period since 1984, the date when Indira's son, Rajiv Gandhi, took the helm of the Congress Party following his mother's assassination. This period is marked by the waning of the Congress Party's dominance and the rise of two seemingly contradictory trends, one toward gradual economic liberalization and increasing integration into the global economy, and the other toward a more pronounced assertion of traditional identities and cultural distinctiveness.

## PRE-INDEPENDENCE INDIA: CIVILIZATIONS, EMPIRES, AND THE ENCOUNTER WITH THE WEST

Most of South Asia is comprised of the Indian subcontinent, a large peninsula encompassing the present-day countries of Bangladesh, India, Pakistan, and neighboring territories. The term "India" has its origins in one of the world's great ancient civilizations that developed in the Indus Valley region to the northwest of present-day India (in the southern part of present-day Pakistan). The Indus Valley civilization, thought to have emerged as early as 4000 B.C., flourished around 2500–2000 B.C., developing its own system of culture, language, irrigation, municipal administration, and even intercity communications networks. This civilization seems to have gone into decline by 1500 B.C., just when several waves of Indo-

Aryan invasions and migrations into the heart of the subcontinent ushered in a new era in the making of South Asian civilization.

## South Asian Civilization: The Sources of Identity and Unity

One of the great divides in Indian society has its roots in the arrival of Indo-Aryan groups in the heart of the Indian subcontinent. The lighter-skinned Indo-Aryans settled down in the northern and central plains, and they developed languages that were loosely related through their common roots in ancient Sanskrit. The darker-skinned Dravidians, who were native to the Indian subcontinent and spoke languages based on an entirely different script, were forced into the southern part of India. This difference, although it was exaggerated by British historians and anthropologists, persists to this day, and the separate identities and interests of the descendants of the Dravidians continue to influence the political behavior of regional elites, parties, and citizens in the southern states.

Aside from the general divide between the populations concentrated in the north-central and southern regions of India, specific languages and their dialects became the basis for distinct regional kingdoms and local communities. Today, nearly two-thirds of the population (about 64 percent) speak Indo-Aryan languages or dialects, but just over a third of the population (36 percent) speaks Hindi, an official language that also has a popular variant spoken in several of the north-central Indian states (e.g., Bihar, Uttar Pradesh, Rajasthan). Other major languages that share the Sanskritic roots of Hindi serve as official languages of separate states (for example, Bengali in West Bengal, Gujarati in Gujarat, Marathi in Maharashtra, and Punjabi in the Punjab). About 22–3 percent of the population speaks one of the four main Dravidian languages that also serve as the official state languages in the south (Telegu in Andra Pradesh, Tamil in Tamil Nad, Kannada in Karnataka, and Malayalam in Kerela). Urdu (a language that uses most of the vocabulary of Hindi in conjunction with an Arabic script) dates back to the arrival of Central Asian Islamic groups and is now spoken by nearly half of the Muslims in different parts of India (just over 5 percent of the total population). Along with Hindi, English is the other official language of India; although it is spoken by less than 5 percent of the population, virtually all national and regional government documents, as well as several major newspapers, are published in English.

In spite of the formation of diverse linguistic communities, from the time of the Indo-Aryan settlement of the Indian subcontinent, a common civilization began to take shape in the northern and central plains, thanks to the fusion of Aryan and Dravidian beliefs and customs. This process was intensified through the partial political unification of the subcontinent under several dynasties founded by powerful princes who the conquered other regional kingdoms. The first of these empires, formed shortly after Alexander the Great's invasion stalled in India, was founded by Chandragupta Maurya in 326 B.C. The Mauryan dynasty was able to extend its control from the Indus Valley region to all but the most southern regions to the south and, in the process, established a centralized fiscal and military apparatus along with a nonhereditary patrimonial bureaucracy. Subsequent rulers (e.g., the Gupta kings, A.D. 320–550, and King Harsha Vardhana, A.D. 606–47) would also establish large empires that contributed to closer economic and political ties among the diverse regional kingdoms of northern and central India. These empires and their relationships with regional provinces are thought to have set the foundation on which British colonial administration and later Indian federalism would be established.

These periods of dynastic rule also contributed to the flowering of a recognizable Hindu culture throughout much of the Indian subcontinent. What "Hinduism" specifically consists of, and whether Hinduism is more a set of beliefs or a generalized spiritual philosophy, are still the subject of debate among Indian political and cultural elites. The original texts associated with Hindu religious beliefs and philosophical ideas (most notably, the *Vedas)* can be traced back to the centuries following the arrival of the Indo-Aryan invaders. From the time of the Mauryan dynasty onward, the most important beliefs, practices, and moral injunctions associated with Hinduism – ranging from triumphant tales about virtuous princes and divinities to the beliefs about reincarnation – were already becoming widely known throughout India. In addition, discernible forms of Hindu religious practice (e.g. the *puja,* or the worship of gods or deities) were already appearing throughout much of the subcontinent. During the 4th and 5th centuries A.D., priests and scholars under the patronage of their rulers helped to mold a more standardized set of Hindu beliefs and practices, despite the persistence of distinctive local traditions. Even in the southern regions of India, from the 7th century onward, some of the more powerful Dravidian princes, along with Dravidian poets and religious scholars, began to accept and actively promote Hindu beliefs and practices. The result was not a unified body of religious doctrine, as may be the case with Catholicisim or Islam, but it was sufficiently coherent to render many Hindu beliefs and practices recognizable throughout the Indian subcontinent.

Also contributing to the emergence of a recognizable social structure throughout India was the caste system. The Indian caste system originally was no different from rigid social and occupational hierarchies established in Europe or Japan several centuries ago. In the Indian caste system, different groups of families were associated with different traditional occupations ordered along a hierarchical scale of "purity." Those who were most closely connected with the reading of Hindu scripts and the performance of Hindu rituals came to be regarded as a higher-status (more "pure") category of *Brahmins* (priests or literati). Rulers, administrators, and soldiers came to form the second category in the caste hierarchy (the warriors), followed by the merchants/traders, the peasants/artisans, and, finally, a fifth category of "untouchable" families associated with menial tasks that were essential but considered "unclean" or "impure."

These five broad categories were further divided into several subcastes *(jatis)* that represent smaller groups of families engaged in a particular hereditary occupation and occupying a particular hereditary social position *within a given region* (usually consisting of a cluster of nearby villages). In everyday life, it is the jati that traditionally represented the primary source of group identity; it is also one's jati that determined the rules and duties binding individuals (e.g., eating habits, prayer rituals, etc.) and defined the pool of eligible marriage partners within a region. The rules and duties of similarly situated jati varied from region to region, as did the specific patterns of stratification, but throughout most of South Asia, these caste and subcaste categories came to constitute a recognizable hierarchy within which there was theoretically no possibility for mobility or intermarriage.

Although many Indian leaders and scholars (including Mahatma Gandhi) have not viewed the caste system as an intrinsic feature of Hindu ethics, the fact that the socioeconomic structure and religious beliefs and practices were so thoroughly fused for so many centuries contributes to the perception – both in India and abroad – that the caste system is inseparable from Hindu religion and culture. This also accounts for the fact that jati continue to be an important source of identity and division throughout contemporary India even after several decades of industrialization and urbanization, and even after the caste system was formally abolished by the Indian constitution promulgated in 1950. On the other hand, this same source of division paradoxically renders the social structures of diverse regions and communities more or less recognizable to people throughout India. In fact, even some Muslim and Sikh communities have been known to adopt social structures similar to the caste system.

Now, we turn to the origins of what is perhaps the most tense division in Indian society at present: the religious division between the Hindu majority, which accounts for more than 80 percent of the Indian population, and the significant Muslim minority, which accounts for about 11 percent (the remaining 8–9 percent consists of Sikhs, Christians, Buddhists, and members of other religions). This division has its roots in the 11th century, when a group of Muslim Central Asian invaders began to raid the northern plains of India. A more significant and permanent Muslim presence in India came about with the arrival in Delhi of an Afghan Muslim prince named Babur, founder of the Moghul Empire (1526–1757). Babur's grandson, Akbar (1555–1605), extended the Moghul Empire through most of the Indian subcontinent and established an efficient, partly merit-based, imperial bureaucracy along with a practical system of tributary rule. As in the case of earlier Hindu dynasties, political and administrative control was partially centralized, but several layers of provincial and regional rulers were able to exercise considerable autonomy so long as they paid tribute to the Moghul emperor in Delhi. Under Akbar, Islam gained a permanent foothold in India, and Muslim subjects (whether recent arrivals or native converts) formed their own communities alongside the majority Hindus throughout much of the empire. At the same time, Akbar himself adopted certain aspects of Hindu political thought, treated Hindu princes and scholars with respect, and abolished many policies that unfairly discriminated against Hindus. In this tolerant atmosphere, Muslim scholars and artists, too, came to be appreciated by Hindu cultural elites. This period of relatively peaceful coexistence among Hindus and Muslims would be short-lived, partly because of the intolerance of later Moghul rulers, and partly because of the divide-and-rule strategy of British colonial rulers.

In sum, between 1500 B.C. and A.D. 1700, there emerged a host of sociocultural cleavages throughout the Indian subcontinent: between northern Aryans and southern Dravidians, between different linguistic regions in both north and south, between different jati within and across regions, and, finally, between Hindus and Muslims. Yet, it is important to remember that for all the emphasis frequently placed on social divisions and conflicts in modern India, there is a centuries-old civilization that had evolved and spread through most of the Indian subcontinent by the time British colonialism arrived. Even after the arrival of Islam, many of the Muslim communities in India managed to hold onto several traditional attitudes, beliefs, and social practices predating Islam (thus rendering Indian Muslims far more recognizable than those in Saudi Arabia or Morocco to the typical Indian Hindu). These similarities, while they may not be sufficient to overcome conflicts rooted in religion, caste, or region, do distinguish India's precolonial historical legacies and postcolonial nation-building experiences from the more tribally organized communities of precolonial Africa and the more ethnically fractured nations of postcolonial Africa.

## The Impact of the West: British Colonialism and Its Consequences

Although South Asian civilization was formed out of encounters with, and the fusion of, "foreign" cultures (for example, Indo-Aryans, Central Asian Muslims), it was the arrival of British traders that marks South Asia's first significant encounter with the West. During the 17th century as the Moghul Empire went into decline, the British East India Company, a large trading company backed by the British government, began to establish trading stations in such towns as Bombay (in the west) and Calcutta (in the east). The regional princedoms in these areas could not foresee the significance of these trading stations, and they played into the hands of the British by striking deals with them in order to enhance their own political and economic position vis-à-vis neighboring provinces and the Moghul emperor in Delhi. When a Bengali prince finally attempted to challenge the growing economic power of the British East India Company in his region, British troops, led by Robert Clive, scored a decisive victory at the Battle of Plassey (1757). Partly as a result of the disunity among Indian rulers and partly as a result of superior military technology, the British then proceeded to defeat dozens of other regional armies and, by 1840, had established a colonial empire that extended throughout the Indian subcontinent.

The colonial system was originally an informal one. It was established in order to realize two main economic goals: (1) to extract cheap resources (raw materials, labor) with which to fuel the takeoff of Britain's Industrial Revolution, and (2) to force open Indian markets to goods manufactured in Britain, while suppressing the growth of indigenous manufacturing. This system of "indirect rule" functioned through a series of alliances with regional princes who were allowed to keep their titles, possessions, and local authority in exchange for their support for British colonial administrators and their economic activities.

This informal empire turned into a much more formal system of "direct rule" after 1857, when the British had to put down rebellion launched by several regional princes seeking to end Britain's political and economic control in their regions. During the late 19th century, as the British extended their colonial possessions in Africa and Asia, India came to be regarded as an especially important part of the British Empire, "the jewel in the crown." Queen Victoria was crowned the ruler of India, and a British viceroy was appointed to administer India directly. During the next ninety years (1857–1947), the impact of British colonialism became significantly more pronounced as British India became progressively more exposed to the forces of the global economy, and as South Asians of all regions, religions, and castes had to contend increasingly with the influence of Western ideas, institutions, technologies, and lifestyles.

In terms of political institutions, with the exception of certain provinces where "indirect rule" continued (e.g., Kashmir), the British proceeded to set up a centralized colonial administration that would later become the basis for the postcolonial Indian state. One of the most important bodies created during this time was the civil service, which assisted in the administration of the colony and which would later form the Indian Administrative Service (IAS), the core of the highly centralized bureaucracy in postcolonial India. After the World War I, the British also proceeded to establish national and regional assemblies consisting of elected representatives. Although these assemblies were not instrumental in making policy under colonial rule, they provided the basis for the postcolonial system of parliamentary democracy. Also, even though the administrative divisions of postcolonial India would be reconfigured later, the British colonial system of administration provided the foundation for the dynamics of modern Indian federalism; in both British and independent India, formally federal arrangements would be accompanied by measures to ensure the unity of the state and the control of the center.

It is important to note, however, that these political institutions were not established for the purpose of fostering genuine representative democracy or national consciousness in India. The national parliament, for example, had very little say over the most important policies and laws issued by the British viceroy; its main function was to provide a semblance of legitimacy for British colonial policies. Similarly, despite the talk of helping to unify India, the British continued to rely on a "divide and rule" strategy. Certain princes and landlords, for example, would be given special privileges in exchange for their cooperation with British authorities. The British systematically favored certain groups of literate, upper-caste Hindus (e.g., Brahmins) in the recruitment of its administrative staff, while attempting to restrict the social mobility and politicization of lower-caste groups and Muslims. And, most significantly, they manipulated the division between Hindus and Muslims in order to make British colonial administration appear indispensable for the maintenance of order. Thus, while British colonialism provided the institutional framework for the postcolonial state, it also paved the way for a legacy of mistrust between those who had most actively cooperated with colonial rule and those who were most suppressed by it.

British *economic* policies had a more widely felt impact on different segments of the Indian population. Karl Marx once wrote that British colonialism was a progressive force in India since it helped to dismantle feudalism and expedite the formation of capitalism (which had to precede socialism). Indeed, throughout British India, colonial economic activities did contribute to new mining and construction, the building of some machines and factories, and an extensive network of transportation and communication, including what is today one of the world's largest railroad systems. This led to the first sustained exposure for thousands of Indians to industrial machinery and production. A small Indian middle class and a somewhat larger working class also emerged as a result of the increase in British economic activities in India, and these classes constituted a new type of social cleavage that would coexist with and cut across preexisting caste-based divisions.

These were not insignificant changes for a society that had been organized primarily around subsistence agriculture, but Marx may have overestimated just how much British economic activities actually contributed to the development of industrial capitalism in India. As in the case of the political realm, British economic activities were not motivated by an altruistic desire to develop the Indian economy. The original motives that had brought the British East India Company to the subcontinent remained very much in play. Much of the infrastructure set up by the British was designed for resource extraction and the transportation of British-manufactured goods to distant markets. The native Indian middle class was severely restricted in the kinds of economic activities it could independently pursue; for example, the British limited the production of textiles by Indian-owned factories because their products were in competition with the more expensive, imported textiles manufactured in British factories. And the nascent working class was severely exploited as the British took advantage of cheap labor as part of their continuing industrial expansion. The British also established monopolies on the production of several basic necessities (even salt) as part of the strategy to make the native population dependent on the colonial economic apparatus. Thus, while the British did bring modern industry to India, they also contributed to Indian "misdevelopment" because the economic infrastructure they set up was designed for the purpose of colonial exploitation, rather than genuine industrialization. India's economic problems today have many and complex causes, but the continuing economy legacy of British colonialism is certainly one of them.

The social and cultural impact of British colonialism was more limited. Most Indians were affected by British economic policies, but their daily lives were relatively untouched by Western ideas or colonial social policies. The British introduced a series of major social reforms aimed at institutionalizing English law and eliminating some of the more egregious traditional practices (such as the treatment of "untouchables" as slaves and the practice of brides throwing themselves on the funeral pyres of their husbands). The introduction of the English language and English literature also helped to provide a new lingua franca for communication among elites from different regions. These changes did spark some new reform movements among educated urbanites but, for the most part, just did not affect the lives of most Indians who simply continued to live in their villages and adhere to traditional practices.

British colonial policies, however, did have a profound impact on well-educated, mostly Hindu elites whom the British sought to co-opt into their colonial administration. Many of these elites (including key leaders in the Indian nationalist movement) attended British schools and universities and were profoundly influenced by such Western ideas as nationalism, liberalism, and socialism. In fact, one of the ironies of British colonial rule is that the attempt to educate and co-opt educated native elites opened the way for a new political class that would eventually lead the movement for Indian independence. It is to this elite that we now turn for the story of how an independent Indian nation emerged.

## The Indian Nationalist Congress and the Movement for Independence

The Indian National Congress (INC) was originally founded in 1885 in order to pursue demands for greater Indian representation in the colonial administration. The founding members, most of whom were from wealthy families and the majority of whom were highly educated Brahmins, did not originally challenge British rule. Its members were content to promote the position of Indians *within* the system of British colonial administration and to debate the merits of various Hindu traditions in light of social reforms initiated by the British. However, the British rejection of even the most moderate demands ended up strengthening the resolve of the INC, prompting it to embrace officially the goal of independence *(swaraj)* in 1906.

The independence movement started to become a grassroots phenomenon a decade later after Mohandas Karamchand Gandhi (referred to as "Mahatma," or "Great Soul") returned to India in 1915. Gandhi had received a law degree in Britain and had spent several years challenging discriminatory British laws in South Africa. After his return to India, Gandhi quickly became a popular nationalist hero and the de facto leader of the INC by 1920. To demonstrate his conviction that the INC needed to become a mass movement, Gandhi took it upon himself to live as most

Indian villagers did, while engineering acts of civil disobedience that repeatedly landed him in jail and galvanized both INC members and the masses at large.

Gandhi focused on the points that united Indians from different religions, regions, castes, and classes: He emphasized the power of a universal inner truth that all human beings shared, while appreciating the distinctive spirituality shared by all *Indians* despite their diversity. This was not an easy synthesis for most Indians to grasp. Some worried that Gandhi was diluting some of the core tenets of Hinduism, while others saw his spiritualism as catering only to Hindus. Nevertheless, by attempting to downplay divisions based on caste, language, and religion in the course of resisting the British, Gandhi was able to draw millions of previously apathetic South Asians into the campaign for independence. His masterful strategy of nonviolent noncooperation served the dual purpose of directly disrupting colonial administration and demonstrating to the Indian masses that their strength lay in their numbers and their will, rather than in the acquisition of arms. For example, he orchestrated a major nationwide boycott of British cloth, during which millions of Indians began to wear white homespun cotton and burn clothes manufactured in Britain; in fact, most Indian politicians wear white homespun in public to this day. Similarly, Gandhi's famous "salt march" caught the attention of Indians everywhere as he led hundreds of his followers on a 200-mile trek to the sea and made salt on the beaches in defiance of a British law prohibiting Indians from manufacturing their own salt.

Most INC members followed Gandhi, renouncing violence in favor of continued adherence to democratic norms and continued reliance on the tactic of nonviolent noncooperation. The one leader who opted for military action, Subhas Chandra Bose, was elected President of the INC for a brief period in 1938, but he left to organize the Indian National Army (with German and Japanese assistance) to fight British rule. Whether this army might have become more effectual than the INC in the long run is not clear, given the outbreak of World War II and the arrival of Indian independence shortly thereafter. Nor is it clear whether colonial rule would have come to an end when it did in the absence of the impact of the World War II on Britain's own economy and infrastructure. What is clear is that the INC campaign of nonviolent noncooperation made it increasingly difficult and costly for the British to maintain the existing system of colonial administration.

On August 15, 1947, British colonial rule formally ended, and two independent nations emerged: India and Pakistan. Gandhi himself had hoped for a unified nation that would include all Hindus and Muslims, but now that independence was at hand, the unity of the nationalist movement was giving way to new tensions and conflicts. Although some Muslims supported the idea of a unified India, many Muslims simply did not trust Gandhi or the Hindu-dominated INC, fearing that their interests as a minority would be ignored. Mohammad Ali Jinnah, an INC member who helped found the Muslim League in 1920, insisted on a separate Pakistani nation and would become its first leader. On the other side, several Hindu organizations sought to preserve traditional Hindu values during the transition, fearing that Gandhi and the INC were catering to minorities at the expense of the interests and values of the overwhelming (80 percent) Hindu majority.

Fearing civil war, Gandhi agreed to a plan that would form a separate nation, Pakistan, in the more extreme western and eastern parts of the subcontinent where Muslims constituted a majority (the eastern part would secede from Pakistan in 1971 to form the present-day state of Bangladesh). During the partition, millions of people were forced to leave their old homes and migrate to new territories, while thousands died in bloody clashes between Hindus and Muslims. The violence would eventually subside, and in India, a secular constitution, based largely on principles of democratic federalism and English common law, went into effect on January 26, 1950.

## THE "THIRD WAY": POLITICAL AND ECONOMIC DEVELOPMENT IN THE ERA OF CONGRESS DOMINANCE

Many formidable INC leaders died during the period of transition. Gandhi himself was assassinated in 1948 by a Hindu fanatic. Bose, who had advocated armed confrontation with the British and had envisioned a more authoritarian Indian state, is thought to have died in a plane crash after his anticolonial army was disbanded. Sardar Vallabhai Patel, a prominent Congress leader who sought to combine an industrial economy with the preservation of Hindu traditions, died of natural causes. Thus, after the INC had reconstituted itself as the Congress Party, Jawaharlal Nehru became its undisputed leader and shaped India's early political and economic development as the first country's prime minister (1950–64). In slight contrast to the ideological inclinations of Gandhi or Patel, Nehru was driven by a modern worldview and scientific rationalism that would inform his strategy of political and economic development and his vision of India's role in the wider international order.

The global context within which India emerged as an independent nation heavily influenced Indian elites in their thinking about India's national role, its political system, and its development program. The impact of Western political doctrines and institutions, the appeal of the Soviet model of rapid industrialization, and the cold war between the two superpowers and their allies – all paved the way for a development path that was distinct from those followed by the earlier developers in the West or by authoritarian or communist leaders elsewhere. Nehru began to give definition to India's global role by remaining neutral in the cold war between the United States and the Soviet Union, and by opting for a "third way" that would combine features of both capitalism and socialism. With dozens of new nations becoming independent in the 1950s and 1960s, Nehru's approach held tremendous appeal, and he became a prominent international figure as a founder of the nonaligned movement. Although few postcolonial nations were able to maintain the original position of neutrality in an era of superpower competition (in fact, India would later sign a "treaty of friendship" with the USSR), Nehru's international leadership marked India as a leader among "Third World" countries and gave India an identity within the international order that would last into the 1980s.

## The Making of a Secular Nation: Political and Legal Institutions

In domestic politics, Nehru committed India to a secular path. "Secularism" generally suggests that the rule of law, as evident in a written constitution and legal codes (and not traditional norms or hereditary privileges), governs public life. In the Indian context, however, secularism has an additional connotation; it suggests that members of all religions, castes, and regional communities should be equal to one another as members of a unified nation-state. This understanding of secularism incorporates the principle that minorities and previously disadvantaged groups would be allowed special privileges until the playing field became more level. Thus, the caste system was formally abolished by law, and a modest system of "affirmative action" was instituted to help members of the lowest caste groups gain entry into educational institutions and employment. India's Muslims and other religious minorities were granted the right to observe certain religious laws and attend religious schools (a right not extended to the Hindu majority).

In terms of India's political institutions, a system of parliamentary democracy was created, based mostly on the British Westminster model. This system has remained more or less intact. The leader of the majoritarian party or coalition in the lower house (Lok Sabha) of the legistlative branch becomes the prime minister and, together with his cabinet ministers, forms the executive branch. Parliamentary elections are held every five years unless a no-confidence motion is passed against the prime minister's party or coalition. The prime minister is the focus of national politics, responsible for appointing the ministers in his cabinet, launching new initiatives or programs, and making important domestic and foreign policy choices on a day-to-day basis. The president, the formal head of state, is usually a nominee of the victorious party in parliament, but must be elected to a five-year term by an electoral college that gives votes to all members of the national parliament, as well as weighted votes to all members of the state assemblies (to ensure reasonable representation of different regions). The president is not involved in day-to-day affairs of government, intervening occasionally to call new elections or to establish direct presidential rule in unstable regions. Each of the states also has a legislative assembly, headed by a chief minister (the leader of the majority party or coalition), but also watched by a governor who acts as the president's representative at the state level. Table 1 lists all the prime ministers and presidents of India through 2000.

During the Nehru years, the electoral system became firmly entrenched, with voter turnout steadily increasing from a low of 46 percent in the 1952 elections to

## TABLE 1. PRIME MINISTERS AND PRESIDENTS OF INDIA

| Prime ministers | | Presidents | |
|---|---|---|---|
| 1950–64 | Jawaharlal Nehru, Congress | 1950–62 | Rajendra Prasad |
| 1964–66 | Lal Bahadur Shastri, Congress[a] | 1962–67 | Dr. S. Radhakrishnan |
| 1967–77 | Indira Gandhi, Congress-I | 1967–69 | Dr. Zakir Hussain[d] |
| 1977–79 | Morarji Desai, Janata Party | 1969–74 | V. V. Giri |
| 1979–80 | Chandra Shekhar, Janata Party | 1974–77 | Fakhruddin Aku Ahmed[e] |
| 1980–84 | Indira Gandhi, Congress-I[b] | 1977–80 | Neelam Sanjiva Reddy |
| 1984–89 | Rajiv Gandhi, Congress-I[c] | 1980–87 | Zail Singh |
| 1989–91 | V. P. Singh, Janata Dal | 1987–92 | R. Venkataraman |
| 1991–96 | N. P. Narasimha Rao, Congress-I | 1992–98 | Shankar Dayal Sharma |
| 1996–97 | Deve Gowda, United Front | 1998– | K. R. Narayanan |
| 1997–98 | Inder Gujral, United Front | | |
| 1998– | Atal Behari Vajpayee, BJP | | |

[a] Died in office 1966.
[b] Assassinated while in office 1984.
[c] Assassinated during 1991 elections.
[d] Died in office 1969.
[e] Died in office 1977.

more than 55 percent in 1962, reaching about 60 percent in subsequent elections. Relative to turnout rates in the United States, this is an impressive rate of participation, especially considering the literacy rate of 52 percent (38 percent for women). In both the national parliament and the state assemblies, a "winner take all" electoral system based on simple plurality and single-member districts has meant that larger, better-organized parties have been able to convert narrow electoral victories into disproportionately large numbers of seats in the national parliament. In the course of the first three elections, the Congress Party, although never capturing a majority of the popular vote, gained more than 70 percent of the seats in the national parliament, and more than 60 percent of the seats in the state assemblies (see Table 2). This represented a "dominant party system," with the Congress Party holding sway over national politics, and several smaller national or regional parties acting as "parties of pressure" in the national parliament while occasionally capturing a state assembly. But Congress dominance was a far cry from one-party authoritarianism inasmuch as regular elections, orderly leadership transitions, and the rule of law have been upheld for most of India's existence as an independent republic.

India's founders also adopted an independent judiciary, headed by a national Supreme Court. This body consists of a chief justice and twenty-five justices who are formally appointed by the president but are usually chosen by the prime minister in consultation with sitting members of the court. As in the United States, the

TABLE 2. CONGRESS PARTY PARLIAMENTARY MAJORITIES, 1952–1984

| Year | Popular Vote (%) | Seats in Parliament (%) |
|------|------------------|-------------------------|
| 1952 | 45 | 74 |
| 1957 | 48 | 75 |
| 1962 | 46 | 73 |
| 1967 | 41 | 54 |
| 1971 | 44 | 68 |
| 1977* | 35 | 29 |
| 1980 | 43 | 67 |
| 1984 | 48 | 79 |

* *Note:* Congress-I defeated by Janata Party coalition in 1977 elections.

Indian court was originally charged with interpreting the Constitution and ensuring civil liberties. What made the Supreme Court's work difficult was not the task of interpretation (since the Indian constitution is so detailed) but the problem of balancing tensions within the Indian constitution, which stemmed from Nehru's attempts to reconcile the Anglo-American liberal political tradition with the socialist emphasis on distributive justice. Moreover, the parliament has frequently tried to bypass the court's prerogative of judicial review by introducing amendments to the constitution, including Amendment 42 (1976), which prohibited the court from reviewing changes introduced by constitutional amendment. The court also suffered a loss of reputation by failing to oppose the suspension of several constitutionally guaranteed rights during Mrs. Gandhi's "Emergency" rule in the mid-1970s. Nevertheless, barring this eighteen-month period, the Supreme Court and the municipal courts have functioned together in a generally fair, nonpartisan manner, attempting to resist political pressures in their efforts to safeguard the basic spirit of the constitution and the rights of citizens.

## Center-Periphery Relations: Federal or Unitary?

To deal with relations among India's diverse regions, a federal republic was set up, with a central government in New Delhi administering a common development strategy, a common foreign policy, and some common social and economic programs. State governments maintained control over a range of economic and social policies (such as land reform and education). While not unlike federal arrangements elsewhere, it is worth noting two features of Indian federalism that distinguish it from federalism in the United States.

First, although the U.S. and Indian versions of federalism both involve a separation of powers between the national and state governments, the Indian constitution leaves the center with substantial powers that the U.S. federal government does not possess. Although the British federal arrangements set up in 1935 never gave genuine autonomy to the provinces, the framers of the Indian constitution (including Nehru and B. R. Ambedkar, chair of the committee that drafted the Indian constitution) moved toward an even more centralized system of government, probably because of concerns spurred by the postindependence Hindu-Muslim riots, the armed conflict with Pakistan over Kashmir, and the threat of secessionist movements elsewhere. Although certain policies (e.g., land reform, municipal projects, educational curricula) are left to the state governments, several articles in the constitution cover a range of circumstances that would transfer power from the states to the central government, effectively transforming the federal system into a unitary one. For example, state governors appointed by the president (often at the behest of the prime minister) oversee the activities of the elected state assemblies and the state chief minister, and several articles allow for the transfer of executive power back to the center in the event of political turmoil. Article 356, which establishes "President's Rule" in troubled states, has been invoked on dozens of occasions, often for no other reason than to oust uncooperative state legislatures. Moreover, the constitution treats the union as indestructible, but it allows the national parliament to alter the boundaries of the states. Also, in contrast to the U.S. Congress, the Indian national parliament (and not the state governments) retains the residual powers of legislation and can preempt any state legislation that contradicts a parliamentary act or federal law.

The second major difference between Indian and U.S. federalism has to do with the manner in which the constituent units – that is, states – are defined. The 1956 States Reorganization Act, which established fourteen states and six territories (now twenty-five states and seven territories), mandated the internal division of India along lines that corresponded to the concentration of populations speaking a particular regional language. Nehru himself had not been in favor of this plan, but given the provincialism of many of the Congress Party's regional leaders, he agreed to accept the linguistic-regional definition of states so long as the center would play the more significant role in shaping India's development. Thus, whereas the Indian constitution ensured the supremacy of the central government and the indestructibility of the union, the States Reorganization Act ended up institutionalizing the differences among linguistically defined regions. As a result, anytime differences surfaced in the interests of various states (vis-à-vis each other and vis-à-vis the central government), these differences acquired an ethnoregional dimension because the linguistically defined group that was identified with the state felt itself threatened or undermined by other groups.

Three patterns are evident in the manner in which India's "federal" system has come under pressure as a result of competing interests and identities corresponding to the linguistically defined states. *First,* the most serious threat to Indian federalism may be found in the regions where state boundaries also correspond to a non-Hindu religious majority. In these rare cases, differences between the state and the central government have turned into dramatic, even violent, social movements challenging the authority of the central government in New Delhi. This has been the case in at least three important regions in India: the Punjab (where Punjabi-speaking Sikhs constitute 51 percent of the population), Kashmir (which is the only Indian-controlled entity with a Muslim majority), and the northeastern territories (which are economically underdeveloped and inhabited by tribal populations that are racially and culturally distinct from Hindus). Tensions in all three regions have been in evidence since the time of Nehru, and violence continues to plague the latter two.

A *second* pattern involves the emergence of regional political parties that explicitly represent the interests of a linguistically defined group or state and that view the central government as incapable of representing these interests. Rather than demand to secede, however, they use the latent *threat* of secession in order to gain more concessions from the central government. This pattern has been in evidence from the very beginning in the relationship between several southern states and the central government. For example, the two major parties that have dominated in the state of Tamil Nad since the 1960s – the Dravida Munnetra Kazhagam (DMK) and its splinter party, the All-India Anna DMK (AIADMK) – can be traced back to a powerful regional movement during the 1940s and 1950s that aimed at reducing the influence of northern (Indo-Aryan) culture in south India and even called for an autonomous state of "Dravidasthan." Today, however, these parties strike deals with national parties and even jockey for cabinet positions in coalition governments at the center.

The *third* pattern involves the operation of national parties as de facto regional parties. These parties make appeals to the interests of the states in which they are popular, but their official platform is designed to appeal to a broad class of citizens across states, regions, religions, and caste groups. There is no threat of secession to invoke in the process of center-periphery bargaining, since the locally popular parties are ultimately defined as national parties with a stake in maintaining the federal system. The fact that they have captured power in one state, however, makes them behave in a manner that is not unlike the behavior of the more ethnically defined regional parties in the south. One of the classic examples here is the domination of the Communist Party of India (Marxist), or CPI-M, in the state of West Bengal since the late 1960s.

## Nehru's "Mixed" Strategy of Economic Development

In terms of economic development, Nehru's development strategy was clearly influenced by the global context in which it was conceived. His development goals, not unlike the goals of leaders in other postcolonial countries, were influenced by the level of wealth and technology evident in the West. And his strategy for achieving those goals was simultaneously influenced by the efficiency evident in Western capitalism and by the dramatic achievements engineered by socialist planners in the USSR in the 1930s–40s. Nehru's overarching faith in scientific rationalism and his commitment to a "third way" paved the way for his "mixed" strategy of economic development, combining the best of two modern economic systems.

Thus, while the economic system was generally based on the principle of private property and allowed private economic activity, there was also a large bureaucratic apparatus that produced "Five-Year Plans" for economic development in much the same manner that the Soviet central planners did. The gross domestic product was split between a growing private sector and a powerful, state-controlled public sector: That is, about one half of the economy was accounted for by the private sector, concentrated primarily in the production of agricultural and light industrial (or consumer) goods, and the other half was accounted for by the public sector, concentrated primarily in heavy industry (i.e., the large-scale production of major industrial goods, ranging from iron and coal mining to the construction of steel, power stations, railroads, and so forth). Moreover, as was the case with "import-substituting industrialization" development strategies in other postcolonial countries, both the public and private sectors were protected and regulated by the Indian government so that they could contribute to the expansion of industrial production while being shielded from competition against firms from more advanced industrial countries. The assumption was that since colonialism and economic backwardness had made the playing field uneven, a postcolonial economy could not hope to catch up to that of its former colonizers without state protection and coordination of domestic industry and without tight restrictions on foreign imports. Also, in keeping with his commitment to socialist egalitarianism, Nehru embraced laws that prevented workers from being fired, guaranteed legal protection for trade unions, provided generous welfare benefits for public-sector employees, and established a progressive system of taxation.

Although Nehru provided the outlines of a "mixed" development strategy, his specific policies and programs left much to be desired, however. Despite some important gains in heavy industrial projects, the performance of the Indian economy was not impressive enough to close the gap between India and the advanced industrial economies of the West. The high import tarriffs and strict licensing requirements did enable many public-sector enterprises and several private-sector conglomerates to take off in a mighty way. But, as in the case of the Soviet Union, most of these firms later proved to be inefficient, wasteful, and incapable of producing goods of consistently high quality. More importantly, Nehru's egalitarian orientation never did get translated into actual progress towards socioeconomic equality, inasmuch as the emphasis on rapid industrialization through large-scale factories disproportionately benefited certain business families in certain sectors, while the vast majority of India's population remained impoverished.

From the point of view of most citizens, Nehru's development strategy not only failed to live up to the expectations it had initially engendered following independence, but it also failed to bring about dramatic material improvements in their day-to-day lives. The fixation on heavy industry also meant that there was very little investment in the agricultural sector in which most of India's rural masses worked. As a result, in the early 1960s, when severe droughts struck, there was not enough of a cushion to prevent famine in many parts of the countryside. Members of lower-caste groups were able to gain some degree of upward mobility through the public-sector positions reserved for them, as we shall see, but the vast majority of individuals belonging to lower-caste communities did not gain the benefits of economic development. Moreover, while the jobs and incomes of regular employees in large industrial firms were protected, the bulk of the working masses (seasonal workers, or workers in the agricultural or informal sectors) were left unprotected and remained impoverished. Thus, after his death in 1964, Nehru's successors were faced with the task of adjusting India's development policies albeit within the "mixed" economy framework.

## The Indira Gandhi Era: Populism, the "Emergency," and the Janata Interregnum

Nehru's immediate successor as prime minister, Lal Bahadur Shastri, had not been a unanimous choice to begin with, and his unexpected death just two years later (in 1966) left the Congress Party scrambling to identify a suitable prime minister. Indira Gandhi (not directly related to the INC leader) emerged as a compromise candidate in part because, as Nehru's daughter, she could increase the Congress's popularity in upcoming elections, and in part because she was seen as someone the established party bosses could manipulate. Although Congress's popular support declined to an all-time low of 41 percent during the 1967 elections, Congress Party candidates did win a plurality of votes and were able to form a government with Indira Gandhi serving as prime minister. Once in power, however, Indira Gandhi surprised and upset the party bosses by announcing her own policy agenda and elevating individuals personally loyal to her at the expense of the older party elites. The rift between Indira Gandhi and the old bosses was so deep that the Congress Party split into two distinct parties: One, following Mrs. Gandhi, reconstituted itself as Congress-I (henceforth referred to as Congress) and inherited the bulk of the old Congress grassroots membership; the other, the Congress-O (for organization) was formed around several of the old party leaders, but became reduced to the role of a coalition partner in opposition to Mrs. Gandhi.

Under Nehru, the Congress Party had evolved from a grassroots independence movement into a dominant political party with a semibureaucratic party machinery built on the ties among local, regional, and various national-level party leaders. But given the split with the old party bosses, Indira Gandhi now had to find other mechanisms for building political support. Although some of the regional political dynamics seen under Nehru – the political bargaining among party candidates, regional "big men," and leaders of various caste or tribal communities – continued to be an important factor, two additional features became increasingly evident in Indian politics.

The first was Mrs. Gandhi's efforts to mobilize the masses directly by means of populist campaigns that appealed to the economic interests of the lower classes (peasants, workers) and to nationalist sentiments. Unable to rely on electoral support generated by the local ties between regional party leaders and communities, Mrs. Gandhi had to create a new message that she could take directly to the masses, and this message had to satisfy the interests of hundreds of millions of lower-class and lower-caste groups that had felt "squeezed" by Nehru's heavy-industry–focused development program. Indira Gandhi's populist campaign to boost agriculture and reduce poverty served to capture the support of the impoverished rural masses, as well as the urban underclasses, during the national elections of 1971 and also the state legislative elections of 1972.

Also worth noting is that Mrs. Gandhi's populism increasingly came to include appeals to Indian national identity in order to buttress her authority. This was especially evident in her rising popularity following the 1971 war against Pakistan (the third since independence), in which India politically and militarily supported efforts to create an independent Bangladesh out of what had previously been East Pakistan. In her second stint as prime minister (1980–4), Mrs. Gandhi was even more explicit in appealing to Hindu nationalist themes to boost her popularity, although this also had a destabilizing effect in regions where the majority population was non-Hindu (such as the Sikh-majority state of the Punjab).

The second dynamic that came into evidence during Mrs. Gandhi's rule was her active personal involvement in the appointment of several key national and state-level government officials, not on the basis of their competence or their loyalty to the Congress Party as a whole, but on the basis of their *personal* loyalty to her in exchange for her political patronage. She and her advisors reviewed personnel files to identify Congress members loyal to Mrs. Gandhi, as well as individuals who might challenge her authority. This process, too, served to compensate for her split with the political elites who ran the old Congress machinery. Although patron-client networks had always permeated organizational ties between central and local elites, what now emerged were more steeply hierarchical, individualized, patronage networks, centered on Mrs. Gandhi and her closest advisers. India's political institutions remained intact, but Mrs. Gandhi ended up shifting the focus to personal ties and loyalties.

In the mid-1970s, this approach would lead to a new confrontation that almost undermined the legal and institutional bases for Indian politics. During 1974, some of the older Congress bosses (Congress-O leaders) and other opposition leaders joined together to accuse Mrs. Gandhi of corruption and campaign violations. One of these leaders, J. P. Narayan, once a devout follower of Mahatma Gandhi, organized frequent protests and even called upon the Indian army to oust the prime minister. In response, Mrs. Gandhi declared a national "Emergency"; many of the opposition leaders were arrested, censorship was introduced, and several parts of the constitution were suspended, although Mrs. Gandhi did promise to hold elections once order had been restored. Mrs. Gandhi's rule over the next eighteen months represented the only period during which postcolonial India functioned more like an authoritarian regime than a parliamentary democracy. In contrast to many other postcolonial dictators, however, Mrs. Gandhi did not seek to destroy or dismantle all opposition parties or rewrite the constitution. Nor did she suspend all individual liberties guaranteed under the constitution.

In 1977, Mrs. Gandhi finally called for national elections, perhaps believing that the voters would overlook her actions and that Congress would remain the dominant party. However, these elections marked the first time that the Congress Party was unable to gain anything close to a parliamentary majority. Instead, a coalition of opposition forces was able to unite temporarily – in the form of a loosely organized umbrella party known as the Janata Party – to form a national government. Just as the single-member districts had previously enabled Congress to convert pluralities of votes into a majority of seats, the Janata coalition managed to convert 43 percent of the popular vote into 55 percent of the seats in parliament.

This election demonstrated that Congress's previous electoral success was at least partly a result of the fragmented and poorly organized opposition. Once the opposition united, it was able to unseat Congress. At the same time, these elections underscored the continuing inability of any *single* party to compete directly with Congress in national elections. The Janata Party was a hastily formed coalition of parties that tried to satisfy various interests simultaneously but found little common ground when it came to the trade-offs between such imperatives as reducing central planning and finding mechanisms to redistribute wealth (with the left parties tending to focus on the latter). Moreover, the two Janata prime ministers, Morarji Desai (1977–9) and Charan Singh (1979–80), had neither the political support nor the personal appeal of Mrs. Gandhi. Opposition to Mrs. Gandhi proved sufficient to gain a victory during an election when the public had been angered by Mrs. Gandhi's "Emergency" rule, but it was not sufficient to enable the Janata coalition to implement a coherent set of policies. Not surprisingly, Congress dominance was reasserted in the 1980 elections as Indira Gandhi was able to engineer a triumphant comeback, with the Congress once again managing to capture two-thirds of the seats in the national parliament.

Following her return to power, Mrs. Gandhi sought to rebuild her political base by increasingly playing up Hindu nationalist themes. As in the case of her populist antipoverty campaigns of the early 1970s, this tactic was intended to boost her personal popularity by appealing to as large a segment of the Indian population as possible. Predictably, however, this also triggered fears among India's religious minorities, sparking a militant movement for greater autonomy in the Punjab (where there was a Sikh majority). In her efforts to quell the militants, Mrs. Gandhi ordered the army to storm the Sikh "Golden Temple" at Amritsar (where the militants had holed up), sparking Hindu–Sikh riots and providing the motivation for her assassination at the hands of Sikh bodyguards in 1984.

## Mrs. Gandhi's Economic Programs: Variations on the Nehruvian Model

Indira Gandhi's economic policies represented variations on the overarching blueprint established by her father. Public-sector firms continued to be the cornerstone of industrialization, and half of the gross national product (GNP) continued to be accounted for by the state sector. Indian economic bureaucrats continued to devise Five-Year Plans and set public-sector production targets. High import tarriffs remained in place as part of India's protectionist strategy. Within this framework, two shifts in the economy served respectively to provide some substance to Mrs. Gandhi's populist campaigns and to consolidate the central role of the Indian state in the economy.

First, in response to the catastrophic results in agricultural production during the 1960s, the balance of investments was altered slightly so that agriculture would no longer be neglected in favor of heavy industrial production. As part of her effort to appeal to rural interests and boost agricultural production, she launched what came to be known as the "green revolution." The overall goal was to improve the level of agricultural production to the point that India could be self-sufficient in food and India's rural population would not have to face another famine. Through the use of new varieties of seed, new methods of fertilization, and new techniques of crop rotation, aggregate agricultural production was boosted dramatically during the green revolution, making India a net agricultural exporter.

The second shift in India's statist economy under Mrs. Gandhi was the expansion of government regulation and the public sector. More industries, notably the banks, were nationalized. More restrictions were slapped on multinational corporations, prompting many to leave. Even the regulation of the domestic private sector increased through the expansion of the "license raj." The latter refers to the fact that all private firms that had a certain level of assets had to secure a license from the national government in order to operate and to export or import goods in several key sectors. These measures were ostensibly designed to protect larger public- and private-sector firms from foreign competition, but the licensing requirement also reduced the level of competition – and hence, efficiency – by increasing the entry barriers or discouraging expansion among newer, less politically connected entrepreneurs. This also led to a high level of corruption, as bureaucrats frequently sought bribes or special favors in exchange for the expeditious processing of licenses.

On the whole, India's economy did grow in spurts throughout the 1970s and into the 1980s. Food production was substantially increased. The heavy-industrial sector expanded as India developed indigenous automobile and airplane manufacturing facilities, while producing its own steel and chemicals and a wide range of consumer goods. However, in the end, these policies neither produced the rapid economic growth seen in the East Asian Newly Industrialized Countries (NICs), nor made a serious dent in the widespread problems of poverty and inequality. The green revolution disproportionately benefited a small minority of peasants and increased the gap between wealthy farmers and the rest of the rural population. Government funds earmarked for special programs often ended up in the pockets of local bureaucrats and the wealthy local elites with whom they colluded. The license raj also served the interests of the established large firms at the expense of smaller or newer businesses. And aside from the small segment of the workforce that was organized, most of India's workers (among whom were a growing contingent of child laborers) continued to earn extremely low wages, working under dismal conditions.

## INDIA IN THE POST–COLD WAR ERA: THE CLASH OF GLOBAL AND COMMUNAL FORCES

Following Indira Gandhi's assassination in 1984, it was left to her son, Rajiv, who had never shown much enthusiasm for politics, to lead Congress (his younger brother, Sanjay, was being groomed for politics but had died in a plane crash). Rajiv Gandhi led the Congress Party to its largest victory ever as it captured 79 percent of the parliamentary seats. However, just as Indira Gandhi's defeat in 1977 did not signal the end of Congress dominance, the victory of 1984 did not signal its resurgence. In fact, the electoral landslide was based on only a 48 percent popular vote, which, though substantial, was in part a sympathy vote following the assassination of Mrs. Gandhi. This vote marked the last time Congress would be able to capture a parliamentary majority on its own. With Rajiv Gandhi's electoral defeat in 1989, and Congress's popular votes steadily declining in subsequent elections (to a low of 26 percent in 1998), it became clear that the era of Congress dominance was drawing to a close (see Table 3).

The waning of Congress dominance also coincided with a more fundamental transformation of India's development path and its national self-conception within the international order. With the ascendance of Mikhail Gorbachev in the Soviet Union and the subsequent decline of communism, the significance of (and pride associated with) belonging to the "Third World" began to decline, as dozens of countries scrambled to redefine their national interests, identities, and strategies. Moreover, these countries had to reconsider the extent to which they could afford to prop up their inefficient, bloated public sectors within an increasingly interdependent global economy that was now decisively dominated by the liberal capitalist countries of the West. Within this global context, even though India's political institutions have remained in place, and even though the Congress Party has con-

TABLE 3. END OF CONGRESS DOMINANCE, 1989–1998

| Year | Party | Popular vote (%) | Seats in parliament (%) |
|---|---|---|---|
| 1989 | Congress-I | 39 | 38 |
| | *Janata Dal* | 18 | 28 (forms government) |
| | BJP | 11 | 16 |
| | Others | 32 | 18 |
| 1991 | *Congress-I* | 37 | 45 (forms government) |
| | BJP | 20 | 24 |
| | Janata Dal | 11 | 11 |
| | Others | 32 | 20 |
| 1996 | Congress-I | 29 | 26 |
| | "United Front" | 29 | 32 (forms government) |
| | BJP and Allies | 24 | 34 |
| | Others | 19 | 8 |
| 1998 | *BJP and Allies* | 36 | 46 (forms government) |
| | Congress | 26 | 26 |
| | "United Front" | 21 | 18 |
| | Others | 17 | 10 |

tinued to play a significant role, India's development path has gone through a marked transformation, reflecting new visions and ambitions and triggering new questions about the basis for India's national identity.

## Tackling Inefficiency and Corruption: Toward Economic Liberalization

Despite his lack of political experience, Rajiv Gandhi did introduce some important changes in the Congress Party's agenda. The two most important initiatives he took were (1) a major overhaul of Congress's economic development program, and (2) an attack on political corruption. During the 1980s, many countries throughout the developing world abandoned import-substituting industrialization and opted for market-oriented "structural adjustment" reforms (often at the suggestion of the World Bank or the International Monetary Fund, which made loans conditional on such reforms). As other countries moved toward liberalizing their economies, Rajiv Gandhi nudged the Congress Party and the Indian government toward market-oriented reforms that were continued and accelerated during the 1990s.

The most noticeable change that occurred in the late 1980s was the raising of the asset threshold that determined whether a company would require a government license or not. In effect, this meant that many newer and larger companies could be formed without going through the difficult and corrupt process of obtaining a license, and that, as a result, there could be increased competition leading to greater efficiency in production. It was still illegal to shut down state enterprises that were losing money, and there remained what some have called "barriers to exit," referring to the bias against allowing insolvent firms to go bankrupt. Import tariffs remained relatively high, and foreign multinationals still found it difficult to establish factories in India. But at least a new consensus had formed: The original program of statist economic development had to be reformed in one way or another, given the evidence of waste, corruption, and inefficiency, in both the state-controlled public sector and the state-regulated private sector.

Rajiv Gandhi's attempts to root out corruption, however, backfired on him. Not only did it prove extremely difficult to prosecute corrupt politicians in a politically charged atmosphere, but also key Congress officials (including some of Rajiv Gandhi's closest associates) themselves became ensnared in a scandal involving bribes in exchange for an arms contract to a Swedish defense firm. The scandal undermined public confidence in Rajiv and in the Congress Party, sending it to defeat in the 1989 elections. In these elections, a reconstituted Janata Dal (not unlike the Janata coalition formed in 1977 to defeat Indira Gandhi) managed to gain enough votes and allies to form the second non-Congress government in India's history, this time under Prime Minister V. P. Singh, the man who had exposed the scandal involving the Swedish defense contractor.

Singh, although an ardent critic of Congress, proceeded further along the path that Rajiv had begun to take. He was committed to a program of accelerated economic liberalization and attempted a vigorous attack on political corruption. By 1991, however, the unwieldy coalition that had backed him, like the first Janata coalition of 1977–80, fell apart under the pressure of ideological and political splits within the coalition. When a leader of the Hindu fundamentalist BJP (Bharatiya Janata Party) was arrested for demonstrating in favor of replacing a mosque with a Hindu temple, the BJP withdrew its support from the Singh government. Another Janata leader, Chandra Shekhar, temporarily staved off new elections by accepting outside support from the Congress Party (the very party the Janata Party had tried to unseat), but Congress later withdrew its support, and new parliamentary elections had to be called for 1991.

It was during the ensuing elections that Rajiv Gandhi was suddenly and shockingly assassinated just five years after his mother had been killed. On May 21, 1991, as Rajiv left behind his security personnel to go into the crowds as part of a more open campaign style designed to restore public confidence in him and his party, a young woman in the crowd set off a massive bomb strapped to herself. The Tamil group involved in Rajiv's assassination was linked to an organization operating in Sri Lanka with the intention of establishing greater autonomy for the

Hindu Tamil minority there. Rajiv Gandhi had refused to support their cause, in part because he saw the Tamil uprising in Sri Lanka as analogous to the demands for regional autonomy by separatist groups within India (including the militant movement for Sikh autonomy in the Punjab). Thus, in a roundabout manner, Rajiv fell victim to the same kind of dynamic that had claimed his mother's life: Both sought to uphold the principle of a centralized, unitary state in the face of ethno-separatist movements.

After a brief respite to allow for Rajiv's funeral, the elections resumed and Congress's fortunes improved dramatically (again in response to a wave of sympathy, this time for Rajiv). Although Congress managed even fewer popular votes in 1991 than it had in 1989, no other coalition was strong or united enough to form a government, leaving Congress in a position to form the government with the support of a few smaller parties. With no other member of the Nehru dynasty available to take the helm, Narasimha Rao became the prime minister of India.

Congress under Rao continued along the path toward greater economic liberalization. The public sector remained bloated and inefficient, commitments to help laid-off state workers (the National Renewal Fund) proved to be costly, and most major firms remained protected by laws making it difficult for them to declare bankruptcy despite mounting losses. Nevertheless, licensing requirements were relaxed even further to allow for the growth of the private sector, and imports were liberalized more significantly as new incentives began to attract more foreign investment to India. Even the state government of West Bengal, dominated by a leading communist party (CPI-M) since 1967, had to embrace market-oriented policies so as to attract investment and keep up with expanding economic opportunities and activities in neighboring states.

This process of economic liberalization has continued, with economic growth rates averaging around 6 percent per year during the 1990s. Demonopolization has led to the creation of new companies and new wealth. A larger class of entrepreneurs, many of them attracted to the high-tech sector, has had a much easier time establishing new firms, while the movement of foreign imports and exports has increased dramatically with the easing of government restrictions. Foreign companies have come to recognize that the Indian middle class alone, no matter how small it is relative to the population as a whole, represents a huge market compared to most other markets in Asia and Africa. Thus, at least some sectors of the Indian economy, along with some segments of the population, have begun to get more exposed to, and more integrated into, the global capitalist economy.

## Social Forces in a Global Economy: Business, Labor, Women, and Environmental Groups

As part of India's increasing exposure to global forces, it is worth noting the growing importance of modern social classes and interest groups that, even if they overlap with preexisting communities, are comparable in their composition, roles, and interests to similar groups elsewhere. Several of these groups are at the forefront of the process through which India is getting increasingly integrated into the global economy. India's business elites are sophisticated, well educated, attentive to international trends, and eager to compete with (and do business with) foreign firms. The government's economic bureaucrats and bankers are well trained in the dynamics of financial markets. These groups are keenly aware of their economic interests and are very much involved in politics, seeking to protect their assets and gain new economic opportunities and advantages. The younger generation among the wealthier classes are hooked into satellite televisions, own their own computers, and carry around cellular phones, reflecting the spread of certain common tastes, lifestyles, and consumption patterns across borders. In their behavior, attitudes, and level of exposure to international forces, these urbanized upper and middle classes are remarkably similar to their counterparts in other parts of the world, suggesting that at least some segment of Indian society has definitely entered the era of globalization.

In order to gauge the effectiveness of India's institutions in the new millennium, however, it is necessary to consider the manner in which the *rest* of India's huge population is affected by, and is reacting to, global economic forces. The vast majority of India's nearly 1 billion people are not regularly exposed to new ideas, images, or goods as are the urban upper and middle classes. Most have not seen their real incomes rise and have not benefited from the new consumer goods flooding into India's urban markets. In fact, for many groups, globalization – and the accompanying cutbacks in government programs and projects – has brought new uncertainties and greater economic hardship. Within this context, let us turn briefly to some of the "less visible" segments of Indian society: the laboring classes, women, and grassroots environmentalists.

Among India's workforce, organized labor represents a social class that theoretically cuts across regional, religious, and caste-based boundaries and focuses on the interests of workers in the major industrial firms. Although trade-union organizations were organized into federations allied with political parties, and so were unable to act in unison consistently, organized labor has paved the way for a relatively new type of identity that emphasizes the material welfare of individuals sharing a similar socioeconomic position. Now, in an era of globalization with the accompanying pressures to streamline the public and private sectors, trade unions are struggling to protect their members' jobs, incomes, and workplace rights. They have so far been able to stave off large-scale dismissals, but they may be fighting a losing battle as government bureaucrats and business groups succeed in introducing new labor laws to reduce labor redundancy and increase labor mobility.

The vast majority of India's workforce, both urban and rural, is not organized and so does not enjoy whatever protection and benefits organized labor has been able to cling to. Many workers have had to take jobs in the informal sector, working for miserable wages with few or no legal rights. In some cases, delays in the payment of wages have led to the starvation of workers. Similarly, in the agricultural sector, despite the success of the green revolution in boosting food production, poorer farmers still live precariously close to the subsistence level. Recent reductions in government spending, initiated at the behest of international lending organizations, have led to cutbacks in rural development and poverty alleviation programs, and have worsened the predicament of much of the rural population, especially landless farmers. In fact, in the late 1990s, many desperate farmers committed suicide in the face of poor harvests, while caste-based violence escalated throughout the countryside, with reciprocal attacks among members of landowning upper-caste families and poorer lower-caste communities.

These instances highlight the predicament of a large underclass of have-nots that has a far more pressing interest in resolving the problems of poverty and social inequality than in rapidly integrating India into the global economy. Although the World Bank and other international organizations still insist that a more competitive economy will bring about the alleviation of poverty and inequality in the countryside, a variety of social movements – some related to radical socialist organizations, others seeking to advance the position of particular tribal or lower-caste groups – are actively challenging the status quo. Some of these movements have grown rapidly in size and have increasingly relied on violent means (e.g., the Telengana movement in Andhra Pradesh). Although most of these movements tend to be focused on local conditions in rural areas, given the substantial overlap in membership among the lower classes and the lower castes, there is some possibility of large-scale mobilization across states and regions throughout rural India.

The majority of India's women, too, are facing new challenges as a group. India has always been a patriarchal society, with women mostly confined to the domestic sphere. Indira Gandhi and other women who have risen to prominence in national politics have been regarded as extraordinary figures in one way or another, and their political leadership has not paved the way for a fundamental transformation of existing attitudes concerning gender. The literacy rate among women is just half that of men. Employment, education, and public office are all held disproportionately by men. Nevertheless, ever since the INC began to debate social reforms in the late 19th century, women have been becoming more active in the political system. This activism is evident in their participation in the nationalist movement and the increasing number of women voters and candidates since the time of independence. It is also evident in the groups formed by urban middle-class women to educate people and transform entrenched patriarchal attitudes. And it is evident in movements of women from rural districts or urban underclasses who have focused mainly on the redress of grievances for specific instances of injustice (e.g., physical abuse, rape, murder, or dowry-related deaths). These forms of activism may not point to the emergence of a Western-style feminist movement, nor can they be expected to in light of the particular historical circumstances and cultural environments shaping the experiences of Indian women. What is more important is that these women, regardless of their religion, caste, or language, are able to act in different ways to advance the common interests they share in transforming some of the attitudes and practices that restrict their opportunities or endanger their lives. In the era of globalization, as public spending and government programs are cut back, these women's groups will have to play an even more active role in order to preserve the livelihoods of their families and at the same time create new opportunities for themselves in the public realm.

Environmental activists will also have a more crucial role to play in India if pollution and the destruction of forests or other habitats is to be brought under control while government and business leaders seek to get ahead in an increasingly competitive global economy. Until recently, environmental movements were comprised of relatively poor people focused on the protection of their own communities and habitats in the face of specific environmental problems or massive developmental projects. The "Chipko" ("Embrace the Trees") movement, for example, was launched in the early 1970s when a group of poor hill people in northern India stood between trees and loggers' saws in order to prevent the loggers from destroying the forests that constituted their habitats. More recently, several communities in western India banded together to get the World Bank to withdraw financial support for the Narmada River Dam project, pressuring the Indian government to change the original blueprint for the dam. The attention such movements have been receiving, and the common challenges they have undertaken, have now paved the way for more coordinated environmental activism across India, as evident in the emergence of a new, cross-regional network known as the National Alliance of People's Movement. Such networks, while still mainly comprised of local communities concerned with their immediate habitats, are now in greater contact with environmental advocacy groups elsewhere, as they recognize the common challenges they face from the quest for profits and economic growth in the global economy.

## Traditional Identities in a Global Age:
## The Politics of Caste in Contemporary India

Over the past several decades, as economic development has accelerated and the agricultural sector has become a progressively smaller portion of the GNP, the simplified occupational structure linked to caste hierarchies in different regions has given way to a much more complex class structure. India's Hindu politicians and administrative elites, once almost exclusively drawn from the upper castes (e.g., Nehru and the old Congress elite), are now from a much more varied background, with several lower-caste politicians rising to national prominence in such states as Bihar and Uttar Pradesh. India's professional classes and business elites are identified not only with the traditional Hindu merchant caste but also with families from other caste groups and religious minorities; conversely, India's working classes now include many members from higher-caste families. In addition, India's constitution formally rejects caste hierarchies, and a host of laws protects the rights of all citizens, while offering special consideration to members of historically disadvantaged caste or tribal groups.

These are important changes, but they have not led to the disappearance of caste from Indian politics and society. Caste-based identities remain important in social relations throughout India and still guide the social behavior of the vast majority of Indians in such areas as the determination of eligible marriage partners, the operation of community associations, and the continuing correspondence between certain social roles and caste groups among a significant minority of India's population (e.g., Brahmin priests who still perform Hindu rituals and large business conglomerates linked to wealthy merchant castes). Within the context of politics, *two* interesting features demonstrate the manner in which caste-based identities have interacted with secular political institutions in contemporary India: The first has to do with voting behavior and the second with India's version of "affirmative action."

The *first* feature became evident almost immediately after independence in the mobilization of collective identities by the Congress Party's regional "big men," who sought support for their candidates in local elections in exchange for resources being funneled back for local redistribution. This was not merely the pork-barrel politics of the U.S. Congress where representatives attempt to gain special resources for their constituencies in order to increase their support in future elections. It was a pattern of electoral behavior in which many individuals voted as members of traditionally defined jati communities, while the elders in these communities either became co-opted by regional party organizations or were able to negotiate with regional party bosses for certain resources in exchange for electoral support from all of its members.

As a result of the growth of non-Congress Party machines and the processes of social and economic change since independence, caste-based vote banks are no longer clearly identifiable, since electoral preferences do not correspond neatly to localized jati communities. Class-based interest groups, modern ideologies, and new political coalitions have provided new social bases for electoral mobilization. Nevertheless, caste-based identities remain available as an important basis for political mobilization in state-level and district-level elections. This has been most evident in the rise to national prominence of several lower-caste leaders on the basis of appeals to the particular interests of lower-caste members in their constituencies. It is also evident in several of the aforementioned social movements comprised of rural caste groups jointly seeking redress (or vengeance) for their grievances vis-à-vis upper-caste landowners.

A *second* aspect of Indian politics that serves to highlight the continuing importance of caste is the policy adopted to give preferential treatment to members of lower-caste groups deemed to be disadvantaged as a result of preexisting caste hierarchies. Although the caste system was officially banned by India's nationalist leaders, educated upper-caste Hindus dominated the Congress Party, the administrative apparatus, and the institutions of higher education. Thus, an "affirmative action" program was instituted to enable members of the "untouchable" castes (about 20 percent of the population) and "scheduled tribes" to receive a wide range of special privileges in access to education and employment; in addition, members in the next lowest caste category (the peasants/artisans who represent 25 percent of the population) are considered "other backward castes" (OBCs) and receive some (but not all) of these same privileges.

As in the case in the United States (most notably in California where a proposition recently outlawed affirmative action), there are groups throughout India that oppose this system of quotas on the grounds that it ignores merit and represents reverse discrimination. Over the last decade, this opposition has become even more politicized as a result of the release of the Mandal Commission Report, a study that provides a lengthier and more detailed list of caste and subcaste groups to be covered in the program of preferential treatment for the "other backward castes." Implementing the recommendations of this report would result in nearly half the jobs in the government or public sector being reserved for members of the "scheduled castes and tribes" and "other backward castes." In a country where upper-caste Hindus represent less than a fifth of the population, the real effect of implementing the Mandal Report recommendations would be a modest increase in the representation of lower-caste Hindus in universities, public-sector jobs, and the government. Nevertheless, in an environment where the growth of high-paying jobs has scarcely kept up with the rise in literacy rates and college graduates, any change in the status quo that threatens to reduce existing opportunities for employment is going to result in a backlash. Thus, the Indian government's plan to implement the Mandal Report's recommendations in 1990 provoked some stunning reactions, ranging from the suicide of several upper-caste Hindu students to upper-caste individuals changing their names to acquire lower-caste surnames. These dynamics suggest that the system of reservations for historically disadvantaged groups, although initially conceived for the purpose of erasing caste-based differences in wealth and employment, has ended up making Indians simultaneously more conscious of their caste identities and more calculating in terms of the impact of caste-related social policies on their individual interests.

## Religious Fundamentalism and the Rise of the Bharatiya Janata Party (BJP)

The growing tensions over caste-based "affirmative action" is related to the revival of Hindu fundamentalism over the past decade. In fact, one way in which many upper-caste Hindus reacted to the government's plan to establish the larger quotas recommended by the Mandal Report was by gravitating toward a Hindu nationalist party, the BJP, during the 1990s. Since the BJP has become a serious political force, let us now take a closer look at how the party emerged and how it turned religion into a basis for political mobilization within a formally secular nation.

Although the BJP was itself formed in 1984, its roots may be traced to the immediate postindependence period when a small political party, the Jan Sangh, was formed with the support of the Rashtriya Seva Sangh (RSS), a Hindu social organization created in 1925 to preserve and promote Hindu traditions. Although the RSS joined the INC's struggle against British colonialism, after independence it steadfastly opposed Congress's secular vision in favor of the revival of pride in *Hinduttva,* the values and ideals of a centuries-old Hindu culture and civilization.

During the years of the Nehru dynasty, the RSS criticized the government for forcing Hindus to observe secular laws while allowing Muslims, Sikhs, and Christians to observe certain religious laws and set up religious schools. The RSS, especially strong in Hindi-speaking states across northern and western India, cultivated ties to various communities and political organizations and arranged weekly meetings devoted to discussions of nationalist-religious ideology. In the 1970s, the RSS began to coordinate its activities with an international Hindu organization known as the Vishva Hindu Parishad (VHP) which was also promoting Hinduttva among Hindus in India and abroad. When the Bharatiya Janata Party (BJP), created in 1984, also began to echo the themes of Hindu fundamentalism, the RSS and VHP teamed up to put their organizational and financial resources at the disposal of the BJP.

The BJP itself began to gain national attention when it joined in the VHP's discussions over what to do with the various mosques built after the Moghul invasion on sites where Hindu temples had stood. By 1990, BJP General Secretary Lal Kishore Advani (later the home minister in the 1998 BJP government) was publicly exhorting Hindus to come to the town of Ayodhya to (re)build a temple at the site of the alleged birthplace of the Hindu mythical god Rama where the Babri mosque stood since it was erected by Muslims during Moghul rule. Although Advani was arrested, the arrest resulted in the BJP withdrawing support from the Janata Dal government (1989–91), paving the way for new elections in which the BJP was able to garner 20 percent of the popular vote, second only to Congress. Then, in December 1992, BJP supporters (including many RSS and VHP activists), ignoring court rulings that protected the Babri mosque, stormed into Ayodhya and destroyed the mosque. This sparked a huge uproar and resulted in several days of Hindu–Muslim rioting in cities throughout India, while catapulting the issue of Hinduttva – and the BJP itself – into the national spotlight.

It is important to recognize how the Ayodhya incident, rather than discrediting BJP leaders for violating the law and contributing to civil unrest, served to increase their national appeal among many frustrated social groups. The BJP had initially drawn its core of supporters almost entirely from the ranks of Hindu upper-caste groups, including members of merchant/trader caste groups that constitute a sizable portion of the Indian middle class. Despite their diverse economic interests, these groups were unified in their desire to redefine Indian nationalism in terms of the greatness of Hindu culture and civilization. The BJP's ranks swelled during the 1990s, in part due to the growing (though perhaps unwarranted) anxiety of other upper-caste Hindus who feared losing educational and employment opportunities to quotas for lower-caste members. But what made the BJP a genuine contender for control of the national parliament was its ability to mobilize Hindus of different castes and professions as part of the common cause of Hinduttva. In contrast to past opposition coalitions that had momentarily united to unseat Congress, the BJP was gaining strength as a *single* party able to identify an alternative vision, however abstract, to the secular India that Congress and most of its opponents had taken for granted.

While economic liberalization continued and while Congress (and several of its opposition parties) remained committed to secularism, the BJP emphasized the need to restore Hindu culture and the rights of Hindus in a country where more than 80 percent of the population was Hindu, but where members of other religious groups were accorded special rights and privileges simply because of their minority status. BJP leaders repeatedly referred to the illegitimacy of a government that allowed Muslims to follow Islamic law and go to Islamic schools while requiring Hindus to observe secular law. These arguments were sufficiently compelling to prompt more than 40 percent of the lower-caste voters to support the BJP and its allies in the 1998 elections. They were also compelling enough to attract support from many urban workers, students, intellectuals, and members of the professional classes (both in India and abroad). Even members of the business class were attracted to (and helped finance) the BJP's campaign on the strength of the BJP's promise that it would enhance India's national greatness and international standing, while simultaneously promoting economic nationalism and private enterprise. Whichever aspect of the BJP platform they were drawn to, one thing that all of its supporters were attracted to was the idea of a new nationalist ideal that could distinguish Indians from the rest of the world in a way that the Western-influenced, secular nationalism of India's founders simply could not do.

It is in this context that the destruction of the mosque at Ayodhya served as a catalyst in helping the BJP generate broad-based electoral support. In the 1996 national elections (the first since the destruction of the Babri mosque), the BJP and its allies gained 186 seats to Congress's 141. It was only another unwieldy alliance of smaller parties named the "United Front," with outside support from Congress, that prevented the BJP from forming a government. Then, in March 1998, when new elections had to be called after Congress withdrew its support from the United Front government, the BJP and its allies managed to secure 251 seats and form a government with the support of a few of the smaller regional parties. Even though one of these parties would subsequently withdraw support, the BJP managed to form the government again in the 1999 elections.

So far, the most dramatic events over which the BJP government has presided have been the series of underground nuclear tests conducted in May 1998, followed by the conflict in Kashmir between Indian troops and Pakistani-backed insurgents. However, while these events have generated a great deal of anxiety, they should not be regarded solely as an expression of the BJP's ideology and ambition. Previous governments had played a crucial role in setting up the nuclear program, and most Indians – regardless of their political loyalties – applauded the tests. Moreover, while the BJP's particular brand of national assertiveness may make relations with Pakistan and China tense for a while, in the long run, South Asia's nuclearization may also lead to the establishment of new channels of communication and a more responsible approach to unresolved territorial conflicts. In this context, it is worth noting that the 1999 conflict in Kargil (Kashmir) never did escalate beyond a localized, conventional military exchange between Indian troops and Pakistani-backed insurgents. The BJP-led Indian leadership did not press the advantage and cross the "Line of Control" into Pakistani-held Kashmir; nor did the Pakistani military officially enter the conflict to press its claims to Indian-held Kashmir.

In the economic realm, too, radical policy changes are unlikely. The BJP's commitment to making India a more respected regional and international power will require a dynamic economy and continued breakthroughs in science and technology, objectives that may not be so easy to achieve if the BJP spurns international opinion or if it turns to some variant of protectionist economic nationalism. Some level of state intervention may be necessary to redistribute wealth in order to maintain the support of lower-caste or lower-class groups, but this does not necessarily suggest a return to the "mixed" Nehruvian model. Also, given the cozy relationship the BJP has developed with many business groups, and given that its ideology focuses on Hinduttva rather than economic isolationism, it is unlikely that sustained BJP rule would bring about any radical shift in economic policy or organization.

The most serious implications of the BJP's rise to power will have to do with the possibility that BJP leaders may try to transform the secular political and legal institutions created five decades ago. The BJP has already introduced motions to amend the constitution, and if it happens to win a more substantial majority in future elections, it may have a real opportunity to change at least some features of the Indian constitution in keeping with its ideology of Hinduttva. Whatever happens, what is already clear is that the formation of a BJP government in 1998 puts the exclamation point on a shift that began in the mid-1980s as the decline of Soviet communism transformed the international order and called into question the developmental path set in motion after independence. While this shift began with a push toward economic liberalization, the changing paradigm of national development and the economic frustrations experienced by many social groups in the process, provided the

BJP with an opportunity to call into question the secular vision of the Indian nation upheld by India's founders and a previous generation of political elites.

## CONCLUSION: IDENTITIES, INTERESTS, AND THE FUTURE OF INDIA'S SECULAR INSTITUTIONS

During the first three and a half decades of independence, India's political dynamics, economic development strategy, and national self-conception as a leader of the Third World all remained essentially unchanged. Under Nehru and Mrs. Gandhi, India's national identity remained secular, tied to its self-conception as a leader of the Third World on the international stage. The Congress Party, barring the post-Emergency defeat in 1977, consistently dominated national politics and was able to push through its program for economic development. A "mixed" economy with a large public sector remained firmly entrenched. Mrs. Gandhi introduced her own distinctive brand of politics and her own economic initiatives, but these took place within the institutional framework and program of development initiated by Nehru in the 1950s.

During this period, many scholars and leaders – indeed, Nehru himself – thought that traditional sources of collective identity were atavistic, that they would fade away in the course of a nation's progress toward modernity. Thus, although they frequently appealed to identities based on religion, caste, or language for political gain, on the national stage the first generation of national elites generally maintained a secular orientation, expecting traditional identities eventually to become less important relative to the kinds of socioeconomic conflicts and interests evident in advanced industrial countries.

Since the mid-1980s, however, a fundamental shift has been under way in the political and economic dynamics of postcolonial India, linked in part to the decline of communism and the need to contend with a different, increasingly interdependent, global environment. Since the time of Rajiv Gandhi, India's leaders, whether belonging to the Congress or other parties, have steadily (though not necessarily irreversibly) moved away from the Nehruvian model of state-led development toward a more open, market-oriented economy. With the memory and the legacy of the Indian nationalist movement now further removed from the consciousness of political actors, the Congress Party is no longer dominant, with other parties and coalitions now jockeying for power, rather than acting only as "parties of pressure."

In this environment, the idea that particularistic identities and traditional social cleavages are bound to decline in relative importance (vis-à-vis socioeconomic interests and conflicts) remains strong among many scholars and among the leaders of the secular parties in contemporary India. Now, however, the focus has shifted; the dissipation of traditional identities is supposed to be spurred not as a consequence of industrialization, urbanization, and other domestic modernization processes, but as a consequence of globalization. Many now predict (or fear) that greater party competition, market reforms, and increasing interdependence in the global economy will erode the distinctiveness of national and regional cultures, paving the way for a relatively homogeneous world of McDonald's, blue jeans, satellite television, and the Internet.

Certainly, this expectation is not entirely unreasonable. The significance attached to preexisting identities has changed in India over the past several decades, while new sources of identity and interest have emerged. Caste identities and religious beliefs do not dominate each and every decision an individual makes. In fact, the original occupational structure with which caste identities were previously identified has become much more complex and heterogeneous with industrialization and urbanization. Similarly, religion may matter deeply in one's everyday life, but it is not at the forefront of every discussion about jobs or every policy debate. Meanwhile, class interests and conflicts have grown in importance, as workers in India confront many of the same concerns as workers in other developing countries where employers attempt to reduce the workforce and control wages in the fiercely competitive global economy. Similarly, new identities and social movements, corresponding to such universal problems as the rights of women and the protection of the environment, have proliferated throughout India.

Contrary to the expectations of India's secular elites and many scholars, however, these trends do not mean that the traditional sources of identity, such as religion and caste, are irreversibly fading away. The persistence of caste-based mobilization at the local level, along with the ability of the BJP to gain support by appealing to Hinduttva at the national level, both show that traditional bases for collective identity remain available for political mobilization. Traditional caste-based, religious, or linguistic/regional identities may not dictate every political outcome or economic competition, but they are never far from the surface. Anytime an individual feels that his/her status and recognition is linked to that of a particular group within a larger political community, and anytime social or economic inequalities coincide with caste, regional, or religious divides, these latter sources of identity remain very much available as bases for collective action and political mobilization.

Thus, the most important questions facing India in the 21st century will be whether its secular institutions, designed more than fifty years ago and influenced by Western models, will be adequate for reconciling tensions and conflicts among different interest groups and identity groups as the effects of globalization threaten to increase the gap between the "haves" and the hundreds of millions of "have-nots." So far, India's secular institutions have remained stable and, until recently, they may have enjoyed a measure of legitimacy not seen in most other postcolonial countries. Yet the recurrence of ethno-regional confrontations, the emergence of caste- and class-based social movements, and the salience of communal tensions between Hindus and religious minorities (Muslims, Sikhs) – all suggest that the survival of the Indian territorial state by no means guarantees the efficacy of India's secular institutions. Where identities related to caste, religion, or language/region overlap with the interests of economically frustrated social groups and classes, there remains the potential for explosive confrontations that may not physically destroy the territorial state but may very well undermine the legitimacy and effectiveness of India's secular institutions.

## BIBLIOGRAPHY

Anderson, Walter K., and Shridhar D. Damle. *The Brotherhood in Saffron: The Rashtriya Swayamsevak Sangh and Hindu Revivalism.* Boulder, CO: Westview, 1987.

Basu, Amrita. *Two Faces of Protest: Contrasting Modes of Women's Activism in India.* Berkeley: University of California Press, 1992.

Berreman, Gerald. *Caste and Other Inequities.* Meerut, India: Folklore Institute, 1979.

Brass, Paul. *Language, Religion, and Politics in North India.* London: Cambridge University Press, 1974.

     *The Politics of India Since Independence.* New York: Cambridge University Press, 1994.

Carras, Mary C. *Indira Gandhi: In the Crucible of Leadership.* Boston: Beacon, 1979.

Chanda, Asok. *Federalism in India.* London: Allen and Unwin, 1965.

Chatterjee, Partha. *The Nation and Its Fragments.* Princeton, NJ: Princeton University Press, 1993.

Dalton, Denis. *Mahatma Gandhi: Non-Violent Power in Action.* New York: Columbia University Press, 1993.

Dasgupta, Jyotirindra. *Language, Conflict and National Development.* Berkeley: University of California Press, 1970.

Dumont, Louis. *Homo Hierarchicus: The Caste System and Its Implications.* Chicago: University of Chicago Press, 1970.

Frankel, Francine. *India's Political Economy, 1947–77: The Gradual Revolution.* Princeton, NJ: Princeton University Press, 1978.

Galanter, Marc. *Competing Equalities: Law and the Backward Classes in India.* New Delhi: Oxford University Press, 1984.

Gopal, Sarvepalli. *Jawaharlal Nehru: A Biography.* New Delhi: Oxford University Press, 1984.

Guha, Ramachandra. *The Unquiet Woods: Ecological Change and Peasant Resistance in the Himalaya.* New Delhi: Oxford University Press, 1991.

Harrison, Selig. *India: The Most Dangerous Decades.* Princeton, NJ: Princeton University Press, 1960.

Hardgrave, Robert, and Stanley Kochanek. *India: Government and Politics in a Developing Nation.* 5th ed. New York: Harcourt Brace Jovanovich, 1993.

Jaffrelot, Christophe. *The Hindu Nationalist Movement and Indian Politics, 1925–1993.* New York: Columbia University Press, 1996.

Jalal, Ayesha. *Democracy and Authoritarianism in South Asia.* New York: Cambridge University Press, 1995.

Kaviraj, Sudipta, ed. *Politics in India.* New Delhi: Oxford University Press, 1997.

Kohli, Atul. *Democracy and Discontent: India's Growing Crisis of Governability.* New York: Cambridge University Press, 1990.

*The State and Poverty in India: The Politics of Reform.* New York: Cambridge University Press, 1987.

Kothari, Rajni. *Politics in India.* Boston: Little-Brown, 1970.

Kothari, Rajni, ed. *Caste in Indian Politics.* New Delhi: Orient Longman, 1981.

Lewis, John. *India's Political Economy.* New York: Oxford University Press, 1995.

Ludden, David, ed. *Contesting the Nation: Religion, Community, and the Politics of Democracy in India.* Philadelphia: University of Pennsylvania Press, 1996.

Nehru, Jawaharlal. *An Autobiography.* New Delhi: Oxford University Press, 1980.

Parekh, Bhikhu. *Gandhi.* New York: Oxford University Press, 1997.

Roy, Rameshary, and Richard Sisson, eds. *Diversity and Dominance in Indian Politics: Division, Deprivation and the Congress.* New Delhi: Sage, 1990.

Rudolph, Lloyd and Susanne. *In Pursuit of Lakshmi: The Political Economy of the Indian State.* Chicago: University of Chicago Press, 1987.

Sengupta, Bhavani. *Rajiv Gandhi: A Political Study.* New Delhi: Konarak Publishers, 1989.

Srinivas, M. N. *The Dominant Caste and Other Essays.* New Delhi: Oxford University Press, 1987.

van der Veer, Peter. *Religious Nationalism: Hindus and Muslims in India.* Berkeley: University of California Press, 1994.

Varshney, Asutosh. *Democracy, Development and the Countryside: Urban-Rural Struggles in India.* New York: Cambridge University Press, 1995.

Wallace, Paul, ed. *Region and Nation in India.* New Delhi: Oxford University Press, 1985.

Wolpert, Stanley. *A New History of India.* 5th ed. Chicago: University of Chicago Press, 1997.

## IMPORTANT TERMS

**Advani, Lal Kishore**   leading figure in the BJP, who served as home minister in the 1998–9 government. He was noted for his public advocacy of the destruction of the Babri mosque in Ayodhya.

**Bharatiya Janata Party (BJP)**   the "Indian People's Party," a political party that has its roots in past Hindu fundamentalist organizations but gradually became a major political force during the 1990s on the strength of its glorification of Hinduttva. It is ideologically linked to such organizations as the Rashtriya Seva Sangh (RSS) and the Vishva Hindu Parishad (VHP).

**Brahmins**   Hindu priests or literati, traditionally considered to be the most "pure" of the caste groups and thus uniquely qualified to perform religious ceremonies.

**caste**   the generic term employed to characterize the inherited status associated with categories in descending order of purity along a fivefold occupational and social hierarchy (from Brahmins and warriors to merchants/traders, peasants/artisans, and "untouchables"). It should be distinguished from the term "jati," which is used to identify groups of families belonging to a particular subcategory of a caste within a locally specific social and occupational hierarchy.

**Congress** the political party that grew out of the Indian National Congress and held power for most of the first five decades after independence. It is used here interchangeably with Congress-I (for "Indira"), which split off from Congress-O (for "organization") after 1967.

**Desai, Morarji** the first non-Congress prime minister of India (1977–9). He led the Janata Party government that was formed following the end of Indira Gandhi's "Emergency" rule.

**dominant-party system** the term employed to characterize India's political system as a result of Congress's steady control over parliament for all but one election between 1952 and 1984.

**Emergency** an eighteen-month period from late 1975 to early 1977 when Indira Gandhi suspended parts of the constitution and arrested opposition leaders in response to calls for her ouster for alleged campaign violations.

**Gandhi, Indira** daughter of Jawaharlal Nehru and Prime Minister of India (1967–7, 1980–4). He was identified with the "Emergency," patronage politics, the green revolution, and antipoverty campaigns. No direct relation to Mohandas K. Gandhi.

**Gandhi, Mohandas K. (Mahatma, or "Great Soul")** British-educated Indian lawyer who became the de facto leader of the Indian nationalist movement and orchestrated numerous nonviolent civil-disobedience campaigns.

**Gandhi, Rajiv** elder son of Indira Gandhi, who became prime minister of India (1984–9) following Indira's assassination. He initiated programs for liberalizing the economy and checking corruption but fell victim to a corruption scandal before being assassinated on the campaign trail in 1991.

**green revolution** the campaign by Indira Gandhi in the early 1970s to promote the use of new seeds and new methods of fertilization and crop rotation in order to boost agricultural production. He made India a net exporter of grain but disproportionately favored wealthier peasants.

**Hinduttva** a term popularized by the BJP and Hindu fundamentalist groups to emphasize the distinctiveness and greatness of Hindu culture and civilization.

**Indian National Congress (INC)** an organization that emerged in 1885 to promote greater Indian representation in the colonial administration and later turned into the main force for the independence movement led by Mahatma Gandhi. It became the Congress Party after independence.

**Janata Dal** the coalition (1989–91) that came to power with the defeat of Rajiv Gandhi and the Congress Party but eventually fell after the withdrawal of BJP support.

**Janata Party** the coalition (1977–9) that came to power following Indira Gandhi's defeat after the "Emergency." Its platform called for reduced planning, local self-reliance, poverty alleviation, and redistribution of wealth, but it fell apart due to splits in the coalition.

**license raj**   an aspect of India's statist economy in which private-sector firms above a certain asset threshold had to obtain a government license to produce, import, or export goods. It is in the process of being slowly dismantled since the mid-1980s as part of economic liberalization.

**Mandal Commission Report**   a report produced during the 1980s that provides a lengthy and detailed list of groups that count as "other backward castes" (OBCs), which would thus qualify for preferential treatment through increased quotas or "reservations" (see term).

**Nehru, Jawaharlal**   leading figure in the Indian National Congress who would become India's first prime minister. He was identified with secular nation-building efforts and a "third way" that theoretically rejected alliances with the superpowers while combining aspects of Western-style capitalism and a Soviet-style command economy.

**President's Rule**   Article 356 of the Indian constitution, which allows the president to authorize intervention by the center in states thought to be experiencing extraordinary political or social unrest. However, it is sometimes invoked to oust uncooperative state legislatures.

**Rao, Narasimha**   prime minister of India (1991–6) under the Congress-led government that came to power immediately after Rajiv Gandhi's assassination. He presided during the period when several reforms were initiated to promote and expand economic liberalization.

**Rashtriya Seva Sangh (RSS)**   a Hindu social organization created in 1925 to preserve and promote Hindu traditions. In the 1980s it became a major force behind the revival of *Hinduttva* (see term) and helped in the BJP's subsequent rise to power.

**reservations**   the term used by Indians to refer to its "affirmative action" system for increasing representation of lower-caste groups in universities and the public sector.

**Shekhar, Chandra**   prime minister of India in the last several months of the Janata Dal government (1991).

**Sikhs**   followers of the Sikh religion, who constitute a slim majority in the state of Punjab. Disaffection with center policies led to the increase in Sikh militancy and the movement for a separate "Khalistan" nation. Sikh bodyguards assassinated Mrs. Gandhi in 1984.

**Singh, Charan**   prime minister of India in the last year of the Janata Party government (1979–80) before Indira Gandhi's electoral comeback.

**Singh, V. P.**   prime minister of India under the Janata Dal government (1989–91). He was identified with efforts to check corruption, promote economic liberalization, and expand the system of "reservations" through formal implementation of the Mandal Report guidelines.

**United Front**   the coalition of secular parties from left, right and center (1996–8), formed to prevent a BJP-led parliamentary majority after the BJP gained the most popular votes in national elections. The coalition fared badly in the 1998 elections.

**Vajpayee, Atal Behari**   prime minister of India from 1998 through 1999. Leader of the first BJP-formed national government, he presided over India's nuclear tests in

May 1998 and the confrontation with Pakistani-backed insurgents in Kargil (Kashmir) in the summer of 1999.

**Vishva Hindu Parishad (VHP)**   an international Hindu organization committed to promoting pride in Hindu culture and civilization *(Hinduttva)*. It helped propel the BJP into the national spotlight through fund-raising abroad and through support for the reconstruction of original Hindu temples at sites where mosques had been erected.


## STUDY QUESTIONS

1. What were the various sources of group identity in South Asia prior to British colonialism?

2. In what ways did British colonial policies influence or undermine postcolonial political institutions and economic development in India?

3. Why was Mahatma Gandhi's leadership important to the success of the Indian National Congress? Why did some groups withdraw support from Gandhi and the INC as independence drew near?

4. What are some of the factors that distinguish Indian democracy and federalism from democracy and federalism in the United States?

5. What new economic initiatives did Indira Gandhi launch within the framework of the Nehruvian model of development? How were these initiatives connected to Mrs. Gandhi's political aims?

6. In what ways does India's political and economic development since the time of Rajiv Gandhi represent a marked departure from the past?

7. Who are some of the "winners" and losers" of India's economic liberalization? On the whole, has economic liberalization contributed to greater political stability?

8. In what ways has India's system of reservations ("affirmative action") for "backward" castes strengthened or undermined traditional and secular sources of political identity?

9. In what ways have India's traditional caste-based, regional, and religious identities intersected with emergent class interests to shape patterns of political participation and mobilization?

10. What factors account for the BJP's electoral triumph in 1998? What does this mean for the future of India's secular political heritage and traditional identities?

# 9

# Iran

~ **Vali Nasr**

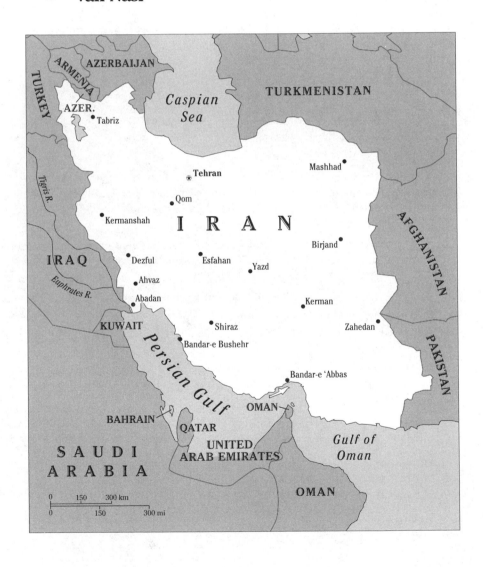

# INTRODUCTION

Iran embarked on the path to development at the turn of the century. Although the goals of that process and many of the means that have been employed to achieve it are typical of other late developers, Iran's experience has proved to be unique. Development was accompanied by ideological conflicts that culminated in a religiously inspired revolution in 1979. In the process, a modernizing monarchy gave place to the theocratic and revolutionary politics of the Islamic Republic. As populism changed the character of the economy and Islamic ideology transformed Iranian society, its norms and institutions and, for a time at least, pursuit of interests were subsumed under that of preservation of identity. Since the revolution, the nature of development has been complex, revealing modernizing impulses tempered by the pressures of Islamic ideology. Beyond its ideological and institutional particularities, the Islamic Republic shares in many of the characteristics and problems of populist authoritarian regimes elsewhere in the Third World: a bloated public sector, mismanagement, and corruption.

There are three distinct and yet interrelated periods in Iran's modern development: the early and later Pahlavi periods: those of Reza Shah (1921–41) and Muhammad Reza Shah (1941–79); and the Islamic Republic (1979–present). There is greater continuity between the first two periods under the Pahlavi monarchs, although there are notable differences as well. The Reza Shah period coincided with the rise of the modern Iranian state, and started the process of development. The Muhammad Reza Shah period continued in the footsteps of the first period but accelerated the pursuit of modernization. Development under the second Pahlavi monarch was, moreover, conditioned by different global influences and domestic sociopolitical identities and interests. The Islamic Republic has been distinct from the earlier periods in its ideological orientation and in many aspects of its economic policies and political characteristics. Above and beyond their differences in ideological orientation or policy choices, the three periods are similar in the dominant role of the state in development. The basis of Iran's path in the modern world is to be found in the circumstances in which Iran first embarked on development.

## THE GLOBAL CONTEXT AND THE RISE OF THE MODERN STATE

Iran is among the handful of Third World countries to escape direct colonialism, but not the impact of imperialism. Throughout the 19th century the ruling Qajar dynasty (1796–1921) was unable to resist Western imperialist penetration; nor could it stave off the gradual loss of territory and control over national assets to foreign powers. This provided the context for the rise of the modern Iranian state and the path to development that it would follow.

Also important was the pivotal role of the monarchy in the 19th century. The monarchy was important to imperial powers who wished to maintain a captive and weak center in Iran. As a result, imperial powers provided strategic support to the monarchy and helped thwart significant challenges to its authority. The broader powers of the monarchy were rooted in the dominant social position of the feudal aristocracy and tribal leaders, who sustained monarchical authority at the center, even as they resisted taxation and defended their autonomy. Of equal importance was the role of the religious establishment. Throughout the 19th century the clergy resisted domination by the monarchy and defended the rights of the nation before imperialist interests that often worked through the monarchy. Still, at a more fundamental level, the clergy defended the sociopolitical position of the monarchy, just as the monarchy protected the socioeconomic interests of the clergy. The nature of relations among the state, the elite, and the religious establishment would change over time with important consequences for the pattern of development.

Concentration of power in the monarchy occurred at a time of weakening of the ruling political establishment as a whole, in large part owing to pressures that were brought to bear on Iranian society and body politic by imperialism. The concentration of power in a decaying center led to circumstances in which neither the state nor social forces enjoyed countrywide domination. This, in turn, produced a crisis for monarchical absolutism. Eventually the monarchy found itself on the defensive against a strong constitutionalist movement that included the intelligentsia – who were the conduit for European constitutionalist ideals – elements of the religious establishment, urban poor, and aspiring members of the bureaucracy and the emerging middle classes. The resultant Constitution of 1906 placed limits on the power of the monarchy and vested much of its authority in a parliament. The Constitutional Revolution would be the first serious attempt to alter the balance of power between state and society. It produced a period of democratic rule in Iran, which proved to be short-lived. By the end of the first decade of the 20th century, Iranian democracy had begun to lose ground to authoritarian tendencies.

The rise of democracy did not produce stable governing coalitions, or well-organized and effective political parties. Democracy intensified political competition at the center, just as it weakened the hold of the center over the country, leading to palpable fears of the country's disintegration. This, along with the collapse of law and order, rampant corruption, and deteriorating economic conditions, limited the prospects for democratic consolidation. Elected governments proved to be just as pliable before imperialist pressure as had absolutist monarchs before 1906. It had further become evident that democracy would not produce rapid modernization. Hence, those social forces that supported the Constitutional Revolution with the hope of bringing both political and economic modernization to Iran were confronted with a zero-sum choice – democracy or socioeconomic modernization. Many opted for the latter, believing that a strong central state would better protect fundamental rights to life and property, integrity of national borders, and national rights before imperialist demands.

In the meantime, the Anglo-Russian rapprochement of 1907 made the division of Iran between the two world powers a distinct possibility, placing greater pressure on the democratic order. This possibility would continue to haunt Iranians until the Bolshevik revolution of 1917 drove a wedge between Russia and the West. Thenceforth, the British would once again take interest in strengthening the political center in Iran. However, by then, the democratic order had been seriously damaged. Consequently, the domestic and foreign efforts to shore up the authority of the center, and the increasing demands for effective modernization and development within Iran – which had been first pursued through the Constitutional Revolution – would now lead to a regime change. The result would be a new political order that would draw heavily on the institutional framework of the absolutist era. Iran would thus embark on its path to development by reconstituting the pre-1906 power structure.

# REZA SHAH PERIOD AND THE BEGINNINGS OF DEVELOPMENT (1921–1941)

The crisis of democracy ended with a military coup in 1921 that was led by Reza Khan (later Reza Shah Pahlavi) in alliance with dissident civilian politicians and intellectuals. Reza Khan quickly consolidated power and in 1926 ascended the throne. The coup ushered in a new period in Iran's history, during which national boundaries became institutionalized, the country committed itself to develop-ment, and its interests, identity, and institutions became defined and entrenched. In many ways, the fundamental characteristics of the modern state and the defin-ing elements of its path to development were outlined during this period.

Reza Shah's monarchy was concerned with two separate though interrelated objectives: first, to assert the power of the center and limit regional autonomy – that is, to ensure law and order and guarantee the territorial integrity of the coun-try; and second, to develop Iran, understood at the time as social modernization and industrialization. The first objective required the establishment of a strong military, and the second objective required the construction of modern bureau-cratic institutions. The realization of both objectives required an increase in state revenue and the mobilization of financial resources through taxation, greater regu-lation of the economy, and attempts to increase the proceeds from oil production and export. Both objectives would in time broaden the state's ability to formulate and implement coherent policies and to reach into society. The two objectives were the most important examples of the state's provision of "public goods" (that is, things that people want but that no individual or group of individuals can pro-vide), in a society where such a concept was largely absent. The provision of these public goods had popular support and helped the state to expand its role in the society and economy, and to organize resources and people effectively. In fact, reshaping identities and value systems in order to better provide those goods became central to the state's conception of its own function.

Reza Shah was largely successful in realizing both objectives. His military cam-paigns defeated separatist movements and subdued autonomous regions and rebellious warlords. In the process, he asserted the primacy of the political center and laid the foundations for strong centralized control of the country. Still, this did not end the obsession with territorial integrity, which at key junctures would translate into xenophobic nationalism, but would otherwise further serve to strengthen state control and nudge Iran in the direction of absolutism. Histori-cally, military-bureaucratic absolutism in Europe had facilitated the mobilization of resources in the face of threats to borders. The same process was evident in Iran as well. Hence early on, the modern Iranian state developed authoritarian ten-dencies in response to international and domestic military threats and the need to mobilize resources to respond to them.

The goal of economic development led the state to extend its control over the economy to mobilize resources for industrialization. Following the examples of Germany and Japan during 1921–41, the state established the very first industries, invested in infrastructure, and tightened its hold over customs, banking, and for-eign trade. The result was a form of state-led capitalism in which the state would see to industrialization, just as it would manage the day-to-day affairs of the economy, although it would provide a role for the private sector.

The objective of economic development both required and promoted administrative and social reform. Reza Shah supported the rise of modern bureaucratic institutions, a new judiciary, and the reform of public health and education. Students were sent abroad and modern educational institutions were established in Iran. In addition, new administrative procedures and secular civil and penal codes were adopted.

Reza Shah was convinced that making Iran strong and fostering its economic development would require fundamental changes in the country's identity and social relations – an ambitious project of cultural engineering that required a coherent state ideology. The state secularized the judiciary and the educational system, and restricted the powers of the clergy. It mandated change of traditional dress to Western dress and promoted secular values. In so doing it hoped to make popular culture compatible with the requirements and goals of development. In place of Islam, the state promoted nationalism, defined in terms of pre-Islamic Iranian identity. Such an identity would be secular and would provide an ideological foundation for both monarchical power and rapid development. The change in identity was also intended to inculcate discipline in the population as a prelude to development. It was then believed, in good part owing to imperialist propaganda, that Iranian cultural beliefs could not promote discipline and the values that are necessary for a modern society. Secular nationalism would remedy that problem. In all this, Reza Shah was deeply influenced by the examples of Germany and Japan, and of Kemalism in Turkey. Global context thus shaped interests, identities, and the relation between the two.

The concern with identity as a necessary prerequisite for successful development would become a hallmark of state-society relations in Iran. As a result, from Reza Shah's regime to that of the Islamic Republic, the state has viewed questions of identity – and hence, issues such as music, dress, popular beliefs, and cultural outlook of the individual – as important to defining the public good and setting the agenda for development. The legacy of the state's cultural policies continue to influence state-society relations in Iran to this day, and hence debates about development begin with struggles over identity.

Giving the state the means to govern effectively was expensive. In fact, how it dealt with financial needs shaped, to a significant degree, the nature of state power. Iran at the time received royalties from the Anglo-Iranian Oil Company, a British company that managed oil production in southern Iran. Efforts to increase royalty payments to the Iranian government proved futile, forcing the state to rely more on tax revenue. Tax farming and unsystematic revenue collections were replaced with a centralized taxation system. The state also turned to foreign advisors to streamline Iran's financial system. Foreign expertise helped the state to extract resources from society and develop plans for economic development; it did not, however, altogether resolve the financial problems confronting the state. Financial constraints encouraged the state to monopolize power in order to increase its ability to extract resources from society and to negotiate more effectively with foreign commercial interests over royalties.

That a strong state did in fact rise in Iran at this time period and that it did so despite significant financial constraints and resistance to central control, and in contravention of foreign interests, is noteworthy. It has been generally accepted that the rise of states is directly correlated with war making, and that societies that experience wars or significant social dislocation are more prone to producing strong states. The rise of the modern Iranian state in the 1920s was closely tied to the military campaigns that consolidated the center's hold over the country, and occurred amid significant hardships – for example, economic hardship, famine, disease, social strife, civil war – that Iranians endured during the first two decades of the 20th century. The campaign to consolidate power at the center and defend the territorial integrity of the country had broad support among many social groups, notably those who had also been the main support for democracy. This allowed Reza Shah to tie the defending of the integrity of state borders to his own consolidation of power. It also allowed his regime to avoid compromises with various social actors – the feudal elite, tribal leaders, merchants – in order to mobilize resources for the military campaigns.

In the 1920s local power in Iran was strong but was unorganized. It was, moreover, dissociated from politics at the center, and in some cases was supported by, and integrated with, foreign interests. It therefore did not serve as a source of support for the parliament during the turbulent years of the democratic period or during the period of regime change in the 1920s. The subsequent weakening of democratic institutions such as parliament during the period of regime change meant minimal oversight by the parliament of the administrative and financial activities of state leaders. Consequently, power accumulated at the center and absolutist tendencies grew unbridled.

The growing dominance of the monarch combined with the social changes that development entailed to create tensions in Iranian politics. In the first place, Reza Shah had been prevailed upon by the clergy to become a monarch, whereas in reality his regime was a "republican monarchy." No sooner had Reza Shah become king than he embarked on secularization and modernization, and also abolished the hereditary titles of the aristocracy. In addition, his campaign to assert centralized control over the country pitted the state against local leaders. He thus moved away from those elite groups and social classes that had until then served as the pillars of the monarchy – the elite, religious establishment, and tribal leaders – and was looking instead to the new middle classes to bolster his regime. The Reza Shah period thus changed the social base of the ruling order. In the economic arena, the same trend was evident. Traditional tradesmen and commercial interests were alienated from the state as it extended its control over the economy. The change in the social base of the monarchy would prove consequential. Disenchanted elite groups, the religious establishment, and small merchants and traders would form the basis of the anti-Pahlavi oppositional coalition. This coalition would eventually serve as the backbone of the revolution of 1979.

Initially Reza Shah allied himself with the new middle classes to take on the elite, local leaders, and the clergy. The new middle classes were then receptive to modernization, secularization, and the nationalist identity that Reza Shah promoted in lieu of Islam. The alliance between the new middle classes and the monarchy, however, failed to provide the state with a countervailing base of support, for these classes were not ideologically committed to the monarchy. As the pace of modernization increased, tensions in the monarchy's relations with the new middle classes grew. By the 1930s, many in these classes were joining pro-democracy and various leftist organizations.

Development spearheaded the rise of modern bureaucratic agencies. At the outset the bureaucracy supported Reza Shah. Over time, however, he became wary of the rising power of the bureaucracy and purged it of its principal leaders. By exercising more control over the bureaucracy, Reza Shah precluded the possibility of the bureaucracy's developing as a legal-rational institution independent of the control of the monarchy. The Iranian state, from this point forward, would display many characteristics of patrimonialism, in which power is concentrated in the ruler whose exercise of authority is only partially influenced by norms and administrative procedures.

In sum, during this period, the global context – in the form of imperialism and the German-Japanese model – combined with the state's need to safeguard territorial integrity and pursue development to shape interests, identity, and institutions in a manner that empowered the state, and hence ensured its domination over Iranian politics.

## THE DEMOCRATIC INTERREGNUM (1941–1954)

The pattern of development that began in 1921 was interrupted with the advent of World War II. The Reza Shah state fell victim to changes in the global context. The Allies were keen to use Iranian territory for supplying the Soviet Union against Germany, and for this it was imperative that they maintain control over Iran. Reza Shah's constant bickering with British oil companies, combined with Iran's reliance on Germany for a number of public projects, had made the British wary of him. The allies demanded that Iran declare neutrality and expel all German citizens, and that Reza Shah abdicate and the Iranian military disarm. In 1941 Reza

Shah was replaced on the throne by his son, Muhammad Reza Pahlavi (known in the West as "the Shah"). Foreign intervention thus ushered in a new era in Iranian politics, one that was characterized by greater openness and new possibilities for state-society relations. Still, foreign intervention did not decisively reshape Iranian politics – rearranging its institutions and altering the balance of power among them – in the manner that the United States would do in Germany and Japan after the war. The British retained the monarchy and did not change the country's constitution or the balance of power among the various social and political actors. That the monarchy would in later years emerge once again as a dominant force in an all-powerful state was therefore not very surprising.

Still, Reza Shah's departure opened the political process and created alternate development paths. During the war, political groups that had been suppressed by Reza Shah – liberals, leftists, and the clergy – organized, and established a place for themselves in the political arena. The parliament, which since 1921 had steadily lost ground to the monarchy, was empowered and once again occupied center stage. The political opening suggested that Iran could develop along democratic lines and that power might permanently shift from the monarchy to the parliament, devolving in the process from state institutions to a broader spectrum of social and political actors. By 1954, however, domestic problems combined with changes in the global context to end the democratic opening.

The 1941–54 period witnessed an intense struggle over the definition of political identity in Iran. The outcome of that struggle would be important for the fate of democracy. Some of the political forces that became dominant during the 1941–54 period were illiberal. Communist, fascist, and religious groups and parties operated in the open political process but were not committed to democracy. In fact, their activities would serve as the pretext for once again vesting the state – and the institution of the monarchy – with greater powers.

Most important in this regard was the communist Tudeh (Masses) Party. Closely allied with the Soviet Union, the Tudeh Party posed a strong challenge to the ruling order and Western interests in Iran. The party was active among the middle classes, labor, intellectuals, and students, mobilizing these social groups in defense of social justice. Its subscription to the cult of Stalin, however, did not favor democracy. The Tudeh Party's ambiguous role in the Soviet Union's attempt to separate two provinces in northern Iran after World War II helped create both popular and Western support for strengthening the political center, which ultimately weakened that party and, in the process, the budding democracy.

The resurgence of religion in politics was equally significant. Religious forces were keen to roll back the secular policies of the Pahlavi state and to institutionalize their role in society and politics. To this end they became active in the political arena, but not with the aim of strengthening democracy. Both the communists and religious forces weakened democracy by engaging in agitational politics: demon-

strations, strikes, and sit-ins in the case of the Tudeh party, and political assassinations in the case of religious activists. By creating political uncertainty, disruptions, and social tensions, the two made the task of democratic consolidation difficult, and helped the monarchy enlist foreign support for its campaign to
consolidate power.

Most damaging to democracy was the oil crisis of 1951–3 and its linkage with
cold war politics. The dispute over royalties with the Anglo-Iranian Oil Company,
which had began in the 1930s, eventually culminated in an impasse in 1951–3. As
the British company refused to accommodate Iran's demands for higher royalties,
nationalist feelings were aroused and they dominated Iranian politics. The monarchy, the military, and some in the business community favored a low-key
approach, believing that a confrontational attitude would not favor Iran. Owing to
British intransigence, however, Iranians demanded more. The popularly elected
nationalist prime minister, Muhammad Mossadeq, and his National Front Party
capitalized on the public mood and nationalized the assets of the Anglo-Iranian Oil
Company in Iran in 1953. The decision was widely popular within Iran and was
supported by the Tudeh Party and religious activists as well.

Britain responded by cutting Iran out of the oil market. The Iranian economy
collapsed, causing social tension and political radicalism. The palpable fear of a
communist takeover changed the political alignment that had dominated Iranian
politics. The clergy, worried about communism, switched sides, as did key segments of the middle classes, commercial interests, and elements of the nationalist
elite. This political realignment facilitated concerted action between the monarchy and the Iranian military in close cooperation with the United States and
Britain. The result was a military coup that toppled the National Front government, ending the democratic interregnum and restoring the monarchy to power.
The 1941–54 period saw the possibility of alternate identities shaping state-society
relations, and Iranian politics developing along a different path. By 1954, however,
those possibilities were no longer present. Foreign intervention first interrupted
and then led to the resumption of the state's development in the direction first
instituted by Reza Shah. Interests, identities, and ultimately institutions were
reshaped by the changing global context.

## RESURRECTION OF THE PAHLAVI STATE (1954–1963)

The 1954–63 period was one of consolidation of monarchical power. Relying on
the military, and with crucial financial and technical assistance from the United
States, the monarchy went on the offensive against its opponents. The National
Front and the Tudeh Party were banned. The military and bureaucracy were
purged of their sympathizers. The campaign also weakened the institutions of civil

society and ultimately the parliament, dimming the prospects for democracy. Cold war considerations led the United States to support these developments in Iran and to help train Iranian military and intelligence agencies to protect the state, which was viewed as a bulwark against communism and the southward expansion of the Soviet Union. Financial aid helped buoy Iran's economy and generated support for the ruling order. The consolidation of power under the monarchy would commit the state to a largely economic vision of development. The spirit of this posture was captured in the Shah's statement: "When the Iranians learn to behave like Swedes, I will behave like the king of Sweden."

Single-minded pursuit of development – the public good whose provision would justify state authority from this point forward – required further streamlining the organization of resources and people, the imperatives that had also propelled the expansion of state-authority formation under Reza Shah. This led the state to reformulate its relations with agrarian elites, who had to this point remained close to the monarchy; the religious establishment, with which the monarchy had only a tenuous alliance; and the middle classes, which were the main agents and beneficiaries of development although they were not committed to the monarchy. The consequences of these reformulations would determine the course of subsequent development.

## ECONOMIC GROWTH AND AUTHORITARIANISM (1963–1979)

Between 1959 and 1963, the Pahlavi state had to weather a number of challenges, the resolution of which both necessitated redoubling its commitment to development and created greater room for pursuing it. The political rumblings occurred at a time when the United States began to waiver in its unconditional support of the Pahlavi state, and viewed some form of reform in Iran as necessary to limiting communist influence in the country. The change in American attitude parlayed into a momentum for wide-scale reform.

In the meantime, an austerity package prescribed by the International Monetary Fund brought on a severe recession during the 1960–2 period. The perceived threat to the ruling order convinced state leaders that they could not afford prolonged economic crises. Oil revenue, even despite modest increases ($555 million in 1963–4 [12 percent of the GNP]), would not remedy the crisis nor satisfy development needs. Hence, reform would have to go hand in hand with, as well as help spur, economic growth. The state began to see its objective of development as integral to sociopolitical reform. This vision culminated in the "White Revolution" of 1963, the term coined to upstage the Left and its promise of "red" revolution.

The White Revolution was a package of sweeping reforms that aimed to change the structure of societal relations in Iran and to enable more effective resource mobilization in the service of development. The most important initiatives were land reform, the enfranchisement of women, and the provision of greater rights and share of industries to labor. Through the White Revolution the state was hoping to institutionalize its hold over the middle classes and among those social groups that might serve as the base of support for an effective communist movement, including the poor, the peasantry, and industrial labor. These reforms, so the argument ran, were necessary for effective development. They would modernize Iranian society, changing it in ways that would help industrialization.

The White Revolution was a risky venture, for the principal losers in the reforms, the landed elite and the clergy, had in the past served as sources of support for the monarchy, whereas the support of the modern middle classes for monarchy had at best been tenuous. The Shah was falling into the same trap that his father had, vesting his political fortunes in a social class whose loyalties would ultimately not rest with the monarchy. In addition, given the Pahlavi state's pro-industry bias, it did not cultivate a base of support among the peasantry that it was enfranchising. Industrial labor, meanwhile, did not as yet possess sufficient power to act as a significant source of support for the monarchy; and if they were to become a force, the monarchy was unlikely to claim their allegiance for long. More immediately, however, the state would rely on the rising power of the bureaucracy, which itself was being modernized from within. The bureaucracy was committed to development, and to that end joined in a ruling alliance with the monarchy. In effect, the state reformulated its linkages with society and also defined the shape of its opposition. The landed elite, the clergy, and the "liberal Left," all of whom opposed the White Revolution or viewed it as the means through which the state might devour their base of support, gravitated toward a united antistate stance. The restoration of power to the monarchy thus reconstituted the oppositional alliance that had first surfaced during the earlier Reza Shah period.

The first expression of this opposition was the protest movement led by the religious cleric Ayatollah Ruhollah Khomeini in 1964. The protest was strongly antistate, but its immediate concern was with the White Revolution. Khomeini characterized the enfranchisement of women as "un-Islamic." He also rejected land reform as a violation of Islamic protection of property rights. The protest movement brought together the landed elite, the religious establishment, and the liberal Left. The first two groups opposed specific points of the White Revolution, whereas the liberal Left viewed the entire reform package as a threat to its political position, and had a vested interest in its failure. The White Revolution sought to change the social structure, in opposition to which they had mobilized support, and to render their political programs obsolete.

The protest movement failed. The state's agenda of social reform and rapid economic development thus unfolded unencumbered. Still, the protest movement had the effect of committing the state to a greater use of force in contending with the opposition. This in turn led to the consolidation of the anti-Pahlavi forces into a more coherent alliance under the unified leadership of the clergy and the liberal Left. Such thinkers as Ali Shariati actually began to formulate a socially conscious religio-ideological perspective that could consolidate an anti-Shah alliance. This opposition would in time become increasingly violent and would, in turn, face greater violence from the state. From this point forward, the security apparatuses of the state, most notably the secret police, SAVAK, would use repressive measures, including detentions and torture, to subdue the opposition. The opposition produced radical communist and Islamist urban-guerrilla organizations, escalating antistate activities to the level of armed conflict and acts of terror. The radicalization of the opposition and the state's use of violence in suppressing it polarized Iranian politics and gradually concentrated power in a limited number of state institutions – most notably its security apparatuses – and in the monarchy.

Economically, however, the 1960s was a period of relative success. Land reform, the overhaul of the bureaucracy, and the weakening of the parliament allowed economic managers to pursue growth aggressively and with greater freedom from outside influence. The result was an industrial transformation, producing growth rates that were unmatched in Iran's history. The GDP for this period grew at an average of 9.2 percent per annum; and industrial growth rates averaging 15 percent per annum were among the highest in the Third World. At the same time, the central characteristics of the economy changed as it acquired medium and heavy industries and a modern private sector.

Economic development in Iran in the 1960s was based largely on import-substituting industrialization (ISI). While ISI produces rapid growth rates early on and helps gets industrialization off the ground, it also poses political and economic challenges down the road. As we have seen earlier in the chapters on Mexico and India, ISI places emphasis on capital-intensive industries, and hence leads to the neglect of small-scale production and the agricultural sector. It can lead to uneven development, overurbanization, and income inequality. It also puts pressure on government finances and the balance of trade, just as it augments state control of the economy. It was partly to address problems born of ISI that Iran decided to support the oil-price hikes of OPEC (the Organization of Petroleum Exporing Countries) in the 1970s.

The rise in oil prices ($958 million in 1968–9 [18 percent of the GNP] in contrast to $20 billion in 1975–6 [35 percent of the GNP]) removed financial pressures from the state and allowed it to spend more freely on various industrial and social projects. It is interesting to note, however, that higher oil prices augmented the challenges before the Shah. They adversely affected the pattern of economic development as the state deepened ISI, but did so with decreasing efficiency. Although the Iranian economy performed well in the 1970s, it veered off the path toward viable industrialization and market development and eventually faced serious crises.

The oil boom created bottlenecks in the economy and led to wasteful spending on grandiose projects. Iran spent billions of dollars on infrastructure and industrial projects. It also spent huge sums on war matériel and public enterprises of questionable economic value. All this eroded trust in the management of the economy. The rapid pace of growth also created social dislocation, cultural confusion, and new political demands with which the state was unequipped to contend. In addition, the newfound wealth encouraged corruption and speculative financial activities. This adversely affected public morale and skewed popular perception about the meaning and intent of entrepreneurial activity. The oil wealth also raised expectations – so much so, that the state not only was unable to gain political support for acquiring the new wealth, but also found itself falling short of fulfilling growing expectations.

The Iranian state began to face political problems associated with "rentier states," that is, states in which income that is external to the productive capacity of the economy accounts for the lion's share of state revenue. Rentier states are generally politically weak, for the state derives little if any of its income from the population, and as a result, does not devise ways to increase revenues through taxation. Nor does it negotiate with the population in order to increase society's contribution to state revenue. Instead, rentier states invest in distributive mechanisms and, having developed a relationship of distribution and patronage with their populations, do not develop meaningful links with society. The population does not credit the government for the generation of wealth, although it expects more from the government in terms of distribution of wealth. Popular support remains contingent on continued flow of "rent."

As oil income dominated the Iranian economy, the Pahlavi state began to face a serious political crisis. On the one hand, its developmental agenda had concentrated power in the state and the monarchy and isolated both from other social groups. On the other hand, the state justified its course of action in terms of provision of a public good: development. Between 1946 and 1979, the state had changed the character of the economy in a fundamental fashion from agriculture to industry. Public planning, urbanization, industrialization, diversification, and infrastructural and human capital investments had produced sustained change and growth. The increase in oil wealth, however, denied the state the ability to claim credit for its economic achievements. It undermined the state's developmentalist claims as it depicted development as synonymous with oil revenue, rendering redundant the political apparatuses that the Pahlavi monarchs had argued were needed for realizing development. All this pushed an already narrowly based state to the brink of collapse. The resultant political tensions erupted in 1977, culminating in the Islamic Revolution of 1979 that toppled the Pahlavi state.

The global context proved important at this juncture as well. The revolution unfolded at a time of change in Iran's relations with the United States. Jimmy Carter, the American president, was unwilling to provide unconditional support to the Shah's regime and instead strongly advocated political reform in Iran. The new U.S. approach created confusion in the Iranian state and emboldened the opposition.

The opposition to the Pahlavi state consisted of liberal and pro-democracy forces, the Left, and religious activists, but it increasingly adopted a strongly Islamic character, especially after Ayatollah Khomeini – then in exile in Iraq – assumed its leadership. Khomeini used his position of authority to put forward a particularly revolutionary and antistate reading of Islam, and used its symbols in mobilizing the masses. Khomeini also built on the traditional role of Shi'i clerics, arguing that given their knowledge of religion, they must rule politically if society were to be Islamic, just, and prosperous. His religio-political crusade was therefore directed at constructing a theocratic form of government.

In promoting his cause, Khomeini strengthened the alliance between the religious establishment and the Left that had been in place since 1964. Khomeini successfully managed to keep the opposition focused on overthrowing the Shah, while postponing the resolution of ideological disagreements and cultural tensions between the religious and secular opposition to the Shah to the postrevolutionary period. His presence on the political scene, however, made religious identity central to politics. In so doing, Khomeini and the revolutionary forces rejected the developmentalist secularism of the Pahlavi state. The revolution owed its success, in large part, to the fact that this stance did not create tensions in the ranks of revolutionary forces, segments of which were politically at odds with the Pahlavi state but shared in its secularism and were themselves products of the Pahlavi state's social engineering. As a result, the revolutionary movement in Iran in 1979 was politically uniform, but was culturally and socially eclectic in that it had both Islamist and secular-liberal and leftist elements in it.

The Shah's failure to divide the opposition along ideological and cultural lines precluded the possibility of negotiations between the monarchy and the liberal Left over a transfer of power. The result was that the political situation continued to radicalize in favor of the religious element in the revolutionary coalition. This did not bode well for democratic development in Iran in 1979. In the end, the Pahlavi state collapsed owing to the Shah's inability to contend with political challenges at a critical juncture. The Pahlavi state had in effect become reduced to the Shah, and his inaction meant that despite broad powers and political possibilities available to the state, it would not survive.

With the fall of the Shah in 1979, the evolution of state authority and function took a new turn. However, despite significant changes in the way in which the state and the economy work in the Islamic Republic, the balance of power between state and society, and the role of the state in socioeconomic change, cannot be understood separate from what occurred in the Pahlavi period. Despite the regime change, ideological shift, and radical social transformation, the path down which the Pahlavi period set Iran continued to shape subsequent development.

## THE REVOLUTIONARY ERA (1979–1988)

The collapse of the monarchy in February 1979 ushered in a new era in Iranian politics. The ideological force of the revolution suggested that the working of the state, the role of interests, and the centrality of identity in development were all likely to change. The revolution promised an axial shift in Iranian politics, a shift that would occur in a changing global context.

The immediate aftermath of the revolution was a period of great fluidity, during which the old order was dismantled and revolutionary forces began to leave their imprint on state and society. Revolutions destroy certain social classes, alter state bureaucracies, and thus make other paths of development possible. In Iran, however, the revolution did not produce a strong state but took over an already existing one and adapted it to its ideology. The central role of the state in development thus remained unaffected. As a result, the postrevolutionary state displayed continuity with as well as change from the past.

Revolutionary forces purged supporters of the old order from various state institutions, public and private organizations, and economic enterprises. The revolution quickly produced institutions of its own. Revolutionary courts and committees and the Revolutionary Guards were organized to serve the functions of the judiciary, the police, and the military. Just as the rise of the Pahlavi state had been closely associated with the creation of the Iranian military, the rise of the new revolutionary state was closely tied to the emergence of these new institutions. Although initially inchoate and disorganized, the new institutions wielded a great deal of power. In time, their presence would create confusion in the state, as the purview of activities of the old military, police, and judiciary would overlap with those of the newly formed revolutionary committees, guards, and courts.

The liquidation of the old order, however, was only a prelude to larger struggles over defining the new order. With the success of the revolution, Ayatollah Khomeini became the undisputed leader of Iran. His supremacy only thinly disguised the intense conflict that was being waged over the definition of the new order. With the triumph of the revolution, the political concord of the disparate groups in opposition to the Shah began to unravel. The liberals, the Left, and the clergy now competed to determine Iran's future.

In March 1979, Iranians voted in a referendum to replace the monarchy with an "Islamic Republic." The term was coined by Khomeini, but it symbolized the struggle among the various factions of the revolutionary alliance over the identity of the

regime that was to rule Iran. Throughout 1979, the struggle became more pronounced in the debates over the new constitution. The resultant document envisioned the Islamic Republic as a modern state with all the constitutional and organizational features of such a state. It provided for a parliament, a judiciary, and an
executive. It delineated the powers of each through a system of checks and balances. But the constitution also made Islamic law supreme. It furthermore recognized Khomeini's position as that of the supreme leader of the revolution (office of
*Vali-e Faqih,* or "supreme guardian-jurisconsult"), an office whose occupant would
not be elected, would not be accountable to any authority, and would have total
veto power over all government decisions and policy making. This arrangement
subjugated the political to the religious in state affairs. It also made identity central
to the question of state authority, above and beyond economic and social interests.

The outcome of the constitutional process suggested that the religious element, led by Khomeini, had gained the upper hand. His domination became more
apparent as the revolutionary regime demanded greater popular observation of
Islamic strictures, especially those concerning women's dress. Religious elites
also mobilized support among the lower middle classes and the poor – groups
with close ties to the religious establishment – to marginalize the modern middle
classes, who served as the social base of the liberal Left. With the victory of the
religious hard-liners in this conflict, the number of clerics in high political offices
grew dramatically.

The final consolidation of power in the hands of the religious element came in
1981–2. Although Islamic activists had already gained the upper hand, it was the
global context in the form of the "hostage crisis" in 1979–80 (when a group of militant "students" took over the U.S. embassy in Tehran and held its employees
hostage for months on end) and the Iran-Iraq war (1980–8) that facilitated their
complete domination. These events diverted popular attention in Iran, and international attention abroad, from domestic power struggles. In addition, both
events created a siege mentality that bolstered the popularity of the religious leadership, who could claim to be defending Iran from American and Iraqi aggression.
In this climate, the liberal Left was portrayed as American stooges, and resistance
to a greater role for Islam in society was depicted as a Western ploy to destabilize
the revolution.

With the purge of the liberal Left, the revolution became a distinctly Islamic
affair. Revolutionary zeal and concern with identity would henceforth define the
nature and function of the state. As in the formation of the Pahlavi state under
Reza Shah, the Islamic Republic, too, justified its power in terms of the provision
of a public good, except that the public good presented by the Islamic Republic
was to be greater Islamization of society and politics, rather than economic development. The Islamic Republic was not interested in rolling back the state's control
over society, nor its ability to penetrate and control it. It, too, believed in a domi-

neering state. In fact, the leadership of the Islamic Republic aimed at expanding rather than contracting the state's control of society.

As in the early Pahlavi state, the Islamic Republic engaged in social engineering as a prerequisite for the realization of its public-policy agenda. It, too, became directly concerned with the dress, music, and cultural outlook of Iranians. It instituted tight control of both the public and private arenas, and viewed social engineering as central to successful policy formulation and implementation. The state's understanding of its function and powers, in some respects, reflected significant continuities with the Pahlavi period.

The centrality of Islamic ideology to state policy made identity and revolutionary fervor central to the flow of politics and the relations between state and society. That fervor, in turn, continued to unfold in the context of the Iran-Iraq war in the 1980s. The war, caused by border disputes and Saddam Hussein's expansionism, was one of the most costly and devastating of this century. During the course of the eight-year war, some 1 million Iranians lost their lives. Iran temporarily lost control of parts of its oil-rich province and incurred significant damage to its urban centers, agriculture, and industrial infrastructure. It was able to turn the tide of the war only at a tremendous human cost. The need to mobilize support and resources for the war pushed the state to emphasize ideology and the revolutionary values that are associated with it. The successful use of ideology in mobilizating for war helped entrench revolutionary zeal and identity in lieu of socioeconomic interests in Iranian politics. Consequently, throughout the 1980–8 period, the workings of the state remained closely tied to the pursuit of Islamization. This, in turn, committed Iran to a confrontational foreign policy and shifted power to the more radical elements in the state leadership. Khomeini supported this trend, for it bolstered his power in Iran and served his ambitions to influence regional and international politics.

Ideological zeal also shaped politics and economics in the Islamic Republic. The Islamic Republic has been different from the Pahlavi state: Despite greater state domination of society, it has avoided personalized rule. Even when Khomeini was at the helm, power was spread among the clerical leaders, who were unified through a patronage network that connected the religious leadership at the center to clerical power brokers. The clerical establishment was committed to the Islamic Republic and to Khomeini's leadership. In fact, Khomeini quickly inculcated group interest in a politically active clergy, thus tying their political ambitions and social position to the fortunes of the Islamic Republic. The clerical leadership ruled collectively – acting as a dominant class – distinguished from the general population by dress and education. The uniform commitment to the Islamic Republic and Khomeini's ideology, however, did not eliminate struggles for power, differences over policy, and disagreements over ideological interpretation among the religious activists and the clerical leadership.

The clerical leadership did not produce a satisfactory way of managing these political debates and conflicts. Before the revolution there had existed no dominant revolutionary party, as had been the case in Russia or China before their communist revolutions. Iran's revolutionary movement was not ideologically and culturally uniform, further limiting the development of a dominant revolutionary organization either before or immediately after the revolution. This revolution, then, turned out to be the first modern revolution to lack a "vanguard" party.

In the absence of a formal organization to manage struggles of power and debates over policy among state leaders, factional politics came out into the open. In the 1980s, three notable factions emerged within the Islamic Republic. The first favored a relaxation of revolutionary vigilance and stabilization of economic relations. Its members came to be known as the "moderates." Those identified with the second faction favored a continuation of revolutionary fervor, but at the same time wished to promote a mercantile economy and the right to private property. They came to be known as the "conservatives." The third faction favored a strong anti-Western policy and the export of the revolution, as well as state control of the economy and limited rights to private property. It came to be known as the "radical" or "hard-line" faction, and was responsible for much of the excesses of the Islamic Republic in foreign policy and expropriation of private property in the first decade of the Islamic Republic. The Iran-Iraq war and Iran's confrontational foreign policy helped the radical faction, whose members were closely allied with the Revolutionary Guards and oversaw Iran's support for revolutionary activism in the Muslim world. The revolutionary fervor espoused by this faction served the aims of mobilizational politics. Although the hard-liners had only a small base of support, mainly in the Revolutionary Guards and in the lower middle and lower classes, they wielded much power in the government and were supported by Ayatollah Khomeini throughout the 1980–8 period. The hard-line faction owed its power to its role in mobilizing support for the war and for the Islamic Republic's foreign policy. That power, derived from the global context in which Iran found itself, worked to increase state domination of the economy and promoted centralized economic planning.

The three factions existed only informally. There has been no actual organization, charter, rules, or platforms to define membership; nor are there any grassroots movements or party structures. The factions have functioned as informal circles within the revolutionary elite, with ill-defined and often changing boundaries. The factions have, however, become protoparty structures, especially because they have shaped electoral results directly.

Struggles for power among these factions occurred for the most part in the parliament, in various consultative forums, in government agencies, in Friday Prayer sermons, and in the media. While debates over foreign policy were restrained, in economic matters the differences were pronounced and the debates were acrimonious. Most notably, the radical faction clashed with the other two factions over the right to property and the legal protection of mercantile activities – all of which was eventually accepted by the revolutionary government.

Factionalism dominated politics in Iran throughout the 1980s. It greatly influenced the distribution of power between the president and prime minister on one side and the parliament on the other. It also influenced the state's relations with society. More important, it influenced the working of the economy, and determined the extent to which interest or identity would shape the state and its policies.

The revolution changed the course of economic development in Iran significantly. The political turmoil of the revolution (1977–9), subsequent domestic political crises, legal uncertainties following the collapse of law and order, meting out of revolutionary justice, debates over property rights, brain drain, the war with Iraq, and international isolation after the hostage crisis all acted to retard the rate of growth. The revolution also radically altered the perceptions of socioeconomic interest and the nature of development. The leftist elements in the revolution viewed economic development under the Pahlavi state as misguided, capitalistic, and, hence, doomed to failure. The religious element was uninterested in development as such and favored replacing it as a national goal with Islamization. Khomeini set the tone in this regard when he commented that "economics is for donkeys" that is, only Islamization matters. The pursuit of interest, he maintained, should be made subservient to identity.

After 1979, therefore, economic development occupied a less prominent place in the priorities of state leaders. To the extent that there was an economic policy in the early years, it was heavily influenced by Marxist models that had been tried in a number of Third World countries. Hence, soon after the revolution, the government nationalized the financial institutions, major industries, and business ventures of those who had been close to the Pahlavi state. By 1998–9, the state owned 80 percent of the Iranian economy, relegating the private sector to small-scale economic activities.

The expansion of the state's control of the economy in time served political ends because the state could distribute jobs to its most ardent supporters. The growth of the public sector also produced new avenues for corruption in the bureaucracy and the political leadership. The net result of this was significantly reduced efficiency. Between 1978 and 1988, the GDP fell by 1.5 percent per year. Put differently, in 1988, the GDP stood at 1974 levels. Industry experienced six years of negative growth. Rapid population growth produced high levels of unemployment, which in 1988 exceeded 30 percent. The weak private sector was unable to create enough jobs to absorb the surplus labor. The government throughout the 1980s addressed the problem by providing employment in the public sector, which by 1988 accounted for one-third of all jobs. In the meantime, oil income fell. The share of oil revenue as a percentage of the GDP fell from 30–40 percent in the 1970s to 9–17 percent in the 1980s, as production levels fell from 5.6 million barrels per day to between 2.2 and 2.9 million. The government increased the rate and scope of taxation, but the economy depended on oil revenues, which continued to account for 85 percent of hard-currency earnings.

By 1988, the economic impact of the war with Iraq, international isolation and economic sanctions, and growing population and declining production presented the Iranian economy with a serious crisis. Shortages in consumer goods had produced a thriving black market that skewed economic interests and the distribution of resources, further reducing efficiency. In addition, the growth of the public sector did not eradicate poverty. By weakening the private sector it did reduce income inequality. But standards of living, especially of the urban poor, did not improve substantially. Inflation and unemployment had effectively undermined the radicals' populism.

While during the 1980–8 period economic hardships could be blamed on the Iran-Iraq war, the conclusion of the war denied the state that excuse. The scope of the economic crisis facing the state now posed serious political challenges. Interests could no longer be easily made subordinate to ideological concerns and the rhetoric of identity politics. Change thus became imperative.

## THE POST-KHOMEINI ERA (1988–PRESENT)

In 1988 the Iran-Iraq war ended with Iraq's unequivocal victory. The following year Ayatollah Khomeini died. These two events had a profound effect on politics in the Islamic Republic. The defeat in the war was a psychological blow to the revolutionary elite. It diminished their legitimacy and reduced the utility of their ideological politics. The population became less tolerant of sacrifices demanded of them, especially since eight years of such sacrifices had ended in an ignoble military defeat. Khomeini's passing from the scene made it more difficult for the ruling order to resist change. As the state began to yield to pressure for change, its policy making became more pragmatic, reflecting greater concern for interests over identity.

After Khomeini died, the president, Ayatollah Ali Khamenei (a member of the conservative faction) became supreme leader, and the speaker of the parliament, Ayatollah Ali Akbar Hashemi-Rafsanjani (a member of the moderate faction) became president (1988–97). The ascendance of the two suggested an alliance between the conservative and moderate factions to marginalize the radical faction. The immediate consequence of Khamenei's and Rafsanjani's assumption of power was the streamlining of the workings of the offices of supreme leader and president. These changes were followed by constitutional reforms that, among other things, integrated revolutionary committees and courts and the Revolutionary Guards with the police, judiciary, and the military, respectively. The Rafsanjani administration also vested greater powers in the bureaucracy and reduced the influence of ideological politics in its day-to-day work. These efforts once again made economic development a central concern of the state, and a justification for its power. The post-Khomeini era thus saw the revival of the Pahlavi conception of the state. These changes did not, however, altogether resolve problems of governance in the Islamic Republic. Most important, the position of the supreme leader limited the power of the president and continued to tie the political system to ideological politics.

The Iranian legislature wields extensive power and limits the scope of the presidency. This is owing to the complexities of the political relations of the ruling elite. From the outset the Islamic Republic did not have the institutional means of distributing power among its various elements and factions. The function that should have been performed by internal party elections was thus performed by general elections. As such, the Islamic Republic itself functions as a party with regular and free elections among "Islamic" candidates. The ruling order has viewed the voters as party members, mobilized through mosque networks and ideological propagation, and the parliament as a "Central Committee" of sorts. Still, the regularity of general elections has helped institutionalize the place of the parliament, the Islamic Consultative Assembly, in the Islamic Republic. Hence, the requirement of deciding over the distribution of power within the ruling regime, and the absence of institutional mechanisms to do so outside of the public arena, by default introduced electoral politics and parliamentary behavior to Iran.

General elections and parliamentary practices, despite all their limitations, have brought about a certain degree of pluralism in the essentially theocratic structure of the Islamic Republic. This means that although Iran is an authoritarian state, far more of its political offices are distributed on the basis of elections – albeit limited elections – and its parliament wields far more effective power than comparable bodies in the Arab world. In fact, one observes two contradictory tendencies working themselves out in the Islamic Republic: on the one hand, the concentration of supreme power in an ideological state, and on the other, democratic practices that are being given significant, if limited, scope for expression within a power structure governed at its apex by a clerical leadership.

It is important to note that elections in the Islamic Republic have not been entirely open, in that there are strict limits on which candidates are allowed to participate. However, once the list of candidates has been set, then the elections have been generally free. This has to do with the combination of the institutional restriction and procedural freedom that characterizes the structure of the Islamic Republic. The state possesses an authoritarian control over society, but is far from constituting a monolith in itself. It is constituted of powerful factions that continuously vie with one another for control. Although the state has been successful in eliminating from the electoral process all those who challenge its fundamental ideological vision, it has not been able to eliminate those who, while sharing this vision, nonetheless challenge various aspects of policy making. Elections are therefore real insofar as they determine the relative influence of the various power centers at the top. They are less than real, however, in that they do not allow for any genuine change in the distribution of power within society, nor do they alter the composition of the leadership of the state.

The importance of the elections and the parliament increased in the post-Khomeini era because Khomeini's passing from the scene intensified factional rivalries. It also increased interest in electoral politics, which reached its climax in the presidential elections of 1997. The intensification of the factional rivalries has in effect nudged the Islamic Republic in the direction of electoral politics and vested greater powers in its representative institutions.

Also important in this regard has been the growing role of economic considerations and, more generally, interests in policy making. Rafsanjani assumed his presidency at a time of economic crisis in Iran. He proposed reforming the Iranian economy and also changing the policy-making environment to better reflect economic interests and pragmatic considerations. His government proposed an extensive privatization program, investment in infrastructure, introduction of free-trade zones, relaxation of currency restrictions, and the attraction of expatriate entrepreneurial talent. The proposals were designed to generate growth through effective state management of the economy, an interesting return to the Pahlavi state's developmentalist approach.

The reform initiative enjoyed some success. Investment in infrastructure increased, management became more efficient, and as a result, the economy began to grow again. In this regard, the institutional and industrial developments of the Pahlavi period were greatly useful to the economic policies of the Islamic Republic. Still, more fundamental reforms proved difficult. The government faced stiff resistance to privatization from the bureaucrats and the myriad quasi-private foundations that manage state-owned enterprises, as well as from labor – and the power brokers who had used public-sector jobs for patronage – who feared loss of jobs. As a result, privatization meant the transference of the ownership of public-sector industries to state-controlled foundations and cronies of the regime. In this way, the state retained control of the industries, even though technically it had privatized them.

The bureaucracy's attempt to assert its autonomy in economic policy making also faced resistance, as it would have reduced kickbacks and patronage, along with profits made by merchants and black marketers. This resistance translated into support for the conservative faction in subsequent elections and pressure to prevent Rafsanjani from running for a third term in 1997.

In the end, Rafsanjani's economic initiative suffered as a consequence of the tightening of Western sanctions against Iran. New efforts to isolate Iran internationally and stop its support of terrorism in the 1990s led to a collapse of the Iranian currency and a decline in the rate of economic growth. The consequence of change in the global context was a heightened debate over Iran's future. Should economic interests continue to be sacrificed in the pursuit of ideological goals, or should Iran subordinate its commitment to identity politics in favor of economic growth? Although there is strong support for continuing Iran's commitment to Islam and the values of the revolution, the scope of economic crises facing the state prevented complacency. By 1998, 65 percent of Iran's population was under twenty-one years of age, the unemployment rate stood at 40 percent, inflation was at 300 percent, and the GDP growth rate lagged behind the population growth rate. Without ending Iran's international isolation as well as undertaking domestic economic reform, Iran could face a political crisis, which could threaten the ruling order and its revolutionary values more seriously than would pragmatism.

By the mid-1990s, revolutionary values and ideological politics came under attack from an unexpected quarter – a resurgence of the secular values of the Pahlavi period. The Islamic Republic has enforced a strict cultural code in Iran. The "Islamization" of society has extended beyond the public sphere and has sought to transform the private lives of Iranians as well. Women's dress, music, public programs, school texts, publications, and all manners of cultural, social, and educational activities have all been subject to state control. This state policy has generated unhappiness and opposition.

The Pahlavi state, too, had sought to transform its citizens, secularizing as well as modernizing them as a prelude to development. Its collapse in 1979, however, has diverted scholarly attention from the extent to which it was successful in transforming Iranian society. In 1979, there existed a peculiar circumstance wherein the Pahlavi state was weak politically but quite strong culturally. That its secular subjects did not have the same political outlook as the rulers weakened the state. The new Islamic Republic, on the other hand, enjoyed far more political appeal among the middle classes than it did cultural support. The Islamic movement in Iran triumphed politically in large measure because it was able to divide secular Iranians along political lines. The Pahlavi state's political failure, however, should not be read as evidence of its cultural irrelevance; for the underlying cultural impact of Pahlavi policies continues to be a major force in Iranian society. Its continued salience is attested to by the inability of the Islamic Republic to establish uncontested cultural hegemony in Iran two decades after the revolution, but also by the fact that pre–revolutionary cultural attitudes have increasingly served as the starting point of important dissenting tendencies in the political arena. Those social groups that continue to live by the norms of the past may be out of power but they remain nonetheless potential contenders for power.

The Islamic Republic was never able to win over the secular social stratum or to eliminate it. It could merely suppress it. Islamic clerics imposed new laws and regulations on the population, largely by force. For instance, new attire for women was imposed after several large demonstrations, one of which drew more than a million women protesters into the streets in 1979. Since then, the strict women's dress code has been enforced brutally by the Revolutionary Guards.

The "Cultural Revolution" in 1980 "cleansed" educational institutions of all those who did not subscribe to Islamic ideology. As far as the liberal Left element within the revolutionary movement itself was concerned, the Islamic Republic eventually resolved that inherent anomaly in the alliance that brought it to power. After an open struggle for power in 1979–81, the Islamist element in the revolutionary alliance purged the secular liberal Left element.

Secular Iranians, among them prominent professionals and intellectuals, were forcibly marginalized, but they remained important as they shifted their activities to the private arena and the important sphere of civil society. In fact, this social stratum has acted in a fashion similar to those groups who spearheaded the uprising in the name of civil society against East European communist states. The refusal to abide by state ideology at the popular and even personal level has challenged the domination of Islamic ideology and is forcing changes on the ruling regime. The cultural influence of the Pahlavi era has continued and remains dominant at the personal level among the middle classes. In recent years, economic crisis and problems of isolation have constricted the ruling regime and weakened its hold over society. Creeping pragmatism in policy making has, moreover, made the secular middle classes and the values they espouse the vanguard force for a decisive movement of political resistance. That economic growth both needs and will empower this social stratum has made it difficult for the Islamic Republic to resist its influence.

## THE PRESIDENTIAL ELECTIONS OF 1997

All of these factors coalesced to determine the outcome of the presidential elections of 1997. These elections were the first to involve a transfer of power at the level of the presidency during the post-Khomeini era. Given the debates over the relative importance of identity and interests in state policy, the elections were viewed as decisive. Early on in the election campaign, the nominee of the conservative faction emerged as the front-runner. The faction had a strong base of support among small businessmen and in the political apparatus of the Islamic Republic, and it also had the backing of Ayatollah Khamenei. In addition, the conservatives posed as a force for continuity, and to some extent retrenchment, of the values and norms of the Islamic Republic. They held to a conservative line on social and cultural issues and supported the thrust of Iran's anti-Western foreign policy. In this way they differed from President Rafsanjani, who had favored easing the strictures that govern social and cultural practices, and who had tried – albeit with little success – to reduce tensions between Iran and the Western powers.

What appeared to be the conservatives' unchallenged march to the presidency, however, soon became a closely contested race with Ayatollah Muhammad Khatami. Khatami did not represent any of the rival factions but appealed to the moderate faction and its followers. In addition, his promise of relaxing the state's ideological vigilance also gained him a following among women, youth, and the secular elements. In many regards, Khatami's platform and following greatly resemble those of Gorbachev in the Soviet Union. Khatami, too, believes in the promise of the revolutionary ideology and hopes that once that ideology is freed from the authoritarian control of the state through reform measures, it will fulfill its promise of progress and prosperity. Many who followed Khatami (again, similar to Gorbachev in Russia) did not share his belief in the promise of revolutionary ideology but liked the implications of his reform proposals.

The intensity of the factional rivalry guaranteed the openness of the elections and paved the way for greater freedom of expression in the media. The election itself, held in May 1997, proved nothing short of an earthquake in Iranian politics. Most observers had expected Khatami to do well but thought that in the end the conservatives would win. This did not come to pass. Khatami won the elections with an overwhelming majority of the vote, 70 percent (some 20 million votes). The defeat of the conservative faction was total and humiliating. Iranians had taken the elections seriously and had voted convincingly in favor of fundamental changes in the nature, structure, and workings of the Islamic Republic. Many saw the elections as a referendum on the Islamic Republic and, at the very least, as a referendum on how its existing leadership ought to understand its mission and relations with society. The vote was also one for interests over identity in the workings of the state.

The election results had important implications. First, this was a unique case in the Middle East: A head of state stepped down from power at the end of his term of office and peacefully handed over power to a successor, elected through constitutional means. The transition of power from Rafsanjani to Khatami has therefore been of tremendous significance in itself. Second, the large turnout – some 30 million, an overwhelming majority of the eligible voters – means that Iranians of all political persuasions had taken the elections seriously, and decided to voice their views and demands within the political process, rather than outside of it. This means that the electoral process has become institutionalized in the Islamic Republic and has become the most important means of integrating various social groups into the political system. It is no longer an artificial appendage to the Islamic state but is very much part of the fabric of its politics.

The decision by so many to use the ballot box to promote change has also strengthened the Islamic Republic, as those who have been unhappy with its achievements have chosen to participate in it rather than opt out of it. The elections and the transition of power have the potential to include greater numbers of Iranians within the Islamic Republic. However, to do so successfully the Islamic Republic must accommodate a broader set of sociopolitical demands, and most notably move farther away from ideological politics and the values of the revolution.

Since Khatami's victory, the leadership of the Islamic Republic has become embroiled in an intense debate. Should the Islamic Republic look to expand its base of support by accommodating the demands of those whom Khatami has brought into the political process? Or should it remain narrowly based in ideological politics and exclude those who seek more open and less identity-based politics? In this debate, the presidency has become the advocate of change and the supreme leader the defender of revolutionary values. Consequently, the debate now involves the relative power of the two offices, and the resolution of the debate over greater liberalization or retrenchment is also likely to resolve the ambiguity of power at the helm of the Islamic Republic.

In addition, the political opening after 1997 occurred when the global context favored reform and restructuring. This, in turn, has increased interest in economic reform and presented the possibility for the current government to pursue this goal more effectively than did the Rafsanjani administration. The worsening of the economic situation in Iran in 1998–9, owing to a decline in oil prices, pushed the ruling regime to take the imperative of liberalization and growth more seriously. Given the ongoing battle over the future of the Islamic Republic, the debate over economic reform is likely to be influenced by, and in turn impact, the debates over political reform. Economic pressures are making interests more important to state policy, and this time they may assist rather than retard democratic development.

Since 1997 Khatami has encouraged freedom of expression and creation of new institutions, believing that greater openness of the political process will foster change in the institutional basis of the Islamic Republic, and anchor development in interests in place of identity. He has, moreover, put forth a more liberal interpretation of the foundational values and ideals of the revolution, such that pluralism – and also normalization of Iran's relations with the West – would be possible within the framework of the Islamic Republic. To this end, in 1998 Khatami took steps to reduce tensions between Iran and the United States. He has publicly asserted that Islam should not be used to justify authoritarianism, but should support the rule of law and pluralism. Khatami's initiatives are designed to broaden his base of support by encouraging those forces that decided the outcome of the 1997 elections to sustain their activity. From early on, Khatami was able to secure control of key state institutions. His government gained control of government agencies that oversee education and culture. It managed to assert some control over the judiciary and intelligence apparatuses. It also presided over the first municipal elections in Iran in 1999, which further strengthened Khatami's followers and their program of change. All of this, however, did not immediately parlay into regime change, nor was it probably meant to do so.

Those who are committed to the values of the revolution, along with the vested interest in state control of the economy, have effectively resisted Khatami's initiatives. They have placed obstacles before his efforts in the parliament and the judiciary. They continue to harass and intimidate pro-democracy forces by means of strong-arm tactics on the streets. As the growing demand for change has confronted concerted resistance, tensions have escalated. In December 1998, death squads assassinated a number of Iranian intellectuals in order to stifle freedom of expression – which was the basis of Khatami's reform initiative. In July 1999, the scope of the conflict broadened, producing open clashes between pro-democracy students and anti-reform forces. The clashes culminated in five days of rioting in several cities. The riots entailed direct attacks on both the supreme leader and the underlying ideology of the Islamic Republic. Although the ruling order was able to contain the uprising, it became evident that its grip on the population's hearts and minds has loosened. There is now greater demand for political freedoms, reduced state control of social relations, and the pursuit of interests in lieu of identity in economic development – all of which require changes in state institutions and state-society relations. Iranians are now engaged in a critical struggle over the future of the state. At issue are the nature of state-society relations and the place of identity and interests in politics.

Looking back at developments since 1988, one can conclude that greater pragmatism has restored the state to its central role in the management of society, politics, and the economy in the name of economic development, as in the earlier Pahlavi era. Still, the possibility of greater democratization of politics suggests that beyond restoration of power to the state and greater attention to the pursuit of economic growth and development, Iranian politics may be developing along a new trajectory. Whether elections will evolve beyond settling struggles of power among ruling factions into a broad-based democratic system will depend on changes in the relative powers of state and society, and the relative importance of interests and identity in shaping institutions and, ultimately, Iran's development path. The pace and scope of economic reform will influence those changes in turn. These considerations have already spurred much thinking about the role that civil-society institutions, the private sector, and other foundational features of democracies must play in the political maturation of the Iranian state. The relations of power that have defined Iranian politics over the course of much of this century will most likely also influence the process of change.

## CONCLUSION

At the turn of the century there existed little in the form of interests, identity, or institutions in the Iranian polity to provide an impetus for development or to chart a path for that process. It was the global context at the time that imbued the

Iranian political process with interests and set the country on its path to development. Those interests, in turn, influenced identity and shaped institutions to give form to the modern Iranian state. Iran looked to Germany and Japan – and also Turkey – as models to follow, and so invested in strong state institutions and promoted secular national identity. As state institutions expanded, they defined interests and identity in order to serve the state's objectives in the economic and the political arenas. Thus early on in the process of development, the global context and interests that emerged from it shaped identity and institutions, guaranteeing the central role of the state in that process.

A changing global context in subsequent years, along with crises that are inherent to development, altered the state in important ways but would not change the state's dominant role in society and politics. Even the Iranian revolution did not reverse this trend. The revolution placed more importance on identity – articulated in Islamic terms – in charting the country's development path. It changed some old institutions and produced some new ones but did not change the role of the state in economic development. The case of Iran shows that the interaction among interests, identity, and institutions – as militated by changes in the global contexts and imperatives of the domestic scene – is more fluid early on in the development process, but becomes increasingly less so over time. As institutions grow in size and reach, they become more rigid. Although institutions continue to respond to the global context, and reflect the influence of interests and identity, they do so with greater infrequency and seldom in major ways. The size and power of the state thus becomes more important in determining the course of development than do interests and identity, the impact of which must now happen through institutions rather than separate from them.

In many ways, the domination of institutions that emerged through Iran's experiment with development – producing a strong and centralized state – account for the fact that Iran has been unable to achieve the end goal of democratic capitalism. Still, in major and minor ways, the global context has shaped interests, and through them identity and institutions, to present Iran with new development possibilities. At the dawn of the 21st century, Iran is yet to arrive at democratic capitalism. However, given the changes in the economic and political spheres in Iran in the past several years, the possibility of realization of that goal is not as remote as it may have been only a short while ago.

## BIBLIOGRAPHY

Abrahamian, Ervand. *Iran Between Two Revolutions.* Princeton, NJ: Princeton University Press, 1982.

Akhavi, Shahrough. *Religion and Politics in Contemporary Iran: Clergy-State Relations in the Pahlavi Period.* Albany, NY: SUNY Press, 1980.

Amuzegar, Jahangir. *Iran's Economy Under the Islamic Republic.* London: I. B. Tauris, 1993.

Arjomand, Said A. *The Turban for the Crown: The Islamic Revolution in Iran.* New York:

Oxford University Press, 1988.

Azimi, F. *Iran: The Crisis of Democracy.* New York: St. Martin's Press, 1989.

Bakash, Shaul. *The Reign of the Ayatollahs: Iran and the Islamic Revolution.* New York: Basic Books, 1984.

Bakhtiari, Bahman. *Parliamentary Politics in Revolutionary Iran: The Institutionalization of Factional Politics.* Gainesville, FL: University Press of Florida, 1996.

Dabashi, Hamid. *Theology of Discontent: The Ideological Foundation of the Islamic Revolution in Iran.* New York: New York University Press, 1993.

Ehteshami, Anoushiravan. *After Khomeini: The Iranian Second Republic.* New York: Routledge, 1995.

Elm, Mostafa. *Oil, Power, and Principle: Iran's Oil Nationalization and its Aftermath.* Syracuse, NY: Syracuse University Press, 1992.

Ertman, Thomas. *Birth of Leviathan: Building States and Regimes in Medieval and Early Modern Europe.* New York: Cambridge University Press, 1997.

Ghani, Cyrus. *Iran and the Rise of Reza Shah: From Qajar Collapse to Pahlavi Rule.* London: I. B. Tauris, 1998.

Karshenas, Massoud. *Oil, State and Industrialization in Iran.* New York: Cambridge University Press, 1990.

Katouzian, Homa. *The Political Economy of Modern Iran, 1926–79.* New York: New York University Press, 1981.

Looney, Robert. *Economic Origins of the Iranian Revolution.* New York: Pergamon Press, 1982.

Migdal, Joel S., Atul Kohli, and Vivienne Shue, eds. *State Power and Social Forces: Domination and Transformation in the Third World.* New York: Cambridge University Press, 1994.

Schirazi, Asghar. *The Constitution of Iran: Politics and the State in the Islamic Republic.* London: I. B. Tauris, 1997.

Skocpol, Theda. "Rentier State and Shi'a Islam in the Iranian Revolution." *Theory and Society* 11, no. 3 (May 1982): 265–83.

## IMPORTANT TERMS

**Anglo-Iranian Oil Company**   the British company that owned the concession to excavate, process, and export Iran's oil until 1954.

**Ayatollah**   literally meaning "sign of God," the title of the highest-ranking religious leader in Shi'i Islam. He has the authority to interpret religious law, and to prescribe proper personal, social, and political behavior.

**bazaar**   the old marketplace in Muslim urban areas. It refers to traditional mercantile and commercial classes.

**Central Committee**   the central decision-making body in a communist party structure.

**Cultural Revolution**   attack by the revolutionary forces on Iranian universities and intellectuals in 1980 in order to purge them of liberal and leftist elements, and to force conformity with revolutionary values. This term originated in China during the purges of the 1960s.

**Friday Prayer**    congregational Muslim prayer on Fridays. In the Islamic Republic it has been used as a political forum to propagate government views and mobilize the masses in support of government policies.

**GNP/GDP**    Gross National Product and Gross Domestic Product, indexes that are used to measure the size and growth rate of an economy. GNP measures the total size of the economy, and GDP measures the size of the economy divided by the number of people in that economy.

**Hashemi-Rafsanjani, Ayatollah Ali Akbar**    revolutionary leader, speaker of the parliament and president between 1988 and 1997. He introduced the first efforts to reform the Islamic Republic.

**hostage crisis**    the crisis initiated in November 1979 when radical students took American diplomatic personnel hostage at the U.S. embassy in Tehran, demanding the handover of the Shah to Iran and recognition of Iran's grievances against the United States for its role in the 1953 coup and support of the Shah. The hostages were released in November 1980 after 444 days.

**import-substituting industrialization (ISI)**    a strategy for industrialization that became popular in the Third World after World War II. It advocates beginning industrialization by producing finished goods, and then expanding the scope of the process by moving to intermediary and primary industrial goods and utilizing protectionism to favor the young industries. It has been associated with several economic and political problems.

**Iran-Iraq war**    an intense war between Iraq and Iraq between 1980 and 1988, during which Iraq first occupied parts of Iran but then was compelled to defend its own territory against Iranian offensives. The most bloody and costly war since World War II, it ended with Iran's defeat.

**Islam**    a monotheistic religion, the world's second-largest faith with more than a billion followers.

**Islamic ideology**    a political doctrine with views on society and government that are drawn from a puritanical understanding of Islam. Advocating that politics should be subservient to religion, it was the guiding ideology of the religious faction of the revolution.

**Islamic Republic of Iran**    the official name of Iran after the revolution. It attests to the centrality of Islam to statecraft since 1979.

**Kemalism**    a model of development that emerged in Turkey in the 1920s. Named after the Turkish president, Mustafa Kemal, its most important features were secularism, nationalism, and a domineering role for the state in socioeconomic change.

**Khamenei, Ayatollah Ali**    revolutionary leader, president, and currently supreme leader of Iran. He is associated with the anti-reform faction since 1997.

**Khatami, Ayatollah Mohammad**    Iran's president since 1997. He has spearheaded efforts to liberalize the Islamic Republic.

**Khomeini, Ayatollah Ruhollah**    the chief architect and leader of the revolution of 1979, who ruled Iran as supreme leader between 1979 and 1988.

**Mossadeq, Mohammad**    the nationalist prime minister at the time of the 1953 coup.

He nationalized Iran's oil industry and led the drive for limiting foreign influence in Iran, and for instituting democracy in the country.

**OPEC**   Organization of Petroleum Exporting Countries, formed in the late 1960s to strengthen the position of oil producers in the international market. It pushed for higher oil prices in the 1970s.

**Pahlavi**   the name of the dynasty that ruled Iran between 1921 and 1979.

**Pahlavi, Muhammad Reza Shah**   the second Pahlavi monarch, who ruled between 1941 and 1979.

**Pahlavi, Reza Shah**   the founder of the Pahlavi monarchy, and initiator of Iran's development in the 20th century. He ruled between 1921 and 1941.

**Rentier state**   a state that earns an overwhelming proportion of its income from sources outside of its domestic economic activity. Such states become autonomous from the society and rely on distributive mechanisms to assert authority. That, in time, will erode their legitimacy.

**Revolutionary Guards**   an ideologically committed militia that was formed after the revolution to perform the functions of the police and the military.

**SAVAK**   Iran's intelligence agency between 1954 and 1979. It was responsible for contending with the opposition, and was associated with the Pahlavi monarchy's human-rights excesses.

**Shah**   king, in Persian.

**Shi'i**   a branch of Islam that dominates in Iran. It places great authority in its religious leaders, and values sacrifice in the path of justice.

**Shariati, Ali**   an intellectual who blended Marxist ideology with Islamic teachings to produce a potent ideology of revolutionary change in Iran in the 1970s.

**Vali-e Faqih**   literally meaning the "supreme guardian-jurisconsult," it is a position that was put forward by Ayatollah Khomeini to embody his belief that it is religiously mandated for Shi'i clerics to rule in the political arena. This view justified the religious nature of the revolution and the constitutional setup of the Islamic Republic.

**vanguard party**   a party that spearheads a revolution.


## STUDY QUESTIONS

1. How has change in identity influenced Iran's development?

2. How has the revolution altered prospects for democratic capitalism?

3. What are most important turning points in Iran's development?

4. Was there greater chance for democratic development in 1977 or in 1997?

5. Has identity been important in Iranian institutional change? If so, how?

6. Does the pursuit of interests produce a more sustainable development path, or does pursuit of identity?

7. Can religious identity sustain secular state institutions and serve developmental goals?

8. How important is the location of Iran to its path of development?

9. In what ways can the global context influence Iran's development from this point forward?

# 10

# South Africa

Michael Bratton

# INTRODUCTION

As one of the world's youngest democracies, South Africa seeks to escape a bitter political legacy. During the second half of the 20th century, its white minority government systematically built a powerful, militarized state around institutions of racial oppression. Starting even earlier, governments helped foster an advanced industrial economy, which thrust Africans and the descendants of European settlers into close contact in the country's burgeoning urban areas. Predictably, political conflicts erupted between blacks, who provided labor, and whites, who benefited from economic growth. Because the old regime was dead set against political change until the late 1980s, the struggle over *apartheid* (as racial segregation was called in South Africa) seemed destined to end in a cataclysm of violence.

That it did not was one of the most remarkable stories of an eventful interlude of global democratization. Against the odds, political leaders from both sides (but especially the visionary Nelson Rolihlahla Mandela, president of the African National Congress) came to recognize that the long-term interests of South Africa's deeply divided communities were inextricably intertwined. Through tough negotiation and painful compromise, hardened opponents forged an elite pact that allowed the country to hold an open election and to install the country's first democratic government in 1994. The world welcomed this transition as marking both the end of colonial rule in Africa and the burial of the last 20th-century government based on myths of racial supremacy.

The years that followed in South Africa have seen a flurry of political creativity. A wide range of new institutions and policies have been designed to redress the exclusions and inequities of the past. But difficult questions remain about the viability of the new order. Do South Africans from different social backgrounds acknowledge their interdependence? Can the government redistribute wealth to blacks without inducing white flight? Does the government have the independence and capacity to deliver the benefits promised in South Africa's expansive new constitution? And, perhaps most importantly, given the absence of a democratic heritage and the persistence of violence, what are the prospects for consolidating democracy?

## THE GLOBAL HISTORICAL CONTEXT

The southernmost tip of Africa, a dry region rich in mineral resources, has supported small hunting and gathering communities from the time that humans first trod the earth. From about 2,500 years ago, the indigenous Khoisan peoples were gradually joined by Bantu-speaking African migrants from the north, who introduced herding, crop cultivation, and iron production. As these groups intermingled, they formed a succession of small-scale chieftaincies which, due to the relative abundance of land, had little need to establish standing armies or other state institutions to enforce claims over territory.

Southern Africa became less isolated from the rest of the world in the late 15th century when – at about the same time that Spain was dispatching Columbus to the Americas – Portuguese mariners rounded the Cape of Good Hope in search of an eastward route to India. Succeeding the Portuguese as the world's top trading power during the 17th century, the Dutch founded the first permanent European settlement there. From the beginning, the Cape Colony was run along lines that established the foundations for modern South Africa: the forced annexation of land and the coercion of labor. This economic system, together with sexual liaisons between white burghers and black workers, gave rise to a complex society stratified along racial and class lines.

The ascendancy of Britain as a global power was marked in southern Africa by its annexation of the Cape Colony in 1806 and the arrival of English settlers on the frontier of the eastern Cape in 1820. At this time, the colony remained predominantly rural, though its economic importance to Britain was as a way station for trade, rather than as an agricultural exporter. The population clustered into four main groups: the English, the Afrikaners (Dutch descendants who had developed their own Africanised culture and dialect), the so-called Cape Coloureds (an emerging community of mixed-race people), and the Xhosa (on the eastern frontier). Political conflicts over land rights among these groups gave rise to demands for government. At the same time, agitation against slavery by English missionaries drove many Afrikaners to trek northward in an effort to escape the reach of regulation.

The first colonial administrations were autocratic: Former military officers drawn from the ranks of the English aristocracy were appointed as colonial governors. An important political precedent was set in 1853, however, when Britain allowed the establishment of an elected legislative council. Henceforth, the country's political evolution would diverge from that in India, where elected institutions were not set up until almost a century later. Instead, the Cape Colony came more closely to resemble Canada (and later Australia and New Zealand), where Britain gradually granted self-government to a small but dominant group of British settlers. Although the first franchise was color-blind – it granted the vote to any adult male who owned property or earned a salary – Africans and Coloureds were effectively excluded from political life because they were poor.

As in other settler colonies (including the United States), contacts with white immigrants at first were devastating for some indigenous peoples. Even during the rule of the Dutch East India Company, the Khoisan hunters and herders of the western Cape had been decimated by European diseases like smallpox and measles. By the mid-19th century, Bantu-speaking groups as far north as the Limpopo River had lost their land, crops, and livestock to European invaders. Foreign conquest was not achieved by strength of numbers – blacks have always greatly outnumbered whites in South Africa – but by the technological superiority of a metropolitan industrial economy that could mass-produce firearms. This is not to say that conquest occurred easily; it was punctuated by hard-fought wars of resistance launched by the Xhosa in the eastern Cape in the 1840s, the Zulu in Natal in the 1850s, and the Sotho, the Venda, and the Pedi in the interior highlands in the 1860s. The Zulu, who had themselves earlier brutally repressed neighboring groups, managed to retain the identity and organization of a warrior nation throughout much of the 19th century.

Initially, four separate settler states were formed in the territory now known as South Africa. Apart from the Cape, the British controlled Natal, a second colony on the eastern seaboard, to which they imported laborers from colonial India (both Hindu and Muslim) to develop sugar plantations and railways. Christian missionaries were particularly active in Natal, establishing schools and hospitals that attracted displaced Africans into modernized lifestyles. On the high-altitude savanna, Afrikaner stock-farmers set up two agrarian republics based on the institutions of individual land title and an armed citizenry: The Orange Free State was a constitutional republic run by an elected assembly of white males under a semblance of legality, whereas the Transvaal was a much more rough-and-ready state held together by roving commandos. The political and religious leaders of these republics constructed a historical mythology of the Afrikaners as a chosen people who had thrown off the bonds of the British Empire and founded their own promised land.

While British colonies and Boer (Afrikaner farmer) republics thus had distinct origins, they nonetheless shared a patriarchal ideology that reduced the relations between the races to those of master and servant. For their part, the African peoples of the region ultimately proved more resilient than the aboriginal populations of the Cape. Shunted into "reserves" of low-quality land, they adapted to the new requirements of an emerging capitalist economy, growing crops for sale to the settlers (both on their own land and as sharecroppers), providing labor on white commercial farms, and adopting not only Christianized religions but also tastes for Western consumer goods. The presence of missionaries, labor recruiters, and tax collectors in the African territories further reduced the influence of hereditary chiefs, whose authority already had been undermined by conquest and colonization.

## THE PATH OF DEVELOPMENT

The economic growth of the region reached a major turning point in 1870 with the discovery in the southern African interior of the world's richest deposits of diamonds and gold. The resultant mining boom generated glittering profits for investors in Britain, Europe, and North America and, by the turn of the century, firmly integrated southern Africa into a global capitalist economy. Industrialization was accompanied by urbanization. Waves of English-speaking immigrants from around the world, and African migrant laborers from as far north as the modern Mozambique, Tanzania, and Zambia, converged on the boom towns of Kimberley and Johannesburg. From the outset, the industrial economy was constructed along racial lines. Whites were awarded skilled jobs with high wages and supervisory responsibilities, while black laborers were poorly paid and housed in spartan, male-only barracks. The joint stock companies that dominated the mining sector found common cause with the colonial governments in controlling the flow of labor by introducing "pass" laws, which ruled that no unemployed African could stay in an urban area without a valid identity document.

Political conflicts intensified over the country's newfound wealth. Despite deep differences between Boer and Briton, the colonists united to crush the last remnants of African resistance. Aided by intelligence reports from the Afrikaners and factionalism in the Zulu royal family – but not without significant military losses – an armed British expedition finally subdued the region's most powerful African kingdom in 1879. The Zulu monarchy was abolished and Zululand was divided into thirteen weakened parts under appointed chiefs. At the same time, Britain was determined to wrest political control of the goldfields from the Afrikaners in the Transvaal; after several unsuccessful attempts at annexation, it resorted to all-out war to guarantee imperial supremacy. The South African (Boer) War (1899–1902) pitted an orthodox British army of almost half a million soldiers against a mobile guerrilla force. A British victory was achieved only when Boer farms were burned to the ground and families were herded into camps, humiliations that rankled long after the war was over.

The peace settlement resulted in the political unification of the region and the creation of the modern state of South Africa. The constitution that established the Union of South Africa in 1910 contained several principles that profoundly shaped the course of subsequent events. First, the constitution followed a British Westminster model in which parliament was supreme within a unitary state (that is, with a single center of power rather than a federation), which gave the political party that controlled parliament considerable latitude. Second, the plural culture of the new state was acknowledged when English and Dutch (later supplanted by Afrikaans) were recognized as official languages of equal status. Finally, and most importantly, blacks (that is, Africans, Indians, and Coloureds, in the local lexicon) were denied a share of political power. The franchise laws of the former colonies remained in place, entirely excluding blacks from government in the new provinces of Transvaal, Orange Free State, and Natal. Voting rights for blacks were protected in the relatively more liberal Cape Province; in practice, however, blacks never accounted for more than one-seventh of the electorate and never elected one of their own to parliamentary office.

Instead, white settlers set about consolidating control of a large and potentially affluent African state whose autonomy from the mother country was further strengthened when the British Parliament abandoned legislative oversight in 1934. The period of the white-run Union (later Republic) of South Africa can be divided conveniently into two periods: first, when English speakers occupied the government (1910–48), and later, momentously, when Afrikaner nationalists took over (1948–94). Public policies during these periods differed in degree rather than kind; both aimed at racial segregation. The post-1948 apartheid regime, however, extended this idea to a deranged extreme by building barriers between the races into the very institutional structure of the state.

These political developments were offset by two countervailing forces. On the one hand, the expansion of the industrial economy required the creation of a stable urban workforce, a process which brought the races into ever-closer economic interdependence. At the same time, the enactment of discriminatory laws was matched at each stage by the emergence of new and gradually more militant forms of black resistance, starting with the formation in 1912 of the organization that became known as the African National Congress (ANC).

One of the first steps of the Union government was to pass a Native Lands Act (1913) that prohibited Africans from buying or leasing farms designated for whites. The effect of this legislation was to reduce the options for rural Africans to a cruel choice between bare subsistence in the reserves or agricultural wage labor. As for the urban areas, the state gave legal effect to the color bars that had become customary in the mining and manufacturing sectors; for example, the

Industrial Conciliation Act (1924) denied Africans the right to engage in collective bargaining. And in 1936, the Natives Representation Act removed Africans from the ordinary voter rolls in the Cape Province, even as white women were being enfranchised nationwide. These indignities fueled campaigns for legislative reform by a small elite of educated Africans – clergy, lawyers, and teachers – who had begun to rally under the ANC banner. They also prompted strikes led by the Industrial and Commercial Workers Union (formed 1928), even though labor actions had been ruled illegal. Indeed, despite segregation, Africans continued to pour into towns, surrounding the prim, white, middle-class suburbs with proletarian squatter settlements that teemed with violent discontent.

World War II (1939–45) deeply divided the white community. Many Afrikaners were distressed that South Africa entered a European conflict on the side of Great Britain, leading extremists in their midst to express open sympathy for Nazi ideas of racial purity. For their part, most English speakers welcomed a chance to mobilize South Africa's resources in support of the Allied war effort, which resulted in the rapid buildup of the country's coal, iron, and garment-manufacturing industries. Seeking to extend economic expansion after the war and recognizing the growing reliance of the economy on black labor, the United Party government of Jan Smuts suggested modest reforms to improve African wages and working conditions. But even these timid steps prompted a right-wing backlash. In the 1948 election, the Afrikaner electorate united behind the National Party (NP), which won a narrow victory, in part because rural voting districts were overrepresented. The government of D. F. Malan came to power at a time when ideas were gaining currency in the Afrikaner churches and secret societies about apartheid (literally, "apart-ness"). A monstrous social experiment to create a government of racial institutions was about to begin.

## THE APARTHEID EXPERIMENT

The National Party government began by packing the state apparatus – the army, the police, the civil service, and the publicly owned railways – with its own supporters. It ensured that Afrikaners would become the prime beneficiaries of agricultural and educational subsidies and of public construction contracts. Thus was state power used to enable social mobility for an Afrikaner population who had always resented the greater economic wealth of the English speakers. These developments, along with the duplication of public services for segregated communities, meant that the state in South Africa became large, strong, and riddled with patronage.

As the basis for apartheid, the government classified every citizen under the Population Registration Act (1950) into one of four racial categories: either African, Coloured, Indian, or White. New laws were introduced to prohibit sex and marriage between people of different races; the authorities even went so far as to break up existing mixed-race families. Under the Group Areas Act (also 1950), thriving multiracial neighborhoods like Sophiatown in Johannesburg and District Six in Cape Town were bulldozed and their inhabitants dispersed. Every public facility was segregated – from bus and train stations and drinking fountains to parks, cinemas, and beaches – by means of demeaning "Whites Only" signs. A Bantu Education Act (1953) effectively abolished mission schools for Africans, replacing them with substandard public institutions. Bent on removing every remaining vestige of political rights for people of color, the National Party did to Coloured voters in 1956 what the United Party government had earlier done to African voters: removed them from the common electoral rolls.

But the architect of apartheid, Hendrick Verwoerd (prime minister, 1958–66) had an even grander vision that called for the complete geographical partition of the races. Under the Bantu Homelands Constitution Act (1957), Africans were stripped of citizenship, expelled from the choicest parts of the country (which constituted 87 percent of the land area), and consigned to ten, scattered, ethnic "homelands." The implementation of this scheme – which included nominal political independence for unviable entities like Transkei and Bophutatswana – amounted to the largest forced movement of population anywhere in the postwar world. Because the impoverished homeland administrations could neither generate employment nor deliver basic services, relocation exacted a harsh toll of malnutrition, disease, and death.

The government's policy of "separate development," however, flew in the face of the reality that South Africa had become an economically integrated society. By 1980, at the peak of apartheid's ethnic cleansing, more than half of the nonwhite population continued to reside in towns, where 6.9 million Africans, 2 million Coloureds, and 700,000 Indians greatly outnumbered 4 million Whites.

Urban dwellers completely rejected the official fiction that Africans belonged in rural backwaters under the tutelage of "tribal" chiefs. Instead, a new generation of young leaders, such as Walter Sisulu, Oliver Tambo, and Nelson Mandela, recommitted the African National Congress (ANC) to multiracial democracy. In 1955 the ANC's Freedom Charter declared that "South Africa belongs to all who live in it, black and white, and that no government can justly claim authority unless it is based on the will of the people." The charter's mix of liberal values (equality before the law, freedom of speech, the right to vote) with more socialist ideas (free education and health care, public ownership of mines and industry), reflected the ANC's openness to various political tendencies. Other liberation movements – like the South African Communist Party (SACP, formed 1921), the Pan-Africanist Congress (PAC, formed 1959), and the Black Consciousness movement, (which coalesced in the 1970s around the ideas of Steve Biko) – sounded more radical and/or Afro-centric themes.

Resistance to apartheid started out peacefully as civil disobedience: Modeled on Gandhian principles of nonviolence, the anti-apartheid movement first took the form of the burning of "passes" or defiance of other discriminatory laws. In response, the police gunned down sixty-seven demonstrators at Sharpeville in 1960 and banned the ANC and PAC. Deprived of all opportunity to organize peacefully, resistance leaders had little choice but to take up arms. The military wings of the PAC and ANC – later known as the Azanian Peoples Liberation Army (APLA) and Umkhonto weSizwe (MK, or the Spear of the Nation) – embarked on bombing campaigns against state installations, such as electricity switching stations and post offices. Convicted for authorizing such attacks, Mandela and Sisulu were incarcerated under life sentences on Robben Island in 1964. There followed a long hiatus while the resistance movement gathered strength again, punctuated by a wave of strikes led by increasingly militant black workers' organizations in 1973, and by a courageous youth uprising in Soweto in 1976. The schoolchildren employed black-consciousness ideas to challenge the use of Afrikaans as a medium of instruction. Within a year, however, the police had arrested, tortured, and killed their hero, Steve Biko.

By the 1980s, apartheid had entered a crisis born of its own contradictions and of new pressures emanating from a changing world. Internally, the economy suffered from recession, currency inflation, and the excessive costs of administering a maze of oppressive social controls. As white professionals began to emigrate and blacks bore the brunt of a second-rate education system, the country encountered shortages of the skills necessary to operate its sophisticated economy. Then the National Party was rocked by a scandal over misappropriated public funds that forced the resignation of Prime Minister John Vorster. His successor, P. W. Botha, pursued a mixed strategy of repression and reform. On the one hand, he enhanced the powers of the presidency at the expense of the cabinet, drew military men into government through the State Security Council, and increasingly used the police as agents of local government. On the other hand, he tried (unsuccessfully) to co-opt Indians and Coloureds into their own separate legislatures and local government councils under a new 1984 constitution. By 1986, Botha had even authorized the repeal of selected "petty" apartheid laws in recognition of the fact that blacks now lived permanently in the heart of all major metropolitan areas.

Botha's strategy did not work because it continued to ignore majority political aspirations. It was overtaken by events as Africans in the urban townships and industrial workplaces took matters into their own hands. By the end of the 1970s, trade unions had won the right to organize legally, and strikes were occurring at unprecedented rates. In 1983, a United Democratic Front (UDF) of trade unions, churches, civic organizations and women's and youth groups coalesced to protest the new constitution. The UDF, considered by many to be a front for the ANC, completely disrupted urban local government through an orchestrated campaign of service and consumer boycotts, although too often, the resultant void of authority was quickly filled by intimidation and violence. Faced with open defiance – symbolized by the militant *toyi-toyi* dance performed en masse at political funerals – the Botha government had no answer except to deploy the army in a nationwide state of emergency in June 1986.

Internationally, South Africa was becoming increasingly isolated. Long gone were the halcyon days of the 1960s and 1970s when British traders and investors (followed by Americans, Germans, and Japanese) were attracted by a stable business climate. Gone, too, was the political support of U.S. President Richard Nixon, who had earlier concluded on the advice of Secretary of State Henry Kissinger that white settlers had a long-term future in southern Africa and were a valuable bulwark against communism. In place of these allies, South Africa faced an increasingly hostile Organization of African Unity (the international body of black African states) and Commonwealth (the association of former British colonies, many from Asia and Africa, from which South Africa had withdrawn in 1961 when it declared itself a republic). The United Nations was clamoring for South Africa to surrender its mandate over neighboring Namibia, to withdraw its troops from Angola, and immediately to dissolve apartheid. The Jimmy Carter administration in the United States came out openly for majority rule and, in 1986, the U.S. Congress overrode a veto by President Ronald Reagan in order to impose comprehensive economic sanctions against South Africa. The inflow of investment capital turned into an outflow. Not only at home, but also abroad, the South African state had become a pariah.

## AN UNEXPECTED TRANSITION

As political attitudes hardened on all sides, a race war seemed inevitable. Yet nothing that had gone before prepared South Africans for what was to come. Recognizing that further violence would devastate Africa's most productive economy, the leaders of the country's opposing political forces stepped back from the brink. Driven by their intertwined self-interests, they unexpectedly forged a peaceful passage that granted black majority rule in return for a continued place for whites in South Africa's bright economic sun. Against the backdrop of the end of the cold war, South Africa made a sudden transition to multiracial democracy in the mid-1990s.

Events in the 1980s had created the climate for negotiation and compromise. Cut off from flows of international capital, the economy began to shrink, driving the South African government to seek rehabilitation in the eyes of the Western world. The collapse of communism in the Soviet Union and Eastern Europe deprived the ANC of its main sources of political, financial, and military support. Because both sides therefore lacked the means to win an outright military victory, each began to see virtue in coming to terms. Thus, political contacts were initiated: openly, between white businessmen and the ANC leaders in exile, and secretly, between government officials and ANC prisoners within the country. These encounters reassured the government that Nelson Mandela would not insist on a winner-take-all solution and would respect minority (i.e., white) rights. Soon after acceding to the leadership of the National Party, Frederick Willem (F. W.) de Klerk decided to gamble on political reform while Afrikaners were still enjoying a measure of control over the political situation. On February 2, 1990, he announced that Mandela would be released, banned parties could resume political activities, and negotiations for an inclusive new political order would begin. Nine days later, in the glare of global television coverage, Mandela walked free.

Negotiations over the country's political future began at the end of 1991 when delegates from the government, the ANC, and seventeen other political organizations, including leaders from the ethnic homelands, gathered in the Convention for a Democratic South Africa (CODESA). Some political parties held back: Leftist black-power movements, such as the PAC, continued to favor armed struggle ("one settler, one bullet"); and conservative groups, such as the Inkatha Freedom Party (IFP), which appealed to Zulu traditionalists, launched attacks on ANC supporters with the covert connivance of the South African security forces. CODESA and the multiparty forums that followed were "on-again, off-again" affairs, regularly breaking down in the face of violent incidents (like the massacre of shack dwellers at Boipatong in 1992 and the 1993 assassination of the popular Communist Party secretary general, Chris Hani). It is ironic, however, that the ever-present specter of escalating disorder repeatedly helped to drive the parties back to the negotiating table.

At issue in negotiations was the shape of the political order. The two major parties could agree on a few basic points – one person–one vote, an independent judiciary, and the reintegration of the homelands – but on little else. Whereas the ANC insisted on a unitary state, the NP (at first) and IFP (throughout) favored federalism. Whereas the ANC wanted majority rule, their opponents called for a rotating presidency and minority vetoes. These differences were ultimately resolved through a series of behind-the-scenes pacts: a political pact to share power in a government of national unity (GNU) for five years; an economic pact to guarantee property rights and civil-service positions and pensions; and a military pact to extend amnesty to individuals on all sides who confessed to politically motivated crimes. While these deals were struck largely as a result of the self-interested calculations of South African elites, the international community kept nudging the peace process forward with promises of diplomatic recognition, aid, and investment.

The multiparty negotiating forum of 1993 eventually produced a transitional government, an interim constitution, and a timetable for the country's first open elections. The interim constitution was modeled on a variety of sources – German, American, and Indian, among others – but, more than anything, it reflected the art of the possible in South Africa's complex society. It was a quasi-federal document that provided for nine provincial legislatures and eleven official languages. It imported conventional ideas from abroad, such as proportional representation, according to which seats were allocated in the national and provincial assemblies based on the share of the electoral votes won by each political party. But it was original in its provisions for a GNU, whereby parties also obtained seats in a coalition cabinet on the basis of their share of the vote.

The election was scheduled for April 27, 1994. From the outset, the campaign was fraught with uncertainty. Inkatha and the far-right Conservative Party announced that they would not take part because the new constitution did not provide autonomy for either a Zulu kingdom or an Afrikaner republic. As a result of growing armed clashes between supporters of the IFP and the ANC, a state of emergency was declared in the Natal province. Chief Mangosuthu Buthelezi, the leader of most rural Zulus, was effectively sidelined from negotiations by Mandela and de Klerk. In return, he appeared willing to risk civil war and to sacrifice South Africa's transition to democracy in pursuit of personal political ambitions and his people's regional interests. Eventually realizing that the transition would occur without him, however, Buthelezi ended his brinkmanship barely one week before the election by announcing that the IFP would take part.

In the event, the 1994 election in South Africa was a celebration, both solemn and jubilant, of a momentous historical shift. For the first time ever, South Africa's diverse peoples participated as political equals in the democratic ritual of choosing their own leaders. The election brought an end to 350 years of settler colonial rule and, with it, the perverse idea that the right to self-government was the preserve of some races but not others.

To be sure, South Africa's founding election did not run entirely smoothly: Voters had to wait in long lines to cast their ballots, some for several days; and the result in Kwazulu-Natal probably owed as much to an elite political bargain as to a valid vote. Nevertheless, the high voter turnout (86 percent of all adults) and the peacefulness at the polls throughout the country enabled the Independent Electoral Commission to declare the election "substantially free and fair." The ANC won a solid majority (62.7 percent of the vote), followed by the National Party and the IFP (20.4 percent and 10.5 percent, respectively), each of which secured control of at least one provincial legislature (in the Western Cape and Kwazulu-Natal, respectively). These three parties formed the Government of National Unity, with Nelson Mandela as President and F. W. de Klerk as his second executive deputy. Against all expectations, these farsighted and level-headed leaders – who deservedly shared the 1992 Nobel Peace Prize – had averted revolution, created a culture of compromise, and – unexpectedly – pulled democracy out of the hat.

# THE SOCIOECONOMIC STRUCTURE

Despite the drama of the democratic transition, change in the political sphere was offset by socioeconomic continuities. South Africa's first elected government inherited a society and economy whose population was mutually estranged, not only in terms of race but also by wealth and well-being. The economy had never been designed to serve a black majority – including a vast, impoverished under-class – that now clamored for jobs, houses, and education. Could South Africans from different social backgrounds emerge from a bitter political conflict and put old divisions behind them? Whereas whites tended to see the democratic transi-tion as the end of a difficult process of change, blacks saw it as just a beginning.

South Africa has always been a predominantly African country, though official policies acknowledged this only after 1994. According to the 1996 census, the total population is just over 40 million persons, of whom some 77 percent are African, 11 percent are White, 9 percent are Coloured, and 3 percent are Asian. The most commonly spoken languages are Zulu (23 percent), Xhosa (18 percent) and dialects of Sotho (17 percent), followed by Afrikaans and English (14 and 9 percent, respectively). Although South Africans are relatively well-educated – 73 percent are literate – many people have received poor-quality schooling and remain uncomfortable in English, the country's main language of government and business. Yet over one-half live in towns (54 percent), and the urban areas are growing at more than twice the rate of the nation as a whole (4.9 percent versus 2 percent).

With the largest and most sophisticated economy on the continent and a gross national product (GNP) of rand 6,854 per person in 1994 (then about $1,950), South Africa is a middle-income country. It features bustling cities with gleaming skyscrapers, modern highways filled with fancy German and Japanese automo-biles, and vast irrigated farms employing the latest agricultural technologies. Indeed, the country's stock of physical infrastructure (roads, railways, harbors, power grids, and water networks), financial institutions (banks, insurance compa-nies, a stock market), and business and technological skills is impressive by inter-national standards. After stalling in the late 1980s and early 1990s, the economy revived after 1994: Over the next three years the GNP grew at a rate exceeding population growth for the first time in two decades. Foreign debt was low and inflation was under control. Importantly, because the South African economy was capable of financing socioeconomic development from domestic resources, the government had little need for aid or loans from international donors.

Contradicting these advantages, however, are poverty and inequality. At least one-third of economically active South Africans lack a formal job, with unemploy-ment being highest among young people, women, and Africans. The average monthly wage of an employed African (rand 1,137 in 1995 or about $300) is barely above the amount needed for the subsistence of a low-income household. Thus, poverty haunts not only the unemployed but also many families with wage earners. Among the African population, 12 percent lack access to clean water, 25 percent have only minimal sanitation, and 53 percent (even more in rural areas) are without electricity. The most common living conditions for the poor are either a mud-and-thatch hut in a bleak and isolated rural backwater or, more commonly, a homemade shack in a garbage-strewn, urban settlement.

Thus, grinding poverty coexists alongside brazen displays of wealth. Among countries that keep reliable records on the gap between the "haves" and the "have-nots," South Africa ranks as one of the most unequal societies in the world, second only to Brazil. The poorest 20 percent of households earns just 3 percent of the country's income, whereas the richest 20 percent earns fully 63 percent. According to the Human Development Index of the United Nations, the lifestyle enjoyed by white South Africans is equivalent to that of New Zealanders, whereas black South Africans live under conditions similar to their counterparts in Congo-Brazzaville. Asians and Coloureds fall somewhere in between.

Such severe social inequalities, combined with a legacy of brutal politics, have bred crime and social violence. South Africa's murder rate – 65 deaths per day in 1997 – leads the world; other manifestations include gang wars, organized bank heists, and an illegal international trade in drugs, guns, and diamonds. The government claims that it has reduced crime, but the facts are mixed: While some offenses like murder may be falling, others like residential burglary continue to climb. Conventional wisdom connects crime with joblessness, but this economic interpretation does not explain the linkage between crime and violence. Here it is necessary to remember that South Africa's seemingly smooth political transition was actually very turbulent. Both the security forces and some anti-apartheid activists adopted tactics of intimidation and vigilantism. A gap in authority opened up between a repressive state and an ungovernable citizenry, into which large numbers of weapons have continued to flow. Fear of crime is pervasive among South Africans, more so, according to public-opinion polls, among blacks than whites.

Scholars have engaged in heated debates about whether South African politics are better understood in terms of social identities like ethnicity or with reference to the interests of economic classes. What seems important, however, is that race and class significantly overlap in South Africa; in social science terminology, social and economic cleavages tend to reinforce rather than cross-cut. To the extent that apartheid was an integrated system that used racial classification not only to exert political control (over blacks) but also to accumulate wealth (for whites), it resulted in particularly deep and lasting divisions.

Thus apartheid's legacy of race-based material inequality remains the starting point for any analysis of the dynamics of the country's contemporary politics. The inherited socioeconomic structure has profoundly shaped the design of political institutions in the country's new constitution. Inequality between the races remains a potentially explosive source of political instability that could still turn South Africa into yet another failed multiethnic state. And the capacity of elected governments to deliver social justice has already become the standard by which many South Africans evaluate the merits of democracy.

## CONTEMPORARY POLITICAL IDENTITIES

To what extent, then, are contemporary South African politics shaped by social identities, particularly race, but also by culture and region? Is it possible to build a shared sense of nationhood in this deeply divided, multicultural society?

Nelson Mandela staked his political career on the proposition that the country belongs to all its people. He used his considerable moral authority to promote a vision of "reconciliation" in which South Africa's diverse groups forgo revenge and live peacefully side by side in a "rainbow nation." To this end, the first cabinet of Mandela's GNU was truly multiracial, made up of sixteen Africans, eight Whites, and six Indians or Coloureds. The transition spawned new symbols of national unity, such as a multicolored flag and an anthem that melds the favorite hymns of the old and new regimes. In this sports-mad country, citizens of all races demonstrate their patriotism by enthusiastically embracing these symbols at national soccer and rugby matches. And in public-opinion surveys, more than 90 percent of respondents agree that they feel "proud" to call themselves "South Africans."

Nevertheless, the same surveys show that most citizens still also identify, first and foremost, with narrower subcommunities. Even as they profess newfound commitments to nonracialism, South Africans still behave politically as if they belong to ethnic blocs. In important respects, for example, the founding election of 1994 was a kind of "ethnic census": Fewer than 3 percent of Whites cast ballots for the (black-led) ANC, and fewer than 5 percent of Africans chose the (White-led) National Party. The fact that two-thirds of Coloured and Indian voters sided with White-led parties suggests that these communities also felt racial distance from Africans and were concerned about the consequences of majority rule. These concerns center on the potential for domination of the electoral process by one demographic group. Because black Africans constitute some 69 percent of the electorate, and because about 75 percent of them express loyalty to the ANC, the ruling party would seem to enjoy a permanent, built-in majority. With a dominant ruling party and a fragmented opposition, it is difficult to see how South Africa can attain an electoral alternation of governments. This aspect of democracy would require the realignment of voter support away from its present racial structure.

Indeed, the salience of race in South African politics has hardly declined since 1994. The government ordered that racial categories be restored in the collection and reporting of official data, arguing that this was necessary if existing inequities were to be addressed. Also introduced were policies of affirmative action to create job opportunities for disadvantaged groups, which, while encouraging the much-needed transformation of institutions throughout society, also helped to keep a consciousness of ethnicity alive. Race relations are marred by harsh stereotypes: Many South African whites believe that their black counterparts lack the technical capacity to operate a complex economy and government; aware of these preju-dices, many blacks are overly sensitive to criticism, tending to dismiss even con-structive dissent as racism. Thus have debates between the government and the opposition – especially in parliament and in the press – too often lapsed into a defensive exchange of epithets.

To South Africa's advantage, however, ethnic groupings do not always coincide completely with territorial boundaries. The requirements of the industrial econ-omy long ago brought blacks and whites together in workplaces across the coun-try and now, increasingly, into residential proximity in the major cities. Economic integration, therefore, continues to dissolve the mutual isolation of the two main racial communities. Some smaller minority groups, however, remain clustered in their own areas: For instance, 83 percent of the Coloureds live in the Cape provinces, especially around Cape Town, and 78 percent of Asians live in Kwazulu-Natal, especially in Durban. In these cases, geographical concentration has proba-bly helped minorities avoid being shut out from politics entirely. In the long run, however, any party that wishes to govern at the national level in South Africa must attract black votes. For these reasons, and following ANC precedents, the emergence in 1997 of a multiracial opposition party called the United Democratic Movement (the first being the ANC) was a seemingly positive development for competitive democracy.

Indeed, ethnic interpretations of South African politics should not be pushed too far. The struggle over the allegiance of the Zulu people is not a simple "black-on-black" tribal conflict. Instead, the Zulu are internally split; while rural folk have been attracted to the Inkatha Freedom Party (which has borrowed symbols of Zulu culture like spears, shields, and leopard skins), many urban Zulus support the ANC. Political killings in the countryside have usually arisen when ANC adher-ents have sought to mobilize support back home, only to invoke a counterreac-tion from Inkatha traditionalists who perceive a threat to the power and status of the *amakhosi* (chiefs). While the level of political violence between the IFP and ANC declined in Kwazulu-Natal after 1994, it began to rise again as the 1999 elec-tions approached. The persistence of violence prompted the top leadership of the two parties to reopen negotiations, including open talk of a governing alliance. To ease tensions and demonstrate trust, Mandela appointed IFP leader Buthelezi not only as minister of home affairs, but also as acting president during the former's absences from the country.

Both Zulu and Afrikaner nationalists now seem to recognize that separation from the South African state is both undesirable and impractical and, instead, have turned their attention to preserving their languages and cultures. Under the interim constitution, Afrikaans was downgraded from one of the two official languages and, when the terms of a permanent constitution were being negotiated in 1996, language rights became a core issue. Afrikaner leaders sought to portray the ANC's multicultural project as an effort to subjugate linguistic minorities (including Zulu speakers and Afrikaans-speaking Coloureds). Thus were racial and ethnic differences bridged by shared cultural concerns. Again, Mandela bent over backward to accommodate differences, recognizing that extremists among cultural minorities could constitute a threat to the stability of the political system if not incorporated within it.

Other potential bases for political identity include religion and gender. As elsewhere in Africa, religious movements that combine Christian and indigenous beliefs have strong popular appeal. The largest voluntary association in the country is the African Zion Church, which has more active members than the ANC or the trade-union confederation. Such independent churches advocate traditional African values, such as *ubuntu* (community), as a sharp rebuke to a pervasive Western consumer culture. Accordingly, religion serves not so much to mobilize people into politics as to encourage withdrawal from a secular world that is seen as excessively materialistic, corrupt, and competitive. The innate social conservatism of many South Africans also expresses itself in the suppression of women. Whether in Afrikaner, Zulu, or Xhosa families, the older males dominate and women are expected to confine themselves silently to the domestic sphere. In cosmopolitan urban areas, disrespect for females is expressed in disturbingly frequent incidents of rape and domestic violence. Despite sweeping guarantees against sexism in the South African Constitution, women in South Africa have yet to organize effectively on the basis of gender identity.

Finally, while racial discrimination is no longer socially acceptable, new forms of exclusion are arising. Even as a new "South African" identity begins to take shape, nationalism reveals its darker side. Xenophobia (fear of the "other") is on the rise against the hundreds of thousands of political refugees and economic migrants from other parts of Africa who have streamed into the country since the democratic transition. In the context of an economy that cannot generate enough employment for local entrants into the labor market, foreigners are too often blamed for job shortages, diseases, and criminal activities for which they are not responsible. Attacks on strangers are on the rise. And respect for equal political rights – both within South Africa's diverse citizenry and between citizens and outsiders – remains in short supply.

## CONTEMPORARY POLITICAL INTERESTS

If the development of an industrial economy helped to dissolve divisions between the races, then it also helped to create social classes. At the same time as South Africans have tried to shrug off the ethnic labels imposed by apartheid, they have devised new forms of political solidarity based on economic interests. As in other capitalist economies, class conflict in South Africa revolves mainly around the divergence of interests between business and labor.

Under apartheid, the government and private companies got together to prohibit African workers from joining trade unions, engaging in collective bargaining, or going on strike. But a vast, semiskilled, industrial workforce with the power to bring economic production to a halt could not be resisted indefinitely. Escalating strikes in the metal, textile, and chemical industries forced the old government to officially recognize African trade unions in 1979 and to acquiesce to the formation of a federated Congress of South African Trade Unions (COSATU) in 1985. By 1990, COSATU's fourteen affiliated unions represented 1.2 million workers. At first, the unions focused on securing better wages and working conditions, refusing to align themselves with any political movement. With the advent of COSATU, however, organized workers entered the "national democratic struggle" under the leadership of the ANC.

As in Poland and Zambia, the labor movement was a key actor in South Africa's late-20th-century transition to democracy. In 1991, COSATU successfully pushed for amendments to the Labor Relations Act that established mediation procedures for settling industrial disputes. When political negotiations over the country's future began to break down in 1992, COSATU orchestrated the "rolling mass action" (marches, stoppages, and stay-aways) that backed up the ANC's bargaining positions. And, in 1994, when the ANC announced lists of candidates for national and provincial parliaments in the GNU, the names of seventy COSATU leaders were included. Because the labor movement played a crucial role in building support for the ANC's electoral victory, COSATU expected the new government to adopt labor-friendly policies.

As it happened, worker interests were not always protected, in part because the ANC had also developed close ties with private capital. Such contacts grew from tentative overtures between business and political leaders in the late 1980s to substantial corporate contributions to the ANC's election campaign in 1994. In the intervening period, entrepreneurs had set up projects to uplift the poor, brought together diverse interest groups to discuss options for the future, and sponsored research on policies for the post-apartheid era. By the time Mandela put together the national unity government, it seemed only natural that he would seek guidance from Harry Oppenheimer – former chairman of Anglo-American Corporation, South Africa's largest conglomerate – about appointments to key economic portfolios in the cabinet.

Though learning occurred on both sides, contacts with business interests – both domestic and international – transformed the ANC's approach to economic policy. The ANC had long preferred a socialist strategy based on the "seizure" of the "commanding heights of the economy" (such as land, industries, and banks). Even as Mandela was being released from prison in 1990, he reiterated the movement's commitment to the nationalization of the means of production and the redistribution of wealth. But moderate voices within the ANC began to question whether it was advisable to grab property and raise taxes in an era of mobile international capital. By late 1991, on a visit to the United States, Mandela was reassuring corporate executives, the World Bank, and U.S. President George Bush that nationalization was no longer in the cards. Instead, the ANC declared that economic growth was the best means for addressing poverty, which in turn was only possible if private companies – local and foreign – felt confident enough to invest.

In revising its economic strategy, the ANC did not completely jettison a role for the state. After all, the new government announced the Reconstruction and Development Programme (RDP) in 1994 that envisaged socioeconomic "transformation" through public investments in education, housing, health care, electricity and other basic amenities. The fact that the RDP was originally a COSATU blueprint is evidence that popular, working-class interests remained critical in shaping ANC thinking. But the RDP was unable to address citizens' (and the unions') most pressing demand: jobs. To this end, the government introduced a set of free-market measures in 1996 known as GEAR (for Growth, Employment and Redistribution). GEAR sought to accelerate South Africa's annual economic growth rate to 6 percent by restraining government spending, deregulating the economy, and selling off state-owned enterprises. In this case, the source of ideas was a report called "Growth for All" authored by the South African Foundation, a body sponsored by the business community.

The South African government thus finds itself at the fulcrum of class conflict. It must perform a delicate balancing act among rival political interests. How can it satisfy the expectations of the downtrodden for improved living standards without at the same time driving away the capital and skills needed to make the economy grow? In search of solutions, the government built on the country's experience with negotiation and compromise. It established a bargaining forum called the National Economic Development and Labour Council (NEDLAC), in which workers, employers, and the state discuss propose legislation before the parliament enacts it. NEDLAC represents what political scientists call corporatism: an institutional arrangement that channels the representation of conflicting interests into a process of cooperative decision making. Because corporatism allows extra weight to groups who are more powerful than their mere numbers would allow, it has led to economic policies in South Africa that are more market-oriented than most ANC supporters would like. At first, COSATU showed restraint at this departure from its interests, but a rising tide of strike actions in the late 1990s suggested that the patience of workers is wearing thin.

The government can make economic adjustments without losing too much political support, however, in part because the class structure is changing. As race barriers are removed, new social groups – notably a black bourgeoisie – are emerging. In the decade before 1994, the personal disposable income of Africans increased by more than 35 percent, while the disposable income of Whites dropped slightly. Since 1994, a new African elite has eagerly embraced money making and American-style consumption, perhaps because private enrichment was so long denied them. Private companies have "unbundled" assets for sale to this new class of investors to the point that blacks now own more than one-tenth of the wealth on the Johannesburg Stock Exchange, though they have still to make headway in operational control of enterprises. As a result, income inequality has risen to almost the same level within the black community as for the society as a whole.

Even the working class is not immune to the allure of the market. COSATU's member unions have established profit-making companies and invested worker retirement funds in the stock market. Trade-union leaders now sit on the boards of major corporations, even in the deeply conservative mining sector. These movements in the class structure have unsettled relations within the trade unions and between unionized workers and the unemployed. Labor leaders face charges that they have "sold out" to capitalism, and calls have started for a new political party of the left. The more militant members of COSATU see their own organization as the vehicle for such a party, openly urging the unions to split from their alliance with the ANC.

For the moment, however, the majority party's hold on the electorate is secure. The 1999 elections produced an increased percentage of votes for the ANC (66 percent) that fell just short of the two-thirds majority needed to change the constitution. Having delivered human dignity and political equality, the ANC can continue convincingly to portray itself as the advocate of the impoverished majority. Indeed, the ANC's support is probably based more on the material interests of its supporters than on their racial identities. After all, the ANC membership, which is overwhelmingly African, elected seven non-Africans to the top ten positions on the party's national executive committee in 1997. Moreover, the Pan Africanist Congress (PAC), which advocates a black-consciousness line, has never been able to garner more than 2 percent of the national vote. Instead, citizens seem to see the ANC as the country's best bet for reducing the gap between the haves and the have-nots. Indeed, the consolidation of democracy in South Africa may well depend on the capacity of the majority party to satisfy exactly these material expectations, an issue that we return to in the Conclusion of this chapter.

# DEMOCRATIC POLITICAL INSTITUTIONS

The purpose of government is to provide authoritative decisions that resolve political conflicts among opposing identities and interests. To govern (to "rule") is to issue decisions ("rulings") that must be obeyed by everyone. Under an authoritarian regime (like the old apartheid system), citizens reluctantly comply with the commands of government because they fear that the state will unleash violence against them if they do not. Under a democratic regime (such as South Africa's political arrangement since 1994), citizens grant compliance more willingly because they regard an elected government as having been legitimately installed. Ideally, a good government is both responsive to popular demands and effective at enforcing its own policy decisions.

Governments convert demands into policies by means of political institutions. Several key institutions are essential to a democracy. These include a constitution with a bill of rights, checks on executive powers, a regular cycle of open elections, and a vibrant and autonomous civil society. Each of these (sets of) political institutions is examined in this section. And special mention is made of two bodies – the Constitutional Court and the Truth and Reconciliation Commission – that have made distinctive contributions to South Africa's development as a democracy.

The South African Constitution, ratified in 1997, is extremely liberal. Widely praised internationally, it was produced by the GNU's Constituent Assembly and is the jewel of the first government's political accomplishments. As well as a full gamut of civil and political rights (e.g, to freedom of speech and association and to voting), the constitution's bill of rights also includes wide guarantees of access to food, water, education, health care, and social security. These social and economic rights are explicitly extended to children. Certain offsetting provisions reflect South Africa's unique history: Freedom of expression is qualified with prohibitions on hate speech; rights to one's cultural heritage are allowed only to the extent that they do not infringe the rights of others; and property rights do not preclude the possibility of redistributive measures (like land reform). Adopted by an overwhelming parliamentary majority, the constitution has won broad acceptance throughout society. Given the generosity of its promises, however, it has yet to be proved fully enforceable.

As in other countries, the constitution of South Africa lays the foundation for the rule of law. It requires a measured separation of central government powers, assigning these conventionally to legislative, executive, and judicial branches of government. It is unconventional, however, in the relative balance ascribed to the executive and legislature, resulting in a democratic system that is neither presidential nor parliamentary, but a hybrid of the two. On one hand, the constitution (rather than the parliament) is now supreme. And the constitution provides for an executive president who enjoys extensive powers of appointment and decision making. On the other hand, the president is not elected directly (but by the National Assembly from among its own numbers), and he or she must select cabinet members from the assembly and dissolve the government if faced with a "no confidence" vote. Because of these formal limitations, the South African chief political executive looks more like a Commonwealth prime minister than the "superpresident" commonly found in other African republics.

In practical political terms, however, the ANC's large working majority in the parliament has enabled the executive to control the legislature. In South Africa, the parliament is bicameral, meaning that it has two houses: the National Assembly and the National Council of Provinces, both currently based in Cape Town. The parliament has been active since 1994, passing an average of 108 laws in each of its first three annual sessions, many of which reversed the thrust of apartheid legislation. But almost all bills originated from the president's office or from other departments in the executive branch. Tight political discipline exerted by the ANC's party caucus has inhibited ANC members of parliament (MPs) from questioning their own ministers. Major decisions on economic policy – such as the shift of emphasis from service delivery under the RDP to job creation under GEAR – were made within the executive branch and without consultation with MPs. The ANC's domination of the parliamentary agenda has been aided by opposition MPs, who tend to raise minority issues (e.g., language rights) rather than mainstream concerns (like jobs, education, and housing).

So far, the judiciary has been more independent than the legislature. The Constitutional Court, which has final say on fundamental legal matters, rejected the draft constitution until provisions were included to strengthen the rights of individuals, the autonomy of provincial governments, and public oversight by watchdog agencies. Although being careful to frame its judgments narrowly, the court has already tilted the scales in favor of social justice: In a landmark ruling in 1998, for example, residents of upscale white suburbs in Johannesburg were ordered to accept increases in property taxes that enabled municipal services to be extended to disadvantaged black townships, such as Soweto. To date, the executive branch has abided by the rulings of the judiciary, even when these have required the president to appear personally in court. This commitment to the rule of law is all the more remarkable given that the higher courts are staffed mainly by elderly judges held over from the previous regime. Compared with the nonracial legislature and the executive, the judiciary is the least "transformed" branch of government.

Because South Africa's recent past was marred by gross violations of human rights, the new order included special institutions to deal with this legacy. Again to international acclaim, the new government established the Truth and Reconciliation Commission (TRC) in 1995 under the supervision of Archbishop Desmond Tutu, a Nobel Peace Prize winner in his own right. The TRC was charged with three tasks: to uncover the truth about human-rights abuses under apartheid; to offer amnesty to those who confessed a politically motivated involvement; and to make reparations to victims. The commission sought a creative solution to South Africa's past problems of state-sponsored and intercommunal political violence that would avoid an escalating spiral of punishment and revenge. Armed with the stick of subpoena power and the carrot of amnesty, it was easily the most powerful commission of its kind ever created.

Several thousand victims testified before the TRC's public hearings, which provided a chance for those who had suffered in silence at last to be heard. A stream of low-level apartheid functionaries also came forward to admit, in chilling detail, how they had served as the covert hit men of the old order. The commission also delved into the misdeeds of the liberation movements, including torture in former ANC training camps and the alleged involvement of Winnie Madikizela-Mandela (then Nelson's wife) in several murders in the late 1980s. The TRC's extraordinary achievement was to cast a spotlight on the inner secrets of the apartheid years, making denial difficult and reducing the likelihood that its horrors can ever recur.

By the time the TRC issued its final report in late 1998, however, it faced criticism from across the political spectrum. Unconfessed perpetrators from all political parties cried foul. Because senior figures, such as former Prime Minister P. W. Botha and IFP leader Gatsha Buthelezi, refused to testify, the truth remained obscure about the chain of command in the killing of anti-apartheid activists. The families of some victims also expressed anger at a process that opened old wounds and offered little succor afterward. Indeed, the TRC confirmed that truth does not always lead to reconciliation. The graffito scrawled on a Pretoria underpass – "Tutu has made them confess, now we will kill them!" – surely represents an extreme view, but it nonetheless captures the missing element: justice. For many South Africans, the righting of wrongs will require more than criminal amnesty for official perpetrators; it also requires a meaningful measure of social justice that involves broad sacrifices from apartheid's multiple beneficiaries.

In the context of persistent social divisions, the political institutions of democracy offer one way forward. While democracy requires more than elections, elections are an essential first step in installing democracy. Although imperfectly administered, the April 1994 elections laid the foundations for diverse communities to agree, for the first time, on a constitution of their own making. In both the interim and new constitutions, South Africans chose an electoral system based on proportional representation (PR). This seemed like an appropriate choice, not only because the previous constituency-based, winner-take-all system had helped the National Party rise to power, but also because rules of proportionality ensure that all voices are heard. In practice in South Africa, though, PR has also created new problems. Because candidates for legislative office are not chosen by local districts, but are selected by their parties to run on a national electoral list, citizens have found it difficult to hold MPs accountable. A "representation gap" quickly grew between voters and political elites.

Local-government elections were held in seven of the country's nine provinces in late 1995, though polls had to be delayed until 1996 in the Western Cape and Kwazulu-Natal due to organizational problems or political violence. These elections confirmed ANC control of the major urban areas, while allowing pockets of minority government in some municipalities. The local polls also introduced several innovations, including a voters' register and a mixed electoral system that combined constituency and proportional representation. Voter registration was also required for the elections to national and provincial legislatures held in June 1999. After this date, the government was no longer constitutionally bound to share executive power with minority parties, though the ANC again chose to offer cabinet seats to Inkatha. With its second national election, the country completed a transition to a multiparty democracy featuring a government in power and an out-of-power opposition.

## BUREAUCRATIC STATE INSTITUTIONS

When South Africans refer to "government" (or "Pretoria," the city where most government offices are found), they usually mean the executive. The executive is the branch of government charged with running the country between elections. It comprises the president, the deputy president, the cabinet, and all government ministries and departments. The Department of Finance (in consultation with an independent Financial and Fiscal Commission that oversees the distribution of revenues to provincial and local governments) is responsible for drawing up the national budget.

From the outset, President Nelson Mandela chose to concentrate on solving high-profile political problems and on performing the presidency's ceremonial duties; he delegated policy making and routine administrative decisions to Deputy President Thabo Mbeki. For his part, Mbeki pulled the power of the executive firmly into his own hands by enlarging his staff and instituting procedures for managing the policy process. In a smooth leadership succession, the ANC gradually prepared the country and the world for Mandela's retirement and Mbeki's ascent to the presidency in 1999. While South Africans may never love the technocratic Mr. Mbeki as much as they do the charismatic Mr. Mandela, they are already accustomed to having a new man in charge.

As with the legislature, the executive in South Africa is strongly influenced by the majority political party. The top organs of the ANC – its National Congress, National Executive Committee (NEC), and National Working Committee (NWC) – lay down the policies that the government must follow. The NEC is the party's highest policy-making body between party congresses, and the NWC is responsible for the day-to-day running of the organization. Because most cabinet ministers also serve as ANC officeholders, party ideas regularly find their way into government policy. But if ANC activists aim to blur the line between the executive and the party, senior civil servants seek to define it clearly. The directors-general (DGs) of government departments – the senior civil servants who provide professional advice and management – are often able to influence policy in their own right. Similarly, insofar as government programs are funded by foreign aid, international donors insist on technical requirements that counterbalance the party's political weight.

Precisely because modern governments control considerable resources – such as expertise, budgets, and coercion – the potential always exists for the abuse of power. This threat increases to the extent that the ANC government aims to accumulate and centralize power in order to radically "transform" society. Certainly, South Africa's previous National Party government was highly secretive, an impulse that still guides bureaucrats today; and a culture of corruption took deep root in the former "homeland" governments that have been incorporated into current provincial administrations. A 1996 public-opinion poll revealed that 40 percent of South African citizens saw the new government as equally (or more) corrupt than the one it replaced. A string of corruption cases reported in the national press – theft from a national school-meal program, the illegal sale of drivers' licences, nonexistent "ghost workers" on the state payroll, and violations in contract-tendering procedures in health and housing – suggests that there is substance behind such popular perceptions.

On paper, South Africa's constitution provides plentiful antidotes to the abuse of executive power: A Human Rights Commission is charged with redressing violations and educating the citizenry; a public protector receives citizen complaints about lax or unfair administration; and an auditor-general reports to legislatures on executives' use of taxpayer money. At first, the ANC sought to expand these ample provisions for public oversight, for example by passing a model code of conduct for parliamentarians. With the passage of time, however, the ANC has backed off from early commitments to transparency, for instance by stalling on an Open Democracy Bill that would provide freedom of information about the workings of government. And, in practice, the operations of all public-watchdog agencies have been limited by budgetary constraints imposed by the Ministry of Finance; none functions comprehensively at the provincial or local levels, where most abuses occur. If such institutions cannot be sustained, executive accountability may be difficult to obtain in this new democracy.

At the heart of executive authority is the coercive power of the state. Under apartheid, the South African government had used the state security apparatus – the army, the police, and the intelligence services – not only against neighboring countries but also against its own people. Since 1994, the role of the army has been redefined (to guard against external threats and to keep peace in regional conflicts), and the defense budget has been slashed in favor of social spending. A smaller South African National Defense Force (SANDF) has been built by combin-

ing selected elements from the old regular army and the armed wings of the guerrilla movements. In 1998, General Sipiwe Nyanda, a former guerrilla commander,
was made chief of staff of the SANDF. While not entirely eliminating racial tensions
over promotions and salaries, such appointments have helped the executive
establish civilian control over the military, greatly reducing the possibility of an
illegal coup (seizure of power).

More troublesome are the intelligence services and the police, which still contain elements uncommitted to the new political order, some of whom have
indulged in disruptive "dirty tricks." Citizens have not forgotten that the South
African Police Services (SAPS) were used as paramilitary shock troops to impose
order during the township uprisings of the 1970s and 1980s. The police are widely
distrusted by South Africans of all races because they lack professional training
(for example, in crime control and community relations) and because their ranks
remain riddled with racists and even criminals. This lack of public confidence is
not alleviated by a justice system that regularly fails to convict offenders. Instead,
prosecutors are overworked, witnesses are inadequately protected, hearings are
endlessly postponed, and many badly prepared cases are thrown out of court. As
such, the government is widely regarded as soft on crime.

Which brings us to the biggest challenge faced by the new South African government: building institutional capacity. As stated, governments must be effective
at implementing their own policies and at eliciting citizen compliance. In short,
they must govern. The period following the 1994 transition in South Africa was a
productive interlude of progressive reform during which popular policies were
enacted in almost every governmental sector. But amid the welter of policy
papers, the nagging question remains: Is the executive branch equipped to ensure
proper implementation?

The task of building institutional capacity in South Africa is complicated by the
complex structure of government. In order to accommodate the country's diversity, the constitution establishes three spheres (or tiers) of government: the
national, the provincial, and the local. Each sphere has responsibility for particular public functions. Whereas the national government is responsible for tasks like
defense and most taxation, the provinces are in charge of health and education,
among other things; for their part, local governments must deliver a range of
municipal services, such as street cleaning, road maintenance, and waste disposal. Each tier of government has a legislative body (provincial parliament or
local government council) and an executive body (a provincial executive council
or a city hall/district administration). Simply staffing all these units of government
when the majority population lacks relevant education and experience is only the
start of the capacity-building challenge.

Generally speaking, the state apparatus tends to perform less well as one
moves from well-established institutions at the political center to new and

untested structures in the locality. And yet, South Africa's great social needs arise primarily among poor populations at the grassroots level. The new government, therefore, is trying to take on an expanded range of services to mass populations, at the same time as it is revising public policies and constructing new delivery institutions, often from scratch. As one politician put it, this is akin to moving the furniture into a new house before you have finished building it.

Even at the political center, civil servants sometimes lack the strategic management and technical and financial skills necessary to run a modern state, leading to a heavy reliance on external consultants. The government barely manages to collect income taxes and is heavily dependent for revenues on the voluntary compliance of a small stratum of individuals in professional and business occupations. Customs control at international airports and harbors is breaking down. Basic middle-management skills are even scarcer at the provincial level, where 57 percent of the public budget is actually expended. As a result, most provincial ministries responsible for education and health have been unable to meet their targets of providing universal service coverage ("education and health for all"). Although many previously disadvantaged South Africans have obtained school places or preventive health care for the first time, the quality of such services is falling. In the localities, life goes on much as before: Established suburban areas enjoy a full range of modern services, but informal settlements endure without paved roads, running water, and electricity.

On the surface, the problems of institutional capacity would appear to be financial. In about one-third of urban townships and rural areas, the local authorities cannot collect enough revenues to cover the costs of delivering basic services. Provincial governments are unable to fully spend their annual budgets or to adequately monitor the use of funds that they do actually disburse. But the vacuum of governmental authority is fundamentally political, originating in unresolved struggles from the apartheid era. For example, many township dwellers still continue to resist payment of fees and taxes for services delivered by local councils, even though these bodies are now democratically chosen. And in some rural areas, traditional leaders and their followers refuse to recognize the authority of elected councillors, whom they regard as interlopers in the jurisdiction of chiefs. Thus, among South African citizens, the legitimacy of democratic institutions is far from universally accepted.

## CONCLUSION: CONSOLIDATING DEMOCRACY?

The long-term challenge in South Africa is to consolidate gains made in peace, prosperity, and democracy. Even though the country's transition from authoritarian rule was led by bold political initiatives, the health of its fragile new institutions will hinge on subsequent economic and social developments. Satisfying the material interests of disadvantaged identity groups is the key to the country's future. As President Mandela stated when he opened parliament in 1998, "Our performance should be judged above all on whether our programs are positively affecting the lives of the most vulnerable sections of society."

In this task, the South African government faces several knotty dilemmas. By way of conclusion, we will consider just four: Can the economy be expanded fast enough to enable a redistribution of wealth and opportunity? Can institutions be deracialized at the same time as services are being effectively delivered? Can crime be aggressively fought within a human rights regime? And, can democratic institutions function well if citizens are not strongly attached to democracy? The ways in which these contending priorities are addressed will determine the kind of economy, society, and polity that South Africa will attain in the future.

First, can the economy grow fast enough to enable redistribution? South African political leaders are bound to be preoccupied with the economy, which must generate enough jobs to ease chronic black impoverishment. Yet the formal sector's ability to create employment has slumped, with mining, manufacturing, and agriculture all recently experiencing net job losses. Foreign investment was slow to arrive in South Africa after 1994, and capital took flight from all emerging markets following the Asian financial crashes of 1997. These events undermined the government's strategy for rapid economic growth and strengthened the hand of critics (like COSATU and the Communist Party), who called for the state to play a larger role in job creation. It is ironic, however, that the more the state intervenes in the economy, the less competitive South Africa will become in attracting essential private investment from both domestic and international sources. Such are the narrow policy options available to a government whose economy reentered the world marketplace at a moment when capital had become thoroughly mobile.

Second, can public institutions be deracialized at the same time as services are being effectively delivered? The South African government is trying to "downsize" a bloated bureaucracy while also "transforming" it (i.e., making it more socially representative and politically responsive). Some ministries and departments have been virtually paralyzed by clashes between old-order officials and new civil service recruits, often in disputes over affirmative action. Such logjams contribute to the crisis of institutional capacity that has slowed South Africa's post-transition development. Malaysia's experience suggests that preferences for formerly disadvantaged groups can be implemented with little conflict in the context of a rapidly growing economy. But where job opportunities are shrinking, affirmative action implies real losses to the formerly advantaged, leading those with marketable skills to seek opportunities abroad. Already, South Africa has lost too many doctors, accountants, and engineers whose talents are vital to the country's progress.

Third, can the government fight crime and respect human rights at the same time? Because democratization raises demands for the accountable use of state power, it relaxes controls over society. People who previously feared state repression are free to engage in new pursuits, both legal and illicit. In South Africa, evidence is rising that former combatants from the apartheid conflict – both regular soldiers and guerrillas – are applying their war skills to careers in violent crime. Criminals of all types are taking advantage of the ANC's progressive policies, like the abolition of the death penalty and guarantees against arbitrary arrest and detention. Lacking confidence that the state will punish wrongdoers, citizens in South Africa are increasingly taking the law into their own hands. The response varies across social groups: In the wealthy enclaves, people retreat behind the protection of private security guards; in poorer communities, they are more likely to resort to vigilante action. Quite regardless of whether the government cracks down, crime threatens to undermine many of the gains of democratization.

Finally, how well can democratic institutions function in the absence of a supportive political culture? Observers have hailed the impressive array of democratic institutions embodied in South Africa's new constitution. But the behavior of citizens reveals low levels of political tolerance among competing social groups and strong popular attachments to antidemocratic political traditions. Certainly, there is little in South Africa's political history – whether in Zulu chieftaincy, the apartheid state, or exiled liberation movements – that could have nurtured democratic commitments. We should not be surprised, therefore, that South Africans do not value democracy intrinsically, that is, as an end in itself: Just one-quarter of respondents in a national survey associate democracy with civil and electoral rights. Instead, South Africans tend to regard democracy instrumentally, as a means to other ends: Almost one-half associate it with jobs, education, and housing. And a similar proportion of citizens say they would be willing to give up elections in exchange for a leader who would provide these material goods.

Thus, South Africa has a distance to travel before its formal political institutions are transformed into a living, breathing democracy. Those who expect democracy to deliver social and economic equality may be sorely disappointed. All that democracy bestows is political equality. It does not guarantee that disparities of social and economic status will be redressed, although comparatively, democracies have a slightly better track record at redistributing wealth than do authoritarian regimes. This does not mean that constructing a culture of democracy is a lost cause in South Africa. There are at least two hopeful signs. The first is that South Africans will surely always remember that democratization restored to people of all races the human dignity that apartheid had denied. This they will not surrender easily. The second is that, when push came to shove, South Africans of widely differing backgrounds resorted to negotiation and compromise to find their way out of the country's deepest political crisis. One must, therefore, be confident that in addressing the country's new challenges, South Africa's diverse identity groups will recognize afresh that their interests are inexorably connected.

## BIBLIOGRAPHY

Adam, Heribert, Frederick van Zyl Slabbert, and Kogila Moodley. *Comrades in Business: Post-Liberation Politics in South Africa.* Cape Town: Tafelberg, 1997.

Bratton, Michael. "After Mandela's Miracle in South Africa." *Current History* 97 (May 1998): 214–19.

*Constitution of the Republic of South Africa, The.* Cape Town: Constitutional Assembly, Act 108, 1996.

Friedman, Steven, and Doreen Atkinson, eds. *The Small Miracle: South Africa's Negotiated Settlement.* Randburg, So. Af.: Ravan Press, 1994.

Heyns, Stephen, ed. *Down Government Avenue: PIMS 1998 Guide to Politics in Practice.* Cape Town: Institute for a Democratic South Africa [IDASA], Parliamentary Information Monitoring Service, 1998.

James, Wilmot, and Moira Levy, eds. *Pulse – Passages in Democracy Building: Assessing South Africa's Transition.* Cape Town: Institute for a Democratic South Africa [IDASA], 1998.

Johnson, R. W., and Lawrence Schlemmer, eds. *Launching Democracy in South Africa: The First Open Election, April 1994.* New Haven, CT: Yale University Press, 1996.

Lodge, Tom. *South African Politics Since 1994.* Cape Town and Johannesburg: David Philip Publishers, 1999.

Mandela, Nelson. *Long Walk to Freedom: The Autobiography of Nelson Mandela.* Boston: Little Brown, 1994.

Mattes, Robert, and Hermann Thiel. "Consolidation and Public Opinion in South Africa." *Journal of Democracy* 9, no. 1 (January 1998): 95–109.

Price, Robert. *The Apartheid State in Crisis: Political Transformation in South Africa, 1975–1990.* New York: Oxford University Press, 1991.

South African Institute of Race Relations. *South Africa Survey, 1996/1997.* Johannesburg: South African Institute of Race Relations, 1997.

Thompson, Leonard. *A History of South Africa.* New Haven, CT, Yale University Press, 1995.

## IMPORTANT TERMS

**African National Congress (ANC)**    the political party that led the struggle for majority rule in South Africa.

**African Zion Church**    a mass-based, socially conservative, independent Christian church.

**Afrikaners**    people mainly of Dutch extraction who comprise a distinctive linguistic subculture within the white community.

**Amakhosi**    traditional tribal chiefs, for example of the Xhosa and Zulu.

**Apartheid**   literally, "apart-ness," an oppressive system of racial segregation that denied political and economic equality to blacks.

**Bantu**   a language group that includes Zulu and Xhosa, formerly used by the apartheid regime as a general designation for Africans.

**Buthelezi, Mangosuthu**   president of the Inkatha Freedom Party, whose supporters are mainly rural Zulu.

**Cape Colony**   the first outpost of white settlement, located in the southwest of present-day South Africa.

**Coloureds**   the South African term for persons of mixed race, and an identity group in their own right.

**CODESA**   a multiparty forum convened in 1991 to negotiate the political future of the country.

**Constitutional Court**   the supreme court, charged with deciding constitutional issues.

**COSATU**   the national confederation of trade union organizations, politically affiliated with the ANC.

**de Klerk, F. W.**   the last Afrikaner president, known for releasing Mandela and negotiating a handover of white power.

**GNU**   the Government of National Unity, formed as a coalition of the parties that won the most votes in the founding election of 1994.

**Homelands**   impoverished rural areas to which Africans were banished under apartheid, supposedly to govern themselves.

**Inkatha**   a movement of Zulu traditionalists, represented by its own political party, the Inkatha Freedom Party.

**Mandela, Nelson**   president of the African National Congress and first national president of majority-ruled South Africa. He is widely respected as the father of racial reconciliation in South Africa.

**Mbeki, Thabo**   Mandela's successor as national president, who took office in July 1999.

**National Party (NP)**   right-wing political party supported mainly by Afrikaners that came to power in 1948 and proceeded to implement apartheid.

**NEDLAC**   the National Economic Development and Labour Council, a bargaining forum for discussion of policy proposals among the business, labor, and governmental sectors.

**Population Registration Act (1950)**   the legislative foundation of apartheid, by which the South African people were classified into racial groups: African, Coloured, Indian, or White.

**Pretoria**   administrative capital of the country, shorthand for "government."

**RDP**   the Reconstruction and Development Programme of 1994, which envisaged rapid socioeconomic "transformation" of the lives of poor people.

**Sharpeville**   site of a massacre of peaceful protesters in 1960 and a commemorated landmark of anti-apartheid resistance.

**South African Constitution**   published in 1996 and ratified in 1997, this document promises a wide range of long-denied political, social, and economic rights to the citizens of South Africa.

**TRC**   the Truth and Reconciliation Commission (established 1995) that was charged with investigating the human rights abuses of apartheid.

**Union of South Africa**   formed 1910, the confederation of former colonies that defined the geographical boundaries of the modern South African state.

**United Democratic Front (UDF)**   a social movement of community organizations that confronted apartheid policies during the 1980s.

**Xhosa**   an African language group concentrated in the Eastern Cape Province.

**Zulu**   a centralized African kingdom found in KwaZulu-Natal Province.


## STUDY QUESTIONS

1.   What were the historical origins of South Africa's identity groups? When, where, and how did they first come into mutual contact?

2.   Describe the new political interests that emerged as a consequence of industrial development in South Africa. On whose terms, and how, were differences of interest first resolved?

3.   *Apartheid* has been described as a "system of institutionalized racism." What were its key institutions?

4.   Trace the course of political resistance to racial segregation in South Africa from its beginnings to the release of Mandela in 1990.

5.   What explains the failure of apartheid and the unexpected success of the democratic transition? Consider both socioeconomic developments within South Africa and international influences from abroad.

6.   In South Africa's deeply divided society, which are more important: political identities based on race or the economic interests of social classes?

7.   In what sense was the election of 1994 an "ethnic census"? How does this square with the emerging popular attachment to a "South African" identity?

8.   How are the divergent interests of business and labor addressed in contemporary South Africa? Identify key institutions.

9.   From a comparative perspective, what is new and distinctive about the political institutions created in South Africa since 1994?

10.   How are South Africa's current challenges – creating jobs, building state capacity, and controlling crime – derived from its past?

# ⇜ Stop and Compare

## EARLY DEVELOPERS, MIDDLE DEVELOPERS, LATE DEVELOPERS, AND EXPERIMENTAL DEVELOPERS

Taken together, the chapters you have just read underscore the importance of domestic political responses to international political challenges. In fact, a different title for the book might well have been *Liberalism and Its Challengers*. As we have seen, Britain and France developed first, each with its own institutional variation on the liberal democratic theme. This development, as positively as we may now evaluate it from our own point of view, made these two states powerful and ultimately threatening to Europe and the rest of the world.

Still, because of British and French successes, other countries sought to emulate the experience of the initial developers. In terms of our five-step framework: (1) Although middle-developers Germany and Japan reacted to British and French development, devising variations on the initial British and French innovations, they were never actually able to replicate them for the simple reason that they were trying to catch up from behind. (2) As middle developers, their middle-class interests were weaker, nationalist identity more pronounced, and bureaucratic state institutions stronger and democracy weaker. (3) These different circumstances of development ultimately weakened liberalism in Germany and Japan, which paved the way for the Nazi and fascist responses. It makes sense, therefore, to speak of a fascist path to the modern world. (4) In contemporary democratic Germany and Japan, interests, identities, and institutions grapple with the legacy of authoritarianism. (5) The Nazis and the Japanese launched World War II, which

413

ultimately led to occupation by the core liberal powers and a recasting of domestic identities, interests, and institutions.

The late developers in this book are the communist giants Russia and China. In terms of our five-step framework: (1) Both tried to industrialize their societies in a global order dominated by liberal and fascist capitalist states. (2) As late developers, their middle-class interests were even weaker, nationalist identity more pronounced, and bureaucratic state institutions even stronger and democracy even weaker. (3) These different circumstances of development weakened the possibilities of liberalism and fascism and paved the way for communism – the 20th century's third main contender for a path to the modern world. (4) After desperately trying to repair a basically unworkable communist economic and political model in the decades after Stalin's death, the Russian response was to give up communism and introduce political democracy and markets in the hope of rejoining the liberal, capitalist world system. Under the influence of the other successful semi-authoritarian capitalist states in East Asia, the Chinese response was to introduce markets into their society, while attempting to maintain Communist Party dominance. Whether either country is able to succeed in its newfound flirtation with a complete or partial reintegration with the international liberal order remains to be seen. (5) After an initial flirtation with global dominance, both the Soviet Union and China settled into an effort to legitimate their specific response to liberalism with superior economic performance under communist economic institutions. Both failed.

During the cold war, the countries we have called in this book "experimental developers" tried to develop by seeking a path between the two surviving paths – liberal democracy and communist totalitarianism. They searched for a political middle way between democracy and authoritarianism and an economic middle way between markets and central plans.

## EXPERIMENTAL DEVELOPERS: MEXICO, INDIA, IRAN, AND SOUTH AFRICA

Our final group of countries thus has a distinctive, global, historical heritage and shares common links. Most often, this commonality is colonial or imperial. Mexico, India, Iran, and South Africa experienced the impact of European colonial and imperial power. All now confront the cultural, institutional, and economic pressures of the global economy. Despite these similarities, each of these countries has distinctive, if modal, kinds of political problems that are of great interest to comparativists.

South Africa and India, respectively, conduct democratic politics in countries with very high levels of tribal and ethnic diversity. Both have developed an innovative set of institutional arrangements for adjudicating conflicting ethnic and tribal interests and identities within the parameters of what we normally think of as democratic institutions. Their experiments with multicultural democracy may even provide lessons, both positive and negative, for more industrialized, Western societies. Furthermore, both confront the problem of sustaining democracy in environments of economic scarcity.

Iran experienced decades of steady Westernization under a dictator, the Shah. After an Islamic revolution in 1980, it sought to reshape its society and live under the rules of political Islam. It thus stands as a fascinating case of the religious reaction to global cultural, economic, and political forces. The recent turn to more moderate leadership in Iran illustrates vividly just how powerful are the homogenizing forces of global liberalism. It remains unclear whether these latest developments signal a gradual return to the modernizing path taken before the Islamic revolution, or whether it is a sign that the Islamic revolution is now institutionally stable and has indeed carved out a viable alternative to the liberalism that it consciously rejected.

Finally, Mexico has taken precisely the opposite route of Iran, choosing economically to integrate itself as closely with the United States as it can. Until recently, Mexico has been steadily (if somewhat corruptly) ruled by one party (the PRI). Whether the new social groups that are emerging as a result of rapid economic change will foster democratization, or whether the PRI will manage to retain its leading role remains open to question.

In sum: four countries, four experiments. Mexico's grand experiment is independence: Is it possible for a country to be autonomous when its northern neighbor happens to be the most powerful nation in the world? Iran's grand experiment is Islam: Is it possible for a country to be economically and politically powerful when it has had an Islamic revolution that creates an Islamic state? India's grand experiment is nonrevolutionary democracy: Is it possible for a large postcolonial country to be a democracy when it has had a major independence movement but not a social revolution? And South Africa's grand experiment is interracial democracy: Is it possible for ethnoconstitutional democracy and markets to survive in a country that made a relatively peaceful transition from colonialism and apartheid?

More generally: ten countries, ten experiments. The closer we look, the more we discover that there were ten developmental paths to the modern world. States made their own development choices and evolved local institutional variations of globally dominant political economies. In the words of our framework: (1) The constant of global context influences (2) the types of domestic interests, identities, and institutions, which produce (3) the range of development paths to the modern world, which, in turn, generate (4) comparative-politics feedback effects on domestic interests, identities, and institutions and (5) international-relations feedback effects on the global context.

# Index